GAMSAT-Prep.com

The Gold Standard textbook is a critical component of a multimedia experience including live courses on campus, MP3s, smartphone apps, online videos and interactive programs, *Heaps* of Practice GAMSATs and a lot more.

GAMSAT-Prep.com

The only prep you need.™

Gold Standard Live GAMSAT Courses are held in the following cities:
Sydney • Melbourne • Dublin • London • Brisbane • Perth • Adelaide • Cork

GOLD STANDARD
MULTIMEDIA EDUCATION

* GAMSAT is administered by ACER which does not endorse this study guide.

THE GOLD STANDARD

GAMSAT

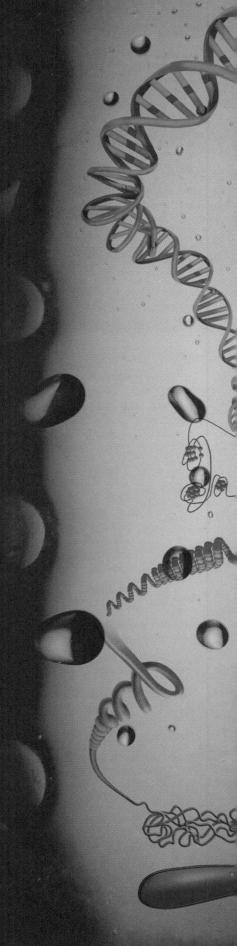

Editor and Author

Brett Ferdinand BSc MD-CM

Contributors

Lisa Ferdinand BA MA
Sean Pierre BSc MD
Kristin Finkenzeller BSc MD
Ibrahima Diouf BSc MSc PhD
Charles Haccoun BSc MD-CM
Timothy Ruger BA MA
Jeanne Tan Te

Illustrators

Harvie W. Gallatiera BSc
Daphne McCormack
Nanjing Design
 • **Ren Yi, Huang Bin**
 • **Sun Chan, Li Xin**

RuveneCo
Inc

Be sure to register at www.GAMSAT-prep.com by clicking on Register in the top right corner of the website. Once you login, click on GAMSAT Textbook Owners in the right column and follow directions. Please Note: benefits are for 1 year from the date of on-line registration, for the original book owner only and are not transferable; unauthorized access and use outside the Terms of Use posted on GAMSAT-prep.com may result in account deletion; if you are not the original owner, you can purchase your virtual access card separately at GAMSAT-prep.com.

Visit The Gold Standard's Education Center at www.gold-standard.com.

Copyright (c) 2017 RuveneCo (Worldwide), 1st Edition

ISBN 978-1-927338-40-7

Address all inquiries, comments, or suggestions to the publisher. For Terms of Use go to: www.GAMSAT-prep.com

The reviews on the back cover represent the opinions of individuals and do not necessarily reflect the opinions of the institutions they represent.

Gold Standard GAMSAT Product Contact Information

Distribution in Australia, NZ, Asia	Distribution in Europe	Distribution in North America
Woodslane Pty Ltd	Central Books	RuveneCo Publishing
10 Apollo Street Warriewood	99 Wallis Road	334 Cornelia Street # 559
NSW 2102 Australia	LONDON,	Plattsburgh, New York
ABN: 76 003 677 549	E9 5LN, United Kingdom	12901, USA
learn@gamsat-prep.com	orders@centralbooks.com	buy@gamsatbooks.com

RuveneCo Inc. is neither associated nor affiliated with the Australian Council for Educational Research (ACER) who has developed and administers the Graduate Medical School Admissions Test (GAMSAT) nor The University of Sydney. Printed in China.

This is not a typical 1st edition textbook.

The Gold Standard GAMSAT, the first GAMSAT textbook ever, had already gone through 5 editions with significant revisions. In the last edition, hundreds of new pages were added and it grew to just over 3 kilograms (the weight of a healthy baby!). Unfortunately, that met with some student complaints, it had become unwieldy - especially if the aim was to review a small section of the book on campus or at work. Meanwhile, we had plans to revise and expand the book yet again.

And so, with more content, more images and more practice questions, the 1 textbook has become 3. We hope that studying will now be more convenient!

Besides adding more content, we have added more online access. Previous editions had 10 hours of video access over the 1-year online access period. Throwing caution to the wind, for the first time ever, we have increased access to unlimited viewings of our hundreds of online videos during the 1-year access period.

Over 8 years, we have been teaching monthly GAMSAT webinars, science review GAMSAT courses on campuses in Australia, the UK and Ireland, as well as producing over 100 YouTube videos providing step-by-step worked solutions to the official (ACER's) practice materials for the GAMSAT. We have met the full range of GAMSAT students: 'young' and 'old', hoping for a career vs. having built one already, arts vs. science, experts vs. neophytes, etc. In all likelihood, we have heard your voice expressed, to one degree or the other, among the thousands of students that we have taught over the years. Each time, we grew and improved with that voice in mind.

We hope to impart to you our excitement about the awesome beauty of learning, and of sharing the mental manoeuvres of those who are still here, and others throughout history from Aristotle to Pythagoras, and from Freud to Newton.

Your formula for GAMSAT success comes in 3 parts: content review, practice problems, and full-length testing. We will guide you through the process.

Let's begin.

– B.F., MD

GAMSAT SCORE!

Good, we have your attention! We just want to be sure that you understand that not every student needs the same Section 3 (science) score in order to be admitted to medical school. Some science students must ace Section 3 to be admitted while some non-science students can gain admittance with an average Section 3 score because of an exceptional performance in the non-science sections. This book is for all students. This means that there may be some science chapters that might not be "worth it" for the non-science student. So we have colour-coded the importance of chapters in providing pertinent background information based on our experience.

HIGH   MEDIUM   LOW

Now you can use your own judgement based on how much time you have to study and our assessment of the **importance** of that chapter. You will find this coding system particularly helpful when studying Biology. Also, if you have no science background in any of the subjects then we highly recommend taking advantage of the hours of online video time that comes with this textbook. In addition, we suggest that all students complete the non-science problem sets in this textbook as well as the science chapter review questions with worked solutions that are online. Reviewing content only provides the background needed for science reasoning. In order to move to the next level, you must do problem sets followed by timed, full-length practice. Review, practice and full-length testing can help you obtain an exceptional GAMSAT score.

As of the publication date of this textbook, calculators are no longer permitted.

To further discuss any of the issues above: gamsat-prep.com/forum.

The Graduate Medical School Admissions Test (GAMSAT) is a paper-based test (no calculators are allowed) and consists of 2 essay writing tasks and 185 multiple-choice questions. This exam requires approximately 5.5 hours to complete and is comprised of 3 Sections. There is no break between Section I and II. There is a lunch break between Section II and III. The following are the three subtests of the GAMSAT exam:

1. **Section I: Reasoning in Humanities and Social Sciences - 75 questions; 100 min.**

   - Interpretation and understanding of ideas in socio-cultural context. Source materials: written passages, tabular or other visual format.

2. **Section II: Written Communication - 2 essays; 60 min.**

   - Ability to produce and develop ideas in writing. Task A essay: socio-cultural issues, more analytical; Task B more personal and social issues.

3. **Section III: Reasoning in Biological and Physical Sciences - 110 questions, 170 min.**

   - Chemistry (40%), Biology (40%), Physics (20%). First-year undergraduate level in Biology and Chemistry and Year 12/A-Level/Leaving Certificate course in Physics. Chemistry is equally divided into General and Organic.

> The overall GAMSAT score is calculated using the following formula*:
>
> Overall Score = (1 x Section I + 1 x Section II + 2 x Section III) / 4

* Note: the formula applies to all medical schools that require the GAMSAT in Australia, the UK and Ireland except for the University of Melbourne and University of Sydney which currently weigh all 3 sections equally. Please carefully review the admissions information for all of your target programmes.

Common formula for acceptance:

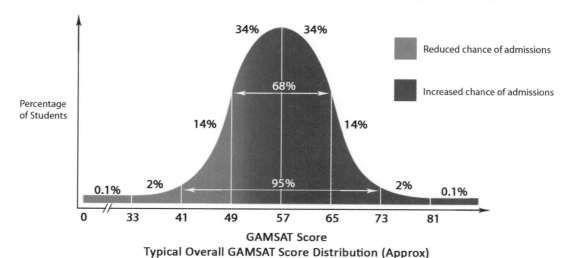

GPA + GAMSAT score + Interview = Medical School Admissions

GAMSAT Score
Typical Overall GAMSAT Score Distribution (Approx)

The GAMSAT is challenging, get organised.

gamsat-prep.com/free-GAMSAT-study-schedule

1. How to study:

1. Study the Gold Standard (GS) textbook and videos to learn
2. Do GS Chapter review practice questions
3. Consolidate: create and review your personal summaries (= Gold Notes) daily

2. Once you have completed your studies:

1. Full-length practice test
2. Review mistakes, all solutions
3. Consolidate: review all your Gold Notes and create more
4. Repeat until you get beyond the score you need for your targeted medical/dental school

Recommended GAMSAT Communities:
- All countries (mainly Australia): pagingdr.net
- Mainly UK: thestudentroom.co.uk (Medicine Community Discussion)
- Mainly Ireland: boards.ie

Is there something in the Gold Standard that you did not understand? Don't get frustrated, get on-line: gamsat-prep.com/forum

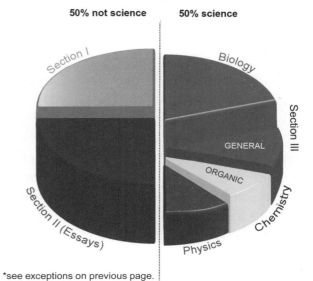

GAMSAT Scores*

50% not science   50% science

*see exceptions on previous page.

3. Full-length practice tests:

1. ACER practice exams
2. Gold Standard GAMSAT exams
3. Heaps of GAMSAT Practice: 10 full-length exams

4. How much time do you need?

On average, 3-6 hours per day for 3-6 months; depending on life experiences, 2 weeks may be enough and 8 months could be insufficient.

To make the content easier to retain, you can also find aspects of the Gold Standard programme in other formats such as:

Good luck with your studies!

Gold Standard Team

THE GOLD STANDARD
MULTIMEDIA EDUCATION

GAMSAT Section 3, Reasoning in Biological and Physical Sciences, is the longest of the 3 subtests on exam day (110 MCQs). 'Biological Sciences', which is the focus of this textbook, refers to Organic Chemistry and Biology. 'Physical Sciences' refers to Physics and General Chemistry. In our experience, most students with a non-science background (NSB) can successfully learn the assumed knowledge for GAMSAT independently, while a smaller number may need to enrol in a short tertiary-level science course.

Essentially, 20% of Section 3 is Organic Chemistry and 40% is Biology. Officially, the level of assumed knowledge is first year university for both subjects. With time, it may become clear to you that despite the preceding statement, the assumed knowledge for Biological Sciences is mostly consistent with A-Level/Leaving Certificate/Year 12 courses. However, the topics explored in the stimulus material during the exam can be quite advanced with the aim being to test your ability to learn on the spot and apply your reasoning skills to novel scenarios.

Break the Wheel: A Different Approach to an Introduction

The Gold Standard GAMSAT Book 1 (Section 1 & Section 2) and Book 2 (Section 3 Physical Sciences) both begin in a rather traditional way: A basic introduction to the structure of each book peppered with study advice. We had that luxury for those 2 books because once the content started, whether it be the Section 1 chapters or the GAMSAT Math chapters, there were a lot of practice questions at GAMSAT standard to set the mood for the rest of the book. In other words, at least the hope was that, seeing GAMSAT-level practice questions early in your preparation will lead you to study differently, to minimise committing details to memory, and optimise your reasoning skills. It is the latter (higher-order thinking skills, 'HOTS') that will be the source of your GAMSAT success.

There is simply more content in the Biological Sciences, especially Biology, as compared to any other GAMSAT subsection. Thus the Biological Sciences ends up being the easiest subsection to get lost in details which often leads to amnesia regarding the purpose of the GAMSAT: reasoning. To prevent that from happening, we will insert GAMSAT-level practice questions in this Introduction and, hopefully, you can adjust the way you study.

We know that many students are apprehensive about trying practice questions because they may have limited or no experience with the content, or, they are concerned that it may affect their confidence moving forward. Medical schools worldwide - to one degree or the other - have been moving towards problem-based learning because research has shown that it is the most effective way to learn and remember new information. Many medical schools begin clinical problem solving on the first day of school even though students have not yet been exposed to any medical knowledge.

If that is not convincing enough, a word from ACER:

"Since problem-based learning techniques are central to modern medical curricula, GAMSAT is constructed with a major focus on the assessment of problem solving ability across a wide range of subject areas."

gamsat.acer.org/about-gamsat/structure-and-content (2017)

The question types for the two sciences that comprise the Biological Sciences could hardly be more different. We endeavour to continually underline the importance of geometric (spatial) reasoning and pattern recognition which underlies most of GAMSAT Organic Chemistry. After that, we will underline the importance of graphs and diagrams (using the example of flow charts) which are amongst the mainstays of GAMSAT Biology.

Take the time that you need. Again, we understand that some of you may have little or no background for the following questions. But keep in mind: The real exam is designed to expose you to new content on the day of the exam to see if you can reason through to a solution. In keeping with 'learning is better by doing', let's begin.

GAMSAT Organic Chemistry

Unit 1, Question 1

A polymer is composed of many simple molecules that are repeating structural units called monomers. Covalent bonds, often symbolized by black lines, hold the atoms in polymer molecules together. If A-B-C-A-B-C-A-B-C were a polymer, we can see that the smallest unit that continually repeats is A-B-C, which is therefore the monomer. Neither shorter segments (e.g. A-B), nor longer segments that are not multiples of the monomer (e.g. A-B-C-A), would accurately recreate the polymer by being repeated.

Rubber, plastics, and many storage macromolecules for sugars such as glucose, are polymers. For example, amylose, a component of starch, is a polymer of glucose:

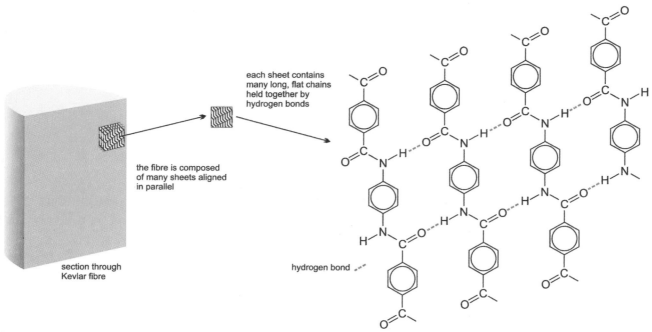

Of course, the molecular structure of amylose continues to the left and right. In fact, the smallest repeating unit, or 'building block', is identified within the square brackets and repeats in the polymer n times, where n can be between 300 and 3000 units. Note that anything smaller than the structure in square brackets would not represent a structure that could be repeated in order to reconstruct amylose.

Kevlar® is a plastic strong enough to stop bullets and knives. Consider the structure of Kevlar®:

each sheet contains many long, flat chains held together by hydrogen bonds

the fibre is composed of many sheets aligned in parallel

section through Kevlar fibre

hydrogen bond

Figure 1: The structure of Kevlar®
essentialchemicalindustry.org (2016)

Note that: Though hydrogen bonds are instrumental to the function of Kevlar®, they are a form of non-covalent bonding.

1. Which of the following represents a monomer (the smallest repeating unit) in the polymer Kevlar®?

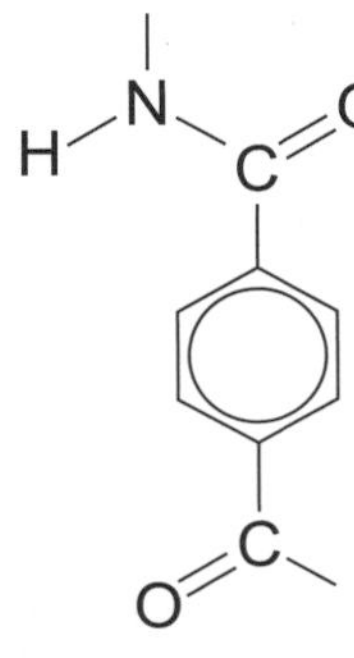

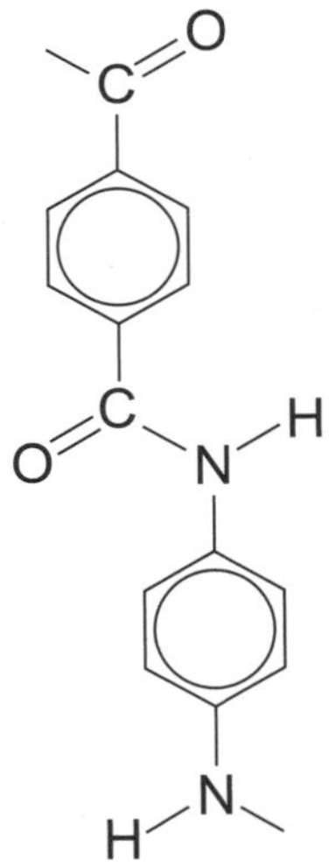

On the Surface: According to the preamble and examples, we are looking for the smallest repeating unit that can be used to recreate the entire structure. Also, according to the preamble, the smallest repeating unit is held together by covalent bonds whereas the blue 'hydrogen bonds', according to the "Note that" following the figure, are *not* covalent. So answer choice B cannot represent a monomer.

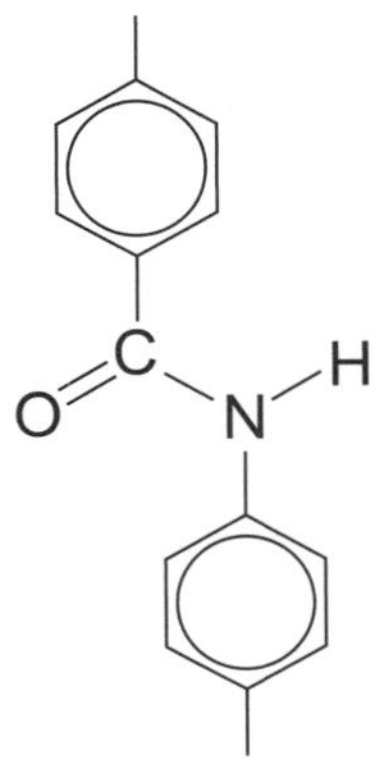

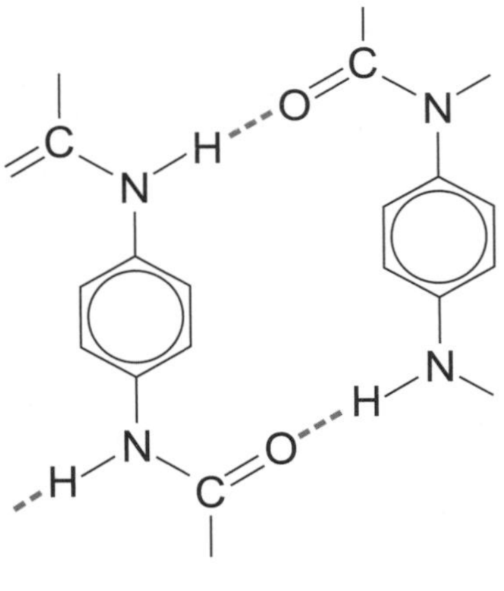

Now it becomes a matter of pattern recognition. Notice that each hexagon (6-sided figure) in Figure 1 has either of the following attachments: 2 N's are directly attached to it or 2 C's are directly attached to it, there are no other possibilities. So whatever the smallest repeating structure is, it cannot simply be a hexagon with 2 N's attached because that does not represent the polymer (i.e., if you kept repeating the hexagon with 2 N's you cannot make Kevlar® because you are missing a key component: the hexagon with the 2 C's attached). Only answer choice D fulfils both the preceding requirements and is thus the correct answer.

For NSB: Think of a gold chain that someone wears around their neck. If you look close enough, you can see a small link in the chain (a monomer) that repeats over and over to form the chain (the polymer). Figure 1 shows us a large, blue structure (section of a fibre) to the left and then we zoom in to take a close look at a very small portion of the whole, just to see a few links in 4 vertical chains. After all, Figure 1 tells us that "each sheet contains many long, flat chains." In other words, we assume that the molecules that we see represent all we need in order to deduce the repeating pattern which must extend upwards and downwards by covalent bonds (black lines), as well as to the left and to the right by hydrogen bonds (blue, dashed lines).

Going Deeper: Those hexagons represent the most famous aromatic compound in Organic Chemistry: benzene. We will explore benzene and aromatic chemistry in GAMSAT Organic Chemistry Chapter 5. Below are different representations of benzene.

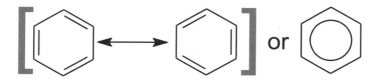

Figure 1 includes two types of bonds that would win any GAMSAT-bond-popularity contest (!!): the hydrogen bond, which is a weaker-than-covalent attraction between a partially positive hydrogen atom and, in this case, a partially negative oxygen atom; and the very covalent amide bond. You can identify the latter in the middle of answer choice D; notice this combination of atoms: O=C-N-H.

That identical arrangement (O=C-N-H), though labelled 'amide' generally, when present in proteins, it is called a 'peptide' bond. Identifying that combination of atoms was not necessary for Question 1 but it is a pattern-recognition skill that would have been of value for almost every past GAMSAT exam. Ideally, you will learn to identify such combinations upside-down, left-right and under a table! The following is a generic dipeptide (ORG Chapter 12) held together by a peptide (amide) bond highlighted in red.

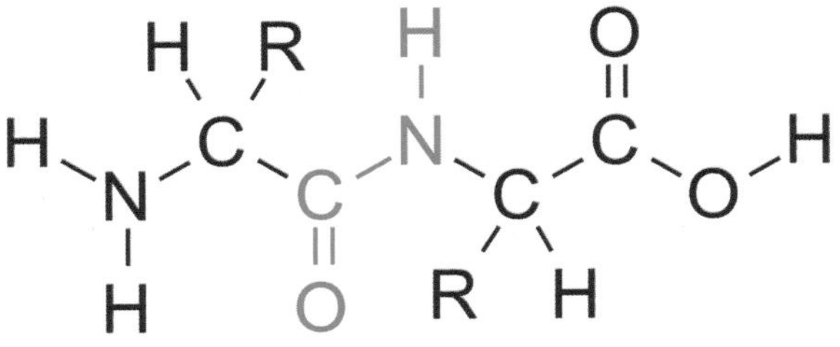

Unit 2, Questions 2 and 3

Carbocations are positively charged carbon ions. Carbocations can be imagined as the neutral alkane form minus 1 hydrogen. The positive charge is then left at a position which can be tertiary, secondary, or primary as represented below:

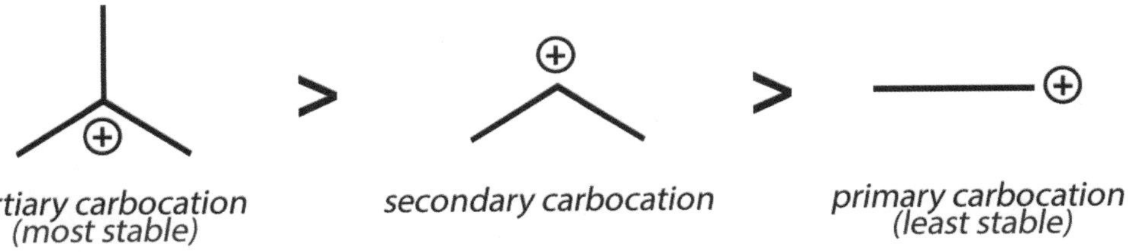

tertiary carbocation
(most stable)

secondary carbocation

primary carbocation
(least stable)

For NSB: There are 2 points for you to consider: 1) notice that the word 'primary' suggests 1; and so the primary position, where the '+' symbol is, has 1 incoming line; the secondary '+' sign has 2 incoming lines; the tertiary '+' has 3 incoming lines; 2) there is one small point that is assumed knowledge: if you were to add a line leading to the center of the tertiary carbocation (the expression would be a 'quaternary' position which does NOT need to be committed to memory), then that position is full. There can never be more than 4 lines going to any position in these structures. Later you will learn that each corner of a geometric figure represents carbon, and carbon cannot bond more than 4 times (ORG Chapter 1). For now, just focus on the number of lines that come into each position (resulting in primary, secondary or tertiary) and the rule: more than 4 lines is impossible.

Consider the bicyclic molecule *norbornane* on the left, AKA bicyclo[2.2.1]heptane, and *camphor* on the right, AKA 1,7,7-trimethylbicyclo[2.2.1]heptan-2-one.

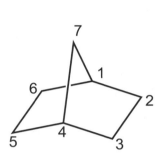
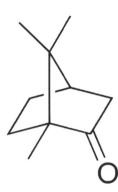

2. If one hydrogen is removed from each of the 7 positions on norbornane, how many of the carbocations would be considered primary, secondary, or tertiary carbocations, respectively?

   A 0 primary, 5 secondary, 2 tertiary
   B 0 primary, 4 secondary, 3 tertiary
   C 1 primary, 4 secondary, 2 tertiary
   D 1 primary, 2 secondary, 4 tertiary

3. As compared to norbornane, camphor has 3 additional carbon positions. How many carbon positions in camphor, if positively charged due to the removal of one hydrogen, would be considered primary, secondary, or tertiary carbocations, respectively?

   A 3 primary, 3 secondary, 1 tertiary
   B 3 primary, 3 secondary, 4 tertiary
   C 2 primary, 4 secondary, 4 tertiary
   D None of the above

On the Surface: Notice in norbornane, positions 2, 3, 5, 6, and 7, each has exactly 2 incoming lines. That represents a total of 5 secondary positions. If one hydrogen was removed from each of those positions, they would become 5 secondary carbocations. Note that positions 1 and 4 each has 3 lines coming into those positions meaning that they are both tertiary. Thus we have evaluated all 7 positions: 0 primary, 5 secondary, 2 tertiary. Answer choice A is correct.

If you did not get Question 2 correct but you can now understand the reasoning, you can try to reevaluate your answer for Question 3. You can always choose to discuss this or any of the subsequent questions on gamsat-prep.com/forum, or review GAMSAT Organic Chemistry Chapter 1 and return to try these questions again.

Now for camphor: Please apply the identical numbering system used on norbornane to camphor so the worked solution will be easier to follow. On camphor, positions 2, 5, and 6, each has exactly 2 incoming lines. Thus they represent a total of 3 secondary positions, if one hydrogen is removed from each of those positions, there would be 3 secondary carbocations. Note that position 1 has 3 lines coming into that position meaning that it is tertiary. Notice that positions 3, 4 and 7, all have 4 lines coming in to those positions: that's not tertiary! The name does not matter (= quaternary!) but the point is that carbon is bonded to its maximum extent and so it could not have a hydrogen at the position that could be removed. The question does not ask about quaternary positions, and we have already determined: 3 secondary, 1 tertiary, which thus far makes answer choice A appealing.

In comparing the 2 structures provided, notice the 3 single lines added to norbornane to create camphor produced 3 primary positions. Because, if we were to remove one hydrogen and thus add a positive charge at the end of each of those lines, just like the example in the preamble, those 3 positions would be primary carbocations.

By the way, yes, ACER infrequently uses "None of the above" or a similar expression and, no, there is no reliable pattern for guessing based on ACER's use of such statements.

Going Deeper: If you complete all your chapter review practice questions, you will learn how to name norbornane and camphor systematically. This is not assumed knowledge; however, it is the kind of question that can come up on the real exam only if the rules are provided first.

Before we go further, let's formalize a point that has been alluded to already: when using 'stick' shorthand drawings, every corner of a geometric figure, and the end of a line with no other atom, is a carbon; carbon is bonded a maximum of 4 times; hydrogen - H - is not always drawn in the shorthand form of molecules but we must assume their presence such that each carbon is bonded 4 times. And so, as an example, the following represents the shorthand skeletal structure and its long form, respectively, for the 6-carbon hydrocarbon *hexane*:

Unit 3, Questions 3-6

'Aldol condensation' is a base catalysed reaction of aldehydes that have α-hydrogens. The intermediate, an *aldol*, is both an <u>aldehyde</u> and an <u>alcohol</u>. The aldol undergoes a dehydration reaction producing a carbon-carbon bond in the condensation product, an *enal* (= alk<u>ene</u> + <u>al</u>dehyde). If the same reaction begins with a ketone, then an *enol* is the intermediate, and an *enone* is the condensation product. Reactions beginning with either aldehydes or ketones are still generally referred to as 'aldol condensation'.

Aldol condensation may be summarized as follows:

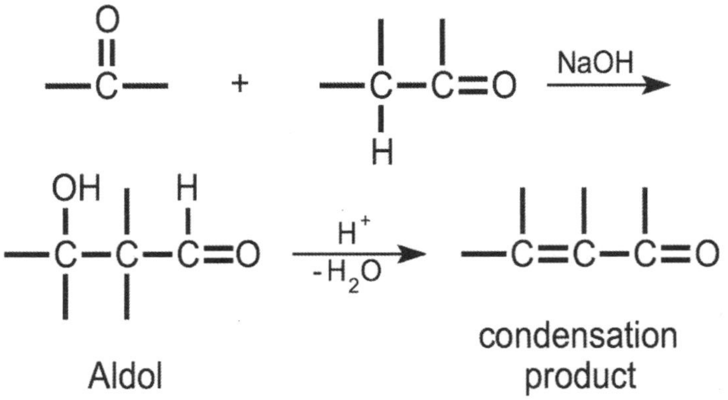

Aldol

condensation product

Note: The α-hydrogen is the hydrogen attached to the carbon (e.g., the α-carbon) next to the carbonyl group (C=O).

Consider the following 5 structures ('Me' represents the methyl group; 'Ph' represents the phenyl group).

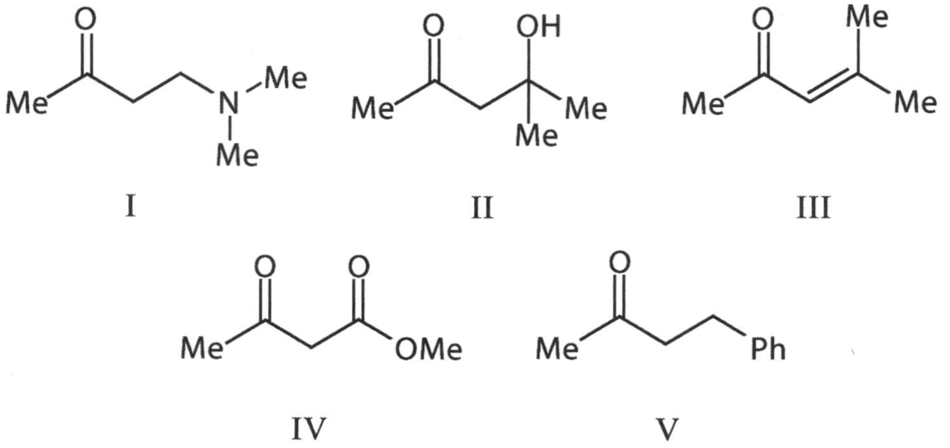

I   II   III

IV   V

3. Which of the structures provided would be consistent with the condensation product and the intermediate (aldol), respectively?

A I & IV
B II & III
C II & V
D III & II

4. For the following reaction, choose the condensation product **Z**:

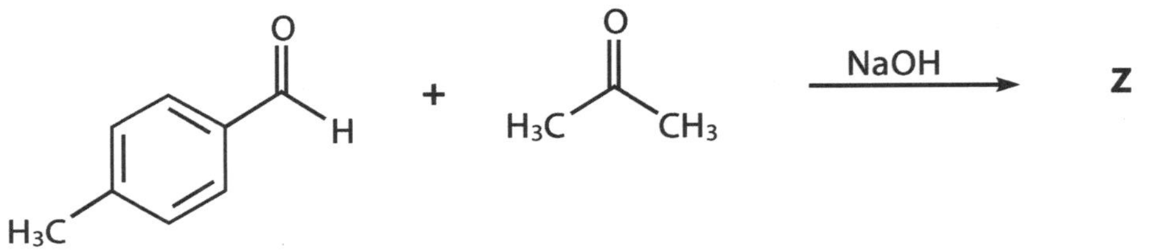

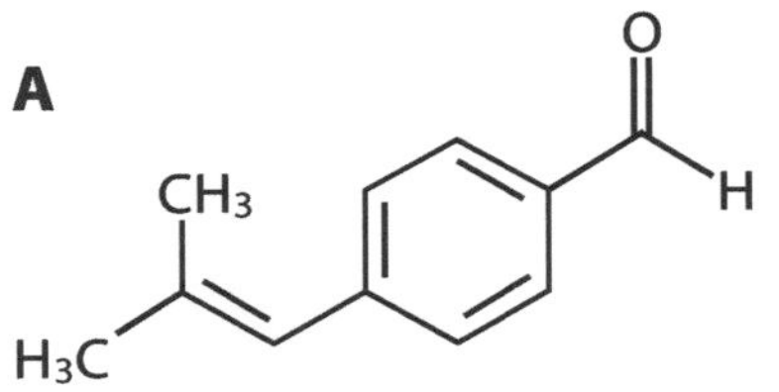

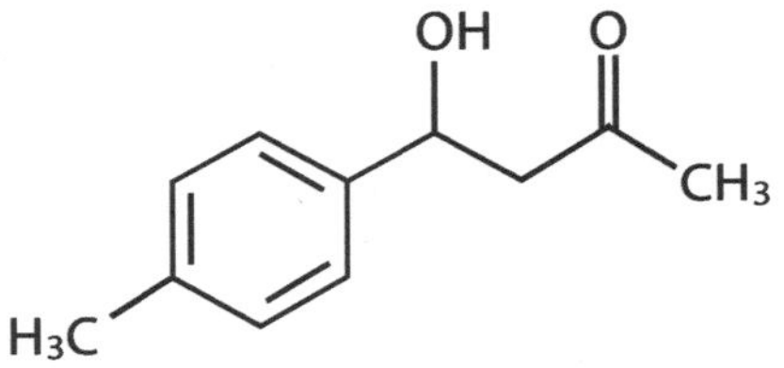

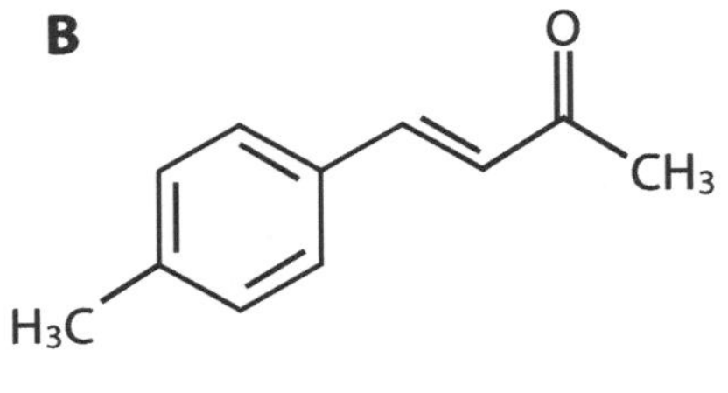

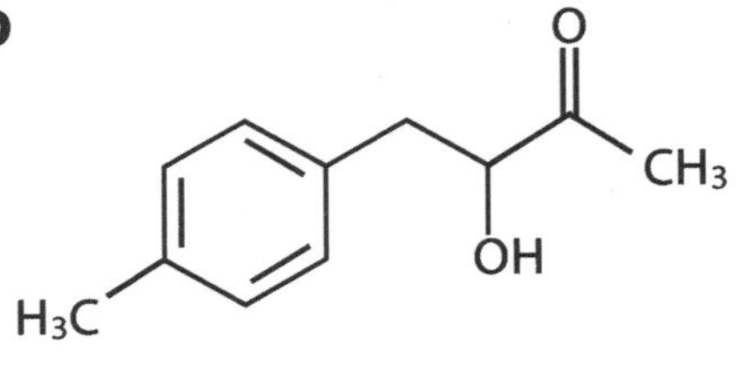

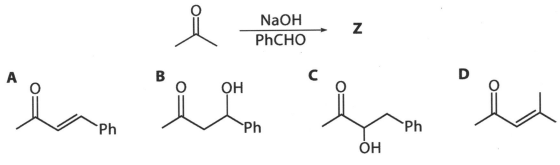

5. For the following reaction, the ketone reacts with PhCHO. Identify the condensation product **Z**:

6. The condensation product from an aldol reaction can also occur in the presence of an acid catalyst in aqueous conditions. For the following reaction, identify the condensation product **Z**:

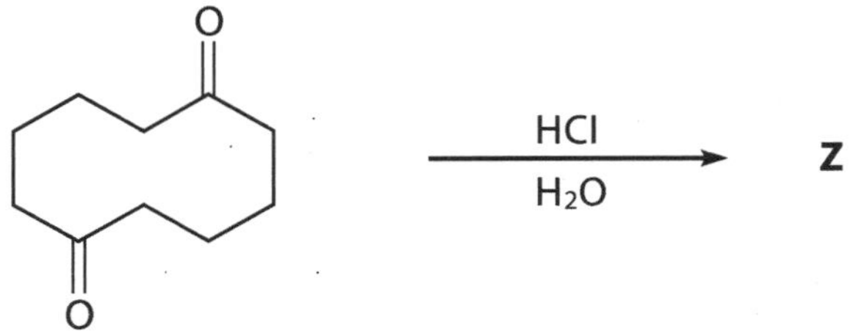

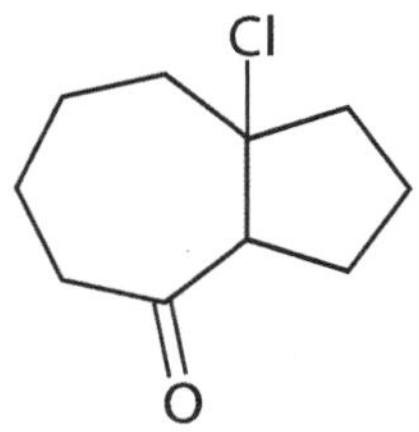

You may have felt that this unit was written in a foreign language! Well, it is our hope to show you that despite the "blah blah blah," the questions can be distilled down to basic pattern recognition and geometric reasoning. Have you ever seen the comics where the illustrator changes a few details from one image to the other as a challenge for you to observe the differences and similarities? If you find those comics easy, then you have already developed an important skill for GAMSAT Organic Chemistry!

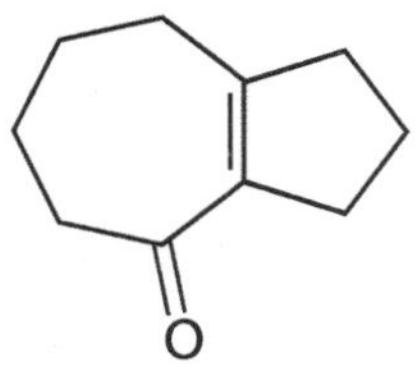

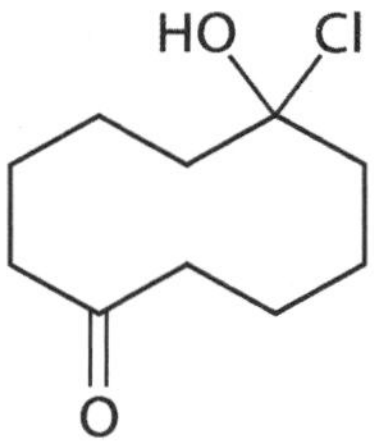

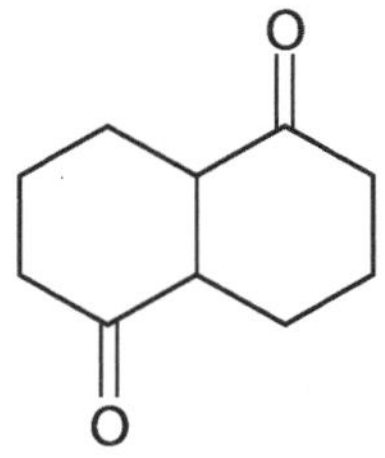

In the reaction summary provided in the preamble, here is the pattern (if it remains unclear to you, please see the string of letters/atoms encircled in red on the next page):

- in the sample reaction provided in the preamble, the final product is called the 'condensation product' and has this arrangement: C=C-C=O (look carefully at the reaction and confirm that you can identify that string of letters and bonds in the condensation product).

- ½ way to the final product must be the intermediate and it is labelled 'Aldol' and has this arrangement: (OH)-C-C-C=O (side note: we put the OH in brackets because it could be written either HO or OH and it has the same meaning; however, 'OH' is simpler to identify in the preamble and questions. If you have a science background then you know that it is the O that must be in between the H and the C, which should be very clear after ORG Chapter 1).

Look back at the reaction provided in the preamble and confirm that you agree with the 2 patterns as described. If you are only now seeing the pattern, consider re-evaluating your answers for Questions 3-6 based on your recognition of the pattern.

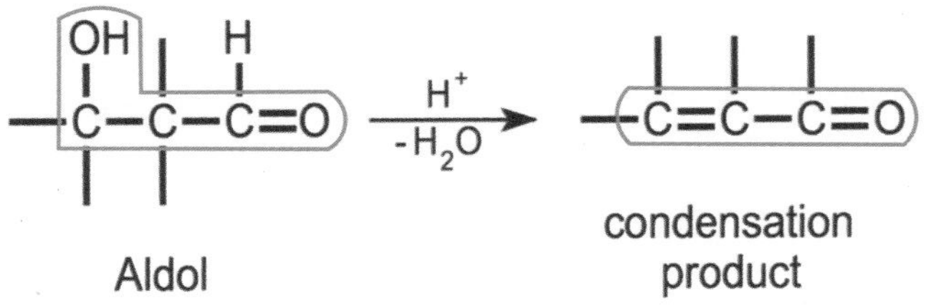

Question 3 asks for "the condensation product and the intermediate (aldol), respectively." Of course, 'respectively' means 'in the order already mentioned' so we must first identify the condensation product.

Thus we look at all 5 structures to find the condensation product with this pattern: C=C-C=O. All 5 structures have 2 lines going to an O (i.e., C=O which is called the 'carbonyl group'), so now we only need to identify C=C. Only structure **III** has a double line (=) that is NOT associated with O, so **III** is the condensation product. Also, for your interest, notice that structure **III** has 1 single line between the 2 double lines just like our pattern: C=C-C=O.

Looking for the aldol (OH)-C-C-C=O in Question 3, notice that there is only one structure, **II**, that has an OH group! So the answer for Question 3 must be D (meaning, the structures are **III** and **II**, in that order).

Also for your interest, notice that for structure **II**, (OH)-C-C-C=O, between the OH group and the carbonyl group, you should be able to count 3 straight, single lines (bonds) consistent with our identified pattern.

If it is 'clicking' now, consider reassessing your other answer choices before continuing.

From this point forward, it only gets easier! Question 4 is looking for the condensation product C=C-C=O which basically means the structure to the right.

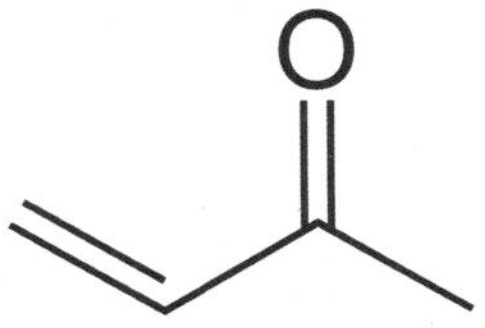

Only answer choice B has a double bond between 2 carbons (C=C) which is then single bonded to a carbonyl group (C=O), and so B is correct. We must maintain the correct order consistent with the pattern that we were provided.

Question 5 is also looking for the condensation product C=C-C=O. There are only 2 options that have the correct pattern, answer choices A and D. So we must identify how they are different from each other and see if we can justify either answer. Answer choice A has 'Ph' attached. We can see 'Ph' under the arrow as part of PhCHO (and the question stem stated that the reaction was with PhCHO making it a good candidate). Answer choice D has 2 separate lines attached (i.e. 2 primary carbons) but how can we justify that? The reactant to the left of the arrow, which has 2 primary carbons, would have had to react with itself. We know the latter did not occur since the question stem stated that the reaction was with PhCHO. Thus answer choice A is correct.

Going Deeper: Just for your interest, answer choice B would be the intermediate of the reaction that would lead to the final condensation product, answer choice A. Later, in the ORG chapters, you will learn that the reaction that goes from answer choice B to A occurs as 3 atoms are lost: $H + OH = H_2O$. When water is lost from a reactant, just like when water is lost from your body, it is called *dehydration*.

The reaction was described in the preamble as 'base catalysed' which refers to the sodium hydroxide (NaOH, a powerful base) above the arrow.

In Question 5, the reactants are (do not worry about nomenclature for now, we will learn how to name these and more complex molecules later):

1) To the left of the arrow is the ketone called 'acetone' (propan-2-one, the active ingredient in nail polish remover and paint thinner; can be smelled on the breath of a diabetic with poorly regulated insulin levels). Among the many ways that the molecular formula for acetone can be presented, here are a few: $(CH_3)_2CO$, $(CH_3)_2C=O$, $CH_3(CO)CH_3$, $CH_3-(C=O)-CH_3$, $H_3C-(C=O)-CH_3$, and so of course, C_3H_6O.

2) Below the arrow is PhCHO. In the preamble, 'Ph' was identified as a phenyl group. Phenyl refers to benzene minus one hydrogen (i.e., normally, benzene as an attachment). PhCHO is shorthand for Ph-(C=O)-H, benzaldehyde (the image to the right). Of course, the preceding information was not necessary to correctly answer the question.

And finally, Question 6 is also looking for the condensation product C=C-C=O: this one has to be the easiest question because only 1 option has a C=C, and so answer choice A is correct. The introduction of the fact that the same reaction can occur in the presence of acid (e.g. HCl) catalyst is simply a distractor. After all, a catalyst increases the rate of a chemical reaction but it is not used up in the process (CHM 9.7), so there can be no Cl attached to the products (i.e. answer choices B and D are impossible for that reason alone).

Going Deeper: Though it was not necessary to notice in order to identify the correct pattern among the answer choices, it is interesting to note that Question 6 presents the only case in this unit where both reactants were in the same molecule! The other reactions were between different molecules, *intermolecular*, while Question 6 had the two necessary components for the reaction within the same molecule, *intramolecular*. The reactant's name is cyclodecane-1,6-dione.

For those of you who want to go even deeper (nomenclature for reactant and product, as well as the overall mechanism that leads to answer choice A): Login to your gamsat-prep.com account, click on Videos in the top Menu, then Organic Chemistry, then "**New: Adjacent to Carbonyl, Practice Problem II with Bicyclic Compound**".

Organic Chemistry at university requires that you recite the names of chemicals used in mixtures (*reagents*), and that you commit to memory what can be added to what to make another what and why (!!) - all of which is largely irrelevant for GAMSAT Organic Chemistry. Although geometric reasoning and pattern recognition are most important, you will hopefully develop other important skills that apply to this exam: the basic rules to name compounds - nomenclature, functional groups, stereochemistry, counting carbons and/or hydrogens to ensure that the reaction makes sense, following the groups in the reactants to see where they end up in the products, etc.

Again, you must largely restrain yourself from trying to commit outcomes to memory (which is a basic requirement in tertiary-level courses) but rather to develop an awareness as to the change in bonding patterns and locations of atoms or groups as the reaction takes place. So, during the real exam, when you are presented with reactions that you are not expected to have seen before, as long as an adequate example is provided, you would have already honed your skills to prepare you to successfully reason the outcomes of novel reactions.

GAMSAT Biology

GAMSAT Biology is primarily concerned with graphs, tables and diagrams (the latter includes flow charts). Undoubtedly, GAMSAT Biology success requires a foundation in GAMSAT Math. Should you have any concerns regarding your basic algebra skills, either you should brush-up on your skills in maths through other resources, or revise the knowledge you once had in secondary school with the Gold Standard (GS) GAMSAT Book 2: The Physical Sciences. In Book 2, there are 2 GAMSAT Math (GM) chapters that will have the greatest effect on your GAMSAT score - GM Chapter 2: Scientific Measurement and Dimensional Analysis, and GM Chapter 3: Algebra and Graph Analysis.

Even if you do not have GS Physical Sciences Book 2, we have created a brand new section of gamsat-prep.com which you can access for free with your GS Online Access Card: GAMSAT Biology Chapter 0. We have placed over 50 MCQs - mostly in video format - with step-by-step worked solutions exploring graph analysis and flow charts.

We are not trying to suggest that all assumed knowledge for GAMSAT Biology is irrelevant. A very basic understanding of cell biology, the circulatory system, and particularly genetics have been proven to be quite helpful topics. However, the majority of questions in the science with the greatest impact on your Section 3 score requires little to no biology-specific assumed knowledge.

In this Introduction, we will explore 2 very common GAMSAT Biology question types: (1) graph analysis, and (2) reasoning through diagrams, a subset of which includes flow charts.

Unit 4, Question 7

Consider Figure 1 and the Michaelis-Menten equation.

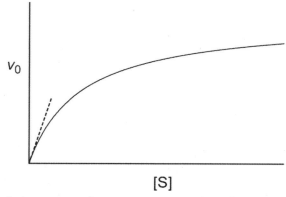

Figure 1: Initial velocity (v_0) versus substrate concentration [S] in an enzyme-catalysed reaction demonstrating Michaelis-Menten kinetics. The dashed line indicates the slope of the curve when [S] $\ll K_m$.

The Michaelis-Menten equation:

$$v_0 = \frac{k_{cat}[\mathrm{E_t}][\mathrm{S}]}{[\mathrm{S}] + K_m} = \frac{V_{max}[\mathrm{S}]}{[\mathrm{S}] + K_m}$$

7.   Which of the following corresponds to the slope of the dashed line in Figure 1?

A $(1/2)[\mathrm{S}]$
B V_{max}/K_m
C k_{cat}/K_m
D $1/V_{max}$

This question touches on many very important parameters in Biochemistry (= Biological Molecules, an important subdivision of Biology). However, this question essentially reduces to a secondary school maths/reasoning problem!

Since we are asked for the slope of the dashed line, we must recall the equation for a straight line where m is the slope (i.e. gradient) and b is the y-intercept: y = mx + b (= a regular visitor to the real exam). Also, from the labelling of Figure 1, we know that $y = v_0$, and $x = [\mathrm{S}]$.

Considering the equation provided in the preamble, let's evaluate the simpler aspect of the equation (the part to the right of the second equal sign) first to see if it can generate an answer. Now we can simplify that part of the equation further by reasoning that if $[\mathrm{S}] \ll K_m$ (which is information given in the caption to Figure 1) then $[\mathrm{S}] + K_m$ (the component in the denominator) is approximately equal to K_m.

Thus the equation provided reduces to:

$v_0 = (V_{max})[\mathrm{S}] / K_m$ and so $v_0 = (V_{max}/K_m) [\mathrm{S}]$ (note the similar form to y = mx + b)

which is a graph of v_0 vs $[\mathrm{S}]$ (i.e. y vs x) with a y-intercept of 0 (see Figure 1 and note that the dashed line intersects y = 0) and therefore the slope must be m = V_{max}/K_m. Thus the correct answer is B.

Note that we did not need, nor could we use, the middle part of the equation since none of the answer choices contained the term $[\mathrm{E_t}]$.

Unit 5, Question 8

The tarpon is among the world's most prized game fish. Adult tarpon are four to eight feet long and weigh 60 to 280 pounds. A graph (Figure 1) has been designed to provide a means to estimate the weight of a tarpon without killing and weighing the fish, using measurements of fork length and dorsal girth.

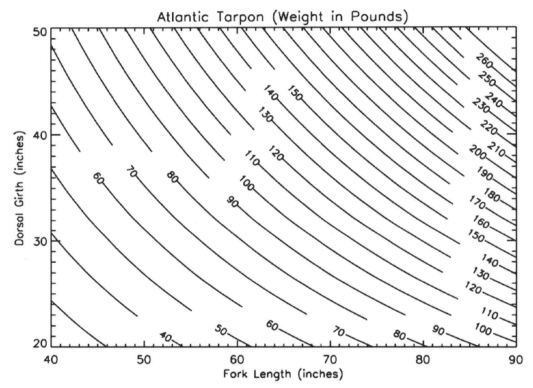

Figure 1: Estimating the weight of tarpon.
Jerald S Ault, PhD; University of Miami

Note that, drawing a straight line from a fork length of 61 inches and then from a dorsal girth of 30 inches intersects the curvilinear line consistent with a weight of approximately 80 pounds.

8. According to Figure 1, which of the following is the best estimate of the dorsal girth in inches of a 210-pound tarpon with a fork length of 83 inches?

   A Less than 39
   B 39
   C 40
   D Over 40

Expect the unexpected! The real GAMSAT will certainly have some graph types that you are not expected to have seen before. In the case of this particular unit, it is a type of nomogram (GM 3.9), which is a diagram showing the relations between three or more variables using a number of scales arranged so that the value of one variable can be found by, for example, drawing a straight line intersecting the other scales. Note that even during the real exam, ACER will typically provide an example as to how to interpret a graph if they expect that they are presenting a graph that is likely novel to you. Pay careful attention when they say: "Note that"!

Some students will use their exam ID (e.g. driver's license) to draw straight lines. We suggest having a long, straight, hexagonal HB pencil (NOT cylindrical because it can roll, and NOT ergonomic because a straight edge is useful for many different types of graph analysis MCQs). Of course, a ruler is not permitted during the real exam.

Using the example provided, drawing a line from a fork length of 61 inches and dorsal girth of 30 inches, results in an intersection at the weight (curvilinear/curved line) of 80 pounds. That brings our attention to the curved lines, how they are continuous and numbered every 10 pounds with varying intervals. In particular, notice the curved line that says '80' has 3 segments: a middle segment that intersects the data points that we evaluated, and the curved line extends to the bottom right and to the top left of the graph. Thus the example helps us interpret the curved lines. You can see our annotation of Figure 1 of the preceding reasoning in green on the next page (*au verso*).

Now when we assess the weight of 210, we must follow that curve upwards until it intersects the vertical line from 83 inches (fork length) and then we can read the dorsal girth, which is 42 inches. Since it is greater than 40 inches, answer choice D is correct.

There is some human biology on the GAMSAT, but fish, birds, bats, and insects are also quite popular!

Notice that Questions 7 and 8 are typically placed in the 'Biology' category but you would be hard pressed to find an introductory-level university course (or any uni. BIO course) that would ask such questions. That is just one of the many reasons that GAMSAT preparation has its own unique path to success.

Please keep in mind: Since some pharmaceutical companies may try to influence the prescribing patterns of doctors by presenting data in complex graphs, tables and/or diagrams, developing a skill for graph analysis will serve both you and your future patients well.

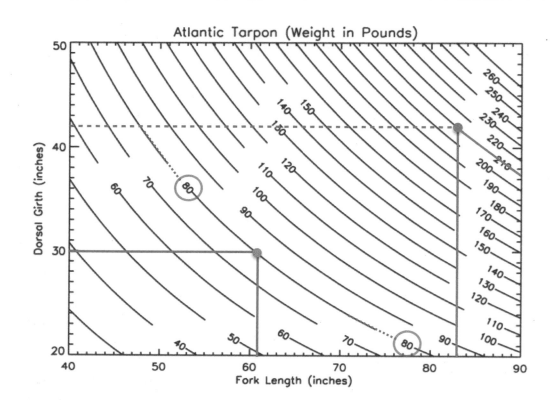

Unit 6, Question 9

In the following branched metabolic pathway, a blue dashed arrow with a minus sign represents the inhibition of a metabolic step by an end product:

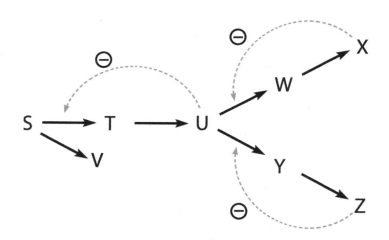

9. Identify the process(es) that would be dominant in the metabolic pathway provided if the 2 end products X and Z were both in relatively high concentrations.

   A T → U
   B S → V
   C U → Y
   D Both W → X and Y → Z

On the Surface: If X and Y are present in high concentrations then, according to the diagram, they will inhibit (i.e. negative feedback) the reactions U → W and U → Y (making answer choice C incorrect). This creates a blockage along the highway so U begins to accumulate. Now U will feedback to block (inhibit) the conversion of S → T (which means less T → U will take place, thus answer choice A is incorrect). Now S accumulates and has only one release valve: S → V (like taking the exit from a highway with loads of traffic).

Going Deeper: Note that answer choice D is not consistent with negative feedback ("inhibition of a metabolic step by an end product" consistent with the diagram). If high concentrations of X and Z resulted in reactions that will make even more X and Z, then that is consistent with positive feedback and is analogous to a runaway, accelerating freight train. It is very important to understand, even if you are just following the arrows in the pathway, the moment that X and Z are elevated, the reaction that makes them is inhibited and therefore cannot be dominant. Potentially, answer choice D would usually be correct when X and Z are in relatively low concentrations.

We will later see classic examples of positive feedback including blood clotting (in the next unit) and contractions in childbirth (BIO 6.3.7). When uterine contraction occurs, the hormone 'oxytocin' is released into the body which stimulates even more contractions. Thus, the result is an increased amplitude and frequency of contractions. The loop is only broken once the baby leaves the uterus.

Side note: There are many different ways to symbolize positive/negative feedback. They may use + or - symbols which may or may not be enclosed in a circle (like the previous image). Or they could use solid or dashed lines with arrow heads, or in the case of negative feedback, it could end with a "T" (for example, the pathway in the next unit). You do not need to commit the various options to memory since a 'key' or legend will be provided or, alternatively, a description will be given as to the meaning of the arrows or connections in the pathway provided.

Unit 7, Questions 10-15

Coagulation (i.e. *clotting*) is the process by which blood changes from a liquid to a cross-linked fibrin gel referred to as a 'blood clot'. This process may stop blood loss from a damaged vessel (*haemostasis*). For normal coagulation to occur, the necessary clotting factors must be present in the blood. There are a number of diseases that arise from disorders of coagulation which can range from bleeding (haemorrhage, bruising) to obstructive clotting (thrombosis).

The coagulation cascade (Figure 1) has two initial pathways which lead to fibrin formation. These are the contact activation (intrinsic) pathway, and the tissue factor (extrinsic) pathway, which both lead to the final 'common pathway' of factor X, thrombin and fibrin. The pathways are a series of reactions in which an inactive protein enzyme precursor, and sometimes its co-factor, are altered to become active components that then catalyse the next reaction in the cascade. Coagulation factors are generally indicated by Roman numerals, with a lowercase 'a' appended to indicate an active form.

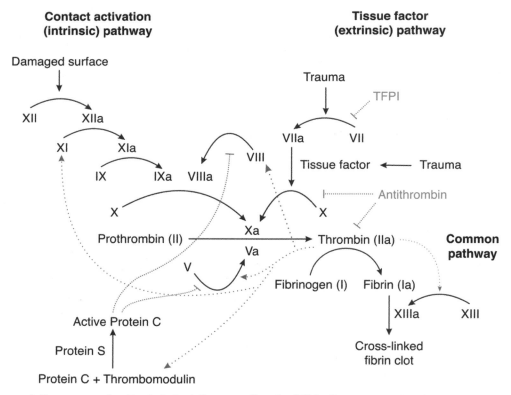

Figure 1: Coagulation cascade. Red dotted lines ending in "T" indicate negative (inhibitory) feedback; green dotted lines ending with an arrow head indicate positive (stimulatory) feedback; curvilinear black arrows indicate 'conversion to'; a factor (or factors) written above and/or below an arrow indicate(s) a catalytic function. For example, factor XIIa catalyses the reaction that converts factor XI to factor XIa. Wikimedia; Joe D, 2007.

10. According to Figure 1, thrombin is directly converted to which of the following?

    A Thrombomodulin
    B Factor VIII
    C Both **A** and **B**
    D Neither **A** nor **B**

11. Vitamin K is required to synthesise factors II, VII, IX and X. A person with a significant deficiency in vitamin K may have:

    A thrombosis due to the activation of both the intrinsic pathway and extrinsic pathway.
    B thrombosis due to the lack of reaction progress in both the intrinsic pathway and extrinsic pathway.
    C haemorrhage due to the lack of reaction progress in either the intrinsic pathway or extrinsic pathway.
    D haemorrhage due to the lack of reaction progress in both the intrinsic pathway and extrinsic pathway.

12. According to the information provided, the final common pathway is most directly activated by:

    A tissue factor and factor VIIa.
    B a blood clot.
    C the activated form of factor XII.
    D antithrombin.

13. In biochemical regulatory mechanisms, negative feedback:

    A is the process of maintaining steady change in one direction.
    B occurs rarely and only in the presence of positive feedback.
    C can operate to maintain a substance's concentration nearly constant.
    D helps to amplify the body's response to a stimulus.

14. A blood clot, formally a 'thrombus', has 2 components: aggregated platelets and red blood cells that form a plug, and a mesh of cross-linked protein. The protein component is largely composed of a more or less equal quantity of factors:

   A   from I to XIII.
   B   in the common pathway.
   C   Ia and XIIIa.
   D   neither **A** nor **B** nor **C**.

15. Which of the following is likely the best treatment option for a person with severe protein S deficiency?

   A   Factor VIIIa
   B   Factor Xa inhibitors
   C   Fibrinogen
   D   Factor XIII activators

Question 10: The caption to Figure 1 states that "curvilinear black arrows indicate 'conversion to'". And so, since there is no curvilinear arrow beginning with thrombin, we have no information as to what thrombin is converted to. Thus answer choice D is correct.

Going Deeper: The caption also states that "a factor (or factors) written above and/or below an arrow indicate(s) a catalytic function" and so we can conclude from Figure 1 that thrombin is the enzyme that catalyses the reaction that produces fibrin. And since the caption states "green dotted lines ending with an arrow head indicate positive (stimulatory) feedback," thus thrombin must stimulate the production of factors VIII and XI, as well as the conversions of V to Va, and XIII to XIIIa, and some stimulatory role with respect to thrombomodulin. To stimulate or catalyse a reaction is wholly different from being the chemical (or substrate/reactant) converted into another chemical (product). We can see from Figure 1 that thrombin is a very important and central component to the coagulation cascade.

Question 11: According to Figure 1, prothrombin (factor II) produces thrombin in the presence of activated factor X and V as part of the final common pathway. If only factors II and X were deficient, that would be enough to retard the normal progress of both the intrinsic and extrinsic pathways, independently, because the common pathway cannot proceed as usual (like a traffic jam along the highway!). A lack of the factors involved in coagulation, as alluded to in the opening paragraph, would reasonably result in bleeding (haemorrhage). Thus answer choice D is correct.

Question 12: The second paragraph of the preamble states "the final 'common pathway' of factor X, thrombin and fibrin." Taking that information, we can see that Figure 1 shows 2 different ways that factor X can be activated to produce Xa which then activates prothrombin. And now we can see exactly how 2 different pathways come together for the final common pathway (note the placement of the words 'Common pathway' in bold on the same line with factor Xa). We can see that in the extrinsic pathway, factor VIIa works with tissue factor to activate the conversion of factor X to factor Xa which is needed for the common pathway. Thus answer choice A is correct.

Regarding the other answer choices: (B) we do not see an arrow in Figure 1 coming from the end product, 'clot', to suggest positive or negative feedback. However, the objective of the pathway is to make a blood clot so it seems suspicious, once the objective is met, that the clot would feedback to activate the forming of yet more clot. At any rate, we do not have sufficient "information provided" to conclude that the clot most directly activates the common pathway; (C) the activated form of factor XII, which is XIIa, begins a cascade activating several steps which finally produces Xa. Answer choice A is the better answer since it accomplishes the same task in fewer steps ("most directly"); (D) antithrombin clearly inhibits the common pathway making it the least plausible of the options.

Going Deeper: You may have noticed and/or you could be asked about examples in the cascade where a factor needs some help to accomplish its task. Answer choice A is such a situation where an activated factor (VIIa) needs help (tissue factor) in order to activate another factor (X). So tissue factor is called the 'cofactor' of factor VIIa. Using Figure 1 and its caption, can you identify other cofactors with Roman numerals? Also, given that tissue factor is actually factor III, can you identify which Roman numerals are missing from the sequence in the cascade?

The caption states that "a factor (or factors) written above and/or below an arrow indicate(s) a catalytic function." There are 2 instances where 2 factors are clearly written in association with an arrow: factor IXa and its cofactor VIIIa; and factor Xa and its cofactor Va.

The 2 factors missing from the sequence shown in Figure 1, from I to XIII, include Factor IV which is calcium, and factor VI which does not exist!

Question 13: A positive feedback loop causes a self-amplifying cycle where a physiological change leads to even greater change in the same direction (thus answer choices A and D are incorrect). A negative feedback loop is a process in which the body senses a change, and activates mechanisms to reverse that change. Of course, such a process is essential for homeostasis (steady state, thus answer choice C is correct).

Although positive feedback in unlikely to occur in the absence of negative feedback (such as in Figure 1), the reverse is not true (answer choice B is incorrect). In fact, negative feedback is far more common than positive feedback. Throughout the BIO chapters, we will be exploring many pathways governed by negative feedback.

Going Deeper: Positive feedback responds to a perturbation in the same direction as the perturbation. In so doing, there is amplification or growth of the output signal which typically occurs to a point until a negative feedback response takes over and restores order. In other words, we can see the example in Figure 1 that positive feedback occurs first, it is most urgent, the person is bleeding. Negative feedback takes longer but you want it to occur at some point because you do not want blood clots forming uncontrollably since they can block the circulation of blood, and thus result in a lack of oxygenated blood to parts of your body with potential consequences including stroke, gangrene, etc. Thus positive feedback can lead to the rapid loss of internal stability (homeostasis) and is therefore the source of many diseases.

You can deduce the answer to Question 13 just by having considered the events in Figure 1; however, this is one of the less common GAMSAT-style questions where having specific background knowledge is disproportionately beneficial. Later, we will explore metabolic pathways (BIO 4.4-4.10), hormones (BIO Chapter 6), positive and negative feedback (BIO 6.3.6, 6.3.7), blood clotting (BIO 7.5), etc. We will continually try to remind you not to get lost in details, like trying to commit the names and actions of each hormone to memory. Rather, it is the understanding of the big picture and key interactions which will then permit you to more quickly assess flow charts like Figure 1.

Question 14, On the Surface: The end product of the cascade, mentioned in the preamble and shown in the diagram, is fibrin which forms the blood clot. The factors are referred to as proteins in paragraph 2 of the preamble suggesting that fibrin, factor Ia, is a protein and is clearly an integral component of the 'cross-linked fibrin clot' in Figure 1. You might be tempted to believe that factor XIIIa might be part of the clot but recall from the second paragraph of the preamble: "an inactive protein enzyme precursor, and sometimes its co-factor, are altered to become active components that then **catalyse** the next reaction in the cascade."

Thus factor XIIIa, being an enzyme that catalyses the reaction that converts fibrin to a clot ('crosslinks fibrin'), like all enzymes, is not consumed by the reaction (thus does not become part of the product). Thus the protein component of the clot is mainly fibrin and we have no information about any other possible component, thus the correct answer is D.

Going Deeper: Almost all metabolic processes in the cell need enzymes in order to occur at rates fast enough to sustain life. The set of enzymes produced in a cell determines which metabolic pathways occur in that cell. Like all catalysts, enzymes increase the reaction rate by lowering the activation energy but they do not alter the equilibrium of a reaction. Some enzymes can make their conversion of substrate to product occur many millions of times faster. In practical terms, this means that reactions that would normally take years, occur in fractions of a second. Many therapeutic drugs are enzyme inhibitors which aim to correct an aberrant cellular pathway.

Question 15: According to Figure 1, Protein S appears to assist in the production of active protein C which inhibits (negative feedback, mentioned in the caption of Figure 1) the reaction that produces Va (which is a cofactor for Xa) and VIIIa (which is a cofactor for IXa that results in the production of Xa). Thus in both instances, the production of thrombin is inhibited and thus the common pathway which leads to a blood clot (*thrombosis*, alluded to in paragraph 2 in the preamble) is inhibited. And so, we can conclude that a protein S deficiency means that the common pathway is NOT blocked and therefore proceeds uninhibited. For blood, this suggests uninhibited thrombosis.

Thus the solution would be to treat the patient with something that imitates the natural role of protein S. Since we want to inhibit the common pathway, the best answer choice is B. The other answer choices promote the coagulation cascade and thus worsen the condition of blood clotting (thrombosis).

More Fun Awaits!

If you feel like you are on a roll, and you are yearning for another complex pathway flow chart, go to gamsat-prep.com and try the test GS-Free. The first unit has heaps of pathway questions. If you are an NSB candidate, try GS-Free after you have completed BIO Chapter 1 so you will have some basic background to make the unit a little easier. Despite the latter suggestion, please notice how little assumed GAMSAT Biology knowledge was necessary to answer the questions in the last few units.

If it is the first time that you have seen problems like the ones that you have just experienced, then of course it can be quite a challenge. But please remember: there are hundreds of practice questions online from simple to GAMSAT level that come free with this textbook. There are over 1000 practice questions that come with the 3-book GS set, and over 5000 MCQs that we have with various other packages. It is probably not accurate to say 'practice makes perfect' but certainly targeted and efficient practice can help you optimise your

GAMSAT score; ultimately, with the objective being to get you beyond the requirement for the medical or dental school that you wish to attend.

Now that you have seen that it can take dozens of pages just to present 15 MCQs, you can understand how having hundreds of questions online has made this textbook about 1/3 of the size it would have been otherwise, which of course means that there was a significant cost savings to you.

Cross-references…

Wherever possible, as we do with all of our books and videos, we will identify another chapter, section or subsection of the book where you can find more information regarding a particular topic. For the most part, each book is self-contained but there are some exceptional cases where we cross-reference between different GS books. The following table contains a summary of the abbreviations used in the Introduction and throughout the following chapters.

Cross-references in the Gold Standard (GS) books, videos, apps, etc.

Abbreviation	Subject	Gold Standard (GS) Book
ORG	Organic Chemistry	GS Biological Sciences, Book 3
BIO	Biology	GS Biological Sciences, Book 3
GM	GAMSAT Math	GS Physical Sciences, Book 2
CHM	General Chemistry	GS Physical Sciences, Book 2
PHY	Physics	GS Physical Sciences, Book 2
RHSS	Reasoning in Humanities & Social Sciences	GS Section 1 & 2, Book 1
WC	Written Communication	GS Section 1 & 2, Book 1

For example, BIO 6.3.7 means that you will find more information by looking at the GS Biological Sciences textbook, Chapter 6 Biology, in the subsection 6.3.7. After a few chapters, you will find the system to be quite straightforward and, often, helpful.

Note: Despite the many new additions throughout this textbook, it remains 99% error-free. Should you have any doubts, join us at gamsat-prep.com/forum.

A Quote with a Dual Purpose

Here is a beauty that you can use for GAMSAT Section 2 (Written Communication) and, hopefully, it will provide some exhortation as you face Gold Standard GAMSAT Book 3 of 3!

Now this is not the end. It is not even the beginning of the end. But it is, perhaps, the end of the beginning.

Winston Churchill

Good luck!

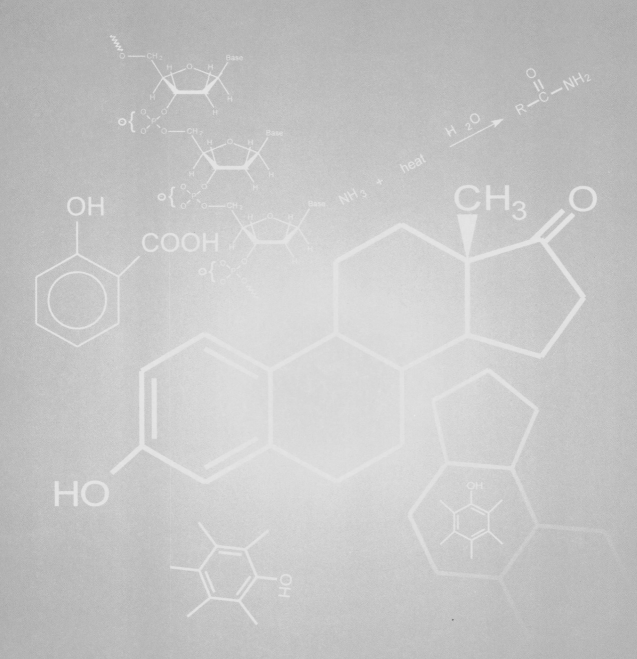

GAMSAT-Prep.com

ORGANIC
CHEMISTRY
PART IV.B: BIOLOGICAL SCIENCES

IMPORTANT: The beginning of each science chapter provides guidelines as to what you should Memorize, Understand and what is Not Required. These are guides to get you a top score without getting lost in the details. Our guides have been determined from an analysis of all ACER materials plus student surveys. Additionally, the original owner of this book gets a full year access to many online features described in the Preface and Introduction including an online Forum where each chapter can be discussed.

MOLECULAR STRUCTURE OF ORGANIC COMPOUNDS
Chapter 1

Memorize	Understand	Not Required *
* Hybrid orbitals * Periodic table trends * Define: Lewis, dipole moments * Ground rules for structures, resonance and reaction mechanisms	* Delocalized electrons and resonance * Multiple bonds, length, energies * Structures and basic stereochemistry * Principles for reaction mechanisms	* Knowledge beyond introductory-level (first year uni.) course * Hybrids involving d, f, etc.

GAMSAT-Prep.com

Introduction

Organic chemistry is the study of the structure, properties, composition, reactions, and preparation (i.e. synthesis) of chemical compounds containing carbon. Such compounds may contain hydrogen, nitrogen, oxygen, the halogens as well as phosphorus, silicon and sulfur. To give some perspective, it is interesting to note that almost 99% of the mass of the human body is made up of just six elements: carbon, hydrogen, oxygen, nitrogen, phosphorus, and calcium. If you master the basic rules in this chapter, you will be able to conquer GAMSAT Organic Chemistry with little further memorization.

Additional Resources

Free Online Q&A + Forum

GAMSAT-prep.com Videos

Flashcards

CARBON ATOM

Special Guest

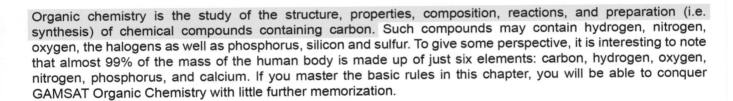

1.1 Generalities

You have never heard of a 'helium tax' or an 'oxygen tax', etc., but you have likely heard of a 'carbon tax'. There are more than 100 elements in the periodic table, but one is the focus of international diplomacy. This is related to the fact that the chemistry of carbon, organic chemistry, is the chemistry of life itself.

That 'carbon tax' is mostly due to the fact that hydrocarbon (hydrogen + carbon) fuels (coal, petroleum, and natural gas) are largely converted (by burning = *combustion*; ORG 3.2.1) to water (H_2O) and carbon dioxide (CO_2). We do not complain about the water, but even the media has identified excess carbon dioxide as a heat-trapping 'greenhouse' gas responsible for climate change. You may also have heard that fuels, 'fossil fuels', are not just hydrocarbons, but they are formed from the fossilized remains of ancient plants and animals - hundreds of millions of years old - and are thus limited in supply. Thus we can deduce that plants and animals make complex molecules involving carbon, hydrogen and oxygen and that is why, when burnt, molecules such as CO_2 and H_2O can be released.

And so, irrespective of your academic background, you have been exposed to many notions related to organic chemistry just by being informed and aware.

Fuels include a category of organic chemicals called 'alkanes' and, we will see later (Chapter 3), when naming alkanes, the suffix -*ane* is used. There tends to be public awareness of many alkanes: methane (the simplest alkane), propane (a fuel for barbecue grills), butane (lighter fuel for cigarettes),

octane (used to improve engine performance and, when high, has entered English vernacular for 'intensity'!). Like acetone (think: nail polish remover, paint thinner), these alkanes evaporate quickly (= *volatile*) because the molecules in the liquid cannot hold each other together. Their volatility relates to that strong smell of acetone or propane, but why? Why isn't water turning to steam at room temperature?

The ability of molecules to interact and the impact that has on a substance's volatility (and therefore boiling point; CHM 4.4), will be discussed every time we present a new category of compounds. Hopefully, you recall from your General Chemistry review, that hydrogen bonds (CHM 4.2) are the key and water is unusually efficient at H-bonding, while hydrocarbons are incapable since they do not have the necessary components, for example, -OH.

Due to differences in electronegativity (CHM 3.1.1, 3.3, 4.2; ORG 1.5), the attraction of the partially positive (= δ^+) hydrogen from one molecule to the partially negative (= δ^-) oxygen of another forms the basis for water's H-bonding (*dashed line*):

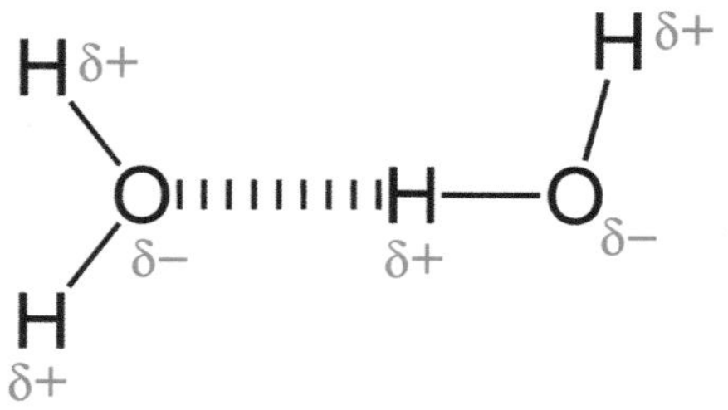

The human body is about two-thirds water. Thus water is the solvent that permits most of life's chemistry to take place.

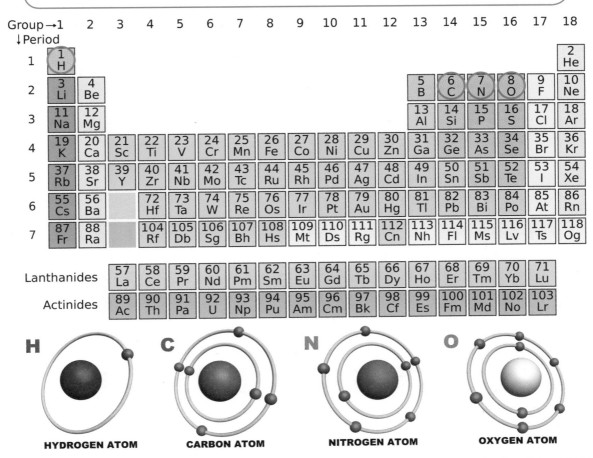

PERIODIC TABLE OF THE ELEMENTS

96% of the mass of the human body is composed of: H, C, N, and O

Figure IV.B.1.0: The periodic table (CHM 2.4) and the most important atoms in organic chemistry. (1) Group 1: alkali metals, red; Group 2: alkaline metals, beige; Groups 3-12 transition metals, peach; olive: metalloids; bright green: nonmetals; other nonmetals include the halogens in yellow (AKA 'halides' as anions), and noble gases in the last group (relatively unreactive, inert). For GAMSAT purposes, since a periodic table is NOT provided, you should be familiar with the location of the first 20 elements + the halogens Br and I. (2) Models (cartoons!) of H, C, N and O with red electrons in orbit around a central nucleus: Notice that the number of electrons matches the atomic number in the periodic table since the atoms are neutral (PHY 12.1; CHM 2.1; i.e. the negatively charged electrons = the number of positively charged protons = the atomic number in the periodic table). Chemical reactions/bonding do not include the nucleus - nor the inner ring of electrons - but rather the outer ring or *valence* electrons. Despite the cartoon, atoms are not like the solar system, as previously thought, where there is a nucleus like the sun and outer electrons like planets revolving in predictable orbits. Instead, electrons are described as probability distributions (ORG 1.2; CHM 2.1, 2.2). Verify the number of electrons in the outer rings: H, 1; C, 4; N, 5; O, 6. When these atoms bond together, we can represent the entirety of each atom as a sphere.

You are the stuff of stars and diamonds!

Let's talk about carbon! What is so special about carbon? Why is it that all life, as we currently understand, must use carbon as the backbone for molecules?

Carbon, like other atoms, was forged in the heart of stars billions of years ago and blasted throughout space. All the atoms in your body are billions of years old and originate from another galaxy. On our planet, natural forms of carbon include graphite (the main component of 'lead' in pencils) and diamonds.

Bonds between carbon atoms are strong and versatile. Carbon has 4 valence electrons (= outer shell electrons, where all the bonding action takes place). Since every bond - symbolized by a line between 2 atoms - contains 2 electrons, and atoms tend to share electrons in bonds, that means that carbon can bond with a maximum of 4 other atoms (= *saturated*). Keeping this simple fact straight and using your eagle eyes to notice when and how the rule is applied, is the source of several straightforward GAMSAT questions every year.

Part of your training includes, throughout this chapter and those to come, identifying carbons and ensuring that every neutral carbon has 4 bonds. In fact, the following table summarizes different, common states for important atoms. After reading a few chapters, you should come back to this table to ensure your understanding.

Atom	Neutral	Cationic	Anionic
C	$-\overset{\displaystyle|}{\underset{\displaystyle|}{C}}-$	$-\overset{\displaystyle|}{\underset{\displaystyle|}{C}}{}^+$	$-\overset{\displaystyle|}{\underset{\displaystyle|}{C}}{:}^-$
N	$-\overset{\displaystyle|}{N}:$	$-\overset{\displaystyle|}{\underset{\displaystyle|}{N}}{}^+$	$\diagup\overset{}{N}\diagdown$
O	$\diagup\ddot{O}\diagdown$	$-\overset{\displaystyle|}{O}{:}^+$	$-\ddot{O}{:}^-$
X	$-\ddot{\underset{..}{X}}:$	$-\ddot{\underset{..}{X}}{}^+$	$:\ddot{\underset{..}{X}}{:}^-$

X = halides (i.e. F, Cl, Br, I)

How strong is a carbon bond? Despite what you may have heard in a comic-book based movie, the hardest material known to humanity is still diamond: pure carbon. Diamond is so strong it is used on the tips of machines to drill through metals, rock and concrete.

Why so strong? The bond between carbon atoms is very strong and the shape, the *tetrahedron*, creates both added strength and the ability to form an incredible array of chains and branches. Not only is the tetrahedron key to the strength of diamonds, it is the most common shape carbon takes in the molecules of life (consider spending a few minutes looking at the pictures - from simple to complex structures - in Chapter 12, Biological Molecules).

The tetrahedron is a pyramid (3D) with a triangular base, and carbon is right in the middle! Whenever carbon is bonded 4 times, which is often the case, each carbon is at the center of a tetrahedron. Consider the following image of methane, CH_4.

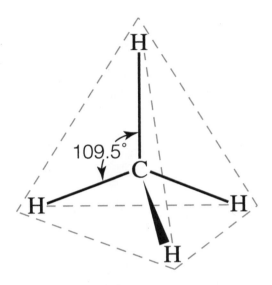

Note: in organic chemistry, a dark triangle means that the bond is coming towards you (i.e. it is coming OUT of the page), a straight line means that the bond is in the same plane as the page, and a dashed triangle means that the bond is going away from you. However, as we will see, there are many shorthand ways to draw molecules that ignore these rules for the sake of expediency. Here are just a couple of such shorthand representations of methane:

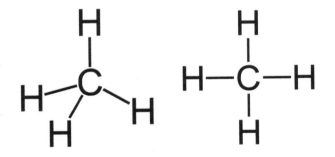

Organic chemistry requires a lot of imagination. Most students will be able to look at the hundreds of illustrations in this book without any difficulty. Some students prefer something more tangible: for example, either purchasing a molecular model set/kit, or making one with the help of YouTube, plasticine and/or Styrofoam. Here is tetrahedral methane using a molecular model set (notice that it is quite similar to the ball-and-stick model of the molecule, see Table IV.B.1.1 *au verso*):

In considering real molecules, how representative are models, skeletal structures and other illustrations? Well, they are really cartoons. How much does Bugs Bunny represent rabbits? I suppose there are some basic features in common, but...

The illustrations of molecules are all simplified representations that, of course, share important characteristics with the real thing. Ideally, you will develop the flexibility to seamlessly go from one way to represent a molecule to another, while reflexively accounting for the key atoms and bonds. By developing your observational skills, as opposed to trying to commit details to memory, you will have a much easier time when faced with typical GAMSAT exam questions.

Table IV.B.1.1: Various ways to represent the structures of carbon-based molecules.

STRUCTURES OF COMMON HYDROCARBONS Hydrogen + Carbon = Hydrocarbons			
	Methane, CH_4	Ethane, C_2H_6	Pentane, C_5H_{12}
Space-filling model Most accurately represents real molecules - compared to other models - but least used since it is not easy to draw and not all atoms or bonds are visible; C: grey, H: white.	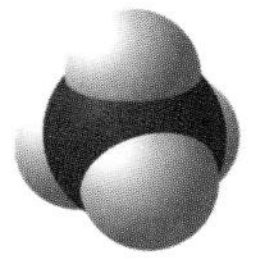		
Ball-and-stick model Atoms, bonds and shapes are clearer (in each case, C is in the center of a tetrahedron); not any easier to draw!	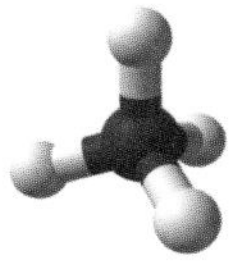	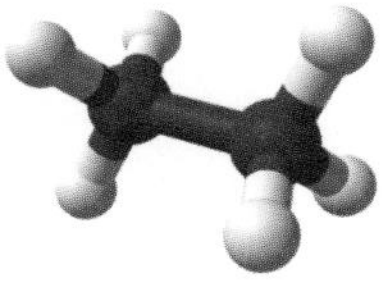	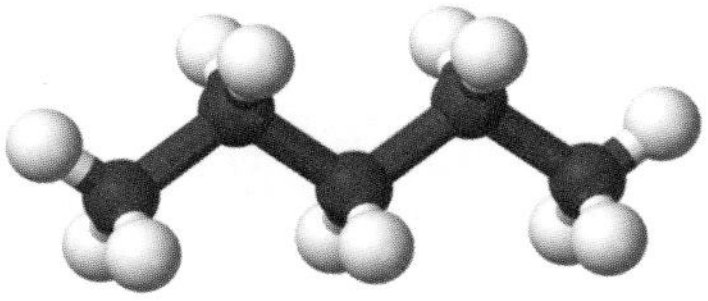
Skeletal structure AKA structural formula, line diagram, etc.; this form preserves the 3D shape with solid (*towards you*) and dashed (*away from you*) triangles.	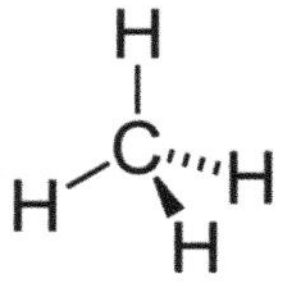	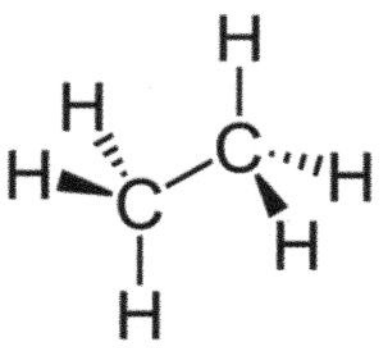	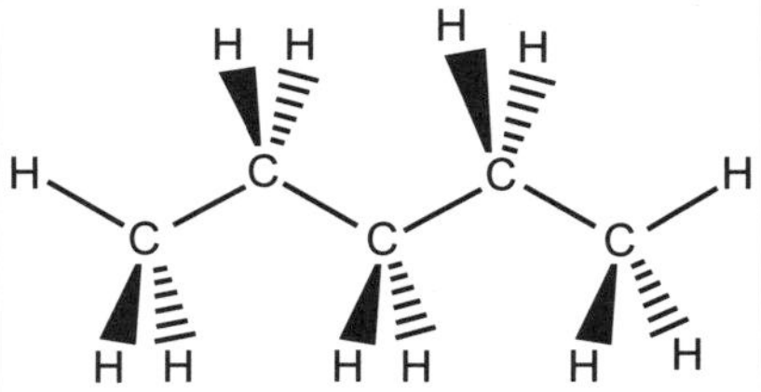
Skeletal structure During the real exam, you would usually use this form (+/- the H's) and/or the shorthand form below. 3D shape is not preserved.	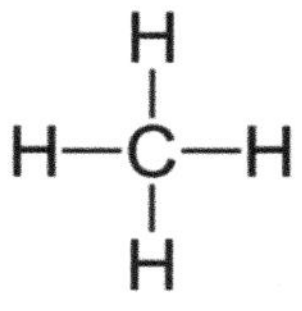	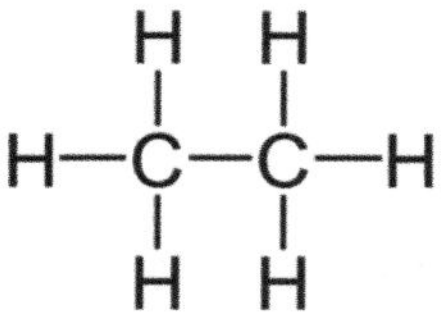	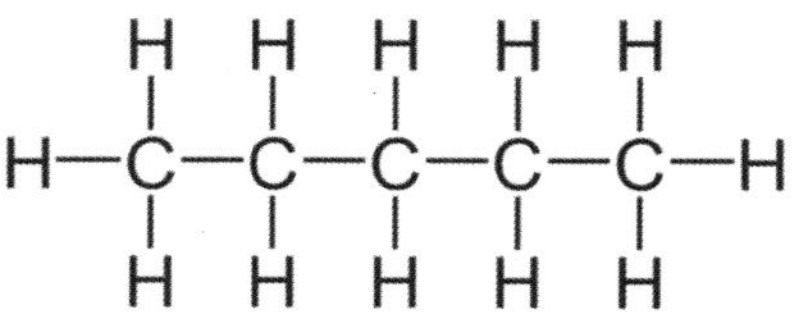
Shorthand Imagination and discipline: Every corner of a geometric figure is a carbon as well as the end of a line*. H's are assumed using the rule: 4 bonds to each C.	N/A		
Miscellaneous	N/A	CH_3CH_3, CH_3-CH_3 H_3C-CH_3	$CH_3CH_2CH_2CH_2CH_3$ $CH_3(CH_2)_3CH_3$

*That is, as long as no other atom is present at the end of a line, then it can be assumed that carbon is present, and as many H's are bonded to that carbon so that neutral C has 4 bonds.

1.1.1 Overview: A Closer Look at the Atoms of Organic Chemistry

Carbon (C), hydrogen (H), oxygen (O), nitrogen (N) and the halides (i.e. fluorine – F, chlorine – Cl, bromine – Br, etc.) are common atoms found in organic compounds. The atoms in most organic compounds are held together by covalent bonds (*the sharing of an electron pair between two atoms*). Some ionic bonding (*the transfer of electrons from one atom to another*) does exist. Common to both types of chemical bonds is the fact that the atoms bond such that they can achieve the electron configuration of the nearest noble gas, usually eight electrons. This is known as the *octet rule*.

A **carbon** atom has one s and three p orbitals in its outermost shell, allowing it to form 4 single bonds. As well, a carbon atom may be involved in a double bond, where two electron pairs are shared, or a triple bond, where three electron pairs are shared. An **oxygen** atom may form 2 single bonds, or one double bond. It has 2 unshared (lone) electron pairs. A **hydrogen** atom will form only one single bond. A **nitrogen** atom may form 3 single bonds. As well, it is capable of double and triple bonds. It has one unshared electron pair. The **halides** are all able to form only one (single) bond. Halides all have three unshared electron pairs.

Throughout the following chapters we will be examining the structural formulas of molecules involving H, C, N, O, halides and phosphorus (P). However, it should be noted that less common atoms often have similar structural formulas within molecules as compared to common atoms. For example, silicon (Si) is found in the same group as carbon in the periodic table; thus they have similar properties. In fact, Si can also form 4 single bonds leading to a tetrahedral structure (i.e. SiH_4, SiO_4). Likewise sulfur (S) is found in the same group as oxygen. Though it can be found as a solid (S_8), it still has many properties similar to those of oxygen. For example, like O in H_2O, sulfur can form a bent, polar molecule which can hydrogen bond (H_2S). We will later see that sulfur is an important component in the amino acid cysteine. {*To learn more about molecular structure, hybrid orbitals, polarity and bonding, review General Chemistry chapters 2 and 3*}

Mnemonic: **HONC** increasing bonds for neutrality . . .
H requires 1 more electron in its outer shell to become stable:
thus hydrogen is neutral when bonded once
O requires 2: thus oxygen is neutral when bonded twice
N requires 3: thus nitrogen is neutral when bonded 3 times
C requires 4: thus carbon is neutral when bonded 4 times

1.2 Hybrid Orbitals

In organic molecules, the orbitals of the atoms are combined to form **hybrid orbitals**, consisting of a mixture of the s and p orbitals. In a carbon atom, if the one s and three p orbitals are mixed, the result is four hybrid sp^3 orbitals. Three hybridized sp^2 orbitals result from the mixing of one s and two p orbitals, and two hybridized sp orbitals result from the mixing of one s and one p. The geometry of the hybridized orbitals is shown in Figure IV.B.1.1.

Take-home message regarding geometry and hybrids: When carbon is bonded 4 times, all 4 bonds are sp^3 and C is in the center of a tetrahedron; when neutral carbon is bonded to 3 atoms, the 3 hybrids are sp^2 and C is in the center of a flat triangle (= *trigonal planar*); when neutral carbon is bonded to 2 atoms, the 2 hybrids are sp and C is in the center of a straight line.

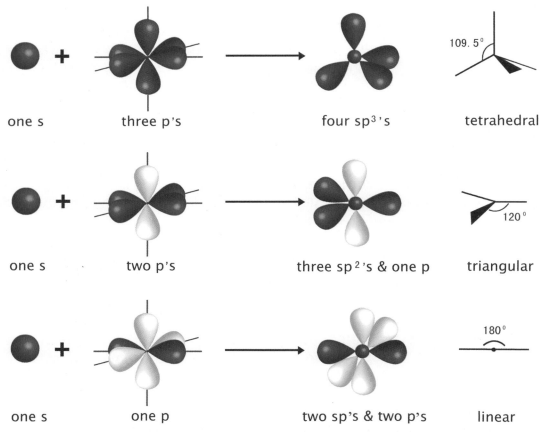

one s	three p's	four sp^3's	tetrahedral
one s	two p's	three sp^2's & one p	triangular
one s	one p	two sp's & two p's	linear

109.5°

120°

180°

Figure IV.B.1.1: Hybrid orbital geometry

NOTE: For details regarding atomic structure and orbitals, see General Chemistry (CHM) sections 2.1, 2.2. For more details regarding hybridized bonds and bond angles (especially for carbon, nitrogen, oxygen and sulfur), see CHM 3.5. Notice in the first line of the image there are three p orbitals occupying the x, y and z axes (GM 3.6) thus p_x, p_y and p_z.

Sigma (or single) bonds are those in which the electron density is between the nuclei. They are symmetric about the axis, can freely rotate, and are formed when orbitals (regular or hybridized) overlap directly. They are characterized by the fact that they are circular when a cross section is taken and the bond is viewed along the bond axis. The electron density in pi bonds overlaps both above and below the plane of the atoms. A single bond is a sigma bond (e.g. C-C); a double bond is one sigma and one pi bond (e.g. C=C); a triple bond is one sigma (σ) and two pi (π) bonds (e.g. C≡C).

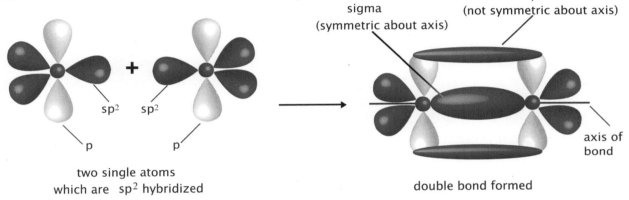

Figure IV.B.1.2a: Sigma and pi bonds. The sp^2 hybrids overlap between the nuclei to form a σ bond; the p orbitals overlap above and below the axis between the nuclei to form a π bond. The product above illustrates the probability distribution (i.e. the likely locations) for the electrons of 2 carbon atoms engaged in a double bond (e.g. the hydrocarbon *ethylene*).

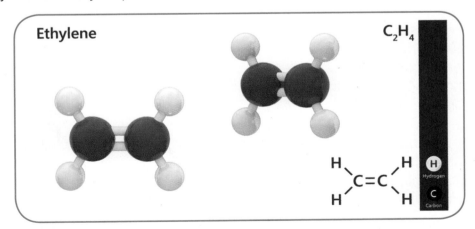

Figure IV.B.1.2b: Ethylene (AKA ethene, $H_2C=CH_2$). Note that each carbon is in the center of a flat triangle: the corners of the triangle being 2 H's and the other C. The carbon-carbon double bond has 2 lines, C=C, one signifies the sigma bond (sp^2-sp^2) and the other is the pi bond (p-p). You may wonder: why does the pi bond only get 1 line when Fig. IV.B.1.2a shows p-p bonding above *and* below the sigma bond? Imagine each carbon like a block of wood with a big screw between the 2 blocks holding them together. The screw is 1 sigma bond. Imagine a very thick rubber band placed around the blocks, encompassing the two blocks thus reinforcing their bond. The rubber band, which goes above and below the screw, is just 1 bond, the pi bond. Side note: as a screw is stronger than a thick rubber band, sigma bonds are stronger than pi bonds.

1.3.1 The Effects of Multiple Bonds

The pi bonds in doubly and triply bonded molecules create a barrier to free rotation about the axis of the bond. Thus multiple bonds create molecules which are much more rigid than a molecule with only a single bond which can freely rotate about its axis.

As a rule, the length of a bond decreases with multiple bonds. For example, the carbon-carbon triple bond is shorter than the carbon-carbon double bond which is shorter than the carbon-carbon single bond.

Bond strength and thus the amount of energy required to break a bond (= *BE, the bond dissociation energy*) varies with the number of bonds. One σ bond has a BE ≈ 110 kcal/mole and one π bond has a BE ≈ 60 kcal/mole. Thus a single bond (one σ) has a BE ≈ 110 kcal/mole while a double bond (one σ + one π) has a BE ≈ 170 kcal/mole. Hence multiple bonds have greater bond strength than single bonds, although a sigma bond is clearly stronger than a pi bond.

1.4 Delocalized Electrons and Resonance

Delocalization of charges in the pi bonds is possible when there are hybridized orbitals in adjacent atoms. This delocalization may be represented in two different ways, the molecular orbital (MO) approach or the resonance (*valence bond*) approach. See Fig IV.B.1.3 and consider reviewing 'covalent bonds' (CHM 3.2).

The MO approach takes a linear combination of atomic orbitals to form molecular orbitals, in which electrons form the bonds. These molecular orbitals cover the whole molecule, and thus the delocalization of electrons is depicted. In the resonance approach, there is a linear combination of different structures with localized pi bonds and electrons, which together depict the true molecule, or **resonance hybrid**. There is no single structure that represents the molecule.

For example, a 'diene' is a hydrocarbon (hydrogen + carbon) chain that has two double bonds that may or may not be adjacent to each other (ORG 4.1). Conjugated dienes (i.e. butadiene) have two double bonds separated by a

Representations of 1,3-butadiene, $H_2C=CH-CH=CH_2$

single bond and are more stable than noncon-jugated dienes because: (1) the delocalization of charge through resonance and (2) hybrid-ization energy. Basically, the positioning and overlap of the pi orbitals strengthen the single bond between the two double bonds.

Along with resonance, hybridization energy affects the stability of the compound. For example in 1,3-butadiene (Fig IV.B.1.3) the carbons with the single bond are sp^2

hybridized, unlike in nonconjugated dienes where the carbons with single bonds are sp^3 hybridized. This difference in hybridiza-tion shows that the conjugated dienes have more 's' character and draw in more of the pi electrons, thus making the single bond stronger and shorter than an ordinary alkane C-C bond. Questions on this concept would always be preceded by an explanatory pas-sage so we will explore s character in the online practice questions.

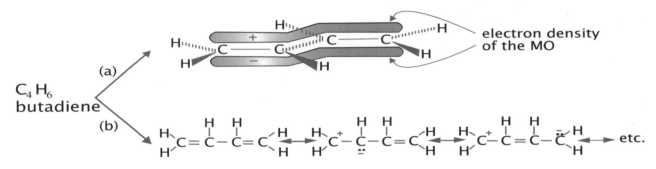

Figure IV.B.1.3: A comparison of MO and resonance approaches. (a) The electron density of the MO covers the entire molecule such that π bonds and p orbitals are not distinguishable. (b) No singular resonance structure accurately portrays butadiene; rather, the true molecule is a composite of all of its resonance structures. Notice that although the bonds can change, atoms do not move in resonance structures. We will be examining reso-nance structures repeatedly throughout the following chapters because they represent typical exam questions.

1.5 Lewis Structures, Charge Separation and Dipole Moments

The outer shell (or **valence**) electrons are those that form chemical bonds. **Lewis dot structures** are a method of showing the valence electrons and how they form bonds. These electrons, along with the octet rule (*which states that a maximum of eight electrons are allowed in the out-ermost shell of an atom*) holds only for the

elements in the second row of the periodic table (C,N,O,F). The elements of the third row (Si, P, S, Cl) use d orbitals, and thus can have more than eight electrons in their outer shell.

Let us use CO_2 as an example. Car-bon has four valence electrons and oxygen has six. By covalently bonding, electrons are shared and the octet rule is followed,

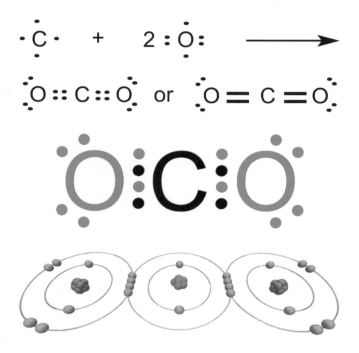

Carbon and oxygen can form resonance structures in the molecule CO_3^{-2}. The −2 denotes two extra electrons to place in the molecule. Once again the octet rule is followed,

In the final structure, each element counts one half of the electrons in a bond as its own, and any unpaired electrons are counted as its own. The sum of these two quantities should equal the number of valence electrons that were originally around the atom.

If the chemical bond is made up of atoms of different electronegativity, there is a **charge separation:**

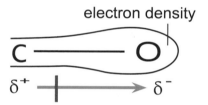
electron density

There is a slight pulling of electron density by the more electronegative atom (oxygen in the preceding example) from the less electronegative atom (carbon in the preceding example). This results in the C−O bond having **partial ionic character** (i.e. *a polar bond; see* CHM 3.3). The charge separation also causes an <u>electrical dipole</u> to be set up in the direction of the arrow. A dipole has a positive end (carbon) and a negative end (oxygen). A dipole will line up in an electric field (PHY 9.1, 10.4).

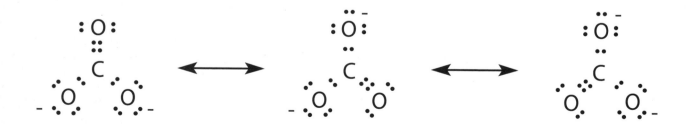

The most electronegative elements (in order, with electronegativities in brackets) are fluorine (4.0), oxygen (3.5), nitrogen (3.0), and chlorine (3.0). These elements will often be paired with hydrogen (2.1) and carbon (2.5), resulting in bonds with partial ionic character. The **dipole moment** is a measure of the charge separation and thus, the electronegativities of the elements that make up the bond; the larger the dipole moment, the larger the charge separation.

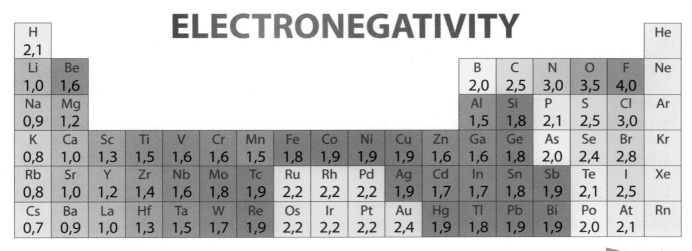

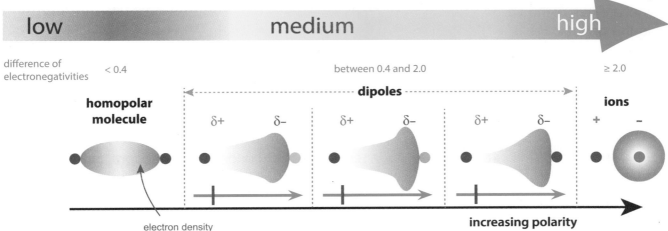

Figure IV.B.1.4: Periodic table showing Pauling's values for electronegativity (CHM 3.1.1) and their impact on bonding. Homopolar - little to no polarity - produces a nonpolar covalent bond whereby the electron density/distribution is symmetric meaning the bond is equally shared (e.g. C-C bond: 2.5 – 2.5 = 0). As described in General Chemistry (CHM 3.1.1, 3.2), a difference in electronegativity between 0.4 and 2.0 creates a separation of charge or dipole. These bonds can be described as polar covalent, or covalent with ionic character, thus the electron distribution is unequal (= asymmetric, not symmetric; e.g. C-O bond: 3.5 – 2.5 = 1.0). When the difference is greater than 2.0, complete electron transfer occurs which results in ionic bonding (e.g. table salt, Na-Cl: 3.0 – 0.9 = 2.1).

No dipole moment is found in molecules with no charge separation between atoms (i.e. Cl_2, Br_2), or, when the charge separation is symmetric resulting in a cancellation of bond polarity like vector addition in physics (i.e. CH_4, CO_2).

A molecule where the charge separation between atoms is not symmetric will have a non-zero dipole moment (e.g. H_2O, CH_3F: *see* below; NH_3 *see* ORG 11.1.2). It is important to note that lone pair electrons make large contributions to the overall dipole moment of a molecule.

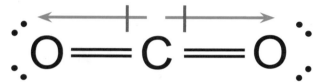

Figure IV.B.1.5: CO_2 - polar bonds but overall it is a non-polar molecule; therefore, CO_2 has a zero dipole moment. Notice that the arrows add to zero like typical vectors (PHY 1.1).

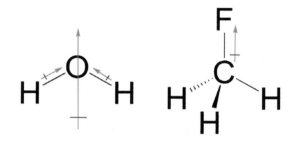

Note: Up to the time of publication, a periodic table has never been provided in a real GAMSAT. One of the purposes of completing the hundreds of chapter review practice questions that are part of the online features of this textbook, is to increase your familiarity with the trends in the periodic table (CHM 2.3; ORG 1.1, 1.5) for the most frequently encountered atoms in GAMSAT Organic Chemistry.

1.5.1 Strength of Polar vs. Non-Polar Bonds

Non-polar bonds are generally stronger than polar covalent and ionic bonds, with ionic bonds being the weakest. However, in compounds with ionic bonding, there is generally a large number of bonds between molecules and this makes the compound as a whole very strong. For instance, although the ionic bonds in one compound are weaker than the non-polar covalent bonds in another compound, the ionic compound's melting point will be higher than the melting point of the covalent compound. Polar covalent bonds have a partially ionic character, and thus the bond strength is usually intermediate between that of ionic and that of non-polar covalent bonds. The strength of bonds generally decreases with increasing ionic character.

Opposites attract. Like charges repel. Such simple statements are fundamental in solving over 90% of mechanisms in organic chemistry. Once you are comfortable with the basics - electronegativity, polarity and resonance - you will not need to memorize the grand majority of outcomes of given reactions. You will be capable of quickly deducing the answer even when new scenarios are presented.

A substance which has a formal positive charge ($^+$) or a partial positive charge ("delta$^+$" or δ^+) is attracted to a substance with a formal negative charge ($^-$) or a partial negative charge (δ^-). In general, a substance with a formal charge would have a greater force of attraction than one with a partial charge when faced with an oppositely charged species. There is an important exception: spectator ions. Ions formed by elements in the first two groups of the periodic table (i.e. Na^+, K^+, Ca^{++}) do not actively engage in reactions in organic chemistry. They simply watch the reaction occur then at the very end they associate with the negatively charged product.

In most carbon-based compounds the carbon atom is bonded to a more electronegative atom. For example, in a carbon-oxygen bond the oxygen is δ^- resulting in a δ^+ carbon (*see* ORG 1.5). Because opposites attract, a δ^- carbon (which is unusual) could create a carbon-carbon bond with a δ^+ carbon (which is common). There are two important categories of compounds which can create a carbon-carbon bond; a) alkyl lithiums (RLi) and b) Grignard reagents (RMgBr), because they each have a δ^- carbon. Note that the carbon

is δ^- since lithium is to the left of carbon on the periodic table (for electronegativity trends *see* ORG 1.5; CHM 2.3). {The letter R typically stands for any hydrocarbon group like alkyl (ORG 3.1), phenyl (ORG 5.1), etc.}

The expressions "like charges repel" and "opposites attract" are the basic rules of electrostatics. "Opposites attract" is translated in Organic Chemistry to mean "nucleophile attacks electrophile". The nucleophile is "nucleus loving" and so it is negatively charged or partially negative, and we follow its electrons using arrows in reaction mechanisms as it attacks the "electron loving" electrophile which is positively charged or partially positively charged. Sometimes we will use color, or an asterix*, or a "prime" symbol on the letter R (i.e. R vs R' vs R'' vs R'''), or a superscript on the letter R (R^1, R^2, etc.), during reaction mechanisms to help you follow the movement of atoms or groups of atoms (the latter may be called *ligands* or *substituents*). Alternatively, an isotope of an atom is used (PHY 12.2). For example, instead of hydrogen, deuterium (^2H or D; PHY 12.2; ORG 14.2.1), or instead of 'normal' oxygen (O-16; ^{16}O), the stable isotope O-18 (^{18}O) is used. Any of the techniques above can be used on an exam question.

For nucleophiles, the general trend is that the stronger the nucleophile, the stronger the base it is. For example:

$$RO^- > HO^- \gg RCOO^- > ROH > H_2O$$

For information on the quality of leaving groups, see ORG 6.2.4.

In organic chemistry, functional groups are specific groups of atoms or bonds within molecules that are responsible for the characteristic chemical reactions of those molecules. The same functional group will undergo the same or similar chemical reaction(s) regardless of the size of the molecule that it is in.

You will find the most common functional groups illustrated below. Again, the shorthand for a carbon atom is each corner of a geometric figure as well as the end of a line. Hydrogens are presumed to be present such that each carbon is bonded 4 times (*see* ORG 1.1). We will be exploring the functional groups below and many others over the following chapters.

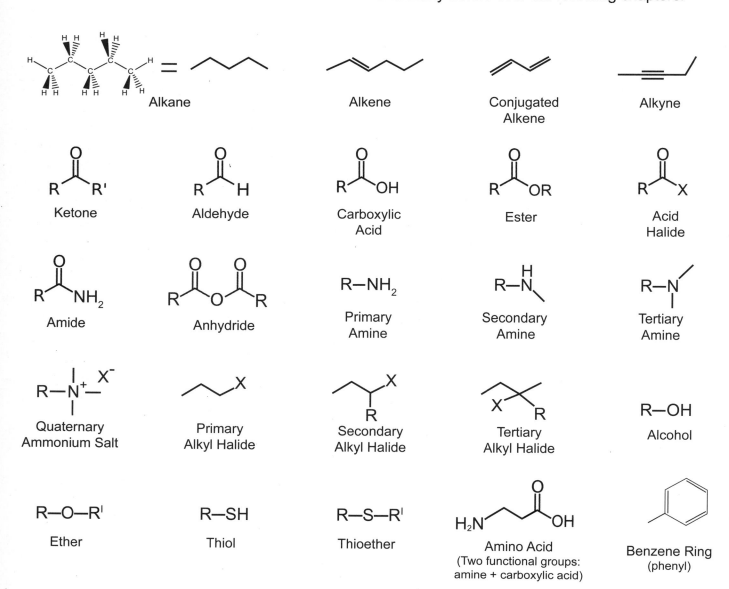

Alkane · Alkene · Conjugated Alkene · Alkyne

Ketone · Aldehyde · Carboxylic Acid · Ester · Acid Halide

Amide · Anhydride · Primary Amine · Secondary Amine · Tertiary Amine

Quaternary Ammonium Salt · Primary Alkyl Halide · Secondary Alkyl Halide · Tertiary Alkyl Halide · Alcohol

Ether · Thiol · Thioether · Amino Acid (Two functional groups: amine + carboxylic acid) · Benzene Ring (phenyl)

1.7 Drawing Molecular Structures of Organic Compounds

As part of GAMSAT Organic Chemistry problem solving, being able to draw basic skeletal structures while maintaining an accurate inventory of all the atoms present in the molecule, is a very important skill. For this exercise, please consider using your carbon-based pencil just in case some erasing is needed! Also, if this is your first time, feel free to re-examine any of the previous sections in this chapter to find information to help you answer (esp. ORG 1.1, 1.1.1, 1.3, 1.4). It is far more valuable to experience the process of problem solving, rather than simply glance at solutions. The worked answers follow the exercise.

For now, do not be concerned with the 3D shapes of the molecules in this exercise. We will be pursuing a detailed examination of molecular shapes in the next chapter on stereochemistry. For now, these skeletal, shorthand line-drawings do not respect spatial orientation, we are only concerned with which atoms are connected to which other atoms (i.e. *connectivity*).

In this exercise, all atoms are neutral so, as discussed at the beginning of this chapter, every H is bonded once, every O is bonded twice, every N is bonded 3 times, and every C is bonded 4 times. If the line diagram shows less than 4 bonds to a carbon, then we assume that H makes up the deficit. If you get tired of drawing every H, feel free to just write H_2 or H_3 when a multiple is present.

For each molecule, draw the expanded structure being sure to account for all atoms including hydrogens. Subsequently, you should also write the molecular formula. Do not worry about naming the molecules for now; however, once you have finished your GAMSAT Organic Chemistry review, consider coming back to this exercise to confirm that most, if not all, of the names make sense to you. We have started with 2 examples below: You can see the shorthand, skeletal formula followed by the expanded form of glycine on the left and proline on the right. They are both amino acids used by the body to produce proteins. Side note: You may notice by looking back at ORG 1.6 that both molecules have functional groups including alkanes, amines (primary for the former, secondary for the latter), and carboxylic acids.

Molecular Formula: $C_2H_5NO_2$

Molecular Formula: $C_5H_9NO_2$

C_4H_8	C_6H_8O	
Molecular Formula:	Molecular Formula:	
C_3H_8	C_4H_{10}	
Molecular Formula:	Molecular Formula:	
C_7H_{12}	C_6H_6	
Molecular Formula:	Molecular Formula:	
C_6H_{10}	C_6H_6	
Molecular Formula:	Molecular Formula:	
C_4	OH $C_5H_{10}O$	
Molecular Formula:	Molecular Formula:	

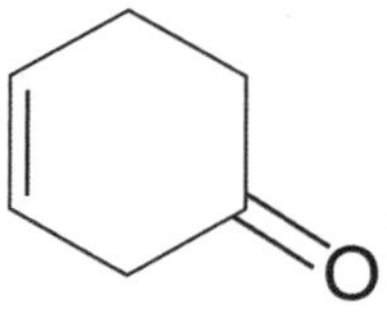

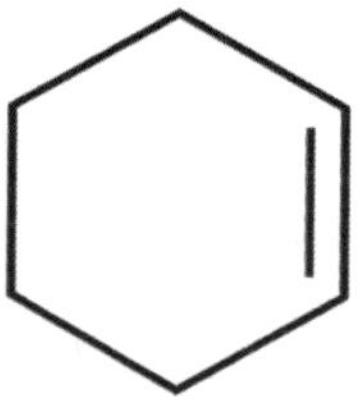

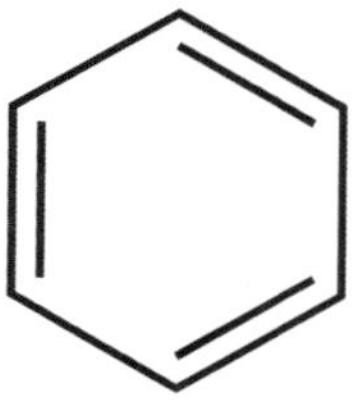

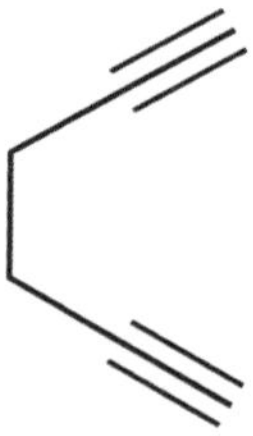

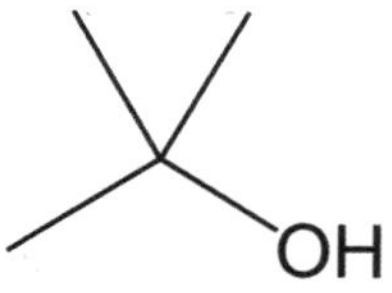

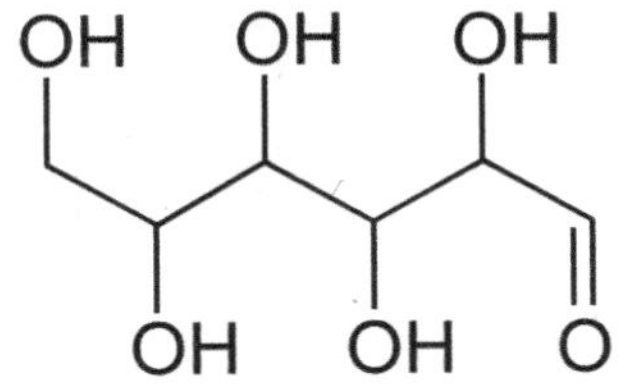

Molecular Formula:

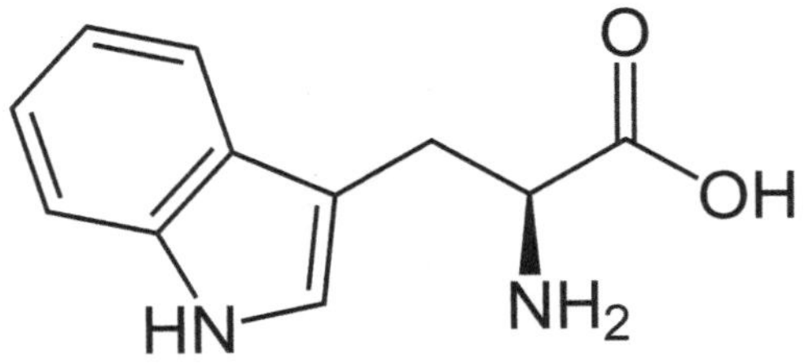

Molecular Formula:

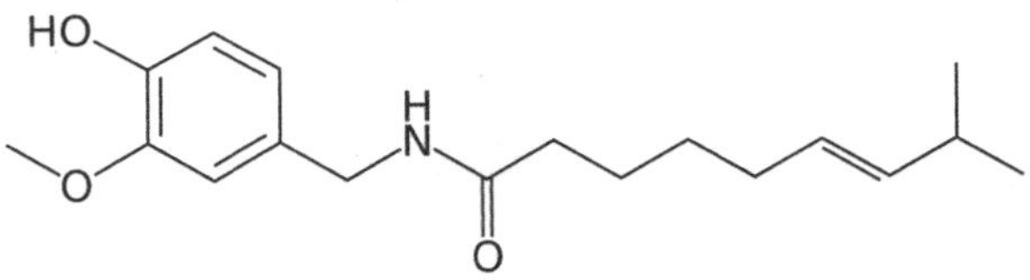

Molecular Formula:

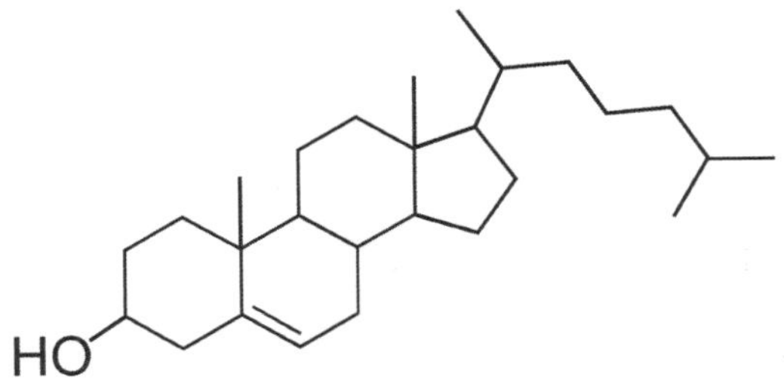

Molecular Formula:

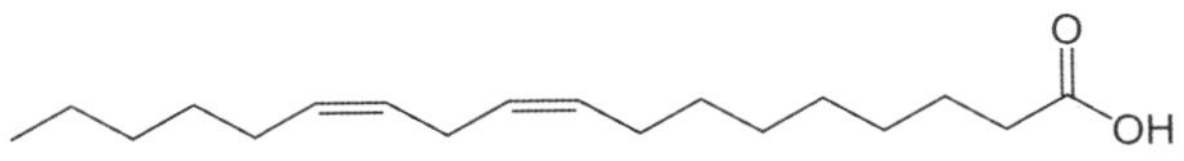

Molecular Formula:

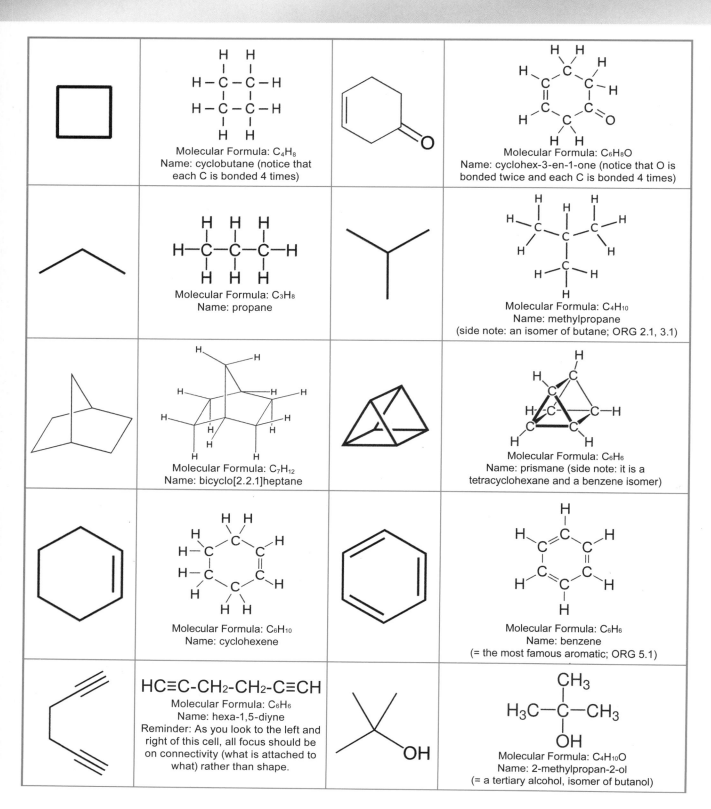

Molecular Formula: C_4H_8
Name: cyclobutane (notice that each C is bonded 4 times)

Molecular Formula: C_6H_8O
Name: cyclohex-3-en-1-one (notice that O is bonded twice and each C is bonded 4 times)

Molecular Formula: C_3H_8
Name: propane

Molecular Formula: C_4H_{10}
Name: methylpropane
(side note: an isomer of butane; ORG 2.1, 3.1)

Molecular Formula: C_7H_{12}
Name: bicyclo[2.2.1]heptane

Molecular Formula: C_6H_6
Name: prismane (side note: it is a tetracyclohexane and a benzene isomer)

Molecular Formula: C_6H_{10}
Name: cyclohexene

Molecular Formula: C_6H_6
Name: benzene
(= the most famous aromatic; ORG 5.1)

HC≡C-CH₂-CH₂-C≡CH
Molecular Formula: C_6H_6
Name: hexa-1,5-diyne
Reminder: As you look to the left and right of this cell, all focus should be on connectivity (what is attached to what) rather than shape.

Molecular Formula: $C_4H_{10}O$
Name: 2-methylpropan-2-ol
(= a tertiary alcohol, isomer of butanol)

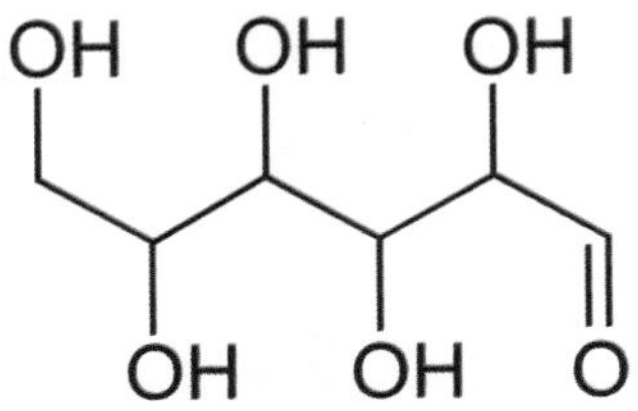

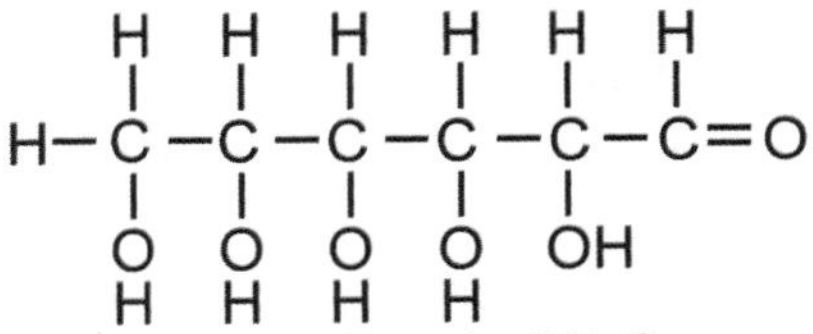

Molecular Formula: $C_6H_{12}O_6$
Name: Glucose (= 2,3,4,5,6-Pentahydroxyhexanal)

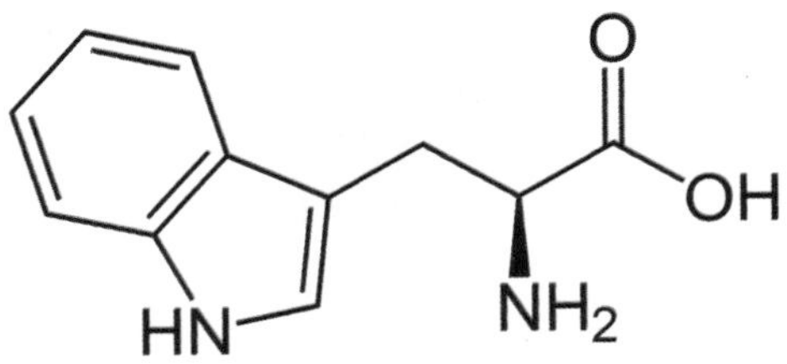

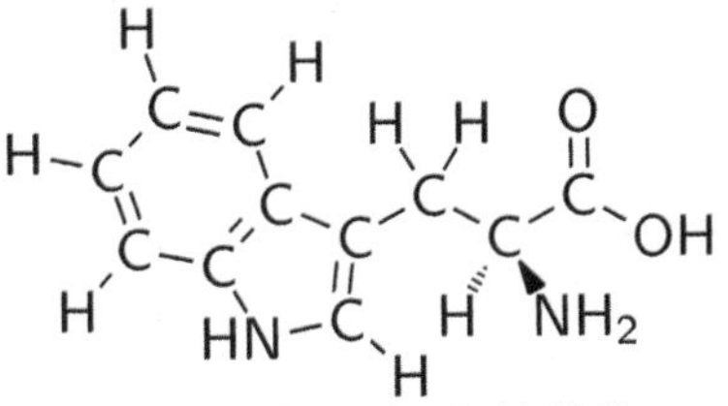

Molecular Formula: $C_{11}H_{12}N_2O_2$
Name: Tryptophan (= an aromatic amino acid essential for the production of proteins in humans; ORG 12.1, 12.2)

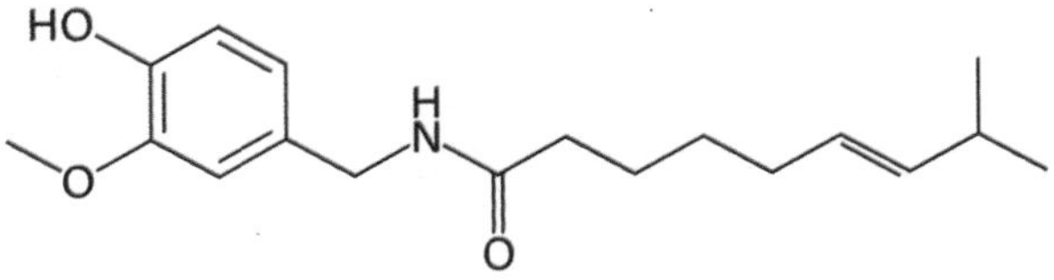

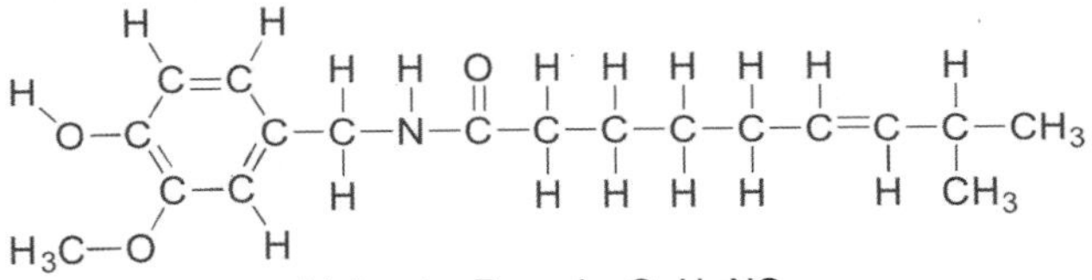

Molecular Formula: $C_{18}H_{27}NO_3$
Name: Capsaicin, AKA: (6E)-N-[(4-Hydroxy-3-methoxyphenyl)methyl]-8-methylnon-6-enamide (= the active ingredient in chili peppers!). Consider going back to ORG 1.6 to see if you can identify the many functional groups in capsaicin: for example, the phenyl alcohol (= *phenol*), amide, alkane, alkene, and the ether in the bottom left of the molecule. Of course, we will be examining all the preceding functional groups over the next 11 chapters, or so.

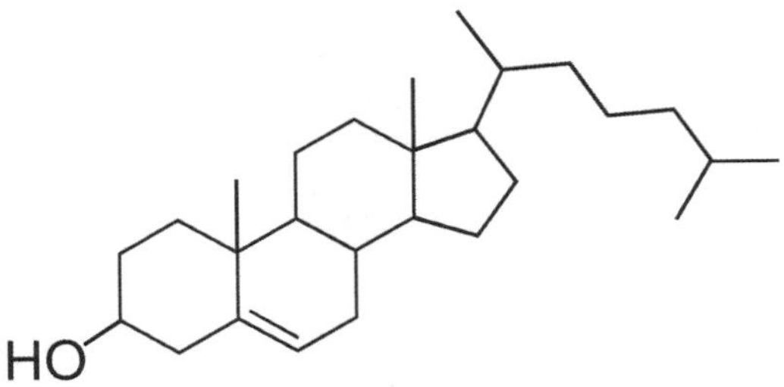

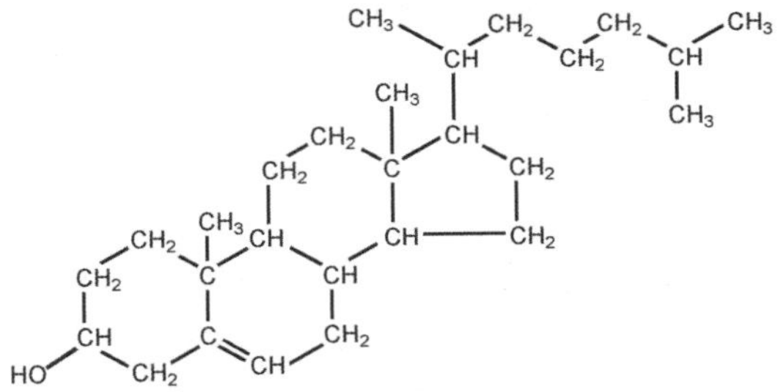

Molecular Formula: $C_{27}H_{46}O$
Name: Cholesterol (the most famous fat! More formerly: a lipid)

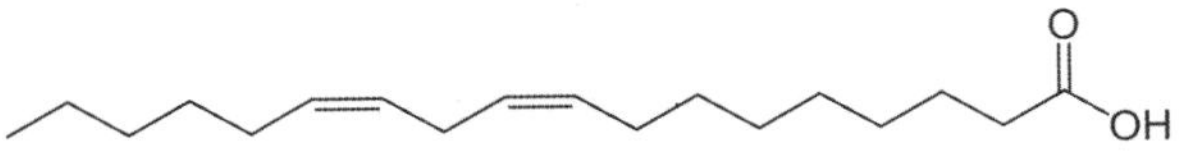

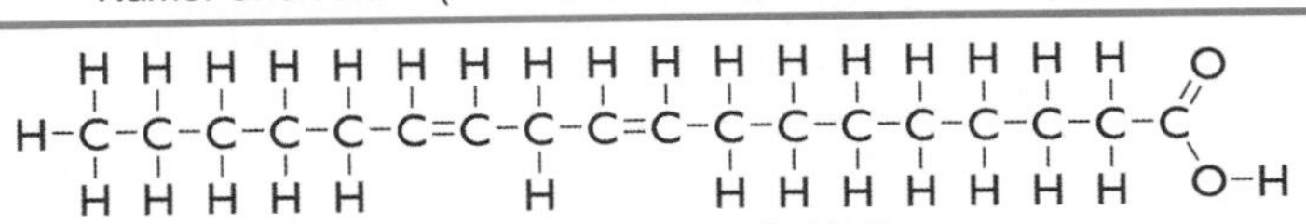

Molecular Formula: $C_{18}H_{32}O_2$
Name: Linoleic acid, AKA: *cis*, *cis* or (9Z,12Z)-octadeca-9,12-dienoic acid; an essential, polyunsaturated (= more than 1 double bond) fatty acid with functional groups: alkane, alkene, carboxylic acid. You may wonder: 'Really, will I ever need to count that many atoms during an exam that provides 1.5 minutes per question in Section 3?' Short answer: Yes, sometimes!

To extend your exercise, consider going back and adding 1 lone pair of electrons on each nitrogen atom and 2 lone pairs on each oxygen atom (ORG 1.1, 1.1.1; for examples: ORG 1.5, 11.1.1, 11.2). Also, just keep in mind that every carbon bonded 4 times has $4sp^3$ hybrids and sits in the center of a tetrahedron; when bonded to 3 atoms, there are $3sp^2$ hybrids and C is in the center of a flat triangle; and finally, when bonded to 2 atoms, there are 2 sp hybrids and C is in the center of a straight line (ORG 1.2). Below is a table with a summary of neutral carbon's bond hybrids.

The selection of molecules that you have now seen foreshadows what you will see as you practice using GS and ACER materials. Of course, the reason for this is that the molecules that you have seen in Chapter 1 - and their derivatives - are frequently part of the real exam.

When bonded to...	Hybridization	Shape	Bond angle
2 atoms	sp	linear	180°
3 atoms	sp^2	trigonal planar (= flat triangle)	120°
4 atoms	sp^3	tetrahedral	109.5°

Reminder: Chapter review questions are available online for the original owner of this textbook. Doing practice questions will help clarify concepts and ensure that you study in a targeted way. First, register at gamsat-prep.com, then login and click on GAMSAT Textbook Owners in the right column so you can use your Online Access Card to have access to the Lessons section.

No science background? Consider watching the relevant videos at gamsat-prep.com and you have support at gamsat-prep.com/forum. Don't forget to check the Index at the beginning of this book to see which chapters are **HIGH**, **MEDIUM** and **LOW** relative importance for the GAMSAT.

Your online access continues for one full year from your online registration.

Memorize	Understand	Not Required*
* Categories of stereoisomers * Define enantiomers, diastereomers * Define ligand, chiral, racemic mixture	* Basic stereochemistry * Identify meso compounds * Assign R/S/E/Z * Fischer projections	* Knowledge beyond introductory-level (first year uni.) course * Memorize specific rotation equation

GAMSAT-Prep.com

Introduction ▌▌▌▌

Stereochemistry is the study of the relative spatial (3-D) arrangement of atoms within molecules. An important branch of stereochemistry, and most relevant to the GAMSAT, is the study of chiral molecules.

More than 1/3 of organic chemistry questions from ACER practice materials test content presented in this chapter. Of course, this does not guarantee the balance of questions on your upcoming exam but it underlines the relative importance of this chapter. Normally, but not always, ACER will reiterate - in the exam's stimulus material - the rules for assigning R/S/E/Z configuration ("stimulus material" refers to the passage, article, graphs, tables or diagrams that precede multiple-choice questions).

Additional Resources

Free Online Q&A + Forum

GAMSAT-prep.com Videos

Flashcards

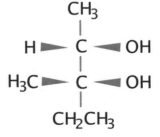

Special Guest

* The real GAMSAT may have advanced level information presented (ie. in a passage) but previous knowledge of said information is not required to answer the questions that would follow. Practice ACER and GS practice GAMSATs can help you clarify this point.

2.1 Isomers

Stereochemistry is the study of the arrangement of atoms in a molecule, in three dimensions. Two *different molecules* with the same number and type of atoms (= *the same molecular formula*) are called isomers. Isomers fall into two main categories: *structural* (constitutional) isomers and *stereoisomers* (spatial isomers). Structural isomers differ by connectivity (= the order and/or kinds of bonds), and stereoisomers differ in the way their atoms are arranged in space (enantiomers and diastereomers; see Fig. IV.B.2.1.1).

2.1.1 Structural (Constitutional) Isomers

Structural isomers have different atoms and/or bonding patterns in relation to each other like the following *chain* or *skeletal* isomers of hexane, C_6H_{14}:

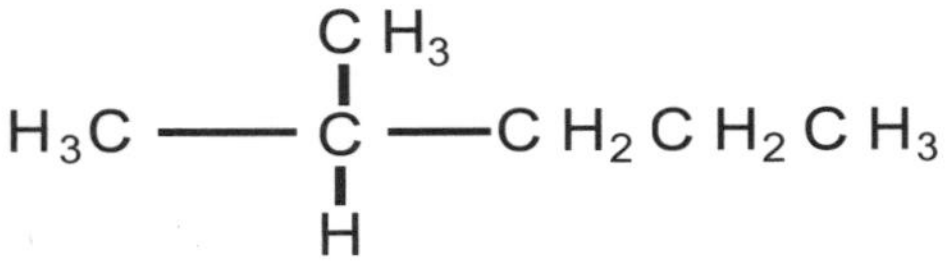

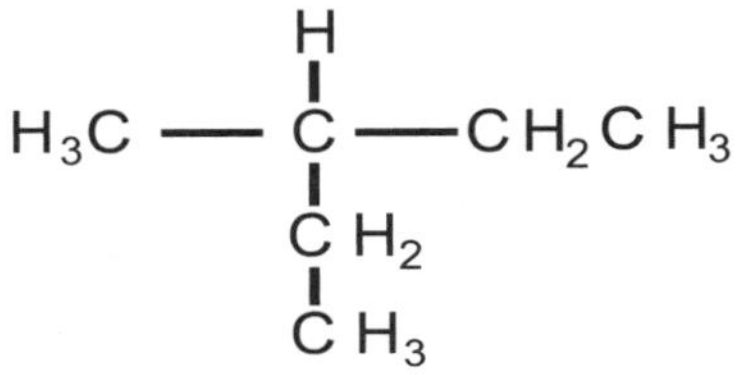

Functional isomers are structural isomers that have the same molecular formula but have different functional groups (ORG 1.6) or *moieties*. For example, the following alcohol (ORG 6.1) and ether (ORG 10.1), $C_4H_{10}O$:

butan-1-ol
(n-butanol)

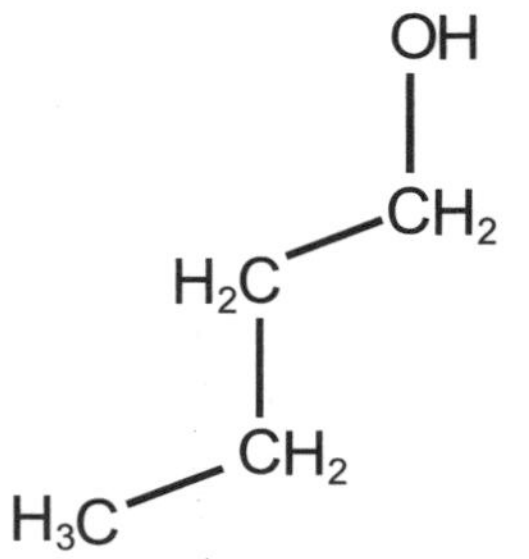

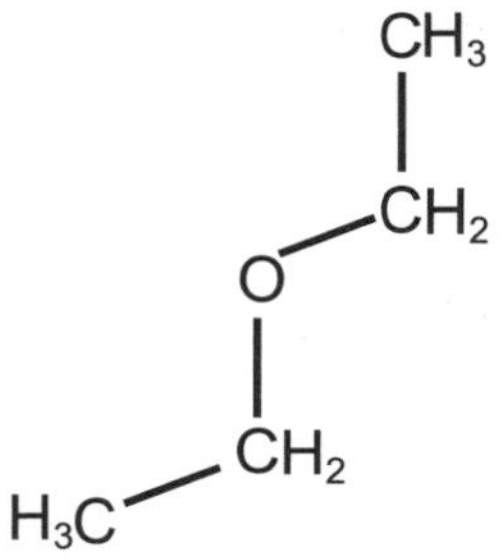

ethoxyethane
(diethyl ether)

Positional or regioisomers are structural isomers where the functional group changes position on the parent structure. For example, the hydroxyl group (-OH) occupying 3 differ-ent positions on the n-pentane (= normal, non-branched alkane with 5 carbons) chain resulting in 3 different compounds, $C_5H_{12}O$:

pentan-1-ol
(1-pentanol)

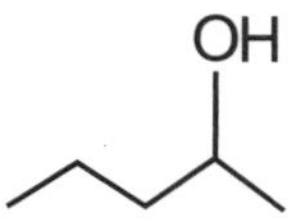

2-pentanol

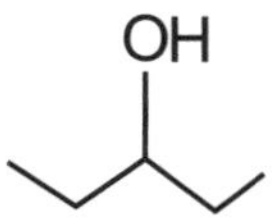

3-pentanol

2.2.1 Geometric Isomers *cis/trans*, E/Z

Geometric isomers occur because carbons that are in a ring or double bond structure are *unable* to freely rotate (see conformation of cycloalkane; ORG 3.3, 3.3.1). This results in *cis* and *trans* compounds. When the substituents (i.e. Br) are on the same side of the ring or double bond, it is designated *cis*. When they are on opposite sides, it is designated *trans*. The *trans* isomer is more stable since the substituents are further apart, thus electron shell repulsion is minimized (ORG 2.4).

cis

cis-dibromoethene   *trans*-dibromoethene

In general, structural and geometric isomers have different reactivity, spectra and physical properties (i.e. boiling points, melting points, etc.). Geometric isomers may have different physical properties but, in general, tend to have similar chemical reactivity.

The E, Z notation is the IUPAC preferred method for designating the stereochemistry of double bonds. E, Z is particularly used for isomeric compounds with 4 different substituent groups bonded to the two *ethenyl* or *vinyl* carbons (i.e. C=C which are sp^2 hybridized carbon atoms). We have just reviewed how to use *cis/trans*. The E, Z notation is used on more complex molecules and, as described, on situations were 4 different substituents are present.

To begin with, each substituent at the double bond is assigned a priority (see 2.3.1 for rules). If the two groups of higher priority are on opposite sides of the double bond, the bond is assigned the configuration E, (from *entgegen*, the German word for "opposite"). If the two groups of higher priority are on the same side of the double bond, the bond is assigned the configuration Z, (from *zusammen,* the German word for "together"). {Generally speaking, learning German is NOT required for the GAMSAT!}

cis-2-bromobut-2-ene
(2 methyl groups on same side)

BUT

(*E*)-2-bromobut-2-ene
(Br is higher priority than methyl)

Mnemonic: Z = Zame Zide; E = Epposites.

Note: From ORG 2.1.1 onwards, until you are in the habit of doing so quickly and efficiently, always make sure that there are 4 bonds to each, neutral carbon (ORG 1.1). When you do not see 4 bonds, like the positional isomers in ORG 2.1.1 or the functional groups presented in ORG 1.6, take the time to work out how many hydrogens – which are not being shown – must be attached to each carbon to complete the rule: '4 bonds to each, neutral carbon'. Similarly, always try to make sure that the number of carbons being presented is correct: either because it matches its isomer (ORG 2.1.1, 2.2) or, if presented, its molecular formula or name (if it is your first time seeing the name of organic molecules, please return to ORG 2.1.1 once you have learned nomenclature in subsequent chapters). Perceiving the correct number of H's and/or C's is a basic requirement for the real GAMSAT.

2.2.2 Enantiomers and Diastereomers

Stereoisomers are different compounds with the same structure (= *connectivity*), differing only in the spatial orientation of the atoms (= *configuration*). Stereoisomers may be further divided into enantiomers and diastereomers. Enantiomers must have opposite, absolute configurations at each and every chiral carbon.

We will soon highlight the easy way to remember the meaning of a *chiral molecule*, however, the formal definition of chirality is of an object that is not identical with its mirror image and thus exists in two enantiomeric forms. A molecule cannot be chiral if it contains a plane of symmetry. A molecule that has a plane of symmetry must be superposable on its mirror image and thus must be *achiral.* The most common chirality encountered in organic chemistry is when the carbon atom is bonded to four different groups. Such a carbon lacks a plane of symmetry and is referred to as a *chiral center*. When a carbon atom has only three different substituents, such as the central carbon in methylcyclohexane, it has a plane of symmetry and is therefore achiral.

A <u>stereocenter</u> (= stereogenic center) is an atom bearing attachments such that interchanging any two groups produces a stereoisomer. If a molecule has n stereocenters, then it can have up to 2^n different non-superimposable (non-superposable) structures (= enantiomers).

<u>Enantiomers</u> come in pairs. They are two non-superposable molecules, which are mirror images of each other. In order to have an enantiomer, a molecule must be chiral. Chiral molecules contain at least one chiral carbon which is a carbon atom that has four different substituents attached. For the purposes of the GAMSAT, the concepts of a chiral carbon, asymmetric carbon and stereocenter are interchangeable.

Enantiomers have the same chemical and physical properties. The only difference is with their interactions with other chiral molecules, and their rotation of plane-polarized light.

Conversely, <u>diastereomers</u> are any pair of stereoisomers that are not enantiomers. Diastereomers are both chemically and physically different from each other.

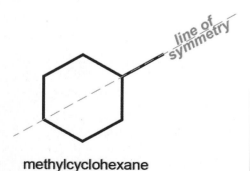

methylcyclohexane

Superimposable vs Superposable: Most exams and many textbooks use these terms interchangeably. On the real GAMSAT, unless the question is preceded by their definitions, then the 2 words have the same meaning. Technically, "superimposable" is to lay or place (something, i.e. a molecule) on or over something else (i.e. another molecule). If the preceding proves that the 2 molecules are identical, then they are "superposable".

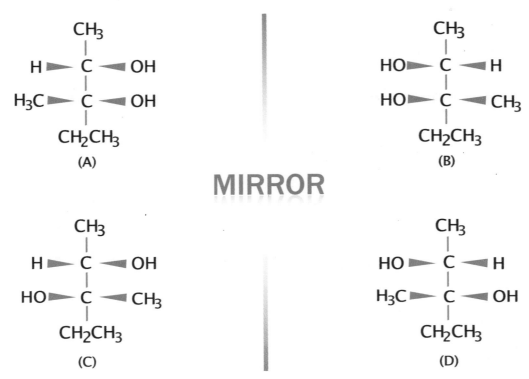

Figure IV.B.2.1: Enantiomers and diastereomers. The enantiomers are A & B, C & D. The diastereomers are A & C, A & D, B & D, B & C. Thus there are 2 pairs of enantiomers. This is consistent with the 2^n equation since each of the structures above have exactly 2 chiral carbons (stereocenters) and thus $2^2 = 4$ enantiomers.

2.3 Absolute and Relative Configuration

Absolute configuration uses the R, S system of naming compounds (*nomenclature; ORG 2.3.1*) and relative configuration uses the D, L system.

Before 1951, the absolute three-dimensional arrangement or <u>configuration</u> of chiral molecules was not known. Instead chiral molecules were compared to an arbitrary standard (*glyceraldehyde*). A molecule was determined to be in its D-form if it has the same relative configuration as D-glyceraldehyde, and its L-form if it has the same relative configuration as L-glyceraldehyde. Thus the *relative* configuration could be determined.

Once the actual spatial arrangements of groups in molecules were finally determined, the *absolute* configuration could be known (ORG 2.3.1).

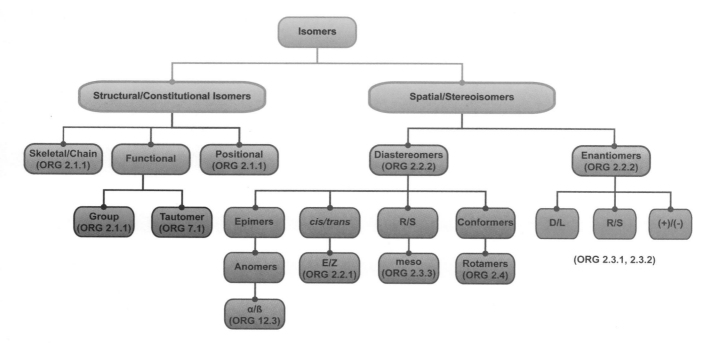

Figure IV.B.2.1.1: Categories of isomers relevant to the GAMSAT.

2.3.1 The R, S System and Fischer Projections

One consequence of the existence of enantiomers, is a special system of nomenclature: the R, S system. This system provides information about the absolute configuration of a molecule. This is done by assigning a stereochemical configuration at each asymmetric (*chiral*) carbon in the molecule by using the following steps:

1. Identify an asymmetric carbon, and the four attached groups.

2. Assign priorities to the four groups, using the following rules (Cahn–Ingold–Prelog priority rules = CIP system):

i. Atoms of higher atomic number have higher priority.

ii. An isotope of higher atomic mass receives higher priority.

iii. The higher priority is assigned to the group with the atom of higher atomic number or mass at the first point of difference.

iv. If the difference between the two groups is due to the number of otherwise identical atoms, the higher priority is assigned to the group with the greater number of atoms of higher atomic number or mass.

v. To assign priority of double or triple bonded groups, multiple-bonded atoms are considered as equivalent number of single bonded atoms:

–CH=CH is taken as

$$-\underset{\underset{C}{|}}{C}H-\underset{\underset{C}{|}}{C}H$$

$$\underset{/}{\overset{\backslash}{C}}{=}O \quad \text{is taken as} \quad \underset{/}{\overset{\backslash}{C}}\underset{\backslash O}{\overset{O}{<}}$$

–C≡C is taken as

$$-\underset{\underset{C}{|}}{\overset{\overset{C}{|}}{C}}-\underset{\underset{C}{|}}{\overset{\overset{C}{|}}{C}}H$$

3. In other words, you must re-orient the molecule in space so that the group of lowest priority is pointing directly back, away from you. The remaining three substituents with higher priority should radiate from the asymmetric carbon atom like the spoke on a steering wheel.

4. Consider the clockwise or counterclockwise order of the priorities of the remaining groups. If they increase in a clockwise direction, the asymmetric carbon is said to have the R configuration. If they decrease in a clockwise direction, the asymmetric carbon is said to have the S configuration {Mnemonic: Clockwise means that when you get to the top of the molecule, you must turn to the Right = R}.

A stereoisomer is named by indicating the configurations of each of the asymmetric carbons.

A Fischer projection is a 2-D way of looking at 3-D structures. All horizontal bonds project toward the viewer, while vertical bonds project away from the viewer. In organic chemistry, Fischer projections are used mostly for carbohydrates (see ORG 12.3.1, 12.3.2). To determine if 2 Fischer projections are superposable (i.e. identical), you can: (1) rotate one projection 180° or (2) keep one substituent in a fixed position and then you can rotate the other 3 groups either clockwise or counterclockwise (3-D configuration preserved):

(3) interchange (switch) the positions of all 4 substituents, in any direction, at the same time:

Assigning R, S configurations to Fischer projections:

1. Assign priorities to the four substituents.

2. If the lowest priority group is on the vertical axis, determine the direction of rotation by going from priority 1 to 2 to 3, and then assign R or S configuration.

3. If the lowest priority group is on the horizontal axis, determine the direction of rotation by going from priority 1 to 2 to 3, obtain the R or S configuration, now the TRUE configuration will be the opposite of what you have just obtained.

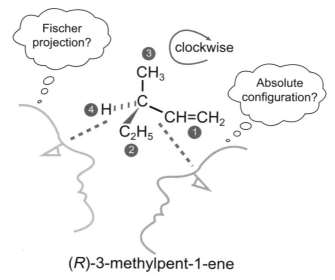

(R)-3-methylpent-1-ene

Figure IV.B.2.2(a): Assigning Absolute Configuration. In organic chemistry, the directions of the bonds are symbolized as follows: a broken line extends away from the viewer (i.e. INTO the page), a solid triangle projects towards the viewer, and a straight line extends in the plane of the paper. According to rule #3, we must imagine that the lowest priority group (H) points away from the viewer.

Fischer Projection

Figure IV.B.2.2(b): Creating the Fischer projection of (R)-3-methyl-1-pentene. Notice that the perspective of the viewer in the image is the identical perspective of the viewer on the left of Figure IV.B.2.2(a). In either case, a perspective is chosen so that the horizontal groups project towards the viewer.

Note: For the GAMSAT, it is not normally expected that you have memorized the rules to assign R, S configurations. They would normally provide the rules and an example before asking questions to confirm that you know how to apply the rules. However, it is normally expected that you know the rules to compare different Fischer projections (ORG 2.3.1). Consider watching the stereochemistry videos at gamsat-prep.com.

2.3.2 Optical Isomers

Optical isomers are enantiomers and thus are stereoisomers that differ by different spatial orientations about a chiral carbon atom. Light is an electromagnetic wave that contains oscillating fields. In ordinary light, the electric field oscillates in all directions. However, it is possible to obtain light with an electric field that oscillates in only one plane. This type of light is known as **plane-polarized light**. When plane-polarized light is passed through a sample of a chiral substance, it will emerge vibrating in a different plane than it started. Optical isomers differ only in this rotation. If the light is rotated in a clockwise direction, the compound is dextrorotary, and is designated by a *d–* or (+). If the light is rotated in a counterclockwise direction, the compound is levrorotary, and is designated by an *l–* or (–). Note that these "d-" and "l-" prefixes are distinct from the uppercase "D" and "L" prefixes (relative configuration, ORG 2.3) and there is no direct correlation between the two systems of nomenclature.

A racemic mixture will show no rotation of plane-polarized light. This is a consequence of the fact that a racemate is a mixture with equal amounts of the (+) and (–) forms of a substance.

Specific rotation (α) is an inherent physical property of a molecule. It is defined as follows:

$$\alpha = \frac{\text{Observed rotation in degrees}}{(\text{tube length in dm}) (\text{concentration in g/ml})}$$

The observed rotation is the rotation of the light passed through the substance. The tube length is the length of the tube that contains the sample in question. The specific rotation is dependent on the solvent used,

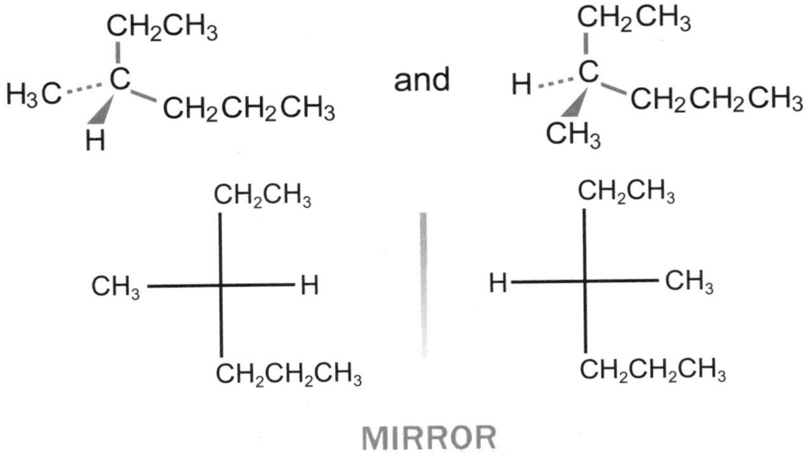

MIRROR

Figure IV.B.2.3: Optical isomers and their Fischer projections: on the left, (R)-(-)-3-methylhexane; on the right: (S)-(+)-3-methylhexane. To prove to yourself that the 2 molecules are non-superposable mirror images (enantiomers), review the rules for Fischer projections (ORG 2.3.1) and compare.

the temperature of the sample, and the wavelength of the light.

It should be noted that there is no clear correlation between the absolute configuration (i.e. R, S) and the direction of rotation of plane-polarized light, designated by (+) or (-). Therefore, the direction of optical rotation cannot be determined from the structure of a molecule and must be determined experimentally. Also note, with the aim to reduce side effects, the stereochemistry of drugs has been increasing in importance over the past few years.

2.3.3 Meso Compounds

Tartaric acid (= 2,3-dihydroxybutanedioic acid which, in the chapters to come, is a compound that you will be able to name systematically = using IUPAC rules) has two chiral centers that have the same four substituents and are equivalent. As a result, two of the four possible stereoisomers of this compound are identical due to a plane of symmetry. Thus there are only three stereoisomeric tartaric acids. Two of these stereoisomers are enantiomers and the third is an achiral diastereomer, called a meso compound. Meso compounds are achiral (optically inactive) diastereomers of chiral stereoisomers.

In a *meso compound*, an internal plane of symmetry exists by drawing a line that will cut the molecule in half. For example, notice that in *meso*-tartaric acid, you can draw a line perpendicular to the vertical carbon chain creating 2 symmetric halves {**MeSo** = **M**irror of **S**ymmetry}.

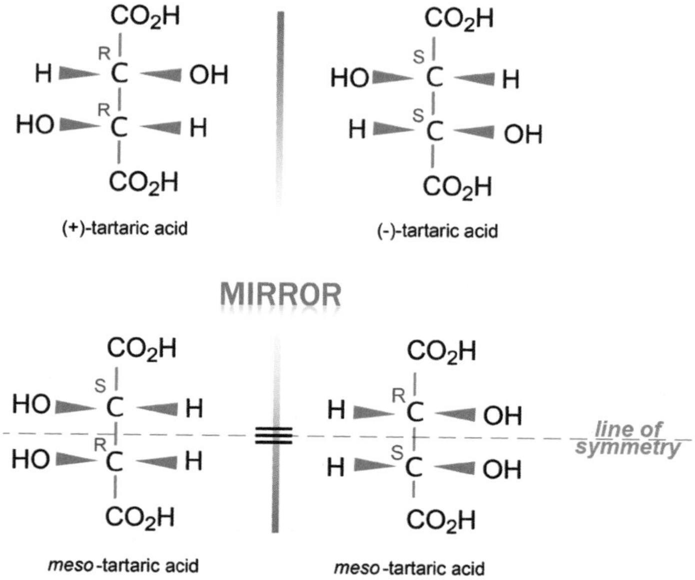

(+)-tartaric acid   (-)-tartaric acid

MIRROR

meso-tartaric acid   *meso*-tartaric acid

line of
symmetry

2.4 Conformational Isomers

Conformational isomers are isomers which differ only by the rotation about single bonds. As a result, substituents (= *ligands* = *attached atoms or groups*) can be maximally close (*eclipsed conformation*), maximally apart (*anti or staggered conformation*) or anywhere in between (i.e. *gauche conformation*).

Though all conformations occur at room temperature, anti is most stable since it minimizes electron shell repulsion. Conformational isomers (= *conformers*, Fig. IV.B.2.1.1) are not true isomers since they are really just different spatial orientations of the same molecules.

Different conformations can be seen when a molecule is depicted from above and from the right, <u>sawhorse projection</u>, or where the line of sight extends along a carbon-carbon bond axis, a <u>Newman projection</u>. The different conformations occur as the molecule is rotated about its axis.

Example 1: Ethane

The lowest energy, most stable conformation, of ethane is the one in which all six carbon-hydrogen bonds are as far away from each other as possible: *staggered*. The reason, of course, is that atoms are surrounded by an outer shell of negatively charged electrons and, the basic rule of electrostatics is that, like charges repel (= electron shell repulsion = **ESR**).

The highest energy, or least stable conformation, of ethane is the one in which all six carbon-hydrogen bonds are as close as possible: *eclipsed*. In between these two extremes are an infinite number of possibilities. As we have previously reviewed, when carbon is bonded to four different atoms (i.e. ethane), its bonds are sp^3 hybridized and the carbon atom sits in the center of a tetrahedron (ORG 1.2, CHM 3.5).

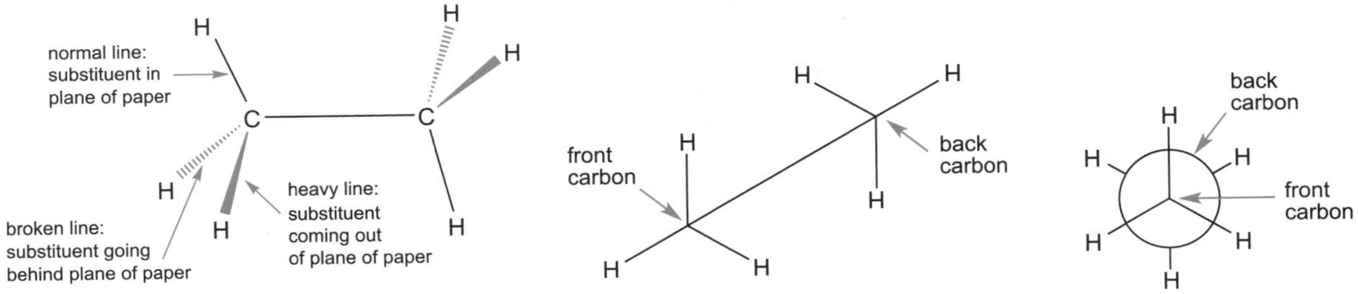

skeletal formula (structure)

sawhorse projection

Newman projection

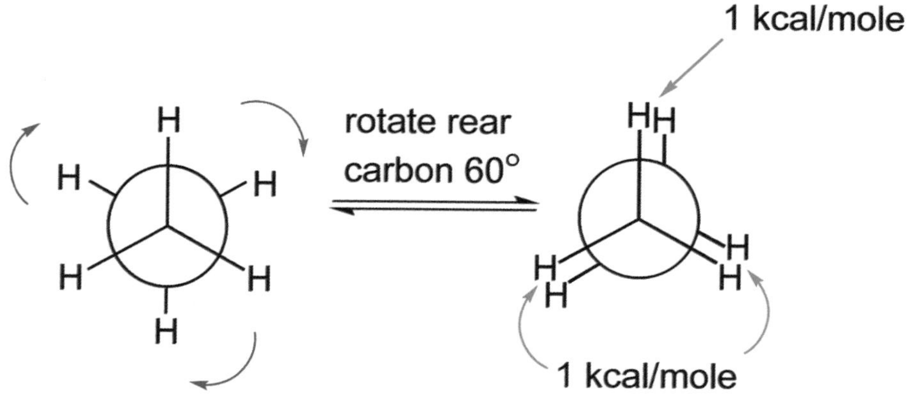

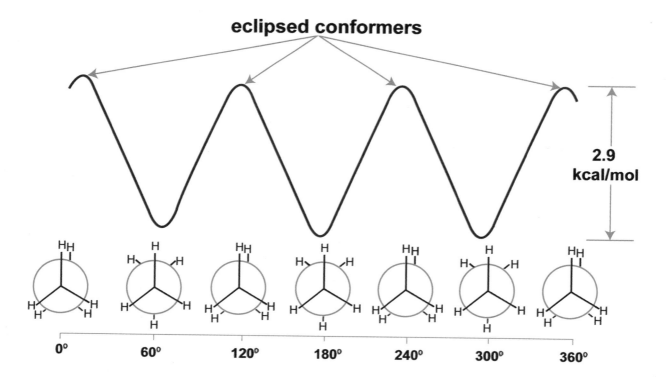

1 kcal/mole

rotate rear
carbon 60°

1 kcal/mole

eclipsed conformers

2.9
kcal/mol

0°   60°   120°   180°   240°   300°   360°

dihedral angle

Example 2: Butane

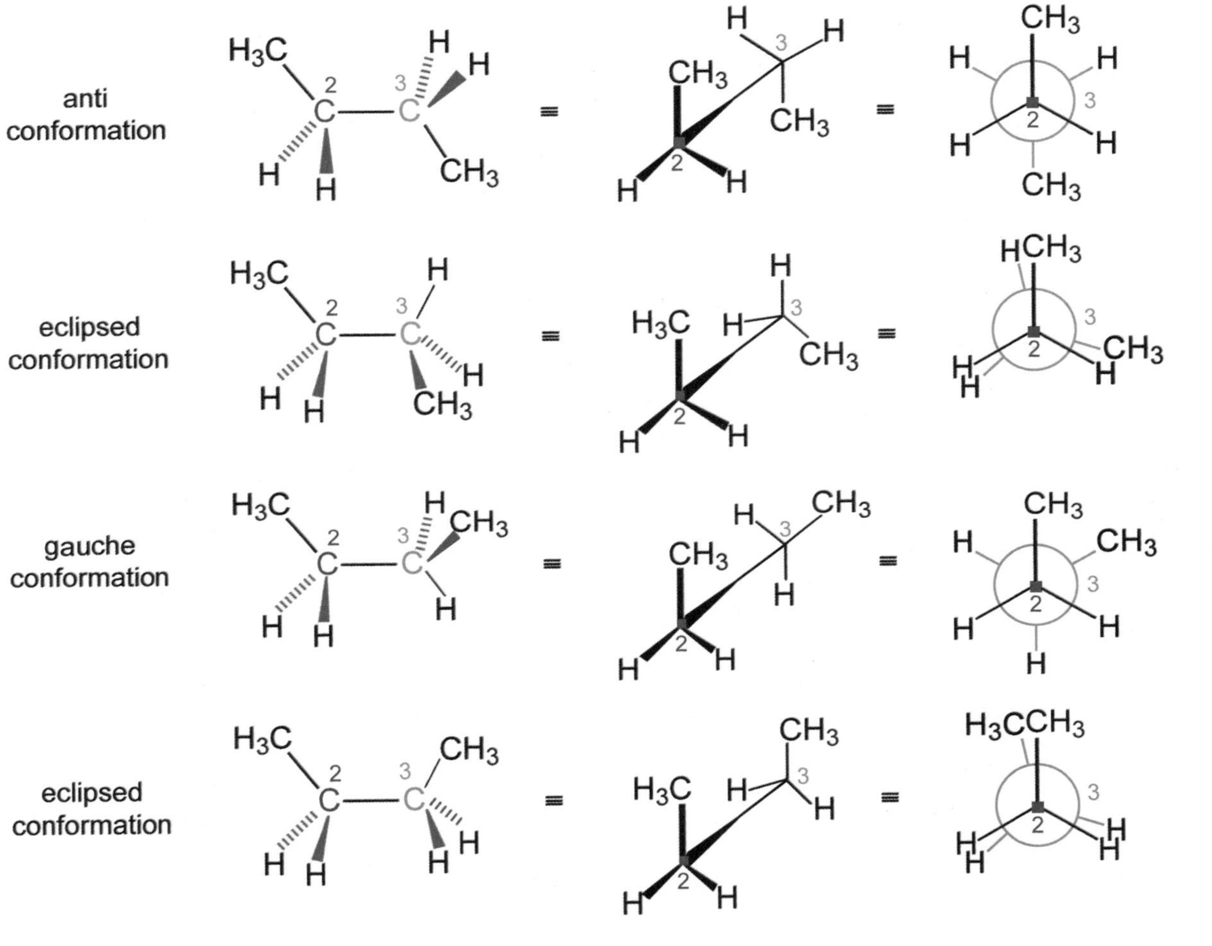

anti
conformation

eclipsed
conformation

gauche
conformation

eclipsed
conformation

The preceding illustration is a plot of potential energy versus rotation about the C2-C3 bond of butane.

The lowest energy arrangement, the anti conformation, is the one in which two methyl groups (C1 and C4) are as far apart as possible, that is, 180 degrees from each other. When two substituents (i.e. the two methyl groups) are anti and in the same plane, they are *antiperiplanar* to each other.

As rotation around the C2-C3 bond occurs, an eclipsed conformation is reached when there are two methyl-hydrogen interactions and one hydrogen-hydrogen interaction. When the rotation continues, the two methyl groups are 60 degrees apart, thus the gauche conformation. It is still higher in energy than the anti conformation even though it has no eclipsing interactions. The reason, again, is ESR. Because ESR is occurring due to the relative bulkiness (i.e. big size) of the methyl group compared to hydrogens in this molecule, we say that *steric strain* exists between the two close methyl groups.

When two methyl groups completely overlap with each other, the molecule is said to be totally eclipsed and is in its highest energy state (least stable).

At room temperature, these forms easily interconvert: all forms are present to some degree, though the most stable forms dominate.

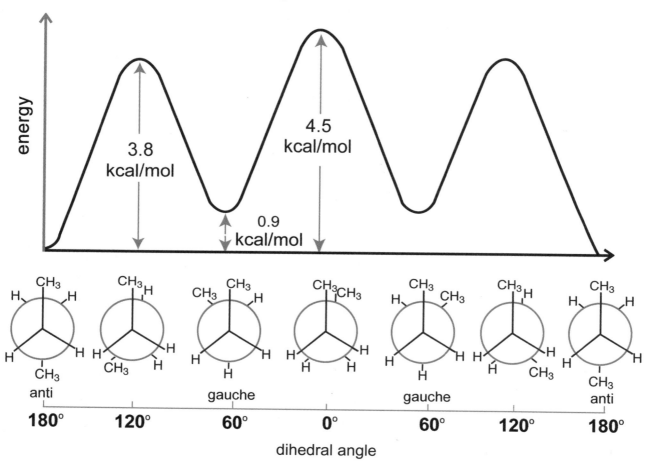

We have seen that conformers rotate about their single bonds. The rotational barrier, or barrier to rotation, is the <u>activation energy</u> (CHM 9.5) required to interconvert a subset of the possible conformations called rotamers. Butane has three rotamers: two gauche conformers and an anti conformer, where the four carbon centers are coplanar. The three eclipsed conformations with angles between the planes (= dihedral angles) of 120°, 0°, and 120° (which is 240° from the first), are not considered to be rotamers, but are instead <u>transition states</u>.

Common Terms

- dihedral angle: torsion (turn/twist) angle
- gauche: skew, synclinal
- **anti**: *trans*, antiperiplanar
- eclipsed: **syn**, *cis*, synperiplanar,
  torsion angle = 0°

"anti" and "syn" are IUPAC preferred descriptors.

There is no need to try to memorize the terms above. If they are required during the exam, the term(s) will be repeated with some context (image or explanatory text). The key is to understand the ideas behind these terms which have been described in this section (ORG 2.4). Again, chapter review practice questions and/or videos will help clarify any doubts and, thereafter, we also have the free forum.

Go online to GAMSAT-prep.com for chapter review Q&A and forum.

ALKANES

Chapter 3

Memorize	Understand	Not Required*
* IUPAC nomenclature * Physical properties	* Trends based on length, branching * Ring strain, ESR * Complete combustion * Free Radicals	* Knowledge beyond introductory-level (first year uni.) course * Technical categorization of "cyclic alkanes"

GAMSAT-Prep.com

Introduction

Alkanes (a.k.a. paraffins) are compounds that consist only of the elements carbon (C) and hydrogen (H) (i.e. hydrocarbons). In addition, C and H are linked together exclusively by single bonds (i.e. they are saturated compounds). Methane is the simplest possible alkane while saturated oils and fats are much larger.

Alkanes are used primarily as fuels (i.e. burned to produce heat or energy), but their derivatives can be found in paints, plastics, cosmetics, cleaners and pharmaceuticals. They are highly combustible and form carbon dioxide and water as they burn. The main components of natural gas are methane and ethane. Propane and butane are used as liquefied petroleum gas. Propane is also used in a propane gas burner (barbecue), butane in disposable cigarette lighters. Other alkanes with more carbons are components in different types of fuels and lubricating oils.

Additional Resources

Free Online Q&A + Forum

GAMSAT-prep.com Videos

Flashcards

Special Guest

* The real GAMSAT may have advanced level information presented (ie. in a passage) but previous knowledge of said information is not required to answer the questions that would follow. Practice ACER and GS practice GAMSATs can help you clarify this point.

3.1 Description and Nomenclature

Alkanes are hydrocarbon molecules containing only sp^3 hybridized carbon atoms (single bonds). They may be unbranched, branched or cyclic. Their general formula is C_nH_{2n+2} for a straight chain molecule; 2 hydrogen (H) atoms are subtracted for each ring. They contain no functional groups and are fully saturated molecules (= *no double or triple bonds*). As a result, they are chemically unreactive except when exposed to heat or light.

Systematic naming of compounds (= *nomenclature*) has evolved from the International Union of Pure and Applied Chemistry (IUPAC). **The nomenclature of alkanes is the basis of that for many other organic molecules.** The root of the compound is named according to the number of carbons in the longest carbon chain:

C_1 = meth	C_5 = pent	C_8 = oct
C_2 = eth	C_6 = hex	C_9 = non
C_3 = prop	C_7 = hept	C_{10} = dec
C_4 = but		

When naming these as fragments, (alkyl fragments: *the alkane minus one H atom*, symbol: R), the suffix '–yl' is used. If naming the alkane, the suffix '-ane' is used. Some prefixes result from the fact that a carbon with *one* R group attached is a *primary* (normal or n –) carbon, *two* R groups is *secondary* (sec) and with *three* R groups it is a *tertiary* (tert or t –) carbon. Some alkyl groups have special names:

C—C—C—   n-propyl (= propyl)

C—C—C—C—   n-butyl (= butyl)

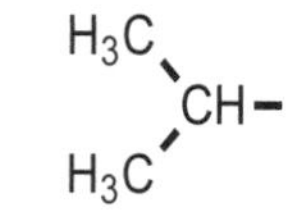

isopropyl
(= 2-propyl or propan-2-yl)

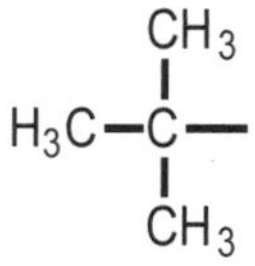

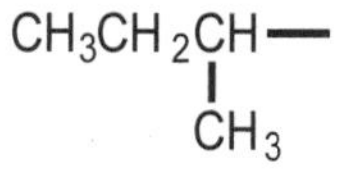

sec-butyl
(= 1-methylpropyl)

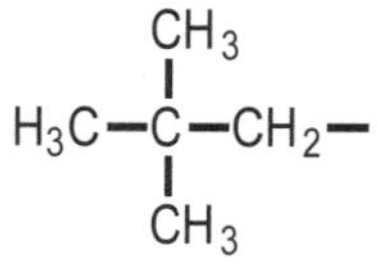

tert-butyl
(= 1,1-dimethylethyl)

neopentyl
(= dimethylpropyl)

Cyclic alkanes are named in the same way (according to the number of carbons), but the prefix 'cyclo' is added. The shorthand for organic compounds is a geometric figure where each corner represents a carbon; hydrogens need not be written, though it should be remembered that the number of hydrogens would exist such that the number of bonds at each carbon is four (ORG 1.1, 1.6).

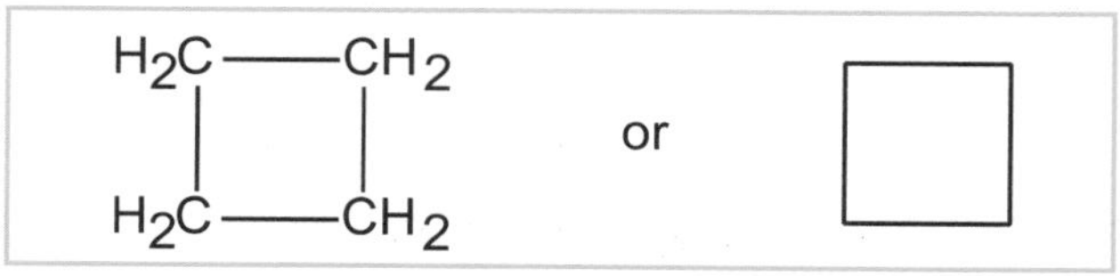

H_2C——CH_2
H_2C——CH_2 or

cyclobutane

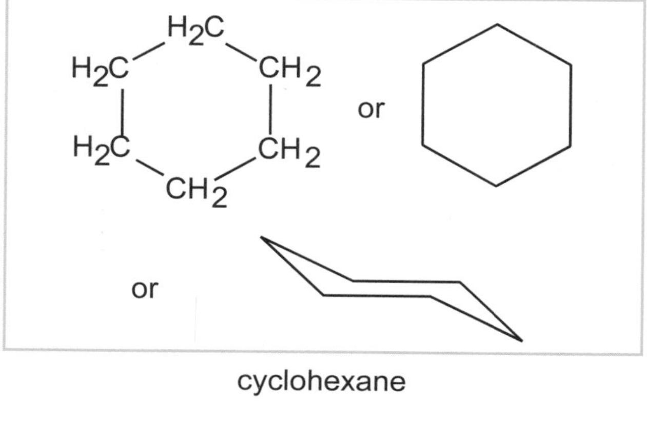

cyclohexane

As mentioned, carbon atoms can be characterized by the number of other carbon atoms to which they are directly bonded. It is very important for you to train your eyes to quickly indentify a primary carbon atom (**1°**), which is bonded to only one other carbon; a secondary carbon atom (**2°**), which is bonded to two other carbons; a tertiary carbon atom (**3°**), which is bonded to three other carbons; and a quaternary carbon atom (**4°**), which is bonded to four other carbons.

The nomenclature for <u>branched-chain</u> <u>alkanes</u> begins by determining the <u>longest</u> <u>straight chain</u> (i.e. *the highest number of carbons attached in a row*). The groups attached to the straight or *main* chain are numbered so as to achieve the lowest set of numbers. Groups are cited in alphabetical order. If a group appears more than once, the prefixes di-(2), tri-(3), tetra-(4) are used.

Prefixes such as di-, tri-, tetra- as well as tert-, sec-, n- are not used for alphabetizing purposes. However, cyclo-, iso-, and neo- are considered part of the group name and are used for alphabetizing purposes. If two chains of equal length compete for selection as the main chain, choose the chain with the most substituents.

For example:

4,6-Diethyl-2,5,5,6,7-pentamethyloctane (7 substituents) or 3,5-Diethyl-2,3,4,4,7-pentamethyl octane (a bit better for keeners!) NOT 2,5,5,6-Tetramethyl-4-ethyl-6-isopropyl octane (6 substituents)

Naming cycloalkanes:

1. Use the cycloalkane name as the parent name. The only exception is when the alkyl side chain contains a larger number of carbons than the ring. In that case, the ring is considered as a substituent to the parent alkane.

2. Number the substituents on the ring to arrive at the lowest sum. When two or more different alkyl groups are present, they are numbered by an alphabetical order.

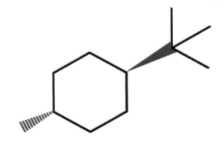

trans-1-tert-butyl-4-methylcyclohexane

3.1.1 Physical Properties of Alkanes

At room temperature and one atmosphere of pressure, straight chain alkanes with 1 to 4 carbons are gases (i.e. CH_4 – methane, CH_3CH_3 – ethane, etc.), 5 to 17 carbons are liquids (e.g. oils), and more than 17 carbons are solid (e.g. wax). Boiling points of straight chain alkanes (= *aliphatic*) show a regular increase with increasing number of carbons. This is because they are nonpolar molecules, and have weak intermolecular forces. Branching of alkanes leads to a dramatic decrease in the boiling point. As a rule, as the number of carbons increase the melting points also increase.

Alkanes are soluble in nonpolar solvents (i.e. benzene, CCl_4 – carbon tetrachloride, etc.), and not in aqueous solvents (= *hydrophobic*). They are insoluble in water because of their low polarity and their inability to hydrogen bond. Alkanes are the least dense of all classes of organic compounds (<< ρ_{water}, 1 g/ml). Thus petroleum, a mixture of hydrocarbons rich in alkanes, floats on water.

3.2 Important Reactions of Alkanes

3.2.1 Combustion

Combustion (CHM 1.4) is typically when a substance reacts with oxygen, releasing energy in the form of heat and light. Combustion includes the burning of hydrocarbons found in fossil fuels like gasoline (i.e. octane and other alkanes for internal combustion engines) and natural gas (i.e. methane and other alkanes for heating, cooking, and electricity generation).

Note that the "heat of combustion" is the change in enthalpy of a combustion reaction. Therefore, the higher the heat of combustion, the higher the energy level of the molecule, the less stable the molecule was prior to combustion.

Combustion may be either complete or incomplete. In complete combustion, the hydrocarbon is converted to carbon dioxide (CO_2) and water (H_2O). If there is insufficient oxygen for complete combustion, the reaction gives other products, such as carbon monoxide (CO) and soot (molecular C). This strongly exothermic reaction may be summarized:

$$C_nH_{2n+2} + \text{excess } O_2 \rightarrow nCO_2 + (n+1)H_2O.$$

3.2.2 Radical Substitution Reactions

Radical substitution reactions with halogens may be summarized (recall E = hf, *see* PHY 9.2.4; also *see* CHM 9.4):

RH + X_2 + uv light (*hf*) or heat → RX + HF

The halogen X_2, may be F_2, Cl_2, or Br_2. I_2 does not react. The mechanism of *halogenation* may be explained and summarized by example:

i. Initiation: This step involves the formation of *free radicals* (highly reactive substances which contain an unpaired electron, which is symbolized by a single dot):

$$Cl:Cl \ + \ \text{uv light or heat} \rightarrow 2Cl\bullet$$

ii. Propagation: In this step, the chlorine free radical begins a series of reactions that form new free radicals:

$$CH_4 + \ Cl\bullet \ \rightarrow \ \bullet CH_3 + HCl$$
$$\bullet CH_3 + \ Cl_2 \ \rightarrow \ CH_3Cl + Cl\bullet$$

iii. Termination: These reactions end the radical propagation steps. Termination reactions destroy the free radicals (coupling).

$$Cl\bullet + \bullet CH_3 \ \rightarrow \ CH_3Cl$$
$$\bullet CH_3 + \bullet CH_3 \ \rightarrow \ CH_3CH_3$$
$$Cl\bullet \ + Cl\bullet \ \rightarrow \ Cl_2$$

Radical substitution reactions can also occur with halide acids (i.e. HCl, HBr) and peroxides (i.e. HOOH – hydrogen peroxide). Chain propagation (step ii) can destroy many organic compounds fairly quick. This step can be inhibited by using a resonance stabilized free radical to "mop up" (*termination*) other destructive free radicals in the medium. For example, BHT is a resonance stabilized free radical added to packaging of many breakfast cereals in order to inhibit free radical destruction of the cereal (= *spoiling*).

The stability of a free radical depends on the ability of the compound to stabilize the unpaired electron. This is analogous to stabilizing a positively charged carbon (= *carbocation*). Thus, in both cases, a tertiary compound is more stable than secondary which, in turn, is more stable than a primary compound.

Also in both cases, the reason for the trend is the same: the charge on the carbon is stabilized by the electron donating effect of the presence of alkyl groups. Alkyl groups are not strongly electron donating, they are normally described as "somewhat" electron donating; however, the combined effect of multiple R groups has an important stabilizing effect that we will see as a critical feature in many reaction types.

$$\bullet CR_3 \;>\; \bullet CR_2H \;>\; \bullet CRH_2 \;>\; \bullet CH_3$$
$$3^\circ \;>\; 2^\circ \;>\; 1^\circ \;>\; methyl$$

Pyrolysis occurs when a molecule is broken down by heat (*pyro* = fire, *lysis* = separate). C-C bonds are cleaved and smaller chain alkyl radicals often recombine in termination steps creating a variety of alkanes.

Please note that the rate law for free radical substitution reactions was discussed in CHM 9.4.

3.3 Ring Strain in Cyclic Alkanes

Cyclic alkanes are strained compounds. This **ring strain** results from the bending of the bond angles in greater amounts than normal. This strain causes cyclic compounds of 3 and 4 carbons to be unstable, and thus not often found in nature. The usual angle between bonds in an sp^3 hybridized carbon is 109.5° (= *the normal tetrahedral angle*).

The expected angles in some cyclic compounds can be determined geometrically: 60° in cyclopropane; 90° in cyclobutane and 108° in cyclopentane. Cyclohexane, in the chair conformation, has normal bond angles of 109.5°. The closer the angle is to the normal tetrahedral angle of 109.5°, the more sta-ble the compound. In fact, cyclohexane can be found in a chair or boat conformation or any conformation in between; however, at any given moment, 99% of the cyclohexane molecules would be found in the chair conformation because it is the most stable (lower energy).

It is important to have a clear understanding of electron shell repulsion (ESR). Essentially all atoms and molecules are surrounded by an electron shell (CHM 2.1, ORG 1.2) which is more like a cloud of electrons. Because like charges repel, when there are options, atoms and molecules assume the conformation which minimizes ESR.

For example, when substituents are added to a cyclic compound (i.e. *see* ORG 12.3.1, Fig. IV.B.12.1 Part II) the most stable position is equatorial (equivalent to the anti conformation, ORG 2.1) which minimizes ESR.

This conformation is most pronounced when the substituent is bulky (i.e. isopropyl, t-butyl, phenyl, etc.). In other words, a large substituent takes up more space thus ESR has a more prominent effect.

Figure IV.B.3.1: The chair and boat conformations of cyclohexane. Some students like to remember that you sit in a chair because a chair is stable. However, a boat can be tippy and so it's less stable.

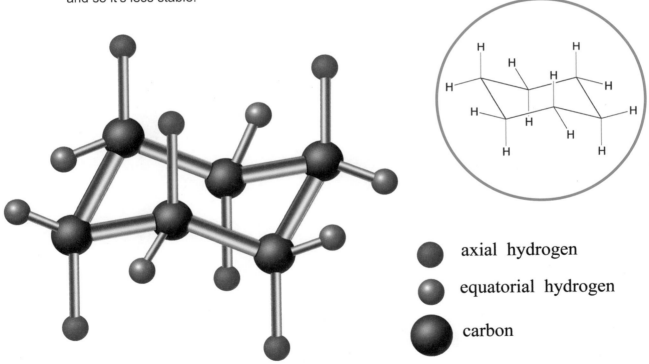

● axial hydrogen

● equatorial hydrogen

● carbon

Figure IV.B.3.2: The chair conformation of cyclohexane. The hydrogens which are generally in the same plane as the ring are <u>equatorial</u>. The hydrogens which are generally perpendicular to the ring are <u>axial</u>. The hydrogen atoms are maximally separated and staggered to minimize electron shell repulsion. Note that the inset (in the circle) shows another way to present a chair conformer: the red bond indicates axial and the blue indicates equatorial. Note that cyclohexane can be presented in all the different ways seen on this page, as well as ORG 3.1.

Go online to GAMSAT-prep.com for chapter review Q&A and forum.

ALKENES

Chapter 4

Memorize	Understand	Not Required*
* Basic nomenclature	* Electrophilic addition, hydrogenation, Markovnikoff's rule, oxidation	* Knowledge beyond introductory-level (first year uni.) course

GAMSAT-Prep.com

Introduction ▛▜▙▟

An alkene (a.k.a. olefin) is an unsaturated chemical compound containing at least one carbon-to-carbon double bond.

Additional Resources

Free Online Q&A + Forum

GAMSAT-prep.com Videos

Flashcards

Special Guest

4.1 Description and Nomenclature

Alkenes *(olefins)* are unsaturated hydrocarbon molecules containing carbon-carbon double bonds. Their general formula is C_nH_{2n} for a straight chain molecule; 2 hydrogen (H) atoms are subtracted for each ring. The *functional group* in these molecules is the double bond which determines the chemical properties of alkenes. Double bonds are sp² hybridized (*see* ORG 1.2, 1.3). The nomenclature is the same as that for alkanes, except: i) the suffix 'ene' replaces 'ane' and ii) the double bond is (are) numbered in the molecule, trying to get the smallest number for the double bond(s). Always select the longest chain that contains the double bond or the greatest number of double bonds as the parent hydrocarbon. For cycloalkenes, the carbons of the double bond are given the 1– and 2– positions.

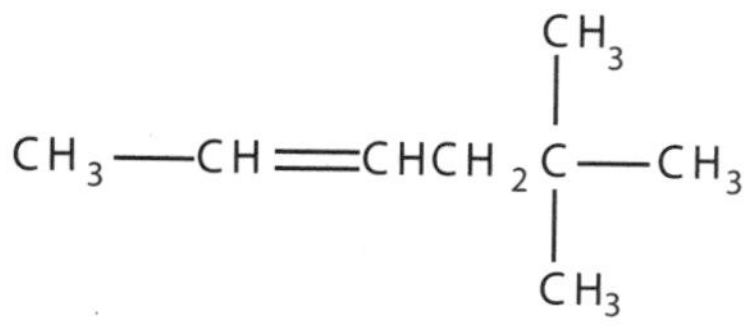

5,5-Dimethyl-2-hexene 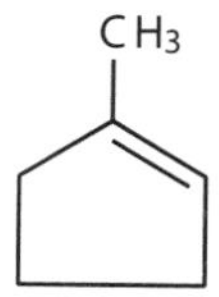   1-methylcyclopentene

Two frequently encountered groups are sometimes named as if they were substituents.

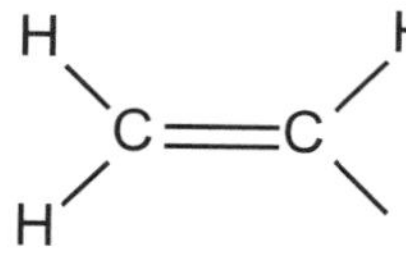

the vinyl group

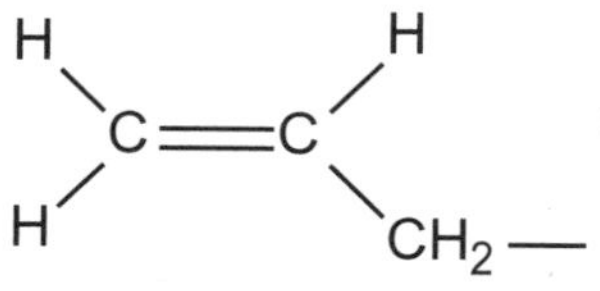

the allyl group

Alkenes have similar physical properties to alkanes. *Trans* compounds tend to have higher melting points (due to better symmetry), and lower boiling points (due to less polarity) than its corresponding *cis* isomer. Alkenes, however, due to the nature of the double bond may be polar. The dipole moment is oriented from the electropositive alkyl group toward the electronegative alkene.

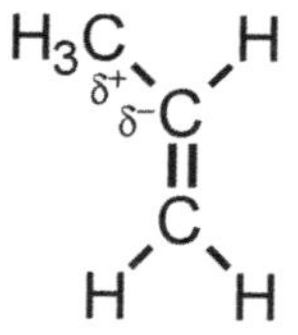

has a small
dipole moment

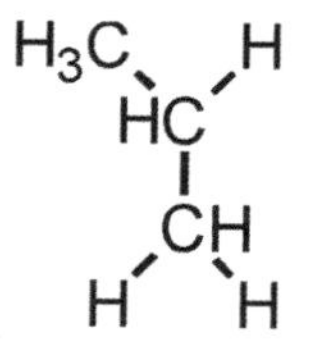

has no dipole
moment

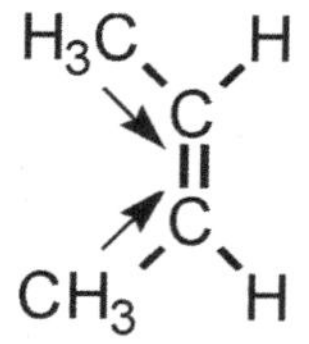

(cis)
small dipole
moment

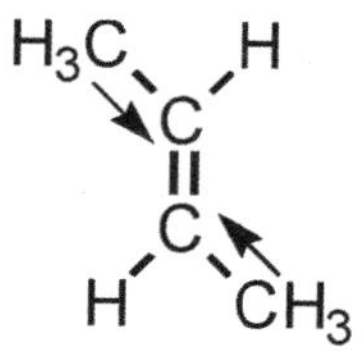

(trans)
no dipole
moment

The greater the number of attached alkyl groups (i.e. *the more highly substituted the double bond*), the greater is the alkene's stability. The reason is that <u>alkyl</u> groups are somewhat electron donating, thus they stabilize the double bond.

An alkene with 2 double bonds is a diene, 3 is a triene. A diene with one single bond in between is a conjugated diene. Conjugated dienes are more stable than non-conjugated dienes primarily due to resonance stabilization (see the resonance stabilized conjugated molecule 1,3-butadiene in ORG 1.4). Alkenes, including polyenes (multiple double bonds), can engage in addition reactions (ORG 4.2.1). The notable exceptions include aromatic compounds (conjugated double bonds in a ring; ORG 5.1) which cannot engage in addition reactions which will be discussed in the next chapter.

- <u>Synthesis of Alkenes</u>: The two most common alkene-forming reactions involve elimination reactions of either HX from an alkyl halide or H_2O from an alcohol (see the following reactions). Dehydrohalogenation occurs by the reaction of an alkyl halide with a strong base. Dehydration occurs by reacting an alcohol with a strong acid.

We will discuss elimination reactions (E1 and E2), which can be used to synthesize alkenes, in the chapter reviewing alcohols (ORG 6.2.4).

4.2 Important Chemical Reactions

4.2.1 Electrophilic Addition

The chemistry of alkenes may be understood in terms of their functional group, the double bond. When <u>electrophiles</u> (*substances which seek electrons*) add to alkenes, carbocations (= *carbonium ions*) are formed. An important electrophile is H^+ (i.e. in HBr, H_2O, etc.).

A <u>nucleophile</u> (ORG 1.6) is a molecule with a free pair of electrons, and sometimes a negative charge, that seeks out partially or completely positively charged species (i.e. a carbon nucleus). Some important nucleophiles are OH⁻ and CN⁻.

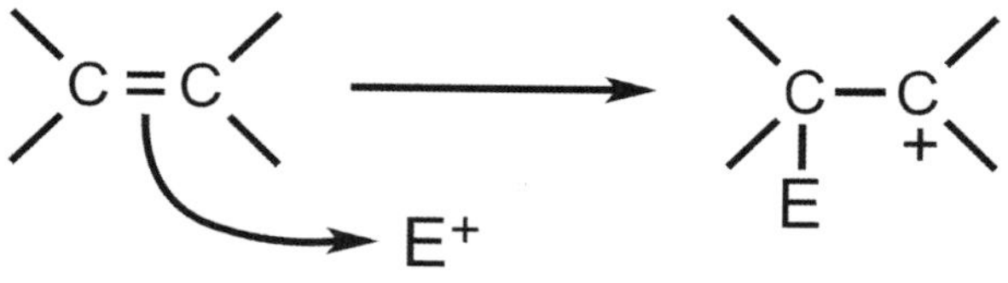

E = electrophile   carbocation (intermediate)

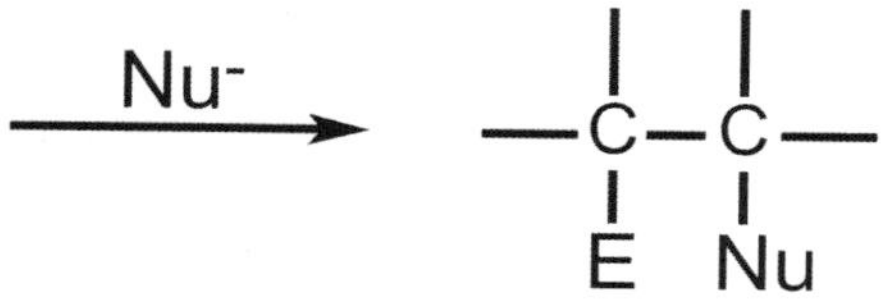

Nu = nucleophile

Note that the carbon-carbon double bond is electron rich (nucleophilic) and can donate a pair of electrons to an electrophile (= "electron loving") during reactions. Electrons from the π bond attack the electrophile. As the π bond is weaker than the σ bond, it can be broken without breaking the σ bond. As a result, the carbon skeleton can remain intact. Electrophilic addition to an unsymmetrically substituted alkene gives the more highly substituted carbocation (i.e. the most stable intermediate). We will soon see that Markovnikoff's rule (or Markovnikov's rule) is a guide to determine the outcome of addition reactions.

Another important property of the double bond is its ability to stabilize carbocations,

carbanions or radicals attached to adjacent carbons (*allylic carbons*). Note that all the following are resonance stabilized:

carbocation

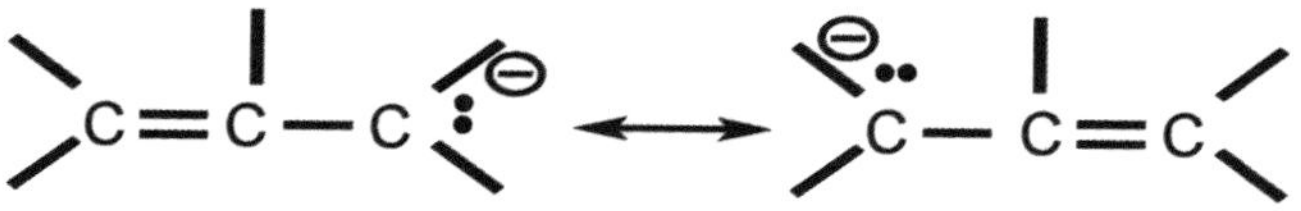

carbanion

carbon radical

The stability of the intermediate carbocation depends on the groups attached to it, which can either stabilize or destabilize it. As well, groups which place a partial or total positive charge adjacent to the carbocation withdraw electrons inductively, by sigma bonds, to destabilize it. More highly substituted carbocations are more stable than less highly substituted ones.

These points are useful in predicting which carbon will become the carbocation, and to which carbon the electrophile and nucleophile will bond. The intermediate carbocation formed must be the most stable. **Markovnikoff's rule** is a result of this, and it states: *the nucleophile will be bonded to the most substituted carbon* (fewest hydrogens attached) *in the product. Equivalently, the electrophile will be bonded to the least* *substituted carbon* (most hydrogens attached) *in the product*. An example of this is:

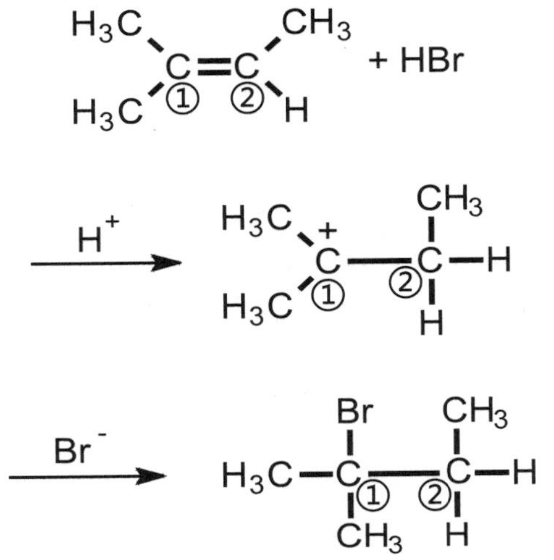

H$^+$ = electrophile
Br$^-$ = nucleophile
① most substituted carbon
② least substituted carbon
① forms the most stable carbonium ion.

The product, 2-bromo-2-methyl butane, is the more likely or major product (*the Markovnikoff product*). Had the H$^+$ added to the most substituted carbon (which has a much lower probability of occurrence) the less likely or minor product would be formed (*the anti-Markovnikoff product*). {Memory guide for Markovnikoff's rule: "Hydrogen prefers to add to the carbon in the double bond where most of its friends are" (this works because the least substituted carbon has the most bonds to hydrogen atoms)}

Carbocation intermediate rearrangement: In both *hydride shift* and *alkyl group shift*, H or CH$_3$ moves to a positively charged carbon, tak-

ing its electron pair with it. As a result, a less stable carbocation rearranges to a more stable one (more substituted).

secondary carbocation → tertiary carbocation

secondary carbocation → tertiary carbocation

Markovnikoff's rule is true for the ionic conditions presented in the preceding reaction. However, for radical conditions the reverse occurs. Thus *anti-Markovnikoff* products are the major products under free radical conditions.

• Addition of halogens: This is a simple and rapid laboratory diagnostic tool to test for the presence of unsaturation (C=C). Immediate disappearance of the reddish Br$_2$ color indicates that the sample is an alkene. The general chemical formula of the halogen addition reaction is:

$$C=C + X_2 \rightarrow X-C-C-X$$

The π electron pair of the double bond attacks the bromine, or X$_2$ molecule, setting up an induced dipole (*see* CHM 4.2) and then displacing the bromide ion. The intermediate forms a cyclic bromonium ion R$_2$Br$^+$, which is then attacked by Br$^-$, giving the di-bromo addition product.

Since the intermediate is a bromonium ion, the bromide anion can only attack from the opposite side, yielding an anti product.

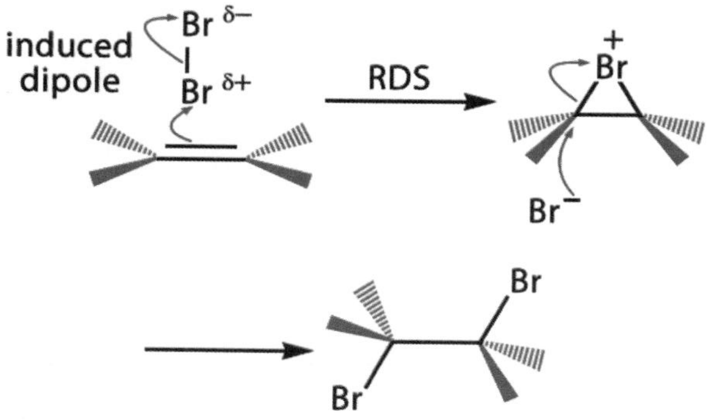

RDS = rate-determining step (CHM 9.4)

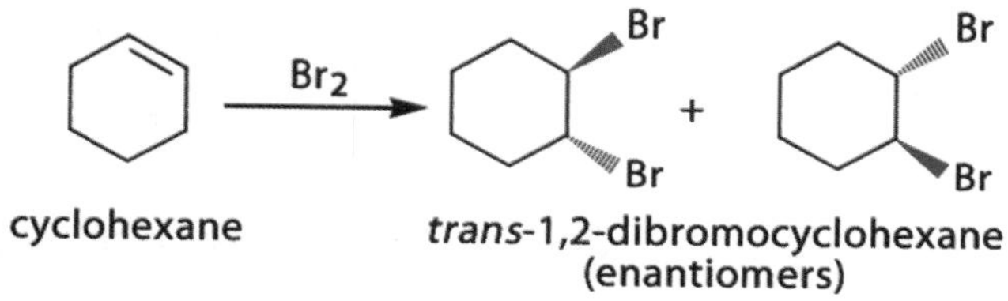

cyclohexane

trans-1,2-dibromocyclohexane (enantiomers)

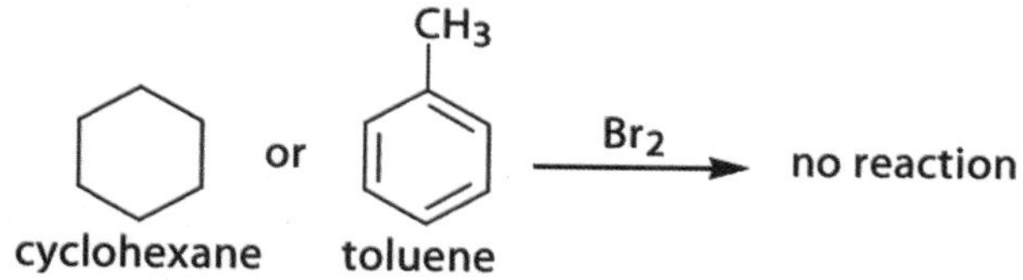

cyclohexane   or   toluene   →Br$_2$→   no reaction

Halogen addition does not occur in saturated hydrocarbons (i.e. cyclohexane) which lack the electron rich double bond, nor do the reactions occur within an aromatic ring because of the increased stability afforded by conjugation in a ring system due to resonance.

• Halohydrin formation reaction: A halohydrin (or haloalcohol) is a functional group where one carbon atom has a halogen substituent and an adjacent carbon atom has a hydroxyl substituent. This addition, which produces a halohydrin, is done by reacting an alkene with a halogen X$_2$ in the presence of water. The intermediate forms a cyclic bromonium ion R$_2$Br$^+$. The water molecule competes with the bromide ion as a nucleophile and reacts with the bromonium ion to form the halohydrin. The net effect is the addition of HO-X to the alkene.

In practice, the bromohydrin reaction is carried out using a reagent called NBS. Markovnikoff regiochemistry and anti addition is observed.

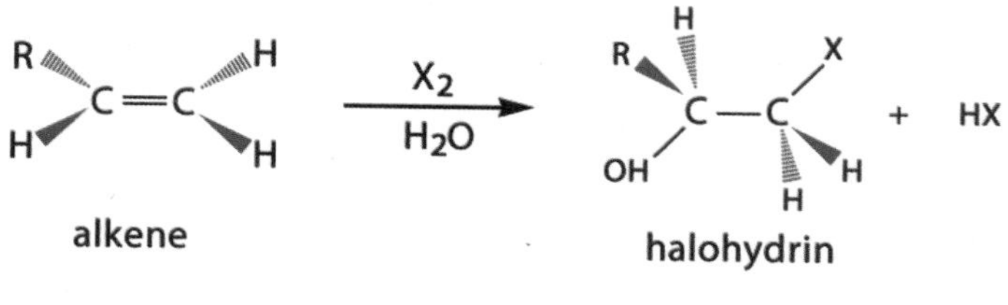

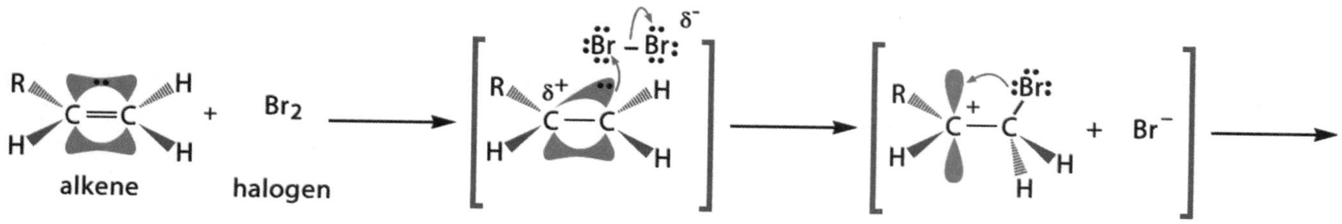

alkene   X$_2$ / H$_2$O →   halohydrin   +   HX

alkene   halogen

cyclic halonium
ion intermediate

halohydrin

"Should I memorize these reaction mechanisms and the ones on the way?"

That would not be very helpful. If a related question were asked, normally the passage or question stem would begin by spelling out the mechanism and then the questions would lean towards your skills involving nomenclature, geometry, pattern recognition and time efficiency. Mechanisms should be followed like a good story that contains a consistent, reasonable plot. The key is to follow the plot, not to memorize it. If the plot can be reasoned then, if given a blueprint and different characters during an exam (or practice), you should be able to determine the conclusion, and how the examiners arrived at that conclusion (i.e. the intermediates when necessary).

Geometry and pattern recognition allow you to follow if an addition is cis (= syn) or trans (= anti, i.e. halohydrin formation). They also help you: follow where the different R groups end up (i.e. alkene oxidation; ORG 4.2.2); recognize unusual product geometries once you have a blueprint (i.e. Diels-Alder reaction; ORG 4.2.4); etc. As often as possible, get in the habit of drawing molecules shorthand while completing your online chapter review practice questions. Drawing and practice questions are important components of GAMSAT Organic Chemistry preparation.

• **Addition of HX**: As we have seen earlier in this section, this reaction occurs via a carbocation intermediate. The halide ion then combines with the carbocation to give an alkyl halide. The proton will add to the less substituted carbon atom, yielding a more substituted (stabilized) carbocation. Markovnikoff regiochemistry is observed. This can be seen in the first two mechanisms shown in this section (ORG 4.2.1).

• **Free radical addition of HBr to alkenes**: Once a bromine free radical has formed in an initiation step (ORG 3.2.2), it adds to the alkene double bond, yielding an alkyl radical. The regiochemistry of this free radical addition is determined in the first propagation step because, instead of H attacking first in electrophilic addition, the bromine radical adds first to the alkene. Thus anti-Markovnikoff addition is observed.

The stability order of radicals is identical to the stability order of carbocations, tertiary being the most stable and methyl the least. Notice that the free radical reaction mechanism that follows uses single headed (blue) arrows to follow the movement of single electrons, as opposed to the normal arrows that we have seen which follow the movement of electron pairs.

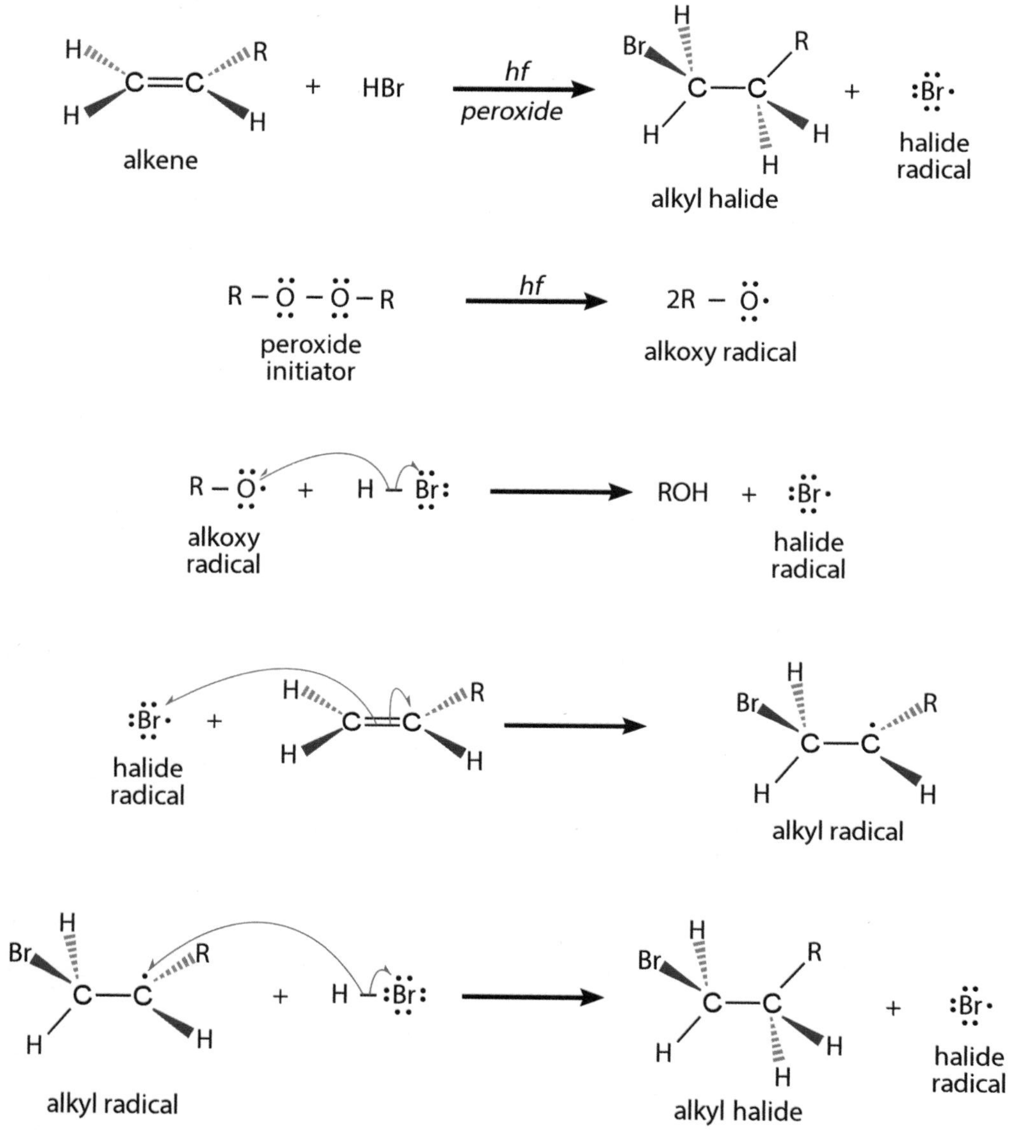

alkene + HBr → (hf / peroxide) alkyl halide + halide radical

peroxide initiator → (hf) alkoxy radical

alkoxy radical + H—Br → ROH + halide radical

halide radical + alkene → alkyl radical

alkyl radical + H—Br → alkyl halide + halide radical

4.2.2 Oxidation

Alkenes can undergo a variety of reactions in which the carbon-carbon double bond is oxidized. Using potassium permanganate ($KMnO_4$) under mild conditions (*no heat*), or osmium tetroxide (OsO_4), a glycol (= *a dialcohol*) can be produced.

In the following chapters, you will learn how to derive systematic nomenclature (these are names of compounds based on rules as opposed to "common" names often based on tradition). IUPAC (official) nomenclature is usually systematic (i.e. ethane-1,2-diol) but sometimes it is not (i.e. acetic acid). Knowing both the common and the systematic names is the safest way to approach the GAMSAT.

The first reaction that follows is the oxidation of ethene (= ethylene) under mild conditions and the second is the oxidation of 2-butene under abrasive conditions.

$$CH_2 = CH_2 + KMnO_4$$

$$\xrightarrow[\text{OH}^-]{\text{Cold}}$$

$$\begin{array}{ccc} CH_2 & - & CH_2 \\ | & & | \\ OH & & OH \end{array}$$

Ethylene glycol
(1,2-ethanediol or ethane-1,2-diol)

Using $KMnO_4$ under more abrasive conditions leads to an oxidative cleavage of the double bond:

$$CH_3 CH = CHCH_3 \xrightarrow[\text{heat}]{KMnO_4,\ OH^-}$$

$$2CH_3 C \overset{\displaystyle O}{\underset{\displaystyle O^-}{}} \xrightarrow{H^+} 2CH_3 C \overset{\displaystyle O}{\underset{\displaystyle OH}{}}$$

Acetate ion   Acetic acid
(ethanoate ion)   (ethanoic acid)

Specifically, cold dilute $KMnO_4$ produces 1,2-diols with the syn orientation. Hot, basic $KMnO_4$ leads to oxidative cleavage of the double bonds with the double bond being replaced with a C=O bond and an O atom added to each H atom that was connected to the central carbon.

$$CH_3 - CH = CH_2 \xrightarrow{KMnO_4} CH_3 - C \overset{\displaystyle O}{\underset{\displaystyle OH}{}} + CO_2$$

acetic acid

$$CH_3 - CH = C \overset{\displaystyle CH_3}{\underset{\displaystyle CH_3}{}} \xrightarrow{KMnO_4}$$

$$CH_3 - C \overset{\displaystyle O}{\underset{\displaystyle OH}{}} + O = C \overset{\displaystyle CH_3}{\underset{\displaystyle CH_3}{}}$$

acetic acid   acetone

$$CH_2 = CH - CH = CH_2 \xrightarrow{KMnO_4} CO_2 + H_2O$$

Ozone (O_3) reacts vigorously with alkenes. The reaction (= *ozonolysis*) leads to an oxidative cleavage of the double bond which can produce a ketone and an aldehyde:

$$\begin{array}{c} CH_3 \\ | \\ CH_3C = CHCH_3 \end{array} \xrightarrow[\text{(2) Zn, H}_2\text{O}]{\text{(1) O}_3}$$

2-Methyl-2-butene

$$\begin{array}{c} CH_3 \\ | \\ CH_3C = O \end{array} + \overset{\displaystyle O}{\underset{}{CH_3CH}}$$

Acetone   Acetaldehyde
(propanone)   (ethanal)

Note that the second step in the reaction uses a reducing agent such as zinc metal. If the starting alkene has a tetra-substituted double bond (i.e. 4 R groups), two ketones will be formed. If it has a tri-substituted double bond, a ketone and an aldehyde will be formed as in the reaction shown. If it has a di-substituted double bond (e.g. R-CH=CH-R), two aldehydes are possible.

The hydroboration–oxidation reaction is a two-step organic reaction that converts an alkene into an alcohol by the addition of water across the double bond. The hydrogen and hydroxyl group are added in a syn addition leading to *cis* stereochemistry. Hydroboration–oxidation is an anti-Markovnikoff reaction since the hydroxyl group (not the hydrogen) attaches to the less substituted carbon.

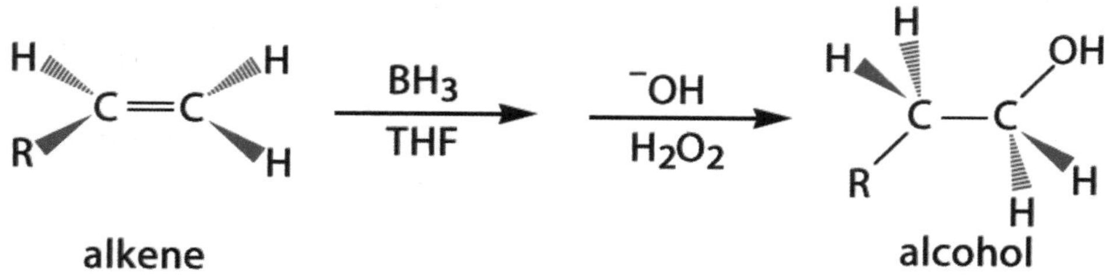

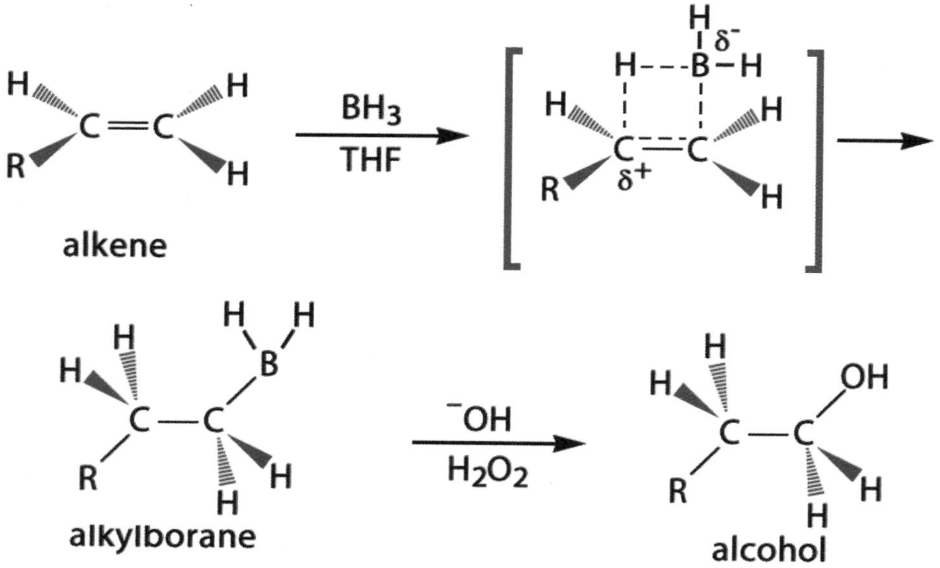

alkene → BH₃ THF → ⁻OH H₂O₂ → alcohol

alkene → BH₃ THF → [intermediate] →

alkylborane → ⁻OH H₂O₂ → alcohol

- **Epoxide Formation**: Alkenes can be oxidized with peroxycarboxylic acids (i.e. CH_3CO_3H or mCPBA). The product is an oxirane (discussed in ORG 10.1.1, ethers).

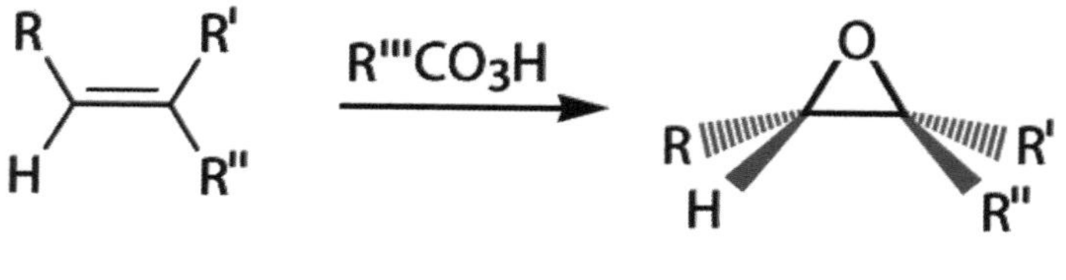

$R'''CO_3H$

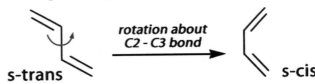

4.2.3 Hydrogenation

Alkenes react with hydrogen in the presence of a variety of metal catalysts (i.e. Ni – nickel, Pd – palladium, Pt – platinum). The reaction that occurs is an *addition* reaction since one atom of hydrogen adds to each carbon of the double bond (= *hydrogenation*). Both hydrogens add to the double bond from the same metal catalyst surface, thus syn addition is observed. Since there are two phases present in the process of hydrogenation (the hydrogen and the metal catalyst), the process

is referred to as a heterogenous catalysis.

A carbon with multiple bonds is not bonded to the maximum number of atoms that potentially that carbon could possess. Thus it is *unsaturated*. Alkanes, which can be formed by hydrogenation, are *saturated* since each carbon is bonded to the maximum number of atoms it could possess (= *four*). Thus hydrogenation is sometimes called the process of saturation.

$$CH_3CH = CH_2 + H_2 \longrightarrow CH_3CH_2 - CH_3$$

Alkenes are much more reactive than other functional groups towards hydrogenation. As a result, other functional groups such

as ketones, aldehydes, esters and nitriles are usually unchanged during the alkene hydrogenation process.

4.2.4 The Diels–Alder Reaction

The Diels–Alder reaction is a cycloaddition reaction between a conjugated diene and a substituted alkene (= the dienophile) to form a substituted cyclohexene system.

Diene + Dienophile = Cyclohexene

All Diels-Alder reactions have four common features: (1) the reaction is initiated by heat; (2) the reaction forms new six-membered rings; (3) three π bonds break and two new C-C σ bonds and one new C-C π bond are formed; (4) all bonds break and form in a single step.

The Diels-Alder diene must have the two double bonds on the same side of the single bond in one of the structures, which is called the s-*cis* conformation (s-*cis*: *cis* with respect to the single bond). If double bonds are on the opposite sides of the single bond in the Lewis structure, this is called the s-*trans* conformation (s-*trans*: *trans* with respect to the single bond).

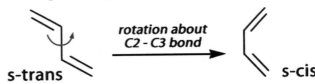

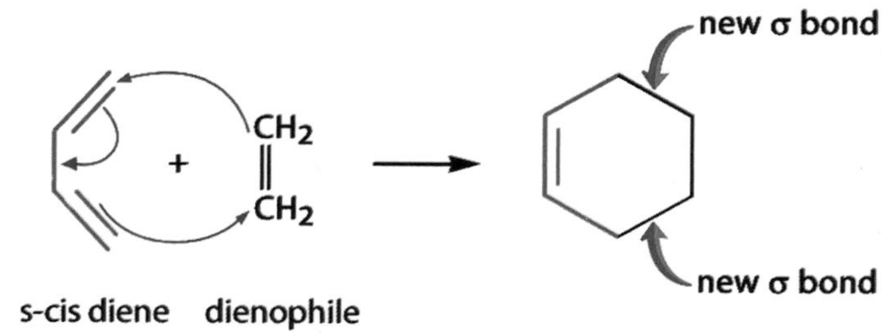

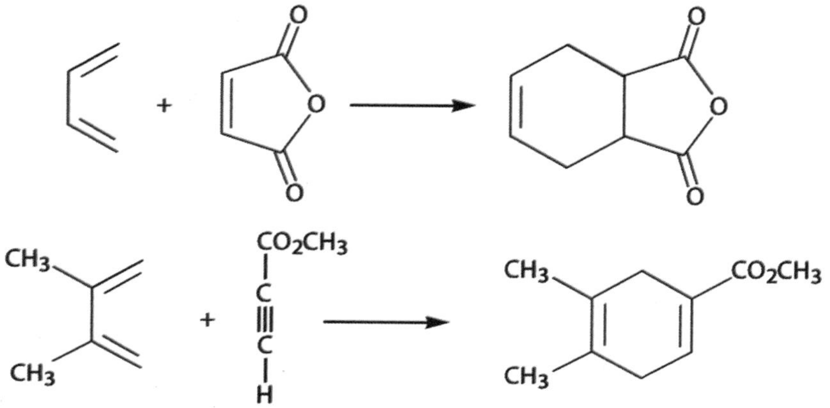

s-cis diene   dienophile

new σ bond

new σ bond

The Diels-Alder reaction is useful because it sometimes creates stereocenters, it always forms a ring, and the reaction is stereospecific (i.e. the reaction mechanism dictates the stereoisomers). For example, a *cis* dienophile generates a ring with *cis* substitution, while a *trans* dienophile generates a ring with *trans* substitution.

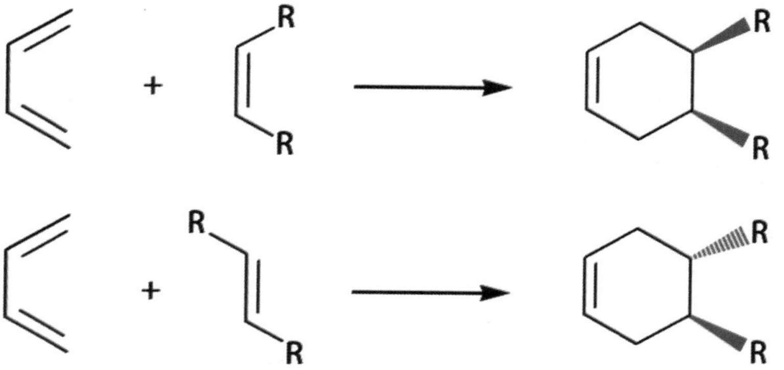

Diels-Alder reactions are reversible (= "Retro-Diels-Alder").

4.2.5 Resonance Revisited

General Chemistry section 3.2 and Organic Chemistry section 1.4 are important to review before you move on to the next chapter on Aromatics. Many exam questions rely on your understanding of resonance and how it affects stability and reactions. It is helpful to remember that the only difference between different resonance forms is the placement of π or non-bonding electrons. The atoms themselves do not change positions, create new bonds nor are they "resonating" back and forth. The resonance hybrid with its electrons delocalized is more stable than any single resonance form. The greater the numbers of authentic resonance forms possible, the more stable the molecule.

4.3 Alkynes

Alkynes are unsaturated hydrocarbon molecules containing carbon-carbon triple bonds (1 sigma + 2 π bonds; ORG 1.3). The nomenclature is the same as that for alkenes, except that the suffix 'yne' replaces 'ene'. Alkynes have a higher boiling point than alkenes or alkanes. Internal alkynes, where the triple bond is in the middle of the compound, boil at higher temperatures than terminal alkynes. Terminal alkynes are relatively acidic.

Basic reactions such as reduction, electrophilic addition, free radical addition and hydroboration proceed in a similar manner to alkenes. Oxidation also follows the same rules and uses the same reactants and catalysts. However, unlike alkenes, alkynes can be partially hydrogenated yielding alkenes with just one equivalent of H_2. The reaction with palladium in Lindlar's catalyst produces the *cis* alkene while sodium or lithium in liquid ammonia will produce the *trans* alkene via a free radical mechanism.

Go online to GAMSAT-prep.com for chapter review Q&A and forum.

Memorize	Understand	Not Required*
Basic nomenclature	* Electrophilic aromatic substitution * How to apply Hückel's rule	* Knowledge beyond introductory-level (first year uni.) course * Memorizing O-P or meta directors

GAMSAT-Prep.com

Introduction

Aromatics are cyclic compounds with unusual stability due to cyclic delocalization and resonance.

Additional Resources

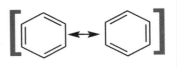

Free Online Q&A + Forum   GAMSAT-prep.com Videos   Flashcards   Special Guest

5.1 Description and Nomenclature

Aromatic compounds are cyclic and have their π electrons delocalized over the entire ring and are thus stabilized by π-electron delocalization. Benzene is the simplest of all the aromatic hydrocarbons. The term *aromatic* has historical significance in that many well known fragrant compounds were found to be derivatives of benzene. Although at present, it is known that not all benzene derivatives have fragrance, the term remains in use today to describe benzene derivatives and related compounds.

Benzene is known to have only one type of carbon-carbon bond, with a bond length of ≈ 1.4 Å (angstroms, 10^{-10}m) somewhere between that of a single and double bond. Benzene is a hexagonal, flat symmetrical molecule. All C-C-C bond angles are 120° and all C-C bonds are of equal length - a value between a normal single and double bond length; all six carbon atoms are sp^2 hybridized; and, all carbons have a p orbital perpendicular to the benzene ring, leading to six π electrons delocalized around the ring. The benzene molecule may thus be represented by two different resonance structures, showing it to be the average of the two:

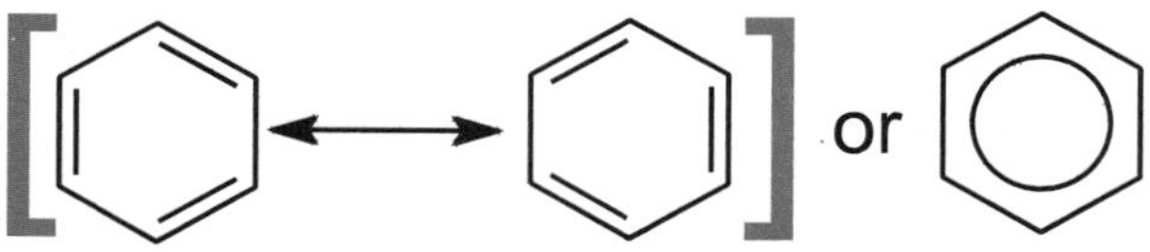

Many monosubstituted benzenes have common names by which they are known.

Others are named by substituents attached to the aromatic ring. Some of these are:

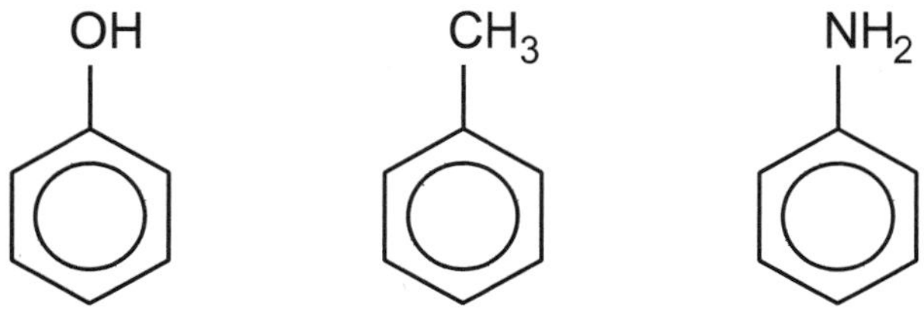

phenol   toluene   aniline

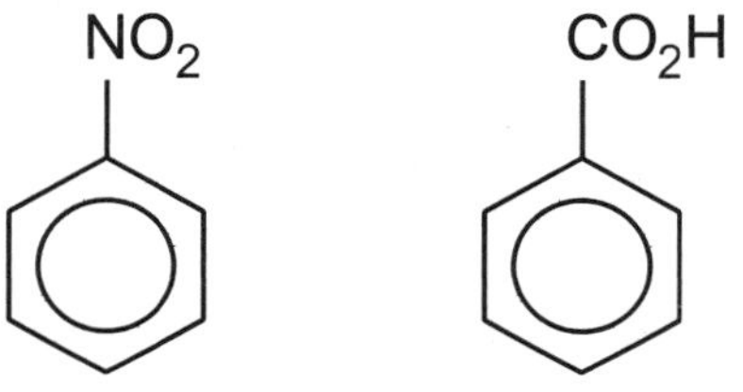

nitrobenzene   benzoic acid

Disubstituted benzenes are named as derivatives of their primary substituents. In this case, either the usual numbering or the ortho-meta-para system may be used. Ortho (*o*) substituents are at the 2nd position from the primary substituent; meta (*m*) substituents are at the 3rd position; para (*p*) substituents are at the 4th position. If there are more than two substituents on the aromatic ring, the numbering system is used. Some examples are:

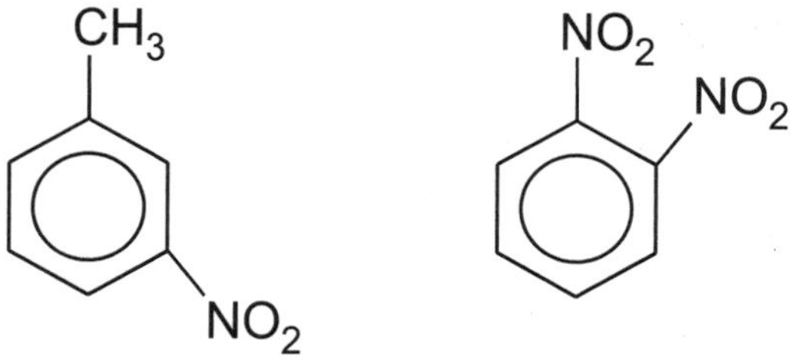

m - Nitrotoluene   o - Dinitrobenzene

NH$_2$ CH$_3$

o - Methylaniline
o - Aminotoluene

CO$_2$H
NO$_2$
OH

3-nitro-4-
hydroxy benzoic acid

When benzene is a substituent, it is called

a *phenyl or aryl group*. The shorthand for phenyl is Ph. Toluene without a hydrogen on the methyl substituent is called a *benzyl group*.

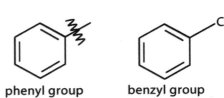

phenyl group   benzyl group

Benzene undergoes substitution reactions that retain the cyclic conjugation as opposed to electrophilic addition reactions.

5.1.1 Hückel's Rule

If a compound does not meet all the following criteria, it is likely not aromatic.

1. The molecule is cyclic.
2. The molecule is planar.
3. The molecule is fully conjugated (i.e. p orbitals at every atom in the ring; ORG 1.4).
4. The molecule has 4n + 2 π electrons.

If rules 1., 2. and/or 3. are broken, then the molecule is non-aromatic. If rule 4. is broken then the molecule is antiaromatic.

Notice that the number of π delocalized electrons must be even but NOT a multiple of 4. So 4n + 2 number of π electrons, where n = 0, 1, 2, 3, and so on, is known as Hückel's Rule. Thus the number of pi electrons can be 2, 6, 10, etc. Of course, benzene is aro-

matic (6 electrons, from 3 double bonds), but cyclobutadiene is not, since the number of π delocalized electrons is 4. Note that a cyclic molecule with conjugated double bonds in a monocyclic (= 1 ring) hydrocarbon is called an annulene. So cyclobutadiene can be called [4] annulene.

[4]annulene
4n π electrons
n = 1
antiaromatic

[6]annulene
4n + 2 π electrons
n = 1
aromatic

[8]annulene (cyclooctatetraene)
4n π electrons, n = 2
non-planar "tub shape"
non-aromatic

A GAMSAT question on Hückel's rule would normally be preceded by Hückel's rule. The point is to verify that you understand its application. There is no need to memorize Hückel's rule.

The number of p orbitals and the number of π electrons can be different, which means, whether a molecule is neutral, a cation or an anion, it can be aromatic. Note that *aliphatic* describes all hydrocarbons that are not aromatic. A cyclic compound containing only 4n electrons is said to be anti-aromatic.

- Cyclopentadienide anion:

Because of the lone pair, there are 6 π electrons, which meets Hückel's number, so it is aromatic. Thus you can see that if an electron pair is added, or subtracted, a molecule can then become aromatic by fulfilling Hückel's rule. Therefore, if 2 electrons are added to [8]annalene, it will then become a more stable molecule. Specifically, the cyclooctatetraenide dianion ($C_8H_8^{2-}$) is aromatic (thus it has increased stability), and planar, like the cyclopentadienide anion, and both fulfill Hückel's rule.

- Cycloheptatrienyl cation:

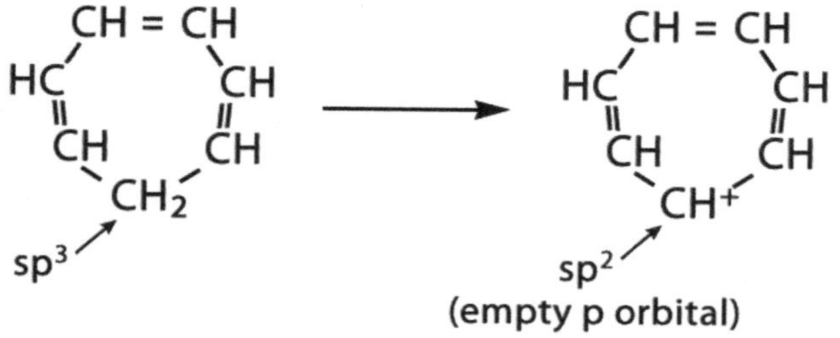

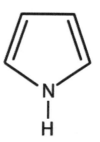

6 π electrons with conjugation through resonance because of the cation, meets Hückel's number, so it is aromatic.

Heterocyclic compounds (usu. = a ring with C + another atom) can also be aromatic.

- Pyridine:

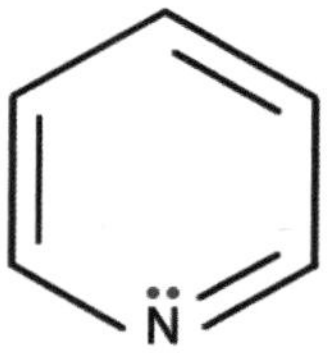

Each sp² hybridized carbon atom has a p orbital and contains one π electron. The nitrogen atom is also sp² hybridized and has one electron in the p orbital, bringing the total to six π electrons. The nitrogen nonbonding electron pair is in a sp² orbital perpendicular to other p orbitals and is not involved with the π system. Thus pyridine is aromatic.

- Pyrrole:

Each sp² hybridized carbon atom has a p orbital and contains one π electron. The nitrogen atom is also sp² hybridized with its nonbonding electron pair sitting in the p orbital, bringing the total to six π electrons. Thus pyrrole is aromatic.

5.2 Electrophilic Aromatic Substitution

One important reaction of aromatic compounds is known as electrophilic aromatic substitution, which occurs with electrophilic reagents. The reaction is similar to a S_N1 mechanism in that an addition leads to a rearrangement which produces a substitution. However, in this case it is the electrophile (*not a nucleophile*) which substitutes for an atom in the original molecule. The reaction may be summarized:

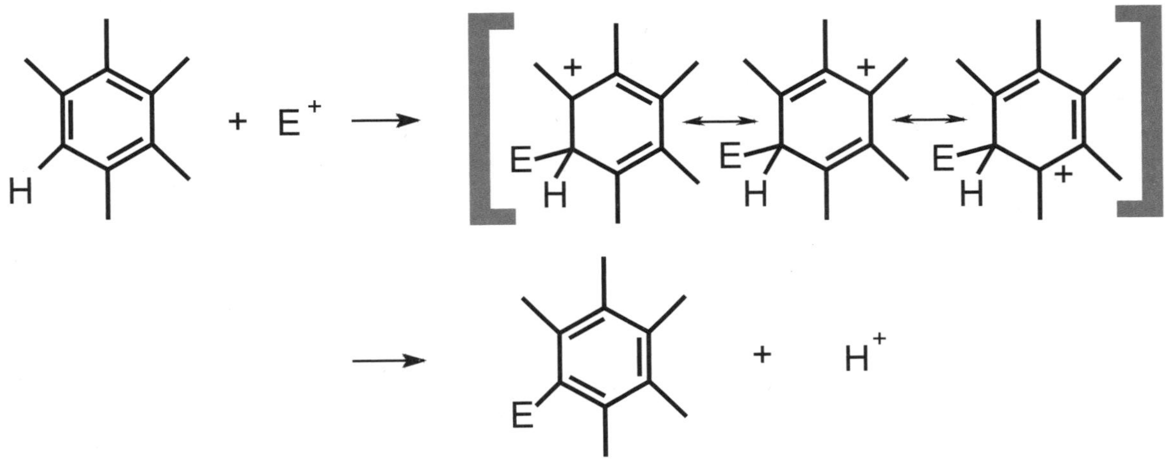

Note that the intermediate positive charge is stabilized by resonance.

It is important to understand that the electrophile used in electrophilic aromatic substitution must always be a powerful electrophile. After all, the resonance stabilized aromatic ring is resistant to many types of routine chemical reactions (i.e. oxidation with $KMnO_4$ – ORG 4.2.2, electrophilic addition with acid - ORG 4.2.1, and hydrogenation - ORG 4.2.3). Remembering that Br, a halide, is already very electronegative (CHM 2.3), Br^+ is an example of a powerful electrophile. In a reaction called bromination, $Br_2/FeBr_3$ is used to generate the Br^+ species which adds to the aromatic ring. Similar reactions are performed to "juice up" other potential substituents (i.e. alkyl, acyl, iodine, etc.) to become powerful electrophiles to add to the aromatic ring.

• Aromatic halogenation: The benzene ring with its 6 π electrons in a conjugated system acts as an electron nucleophile (electron donor) in most chemical reactions. It reacts with bromine, chlorine or iodine to produce mono-substituted products. Fluorine is too reactive and tends to produce multi-substituted products. Therefore, the electrophilic substitution reaction is characteristic of aromaticity and can be used as a diagnostic tool to test the presence of an aromatic ring.

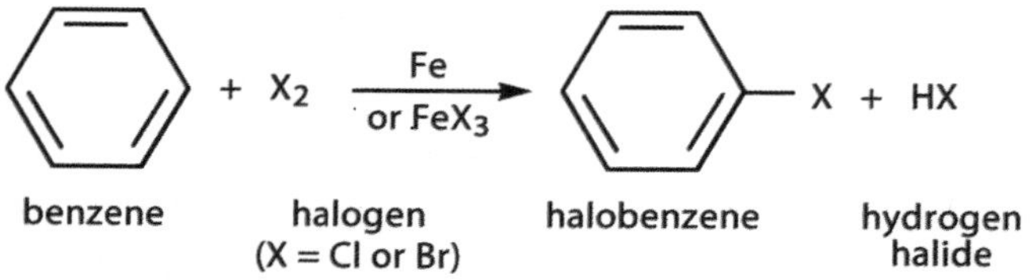

benzene   halogen   halobenzene   hydrogen
          (X = Cl or Br)   halide

- **Aromatic nitration**: The aromatic ring can be nitrated when reacted with a mixture of nitric and sulfuric acid. The benzene ring reacts with the electrophile in this reaction, the nitronium ion NO_2^+, yielding a carbocation intermediate in a similar way as the aromatic halogenation reaction.

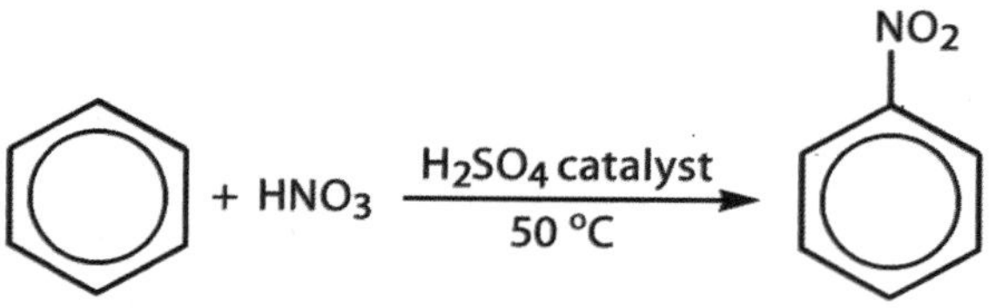

- **Aromatic sulfonation**: Aromatic rings can react with a mixture of sulfuric acid and sulfur trioxide (H_2SO_4/SO_3) to form sulfonic acid. The electrophile in this reaction is either HSO_3 or SO_3.

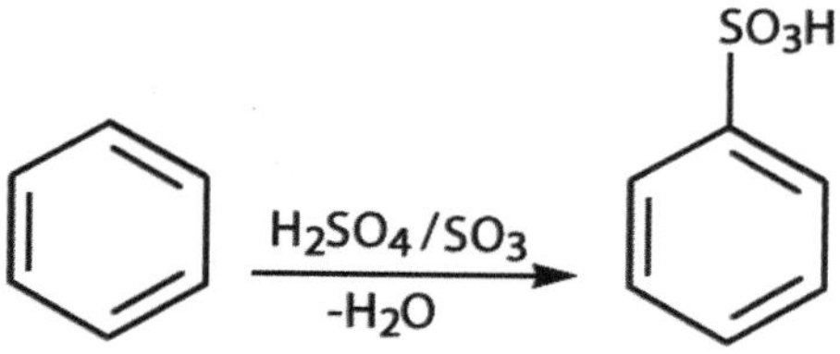

- **Friedel-Crafts alkylation**: This is an electrophilic aromatic substitution in which the benzene ring is alkylated when it reacts with an alkyl halide. The benzene ring attacks the alkyl cation electrophile, yielding an alkyl-substituted benzene product.

There are several limitations to this reaction:

1. The reaction does not proceed on an aromatic ring that has a strong, deactivating substituent group.

2. Because the product is attacked even faster by alkyl carbocations than the starting material, poly-alkylation is often observed.

3. Skeletal rearrangement of the alkyl group sometimes occurs. A hydride shift or an alkyl shift may produce a more stable carbocation (*see* ORG 4.2.1).

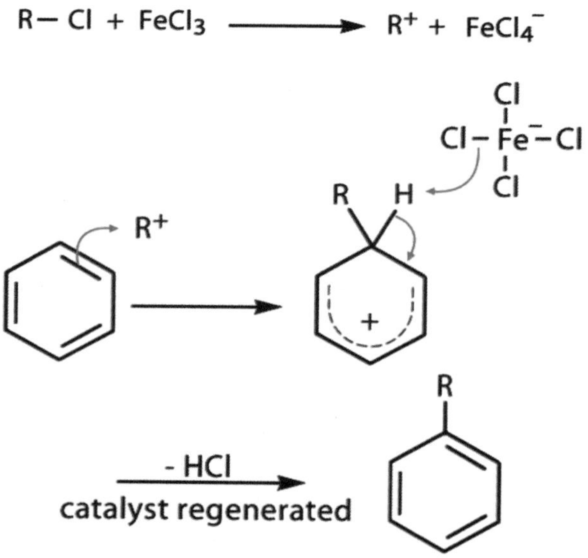

$$R-Cl + FeCl_3 \longrightarrow R^+ + FeCl_4^-$$

- **Friedel-Crafts acylation**: An electrophilic aromatic substitution in which the benzene ring is acylated when an acyl group is introduced to the ring. The mechanism is similar to that of Friedel-Crafts alkylation. The electrophile is an acyl cation generated by the reaction between the acyl halide and $AlCl_3$. Because the product is less reactive than the starting material, only mono-substitution is observed.

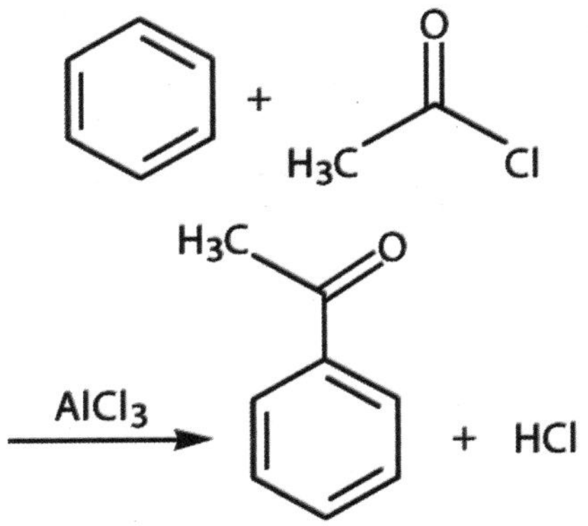

When groups are attached to the aromatic ring, the intermediate charge delocalization is affected. Thus nature of first substituent on the ring determines the position of the second substituent. Substituents can be classified into three classes: ortho-para (o-p) directing activators, ortho-para directing deactivators, and meta-directing deactivators. As implied, these groups indicate where most of the electrophile will end up in the reaction.

5.2.1 O-P Directors

If a substituted benzene reacts more rapidly than a benzene alone, the substituent group is said to be an <u>activating group</u>. Activating groups can *donate* electrons to the ring.

Thus the ring is more attractive to an electrophile. All activating groups are o/p directors. Some examples are $-OH$, $-NH_2$, $-OR$, $-NR_2$, $-OCOR$ and alkyl groups.

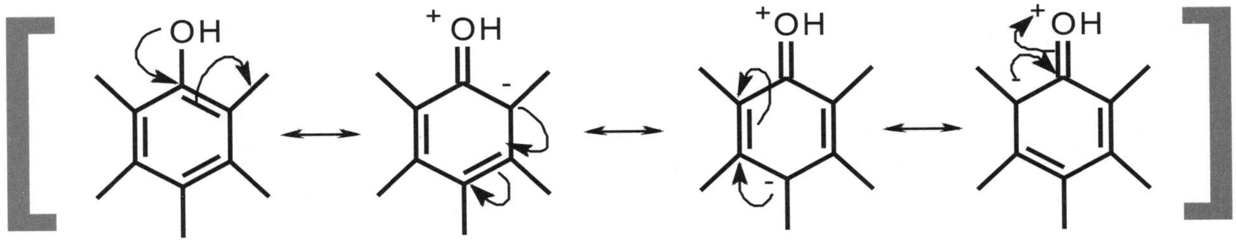

Note that the partial electron density (δ^-) is at the ortho and para positions, so the electrophile favors attack at these positions. Good stabilization results with a substituent at the ortho or para positions preferentially.

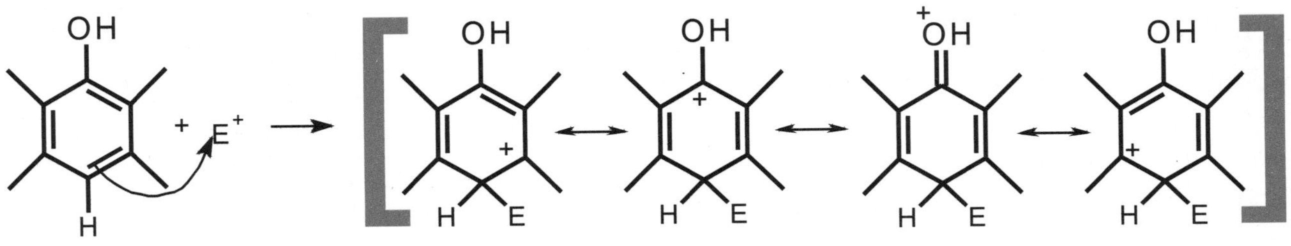

When there is a substituent at the meta position, the –OH can no longer help to delocalize the positive charge, so the o-p positions are favored over the meta:

Note that even though the substituents are o-p directors, probability suggests that there will still be a small percentage of the electrophile that will add at the meta position.

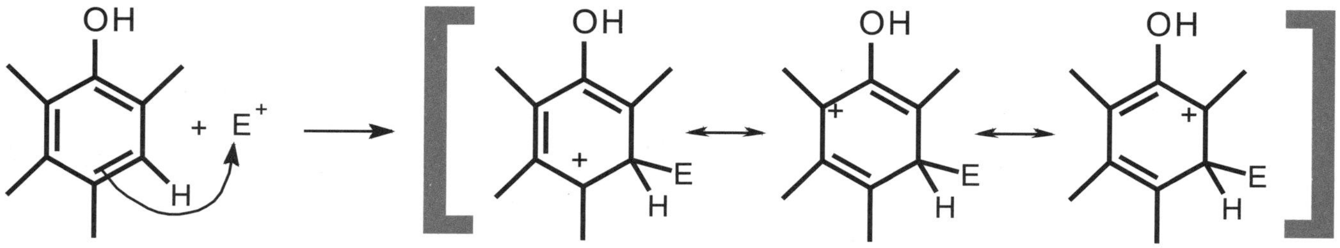

5.2.2 Meta Directors

If a substituted benzene reacts more slowly than the benzene alone, the substituent group is said to be a <u>deactivating group</u>. Deactivating groups can *withdraw* electrons from the ring. Thus the ring is less attractive to an electrophile. All deactivating groups are meta directors, with the exception of the weakly deactivating halides which are o–p directors (-F, -Cl, -Br, -I). Some examples of

meta directors are $-NO_2$, $-SO_2$, $-CN$, $-SO_3H$, -COOH, -COOR, -COR, CHO.

Without any substituents, the partial positive charge density (δ^+) will be at the o–p positions. Thus the electrophile avoids the positive charge and favors attack at the meta position:

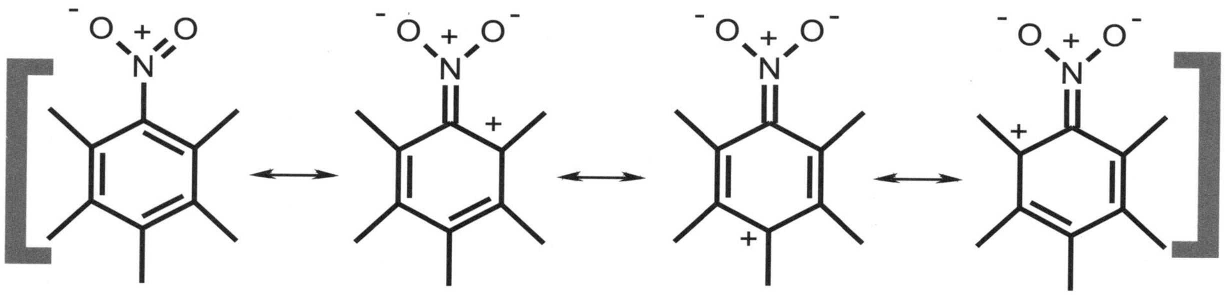

If you are seeking another way to learn, consider logging into your GAMSAT-prep.com account and clicking on Videos to choose the Aromatic Chemistry videos.

With a substituent at the meta position:

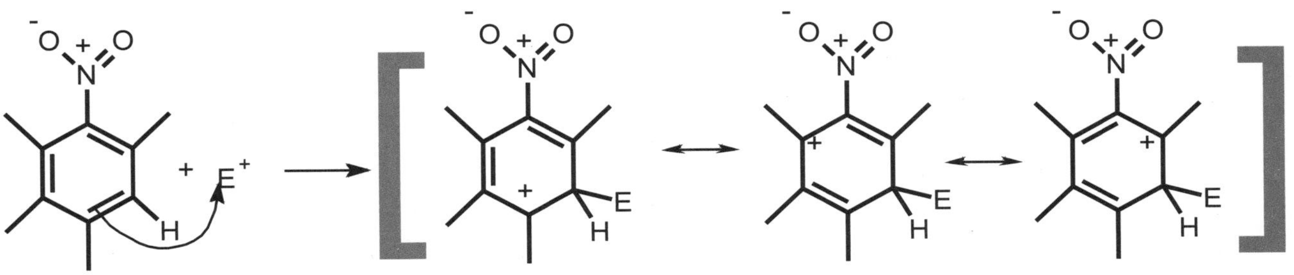

Note that even though the substituents are meta directors, probability suggests that there will still be a smaller percentage of the electrophile that will add at the o–p positions.

5.2.3 Reactions with the Alkylbenzene Side Chain

• __Oxidation__: Alkyl groups on the benzene ring react rapidly with oxidizing agents and are converted into a carboxyl group. The net result is the conversion of an alkylbenzene into benzoic acid.

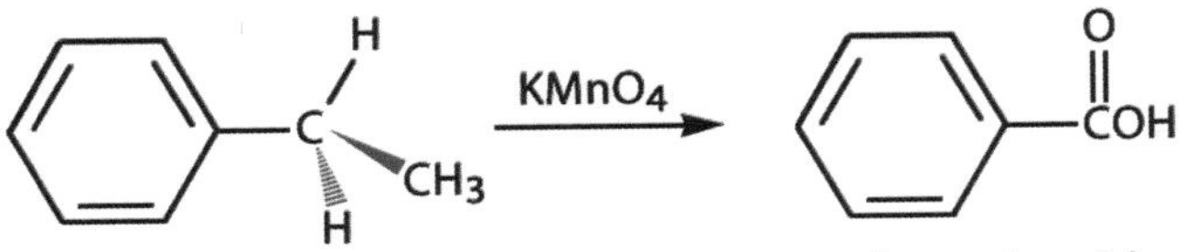

aromatic ring with
alkyl substituent

benzoic acid

• __Bromination__: NBS (N-bromosuccinimide) reacts with alkylbenzene through a radical chain mechanism (ORG 3.2.2): the benzyl radical generated from NBS in the presence of benzoyl peroxide reacts with Br_2 to yield the final product and bromine radical, which will cycle back into the reaction to act as a radical initiator. The reaction occurs exclusively at the benzyl position because the benzyl radical is highly stabilized through different forms of resonance.

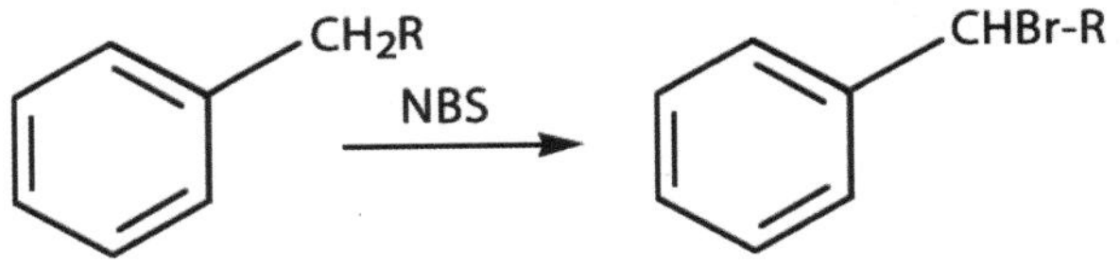

• __Reduction__: Reductions of aryl alkyl ketones in the presence of H_2 and Pd/C can be used to convert the aryl alkyl ketone generated by the Friedel-Crafts acylation reaction into an alkylbenzene.

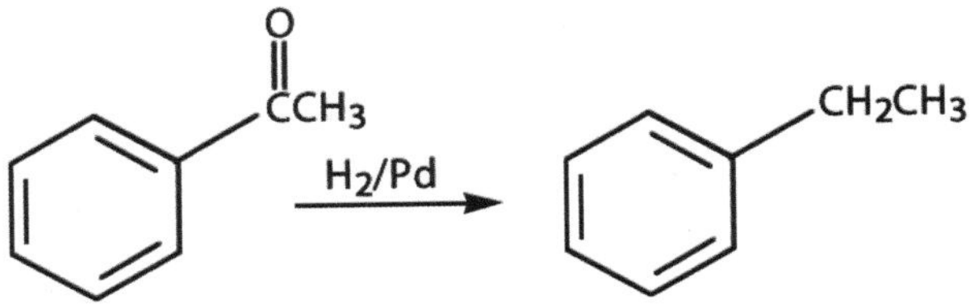

Go online to GAMSAT-prep.com for chapter review Q&A and forum.

Memorize	Understand	Not Required*
PAC nomenclature ysical properties oducts of oxidation fine: steric hindrance	* Trends based on length, branching * Effect of hydrogen bonds * Dehydration, redox reactions * Nucleophilic substitution, elimination	* Knowledge beyond introductory-level (first year uni.) course

GAMSAT-Prep.com

Introduction

An alcohol is any organic compound in which a hydroxyl group (-OH) is bound to a carbon atom of an alkyl or substituted alkyl group. There is an incredibly wide range of 'alcohols' - although originally, the term only referred to the primary alcohol *ethanol* (ethyl alcohol), the predominant alcohol in alcoholic beverages.

IUPAC nomenclature for alcohols applies the suffix *-ol* to organic molecules where the *hydroxyl* group is the functional group with the highest priority; in substances where a higher priority group is present, the prefix hydroxy- is used. The suffix *-ol* in non-systematic names (such as paracetamol or cholesterol) also usually indicates that the molecule includes a hydroxyl functional group and, so, can be termed an 'alcohol'. Some molecules, particularly sugars (e.g. glucose and sucrose, ORG 12.3) contain hydroxyl functional groups without using the suffix *-ol*.

Additional Resources

Free Online Q&A + Forum

GAMSAT-prep.com Videos

Flashcards

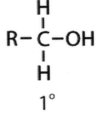

Special Guest

6.1 Description and Nomenclature

The systematic naming of alcohols is accomplished by replacing the –e of the corresponding alkane with –ol.

Alcohols are compounds that have hydroxyl groups bonded to a saturated carbon atom with the general formula ROH. It can be thought of as a substituted water molecule, with one of the water hydrogens replaced with an alkyl group R. Alcohols are classified as primary (1°), secondary (2°) or tertiary (3°) based on the number of carbon atoms connected to the carbon atom bonded to OH:

$$
\begin{array}{ccc}
H & H & R \\
| & | & | \\
R-C-OH & R-C-OH & R-C-OH \\
| & | & | \\
H & R & R \\
1° & 2° & 3°
\end{array}
$$

As with alkanes, special names are used for branched groups:

$$
CH_3-\underset{\underset{\displaystyle CH_3}{|}}{\overset{\overset{\displaystyle OH}{|}}{CH}}
$$

IUPAC: propan-2-ol
- Isopropanol
- Isopropyl alcohol

$$
CH_3-\underset{\underset{\displaystyle CH_3}{|}}{\overset{\overset{\displaystyle OH}{|}}{C}}-CH_3
$$

IUPAC: 2-methylpropan-2-ol
- 2-methyl-2-propanol
- tert-butanol

The alcohols are always numbered to give the carbon with the attached hydroxy (–OH) group the lowest number (choose the longest carbon chain that contains the hydroxyl group as the parent):

$$
CH_3CH_2CH_2\underset{\underset{\displaystyle OH}{|}}{CH}CH_2CH_3
$$

3-hexanol NOT 4-hexanol

$$
CH_3CH_2CH_2\underset{\underset{\displaystyle CH_3}{|}}{\overset{\overset{\displaystyle CH_3}{|}}{CH}}CH_2\underset{\underset{\displaystyle OH}{|}}{CH}CH_2\underset{\underset{\displaystyle CH_3}{|}}{CH}CH_3
$$

2,6-dimethyl-4-nonanol

The shorthand for methanol is MeOH, and the shorthand for ethanol is EtOH. Alcohols are weak acids ($K_a \approx 10^{-18}$), being weaker acids than water. Their conjugate bases are called alkoxides, very little of which will be present in solution:

$$
\underset{ethanol}{C_2H_5OH} + OH^- \rightleftharpoons \underset{ethoxide}{C_2H_5O^-} + H_2O
$$

The acidity of an alcohol decreases with increasing number of attached carbons. Thus CH_3OH is more acidic than CH_3CH_2OH; and CH_3CH_2OH (a primary alcohol) is more acidic than $(CH_3)_2CHOH$ (a secondary alcohol), which is, in turn, more acidic than $(CH_3)_3COH$ (a tertiary alcohol).

Alcohols have higher boiling points and a greater solubility than comparable alkanes, alkenes, aldehydes, ketones and alkyl halides. The higher boiling point and greater solubility is due to the greater polarity and hydrogen bonding of the alcohol. In alcohols, hydrogen bonding is a weak association of the –OH proton of one molecule, with the oxygen of another. To form the hydrogen bond, both a donor, and an acceptor are required:

Sometimes an atom may act as both a donor and acceptor of hydrogen bonds. One example of this is the oxygen atom in an alcohol:

hydrogen bonds

As the length of the carbon chain (= R) of the alcohol molecule increases, the nonpolar chain becomes more meaningful, and the alcohol becomes less water soluble. The hydroxyl group of a primary alcohol is able to form hydrogen bonds with molecules such as water more easily than the hydroxyl group of a tertiary alcohol. The hydroxyl group of a tertiary alcohol is crowded by, for example, the surrounding methyl groups and thus its ability to participate in hydrogen bonds is lessened. As well, in solution, primary alcohols are more acidic than secondary alcohols, and secondary alcohols are more acidic than tertiary alcohols. In the gas phase, however, the order of acidity is reversed.

6.1.1 Acidity and Basicity of Alcohols

Alcohols are both weakly acidic and weakly basic. Alcohols can dissociate into a proton and its conjugate base, the alkoxy ion (alkoxide, RO^-), just as water dissociates into a proton and a hydroxide ion. As weak acids, alcohols act as proton donors, thus $ROH + H_2O \rightarrow RO^- + H_3O^+$. As weak bases, alcohols act as proton acceptors, thus $ROH + HX \rightarrow ROH_2^+ + X^-$.

Substituent effects are important in determining alcohol acidity. The more easily the alkoxide ion is accessible to a water molecule, the easier it is stabilized through solvation (CHM 5.3), the more its formation is favored, and the greater the acidity of the alcohol molecule. For example $(CH_3)_3COH$ is less acidic than CH_3OH.

Inductive effects are also important in determining alcohol acidity. Electron-withdrawing groups stabilize an alkoxide anion by spreading out the charge, thus making the alcohol molecule more acidic. Vice versa, electron-donating groups destabilize an alkoxide anion, thus making the alcohol molecule less acidic. For example $(CH_3)_3COH$ is less acidic than $(CF_3)_3OH$.

Since alcohols are weak acids, they do not react with weak bases. However, they do react with strong bases such as NaH, $NaNH_2$, or sodium or potassium metal.

$$CH_3CH_2OH + NaH \rightarrow CH_3CH_2O^-Na^+ + H_2$$

$$CH_3CH_2OH + NaNH_2 \rightarrow CH_3CH_2O^-Na^+ + NH_3$$

$$2CH_3CH_2OH + 2Na \rightarrow 2CH_3CH_2O^-Na^+ + H_2$$

6.1.2 Synthesis of Alcohols: How to Make Alcohols

1. **Hydration of alkenes:** Alcohols can be prepared through the hydration (= *to combine with water*) of alkenes: **(1)** Halohydrin (one carbon with a halogen and an adjacent carbon with a hydroxyl substituent) formation yields a Markovnikoff hydration product with anti stereospecificity (i.e. the OH nucleophile adds to the most substituted carbon but *opposite* to the halide); **(2)** Hydroboration-oxidation yields a syn stereospecific anti-Markovnikoff hydration product (the OH adds to the least substituted carbon); **(3)** Oxymercuration-reduction yields a Markovnikoff hydration product.

2. **Reduction of carbonyl compounds:** An alcohol can be prepared through the reduction of an aldehyde, ketone, carboxylic acid or ester. Aldehydes are converted into primary alcohols and ketones are converted into secondary alcohols in the presence of reducing agents $NaBH_4$ or $LiAlH_4$ (also symbolized as LAH or LithAl). Since $LiAlH_4$ is more powerful and more reactive than $NaBH_4$, it can be used

as a reducing agent for the reduction of carboxylic acids and esters to give primary alcohols (see ORG 6.2.2).

3. **Addition reaction with Grignard reagents:** Grignard reagents (RMgX) react with carbonyl compounds to give alcohols. Grignard reagents are created by reacting Mg metal with alkyl (aryl or vinyl) halide.

$$R\text{-}X + Mg \rightarrow RMgX$$

A number of different alcohol products can be obtained from Grignard reactions with formaldehyde, other aldehydes, ketones or esters. A carboxylic acid does not give an alcohol product because, instead of an addition reaction, the carboxylic acid reacts with the Grignard reagent giving a hydrocarbon and magnesium salt of the acid.

• Formaldehyde: Primary alcohol

For alkene hydration, reduction of carbonyl, addition with Grignards, and the other reactions, follow the story, follow the geometry, follow the substituents (R, R', R", etc.) as you have been doing with the other chapters. It is extremely unlikely to be asked a GAMSAT question that requires the memorization of a reagent (= the chemical added to bring about the reaction, i.e. Grignard, ether, catalysts, etc.).

- <u>Aldehyde</u>: Secondary alcohol

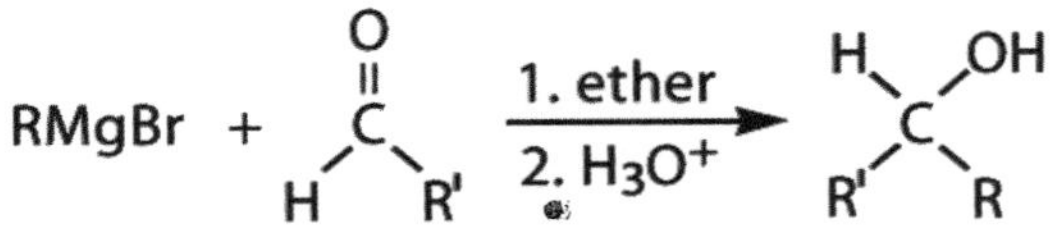

- <u>Ketone</u>: Tertiary alcohol

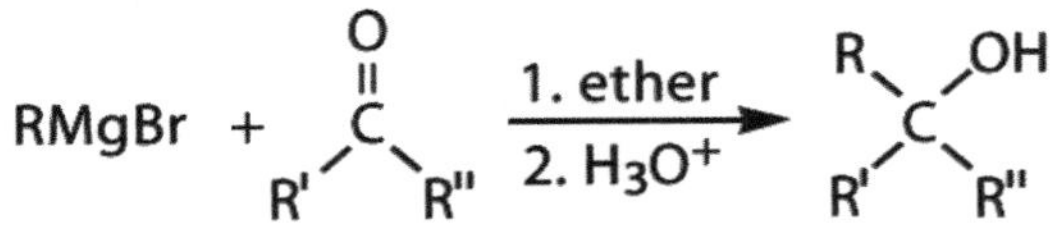

- <u>Ester</u>: Tertiary alcohol

Two substituents from the Grignard reagent are added to the carbonyl-bearing carbon, giving a tertiary alcohol.

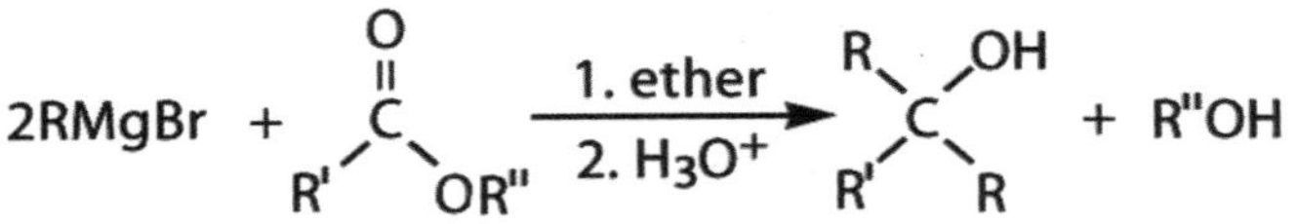

6.2 Important Reactions of Alcohols

6.2.1 Dehydration

<u>Dehydration</u> (= *loss of water*) reactions of alcohols produce alkenes. The general dehydration reaction is shown in Figure IV.B.6.1.

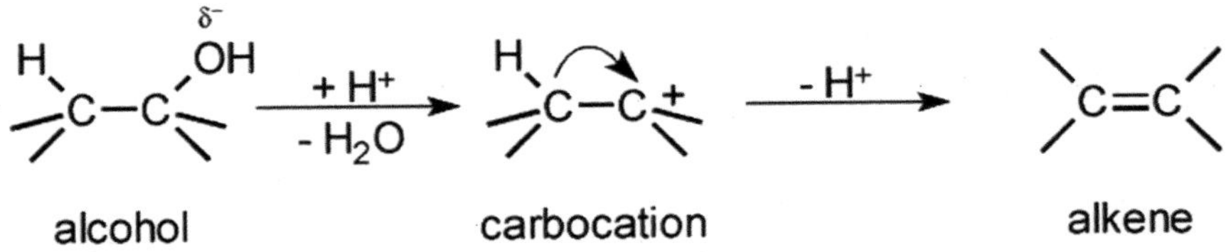

alcohol   carbocation   alkene

Figure IV.B.6.1: Dehydration of an alcohol. The proton (H^+) is attracted to the partial negative charge of –OH thus water is formed which is a good leaving group. Then electrons are attracted to the positively charged carbon causing a proton to leave. Thus the acid (i.e. proton) increases the reaction rate and is regenerated (= *catalyst*; CHM 9.7).

For the preceding reaction to occur, the temperature must be between 300 and 400 degrees Celsius, and the vapors must be passed over a <u>metal oxide catalyst</u>. Alternatively, strong, <u>hot acids</u>, such as H_2SO_4 or H_3PO_4 at 100 to 200 degrees Celsius may be used.

The reactivity depends upon the type of alcohol. A tertiary alcohol is more reactive than a secondary alcohol which is, in turn, more reactive than a primary alcohol. The faster reactions have the most stable carbocation intermediates. The alkene that is formed is the most stable one. A phenyl group will take preference over one or two alkyl groups, otherwise the most substituted double bond is the most stable (= *major product*) and the least substituted is less stable (= *minor product*).

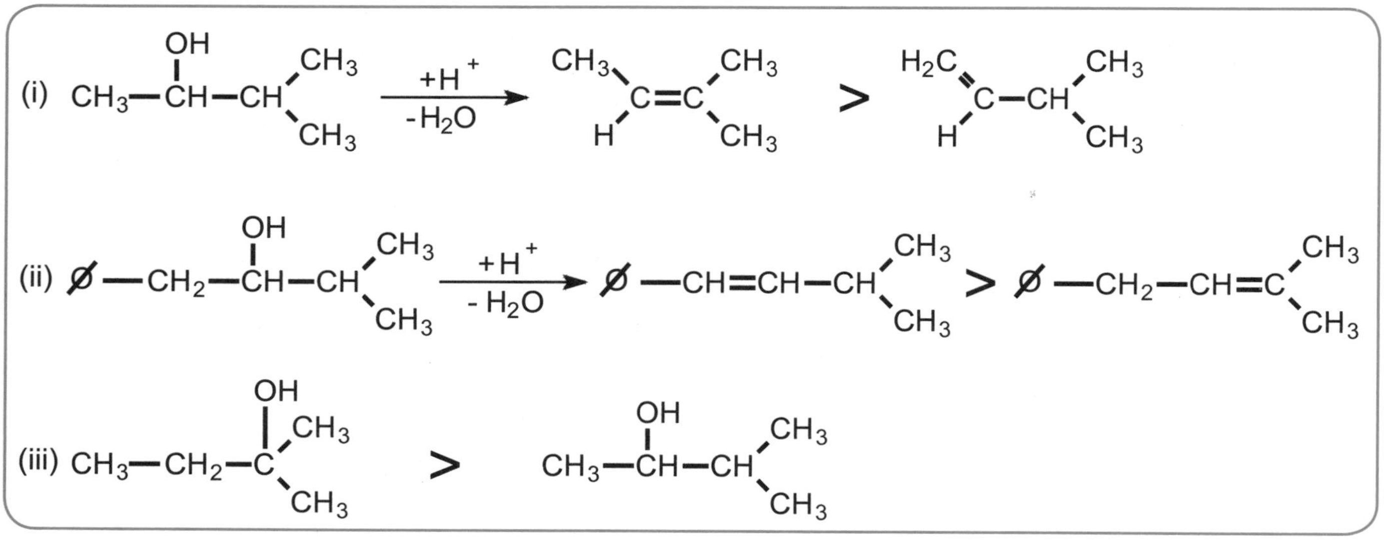

Figure IV.B.6.2: Dehydration of substituted alcohols. Major and minor products, respectively, are represented in reactions (i) and (ii). An example of a reactant with a greater reaction rate due to more substituents as an intermediate is represented by (iii). ϕ = a phenyl group.

6.2.2 Oxidation-Reduction

In organic chemistry, oxidation (O) is the increasing of oxygen or decreasing of hydrogen content, and reduction (H) is the opposite. Primary alcohols are converted to aldehydes using PCC or $KMnO_4$, under mild conditions (i.e. room temperature, neutral pH). Primary alcohols are converted to carboxylic acids using CrO_3 (the mixture is called a Jones'

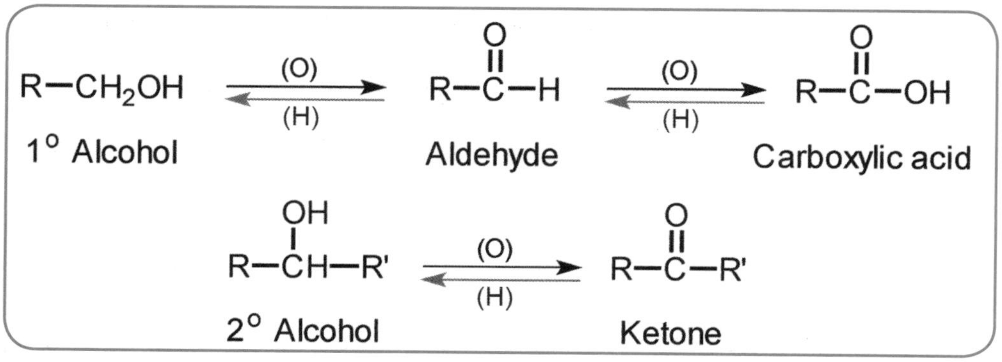

Figure IV.B.6.3: Oxidation-Reduction. In organic chemistry, traditionally the symbols R and R' denote an attached hydrogen, or a hydrocarbon side chain of any length (which are consistent with the reactions above), but sometimes these symbols refer to any group of atoms. For the GAMSAT, when R is used, it is normally defined in the passage preceding the questions.

reagent), $K_2Cr_2O_7$, or $KMnO_4$ under abrasive conditions (i.e. increased temperature, presence of OH^-). Secondary alcohols are converted to ketones by any of the preceding oxidizing agents. It is *very* difficult to oxidize a tertiary alcohol. Under acidic conditions,

tertiary alcohols are unaffected; they may be oxidized under acidic conditions by dehydration and *then* oxidizing the double bond of the resultant alkene. Classic reducing agents (H) include $LiAlH_4$ (strong), H_2/metals (strong) and $NaBH_4$ (mild).

6.2.3 Substitution

In a <u>substitution reaction</u> one atom or group is *substituted* or replaced by another atom or group. For an alcohol, the –OH group is replaced (*substituted*) by a halide (usually chlorine or bromine). A variety of reagents may be used, such as HCl, HBr or PCl_3. There are two different types of substitution reactions, S_N1 and S_N2.

In the S_N1 (*1st order or monomolecular nucleophilic substitution*) reaction, the transition state involves a carbocation, the formation of which is the rate-determining step (CHM 9.4). Alcohol substitutions that proceed by this mechanism are those involving benzyl groups, allyl groups, tertiary and secondary alcohols. The mechanism of this reaction is:

(i) $R–L \rightarrow R^+ + L^-$
(ii) $Nu^- + R^+ \rightarrow Nu–R$

The important features of this reaction are:

- The reaction is first order (this means that the rate of the reaction depends only on the concentration of one compound, CHM 9.2); the rate depends on [R–L],

where R may be an alkyl group, and L represents a substituent or ligand.

- There is racemization (ORG 2.3.2) when a chiral molecule is involved.

- A stable carbonium ion should be formed; thus in terms of reaction rate, benzyl groups = allyl groups > tertiary alcohols > secondary alcohols >> primary alcohols.

- The stability of alkyl groups is as follows: primary alkyl groups < secondary alkyl groups < tertiary alkyl groups.

The mechanism of the S_N2 (*2nd order or bimolecular nucleophilic substitution*) reaction is:

$$Nu^- + R—L \rightarrow [Nu----R----L]^- \rightarrow Nu—R + L^-$$

There are several important points to know about this reaction:

- The reaction rate is second order overall (the rate depends on the concentration of two compounds); first order with respect to [R-L] and first order with respect to the concentration of the nucleophile [Nu⁻].

- Note that the nucleophile adds to the alkyl group by *backside displacement* (i.e. Nu must add to the *opposite* site to the ligand). Thus optically active alcohols react to give an <u>inversion</u> of configuration, forming the opposite enantiomer (ORG 2.2.2, 2.3.2).

- Large or bulky groups near or at the reacting site may hinder or retard a reaction. This is called *steric hindrance*. Size or <u>steric factors</u> are important since they affect S_N2 reaction rates; in terms of reaction rates, CH_3^- > primary alcohols > secondary alcohols >> tertiary alcohols.

The substitution reactions for methanol (CH_3OH) and other primary alcohols are by the S_N2 reaction mechanism.

6.2.4 Elimination

<u>Elimination reactions</u> occur when an atom or a group of atoms is removed (*eliminated*) from adjacent carbons leaving a multiple bond:

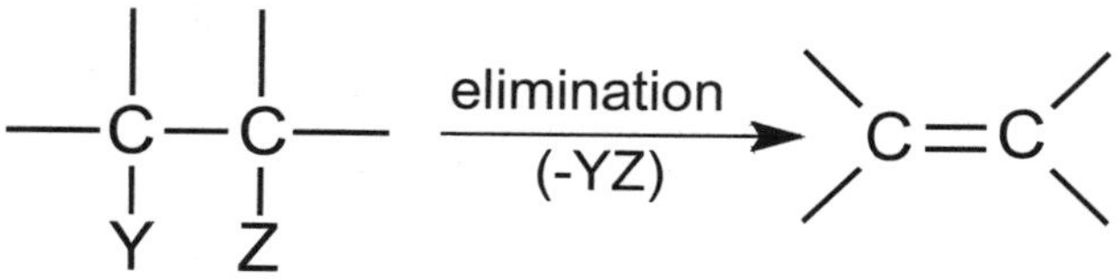

There are two different types of elimination reactions, E1 and E2. In the E1 (<u>E</u>limination, 1st order) reaction, the rate of reaction depends on the concentration of one compound. E1 often occurs as minor products alongside S_N2 reactions. E1 can occur as major products starting with a *substrate* (reactant) like an alkyl halide, or an alcohol:

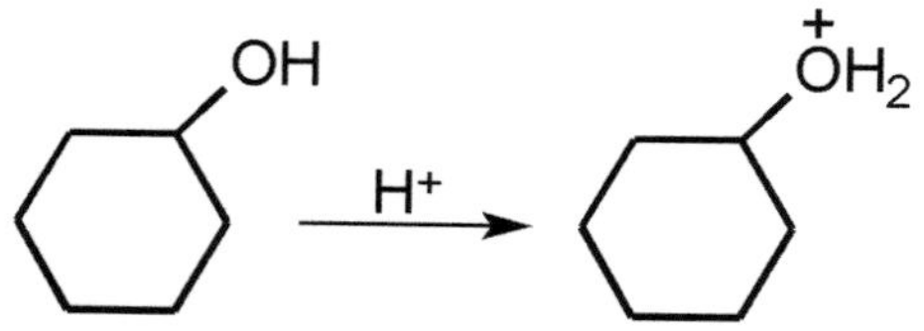

cyclohexanol

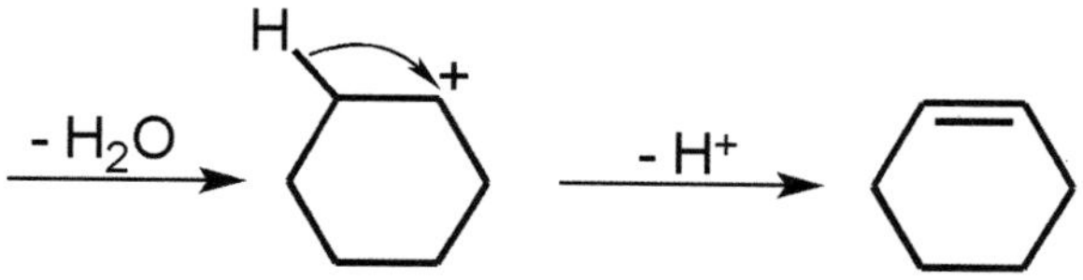

2° carbocation   cyclohexene

The acid-catalyzed dehydration of alcohols is thus an E1 reaction which yields the more highly substituted alkene as the major product. There is a carbocation intermediate formed during the preceding reaction, thus a tertiary alcohol will react faster and yield an alkene in a more stable way than a secondary or primary alcohol.

Secondary and primary alcohols will only react with acids in very harsh condition (75%-95% H_2SO_4, 100 °C). However, they will react with $POCl_3$ converting the −OH into a good leaving group to yield an alkene. This reaction takes place with an E2 mechanism.

In the E2 (<u>E</u>limination, 2nd order)

reaction, the rate of reaction depends on the concentration of two compounds (CHM 9.2). E2 reactions require strong bases like KOH or the salt of an alcohol (e.g. ORG 6.1.1, *sodium alkoxide*). An alkoxide (RO^-) can be synthesized from an alcohol using either Na(*s*) or NaH (*sodium hydride*) as reducing agents. The hydride ion H^- is a powerful base:

$$R\text{-}OH + NaH \longrightarrow R\text{-}O^-Na^+ + H_2$$
$$\text{sodium alkoxide}$$

Now the alkoxide can be used as a proton acceptor in an E2 reaction involving an alkyl halide:

C$_2$H$_5$O$^-$ + H-C-C-CH$_3$ (Br)

ethoxide   2-bromopropane

propene   ethanol

In the preceding reaction, the first step (1) involves the base (ethoxide) removing (*elimination*) a proton, thus carbon has a negative charge (*primary* carbanion, very *unstable*). The electron pair is quickly attracted to the δ^+ neighboring carbon (2) forming a double bond (note that the carbon was δ^+ because it was attached to the electronegative atom Br, *see* ORG 1.5). Simultaneously, Br (*a halide, which are good leaving groups*) is bumped (3) from the carbon as carbon can have only four bonds. {Notice that in organic chemistry the curved arrows always follow the movement of electrons.}

The determination of the quality of a leaving group is quite simple: good leaving groups have *strong* conjugate acids (CHM 6.3). As examples, H_2O is a good leaving group because H_3O^+ is a strong acid, likewise for Br^-/HBr, Cl^-/HCl, HSO_4^-/H_2SO_4, etc.

> Substitution and elimination reactions are the most important mechanisms to understand in GAMSAT Organic Chemistry.

6.2.5 Conversion of Alcohols to Alkyl Halides

Alcohols can participate in substitution reactions only if the hydroxyl group is converted into a better leaving group by either protonation or the formation of an inorganic ester. Tertiary alcohols can be converted into alkyl halides by a reaction with HCl or HBr. This reaction occurs in an S_N1 mechanism.

Primary and secondary alcohols do not react with HCl or HBr readily and are converted into halides by $SOCl_2$ or PBr_3. This reaction occurs in an S_N2 mechanism.

$$RCH_2OH + SOCl_2 \longrightarrow RCH_2Cl + SO_2 + HCl$$
$$RCH_2OH + PBr_3 \longrightarrow RCH_2Br + HOPBr_2$$

Go online to GAMSAT-prep.com for chapter review Q&A and forum.

ALDEHYDES AND KETONES

Chapter 7

Memorize	Understand	Not Required*
JPAC nomenclature edox reactions	* Effect of hydrogen bonds * Mechanisms of reactions * Acidity of the alpha H * Resonance, polarity * Grignards, organometallic reagents	* Knowledge beyond introductory-level (first year uni.) course

GAMSAT-Prep.com

Introduction ▪▪▪▪

An aldehyde contains a terminal carbonyl group. The functional group is a carbon atom bonded to a hydrogen atom and double-bonded to an oxygen atom (O=CH-) and is called the aldehyde group. A ketone contains a carbonyl group (C=O) bonded to two other carbon atoms: R(CO)R'. Consider reviewing the functional groups presented in ORG 1.6.

Additional Resources

Free Online Q&A + Forum

GAMSAT-prep.com Videos

Flashcards

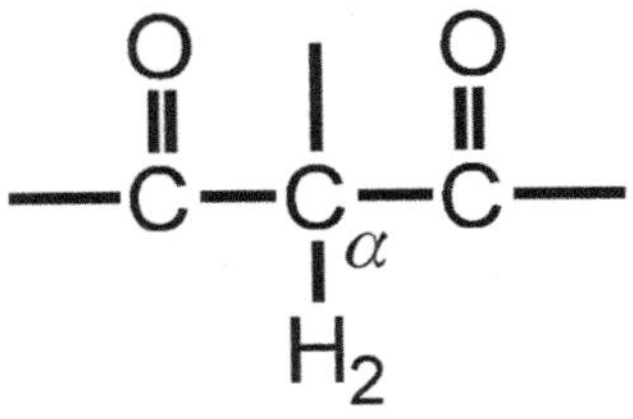

Special Guest

THE BIOLOGICAL SCIENCES ORG-85

* The real GAMSAT may have advanced level information presented (ie. in a passage) but previous knowledge of said information is not required to answer the questions that would follow. Practice ACER and GS practice GAMSATs can help you clarify this point.

7.1 Description and Nomenclature

Aldehydes and ketones are two types of molecules, both containing the carbonyl group, C=O, which is the basis for their chemistry.

The carbonyl functional group is planar with bond angles of approximately 120°. The carbonyl carbon atom is sp² hybridized and forms three σ bonds. The C=O double bond is both stronger and shorter than the C-O single bond.

The general structure of aldehydes and ketones is:

$$\underset{\text{Aldehyde}}{R-\overset{\overset{\textstyle O}{\|}}{C}-H} \qquad \underset{\text{Ketone}}{R-\overset{\overset{\textstyle O}{\|}}{C}-R'}$$

Aldehydes have at least one hydrogen bonded to the carbonyl carbon, as well as a second hydrogen (= *formaldehyde*) or either an alkyl or an aryl group (= *benzene minus one hydrogen*). Ketones have two alkyl or aryl groups bound to the carbonyl carbon (i.e. the carbon forming the double bond with oxygen).

Systematic naming of these compounds is done by replacing the '–e' of the corresponding alkane with '–al' for aldehydes, and '-one' for ketones. For aldehydes, the longest chain chosen as the parent name must contain -CHO group and the -CHO group must occupy the terminal (1st Carbon, or C1) position. For ketones, the longest chain chosen as the parent name must contain the ketone group and give the lowest possible number to the carbonyl carbon. Common names are given in brackets:

$$\underset{\substack{\text{ethanal}\\(\text{acetaldehyde})}}{CH_3\overset{\overset{\textstyle O}{\|}}{C}-H} \qquad \underset{\substack{\text{propanone}\\(\text{acetone})}}{CH_3\overset{\overset{\textstyle O}{\|}}{C}CH_3} \qquad \underset{\substack{\text{2-pentanone}\\(\text{methyl propyl ketone})}}{CH_3\overset{\overset{\textstyle O}{\|}}{C}CH_2CH_2CH_3}$$

The important features of the carbonyl group are:

• **Resonance**: There are two resonance forms of the carbonyl group:

• **Polarity**: Reactions about this group may be either nucleophilic, or electrophilic. Since opposite charges attract, nucleophiles (Nu⁻) attack the δ⁺ carbon, and electrophiles (E⁺) attack the δ⁻ oxygen. In both of these types of reactions, the character of the double bond is altered:

- **Acidity of the α-hydrogen**: The α-hydrogen is the hydrogen attached to the carbon next to the carbonyl group (the α-carbon). The β-carbon is the carbon adjacent to the α-carbon. The α-hydrogen may be removed by a base. The acidity of this hydrogen is increased if it is between 2 carbonyl groups:

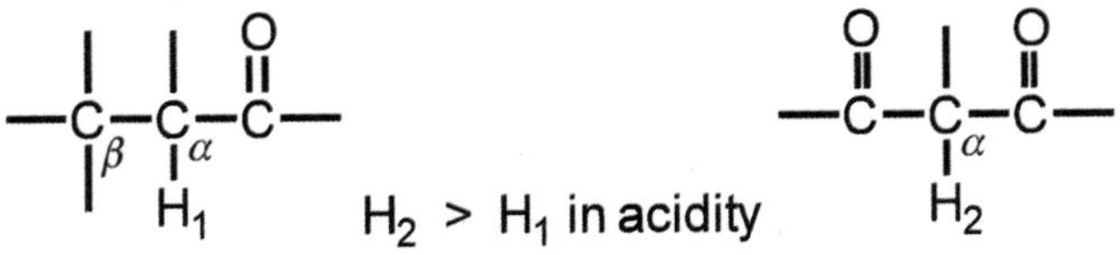

H₂ > H₁ in acidity

This acidity is a result of the resonance stabilization of the α-carbanion formed. This stabilization will also permit addition at the β-carbon in α-β unsaturated carbonyls (*those with double or triple bonds*):

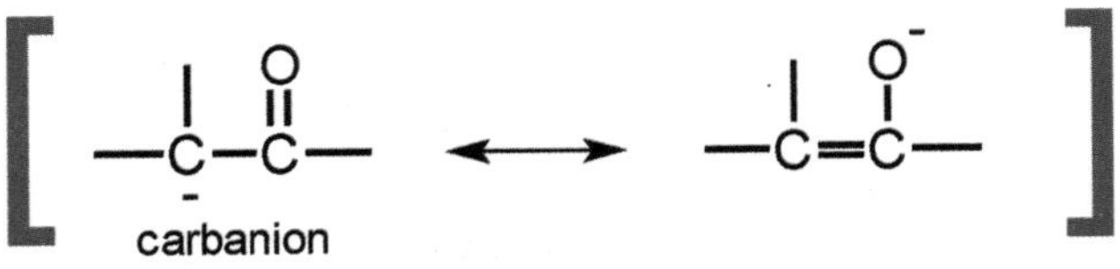

resonance stabilization

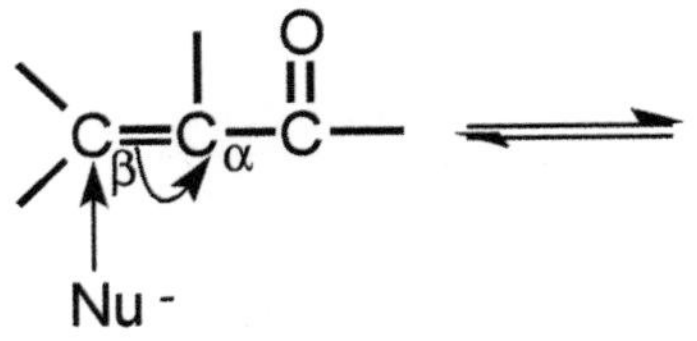

α, β unsaturated carbonyl

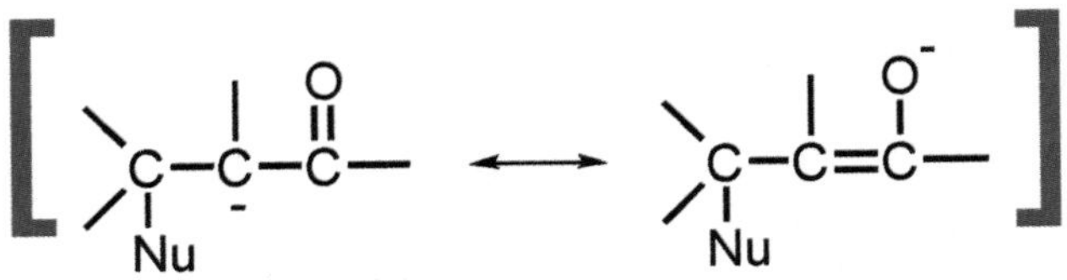

Note that only protons at the α position of carbonyl compounds are acidic. Protons further from the carbonyl carbon (β, gamma - γ, and so on, positions) are not acidic.

- **Keto-enol tautomerization**: Tautomers are constitutional isomers (ORG 2.1-2.3) that readily interconvert (= *tautomerization*). Because the interconversion is so fast, they are usually considered to be the same chemical compound. The carbonyl exists in equilibrium with the enol form of the molecule (enol = alk*ene* + alcoh*ol*).

Although the carbonyl is usually the predominant one, if the enol double bond can be conjugated with other double bonds, it becomes stable (conjugated double bonds are those which are separated by a single bond; ORG 1.4, 4.1):

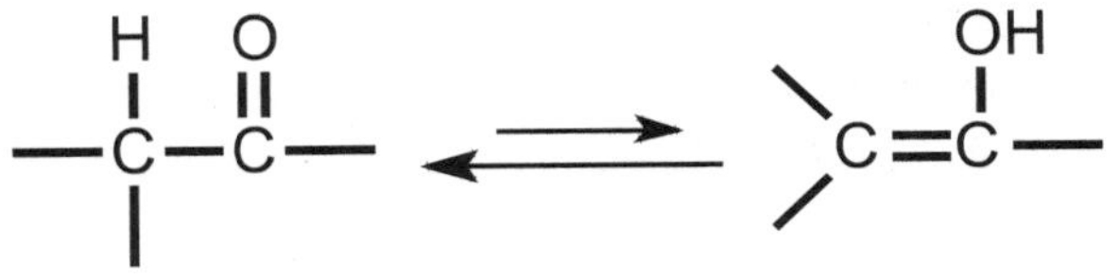

carbonyl   enol

- **Hydrogen bonds:** The O of the carbonyl forms hydrogen bonds with the hydrogens attached to other electronegative atoms, such as O's or N's:

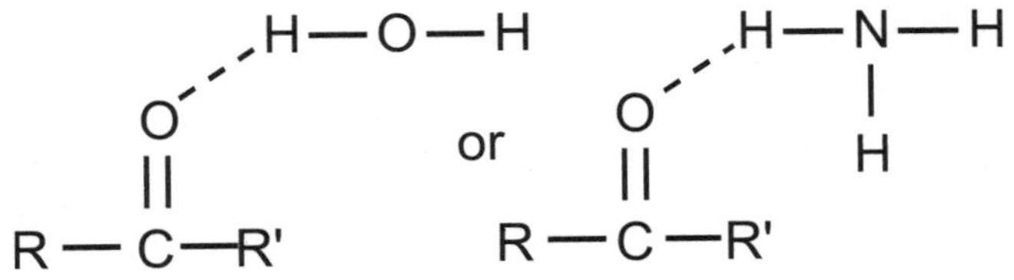

Since there is no hydrogen on the carbonyl oxygen, aldehydes and ketones do not form hydrogen bonds with themselves.

7.2 Important Reactions of Aldehydes & Ketones

7.2.1 Overview

Since the carbonyl group is the functional group of aldehydes and ketones, groups adjacent to the carbonyl group affect the rate of reaction for the molecule. For example, an electron withdrawing ligand adjacent to the carbonyl group will increase the partial positive charge on the carbon making the carbonyl group more attractive to a nucleophile. Conversely, an electron donating ligand would decrease the reactivity of the carbonyl group.

Generally, aldehydes oxidize easier, and undergo nucleophilic additions easier than ketones. This is a consequence of steric hindrance (ORG 6.2.3).

Aldehydes will be oxidized to carboxylic acids with the standard oxidizing agents such as $KMnO_4$, CrO_3 (Jones reagent), HNO_3, Ag_2O (Tollens' reagent). Ketones rarely oxidize. When the Tollens' reagent is used, metallic silver Ag is produced if the aldehyde functional group is present in a molecule of unknown structure, thus making it useful as a diagnostic tool. Therefore, the aldehyde will form a silver precipitate while a ketone will not because ketones cannot be oxidized to carboxylic acid.

There are several methods for preparing aldehydes and ketones. We have already seen ozonolysis (ORG 4.2.2) and the classic redox series of reactions (please review ORG 6.2.2). To add to the preceding is a reaction called "hydroformylation" shown for the generation of butyraldehyde by the hydroformylation of propene:

$$H_2 + CO + CH_3CH = CH_2 \longrightarrow CH_3CH_2CH_2CHO$$

Primary alcohols can be oxidized to yield aldehydes. The reaction is performed with the mild oxidation reagent PCC.

$$CH_3 - CH_2 - OH \xrightarrow[CH_2Cl_2]{C_5H_5\overset{+}{N}H[CrO_3\overset{-}{Cl}]\ (PCC)} CH_3 - \overset{\overset{O}{\|}}{C}H$$

ethanol   ethanal

Secondary alcohols can be oxidized to yield ketones. These reactions are usually performed with PCC, Jones' reagent (CrO_3), or sodium dichromate, which all form H_2CrO_4:

Other reagents include: $K_2Cr_2O_7/H_2SO_4$ or CrO_3/H_2SO_4 or $KMnO_4/OH^-$ or $KMnO_4/H_3O^+$.

Alkenes can be oxidatively cleaved to yield aldehydes when treated with ozone (ORG 4.2.2).

Alkenes can be oxidatively cleaved to

yield ketones when treated with ozone if one or both of the double-bonded carbons is (are) di-substituted (i.e. 2 R groups attached).

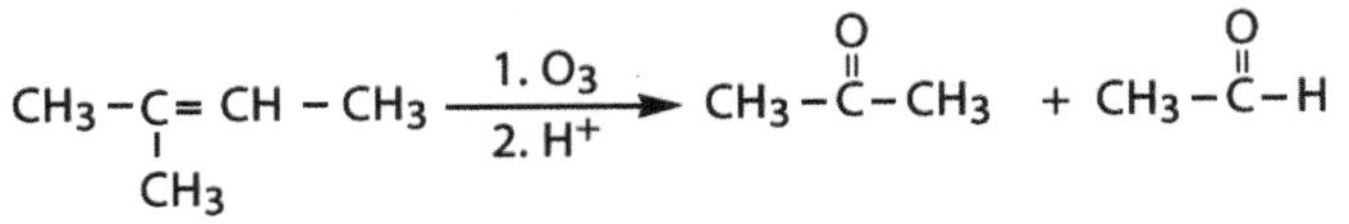

$$CH_3-\underset{\underset{CH_3}{|}}{C}=CH-CH_3 \xrightarrow[2.\,H^+]{1.\,O_3} CH_3-\overset{\overset{O}{||}}{C}-CH_3 + CH_3-\overset{\overset{O}{||}}{C}-H$$

Ketones can also be prepared by Friedel-Crafts acylation of a benzene ring with acyl halide in the presence of an AlCl$_3$ catalyst (ORG 5.2).

Hydration of terminal alkynes will yield methyl ketones in the presence of mercuric ion as catalyst and strong acids. The formation of an unstable vinyl alcohol undergoes keto-enol tautomerization (ORG 7.1) to form ketones.

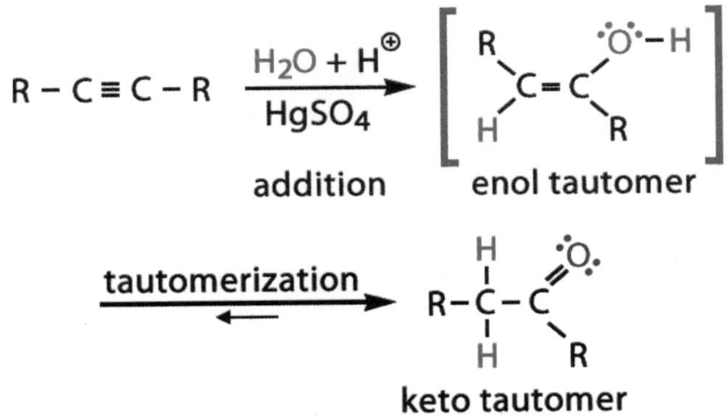

$$R-C\equiv C-R \xrightarrow[HgSO_4]{H_2O+H^\oplus}$$

addition   **enol tautomer**

tautomerization

keto tautomer

There are two classes of reactions that will be investigated: nucleophilic addition reactions at C=O bond, and reactions at adjacent positions.

The most important reaction of aldehydes and ketones is the nucleophilic addition reaction. A nucleophile attacks the electrophilic carbonyl carbon atom and a tetrahedral alkoxide ion intermediate is formed. The inter-

mediate can lead to the protonation of the carbonyl oxygen atom to form an alcohol or expel the carbonyl oxygen atom as H$_2$O or OH$^-$ to form a carbon-nucleophile double bond.

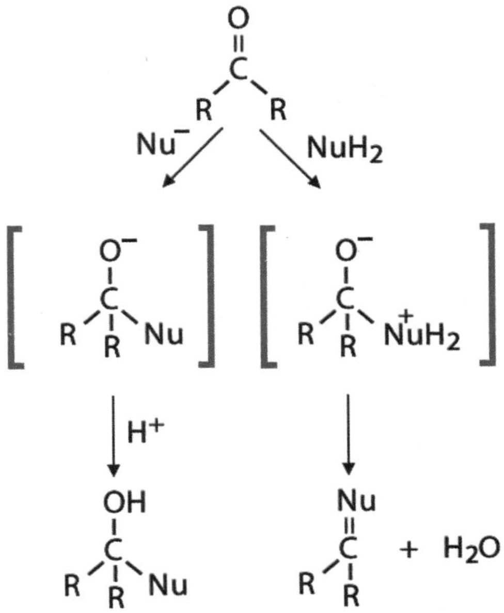

Aldehydes and ketones react with water in the presence of acid or base catalyst to form 1,1-diols, or gem-diols. Water acts as the nucleophile – with or without an acid catalyst – here attacking the carbonyl carbon:

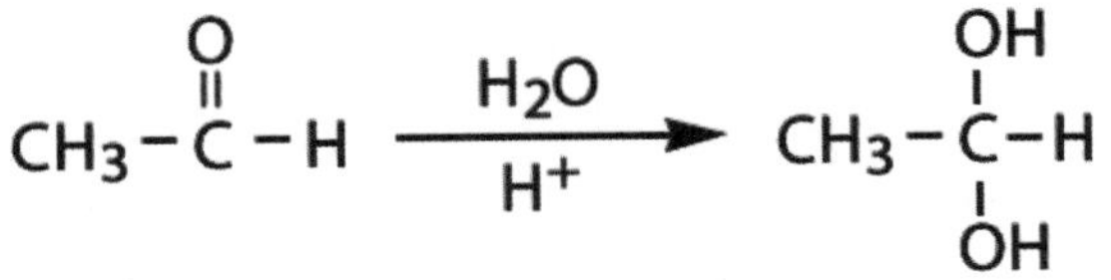

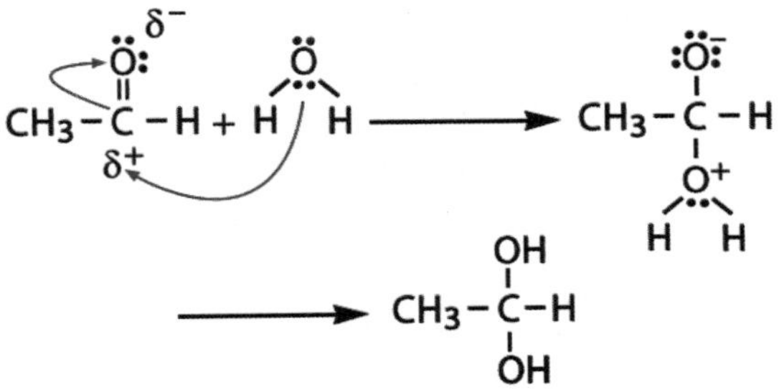

$$CH_3-\overset{\overset{O}{||}}{C}-H \xrightarrow[H^+]{H_2O} CH_3-\underset{\underset{OH}{|}}{\overset{\overset{OH}{|}}{C}}-H$$

Aldehydes and ketones react with HCN to form cyanohydrin. CN$^-$ attacks the carbonyl carbon atom and protonation of O$^-$ forms a tetrahedral cyanohydrin product.

$$CH_3-CH_2-\overset{\overset{O}{\|}}{CH} + HCN \rightleftharpoons CH_3CH_2\overset{\overset{OH}{|}}{\underset{\underset{CN}{|}}{C}}-H$$
propanal

$$CH_3-\overset{\overset{O}{\|}}{C}-CH_3 + HCN \rightleftharpoons CH_3\overset{\overset{OH}{|}}{\underset{\underset{CN}{|}}{C}}-CH_3$$
acetone

Reduction of aldehydes and ketones with Grignard reagents yields alcohols. Grignard reagents react with formaldehyde to produce primary alcohols, all other aldehydes to produce secondary alcohols, and ketones to produce tertiary alcohols.

$$\overset{\delta^-\;\;\delta^+}{R-MgX} + R-\overset{\overset{O}{\|}}{C}-H(R) \xrightarrow{H^+} R-\overset{\overset{OH}{|}}{\underset{\underset{R}{|}}{C}}-H(R)$$

$$\overset{\delta^-\;\;\delta^+}{R-Li} + R-\overset{\overset{O}{\|}}{C}-H(R) \xrightarrow{H^+} R-\overset{\overset{OH}{|}}{\underset{\underset{R}{|}}{C}}-H(R)$$

$$R-C\equiv C^-Na^+ + R-\overset{\overset{O}{\|}}{C}-H(R)$$

$$\xrightarrow{H^+} R-C\equiv C-\overset{\overset{OH}{|}}{\underset{\underset{H}{|}}{C}}-H(R)$$

Reducing agents such as NaBH$_4$ and LiAlH$_4$ react with aldehydes and ketones to form alcohols (ORG 6.2.2). The reducing agent functions as if they are hydride ion equivalents and the H:$^-$ attacks the carbonyl carbon atom to form the product.

$$+ \overset{\overset{O}{\|}}{\underset{H\quad H}{C}} \longrightarrow H-\overset{\overset{OH}{|}}{\underset{\underset{H}{|}}{C}}-H$$

LiAlH$_4$
or
NaBH$_4$

$$+ \overset{\overset{O}{\|}}{\underset{R'\quad H}{C}} \longrightarrow H-\overset{\overset{OH}{|}}{\underset{\underset{R'}{|}}{C}}-H$$

$$+ \overset{\overset{O}{\|}}{\underset{R'\quad R''}{C}} \longrightarrow H-\overset{\overset{OH}{|}}{\underset{\underset{R'}{|}}{C}}-R''$$

7.2.2 Acetal (ketal) and Hemiacetal (hemiketal) Formation

Aldehydes and ketones will form hemiacetals and hemiketals, respectively, when dissolved in an excess of a primary alcohol. In addition, if this mixture contains a trace of an acid catalyst, the hemiacetal (hemiketal) will react further to form acetals and ketals.

An acetal is a composite functional group in which two ether functions are joined to a carbon bearing a hydrogen and an alkyl group. A ketal is a composite functional group in which two ether functions are joined to a carbon bearing two alkyl groups.

This reaction may be summarised:

$$R-\overset{\overset{\displaystyle O}{\|}}{C}-R' \quad + \quad R''OH \quad \underset{-H^+}{\overset{+H^+}{\rightleftarrows}}$$

aldehyde (R' = H)   excess
or ketone (R' = alkyl)   alcohol

$$R-\overset{\overset{\displaystyle OH}{|}}{\underset{\underset{\displaystyle OR''}{|}}{C}}-R' \quad \underset{+H_2O}{\overset{+H^+/-H_2O}{\rightleftarrows}} \quad R-\overset{\overset{\displaystyle OR''}{|}}{\underset{\underset{\displaystyle OR''}{|}}{C}}-R'$$

hemiacetal   acetal
or   or
hemiketal   ketal

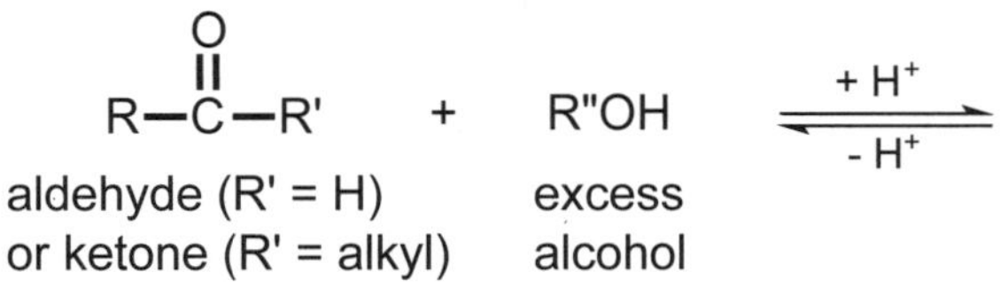

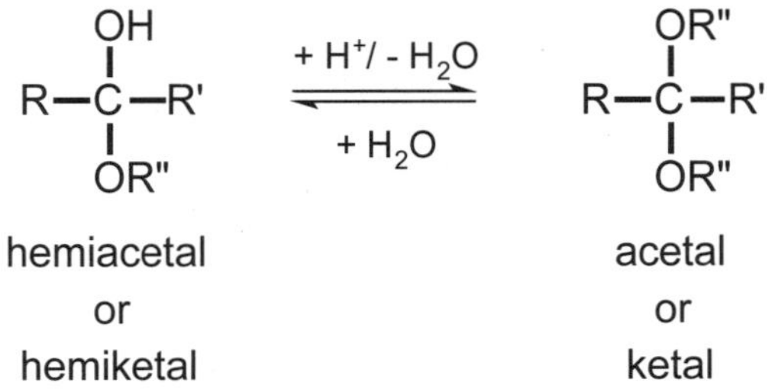

The <u>first step</u> in the above reaction is that the most charged species (+, the hydrogen) attracts electrons from the δ^- oxygen, leaving a carbocation intermediate. The <u>second step</u> involves the δ^- oxygen from the alcohol *quickly* attracted to the current most charged species (+, carbon). A proton is lost which regenerates the catalyst, and produces the hemiacetal or hemiketal. Now the proton may attract electrons from -OH forming H_2O, a good leaving group. Again the δ^- oxygen on the alcohol is attracted to the positive carbocation. And again the alcohol releases its proton, regenerating the catalyst, producing an acetal or ketal.

Aldehydes and ketones can also react with HCN (hydrogen cyanide) to produce stable compounds called cyanohydrins which owe their stability to the newly formed C-C bond.

7.2.3 Imine and Enamine Formation

Imines and enamines are formed when aldehydes and ketones are allowed to react with amines.

When an aldehyde or ketone reacts with a primary amine, an <u>imine</u> (or Schiff base) is formed. A primary amine is a nitrogen compound with the general formula $R-NH_2$, where R represents an alkyl or aryl group. In an imine, the carbonyl group of the aldehyde or ketone is replaced with a C=N-R group.

The reaction may be summarised:

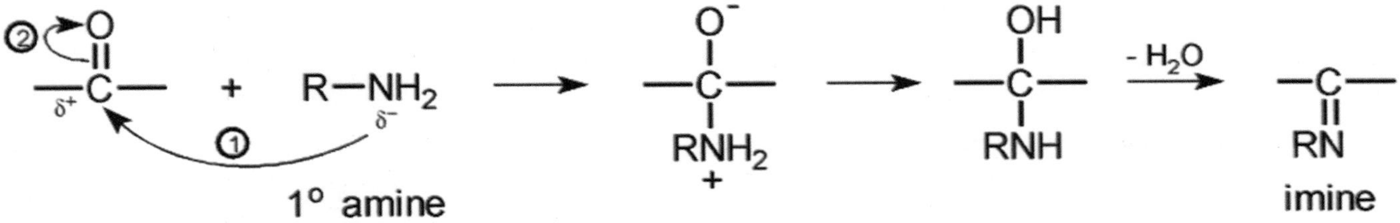

When an aldehyde or ketone reacts with a secondary amine, an <u>enamine</u> is formed. A secondary amine is a nitrogen with the general formula $R_2N\text{-}H$ (*see* ORG 1.6 for functional groups), where R represents aryl or alkyl groups (these groups need not be identical).

Tertiary amines (of the general form R_3N) do not react with aldehydes or ketones.

7.2.4 Aldol Condensation

<u>Aldol condensation</u> is a base-catalyzed reaction of aldehydes and ketones that have α-hydrogens. The intermediate, an aldol, is both an <u>ald</u>*ehyde* and a *alcoh*<u>ol</u>. The aldol undergoes a dehydration reaction producing a carbon-carbon bond in the condensation product, an *enal* (= *alk*<u>en</u>e + <u>al</u>*dehyde*).

The reaction may be summarised:

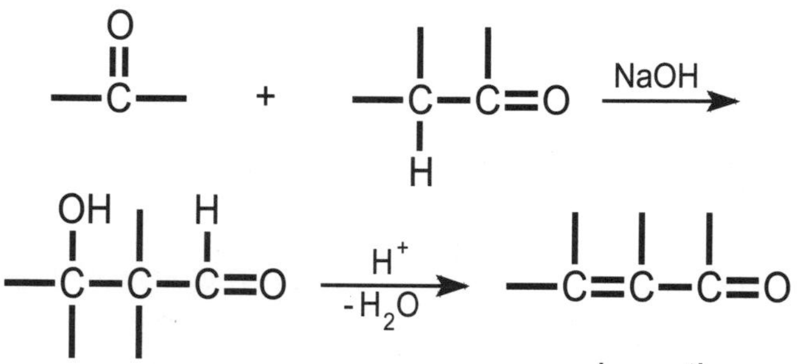

Aldol   condensation product

The reaction mechanism:

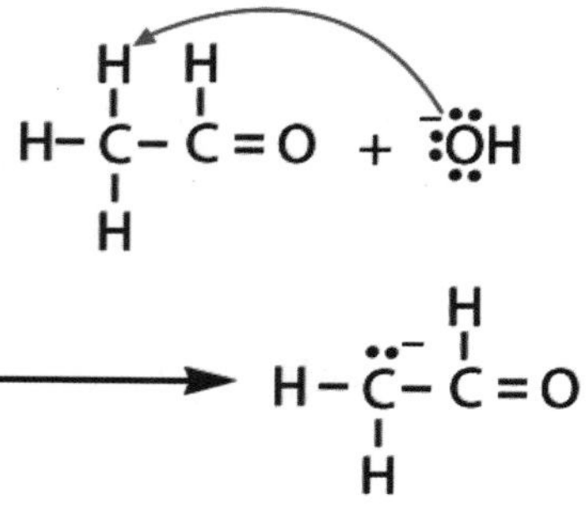

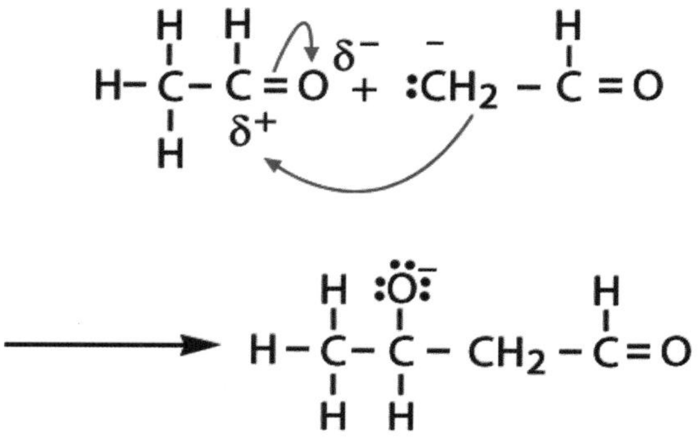

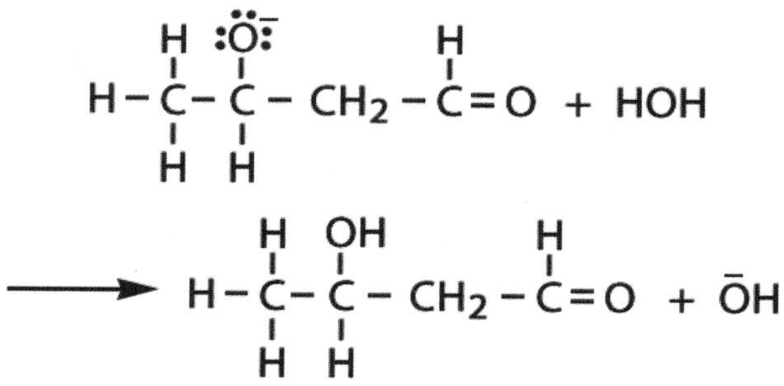

An aldol can now lose H_2O to form a β-unsaturated aldehyde via an E1 mechanism.

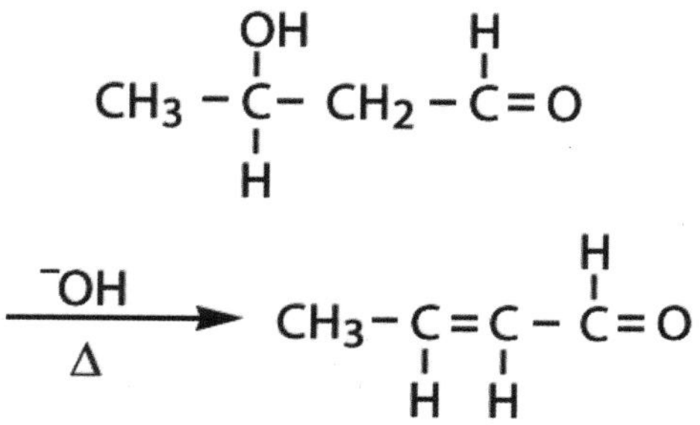

7.2.5 Conjugate Addition to α-β Unsaturated Carbonyls

α-β unsaturated carbonyls are unusually reactive with nucleophiles. This is best illustrated by example:

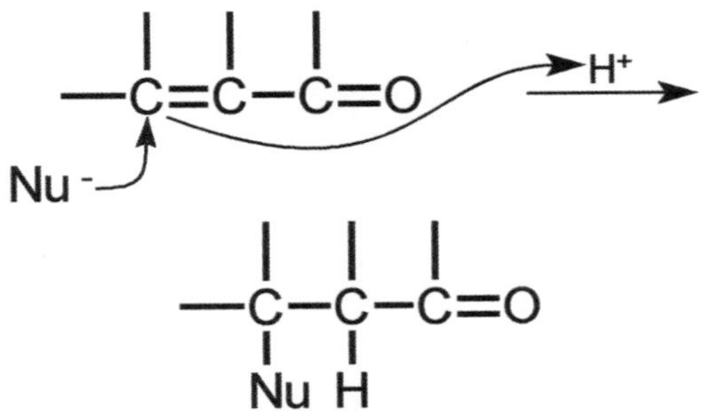

Examples of relevant nucleophiles includes CN^- from HCN, and R^- which can be generated by a Grignard Reagent (= RMgX) or as an alkyl lithium (= RLi).

For example:

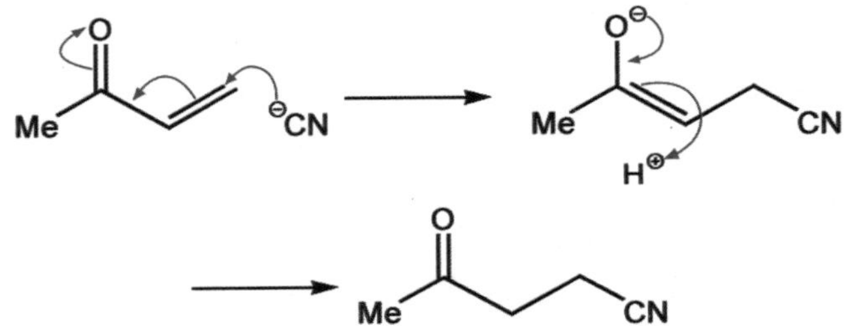

Go online to GAMSAT-prep.com for chapter review Q&A and forum.

CARBOXYLIC ACIDS

Chapter 8

Memorize	Understand	Not Required*
IUPAC nomenclature Redox reactions	* Hydrogen bonding * Mechanisms of reactions * Relative acid strength * Resonance, inductive effects * Grignards, organometallic reagents	* Knowledge beyond introductory-level (first year uni.) course

GAMSAT-Prep.com

Introduction ▪▪▪▪

Carboxylic acids are organic acids with a carboxyl group, which has the formula -C(=O)OH, usually written -COOH or $-CO_2H$. Carboxylic acids are Brønsted-Lowry acids (proton donors) that are actually, in the grand scheme of chemistry, weak acids. Salts and anions of carboxylic acids are called *carboxylates*.

Additional Resources

Free Online Q&A + Forum

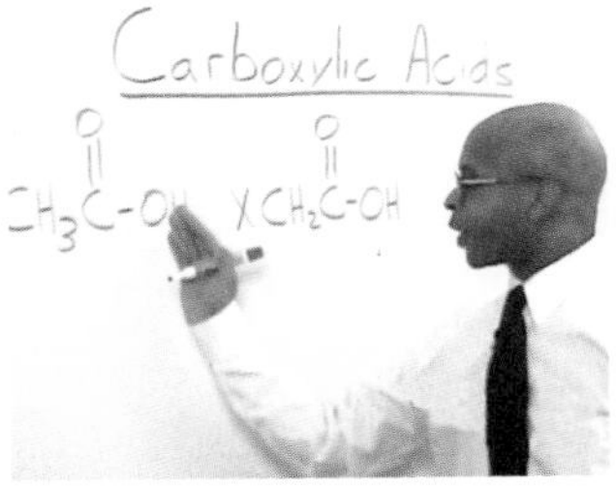

GAMSAT-prep.com Videos

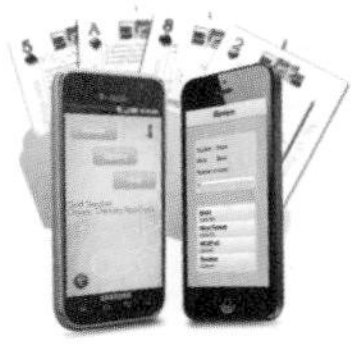

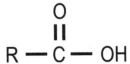

Flashcards

$$R - \overset{\overset{\displaystyle O}{\|}}{C} - OH$$

Special Guest

8.1 Description and Nomenclature

Carboxylic acids are molecules containing the *carboxylic group* (carbonyl + hydroxyl), which is the basis of their chemistry. The general structure of a carboxylic acid is:

$$
\begin{array}{c}
O \\
\parallel \\
R - C - OH
\end{array}
$$

Systematic naming of these compounds is done by replacing the '–e' of the corresponding alkane with '–oic acid'. The molecule is numbered such that the carbonyl carbon is carbon number one. Many carboxylic acids have common names by which they are usually known (systematic names in italics):

$$
\begin{array}{ccc}
O & O & O \\
\parallel & \parallel & \parallel \\
H - C - OH & CH_3 - C - OH & HO - C - OH
\end{array}
$$

formic acid   acetic acid   carbonic acid
methanoic acid   *ethanoic acid*   *hydroxymethanoic acid*

$$
\begin{array}{cc}
O & O \\
\parallel & \parallel \\
HO - C - CH_2CH_2 - C - OH
\end{array}
$$

succinic acid
butanedioic acid

CO_2H

benzoic acid
same: *benzoic acid*

Low molecular weight carboxylic acids are liquids with strong odours and high boiling points. The high boiling point is due to the polarity and the hydrogen bonding capability of the molecule. Strong hydrogen bonding has a noticeable effect on boiling points and makes carboxylic acids boil at much higher temperatures than corresponding alcohols. Because of this hydrogen bonding, these molecules are water soluble. Carboxylic acids with more than 6 carbons are only slightly soluble in water, however, their alkali salts are quite soluble due to ionic properties. As well, carboxylic acids are soluble in dilute bases (NaOH or $NaHCO_3$), because of their acid properties. The carboxyl group is the basis of carboxylic acid chemistry, and there are four important features to remember. Looking at a general carboxylic acid:

- The hydrogen (H) is weakly acidic. This is due to its attachment to the oxygen atom, and because the carboxylate anion is resonance stabilized:

$$
\begin{array}{c}
O \\
\parallel \\
R - C - OH
\end{array}
\rightleftharpoons H^+ +
$$

$$
\left[
\begin{array}{c}
O \\
\parallel \\
R - C - O^-
\end{array}
\longleftrightarrow
\begin{array}{c}
O^- \\
| \\
R - C = O
\end{array}
\right]
$$

resonance forms

- The carboxyl carbon is very susceptible to nucleophilic attack. This is due to the attached oxygen atom, and the carbonyl oxygen, both atoms being electronegative:

$$
\begin{array}{c}
\delta^- \; O \\
\parallel \\
R - C - O - H \\
\delta^{++} \rightarrow \delta^-
\end{array}
$$

$$
\begin{array}{c}
② \quad O \\
\parallel \\
R - C - O - H \\
Nu^- \quad ①
\end{array}
\longrightarrow
\begin{array}{c}
O^- \\
| \\
R - C - O - H \\
| \\
Nu
\end{array}
$$

- In basic conditions, the hydroxyl group, as is, is a good leaving group. In acidic conditions, the protonated hydroxyl (i.e. water) is an excellent leaving group. This promotes nucleophilic substitution:

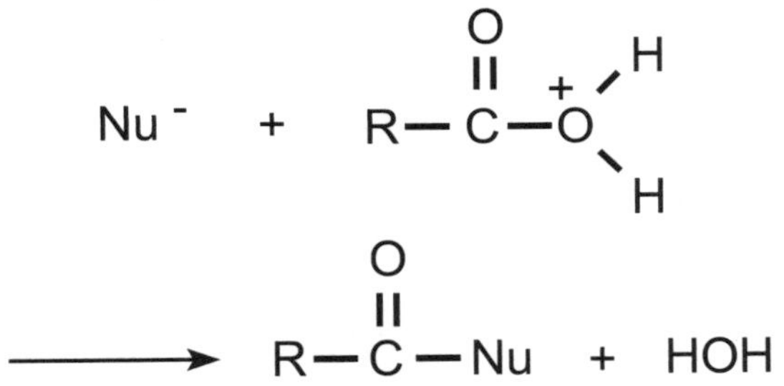

$$Nu^- \ + \ R-\overset{\overset{\textstyle O}{\|}}{C}-\overset{+}{O}\overset{\nearrow H}{\searrow_H}$$

$$\longrightarrow \ R-\overset{\overset{\textstyle O}{\|}}{C}-Nu \ + \ HOH$$

- Because of the carbonyl and hydroxyl moieties (i.e. parts), hydrogen bonding is possible both inter- and intramolecularly:

$$R-\overset{\overset{\textstyle O}{\|}}{C}-OH \cdots HO-\overset{\overset{\textstyle O}{\|}}{C}-R$$

intermolecular (dimerization)

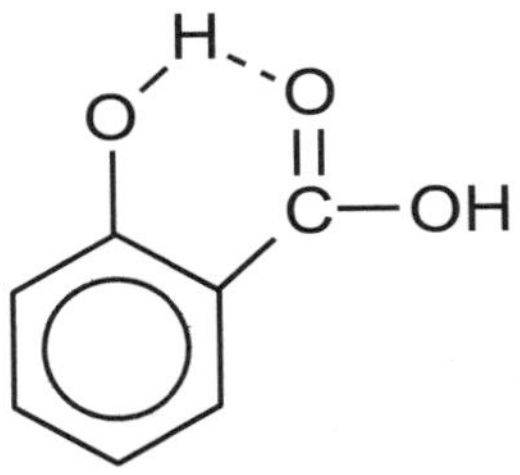

intramolecular

As implied by their name, carboxylic acids are acidic - the most common acid of all organic compounds. In fact, they are colloquially known as organic acids. Organic classes of molecules in order of increasing acid strength are:

alkanes < ammonia < alkynes < alcohols < water < carboxylic acids.

In terms of substituents added to benzoic acid, electron-withdrawing groups such as $-Cl$ or $-NO_2$ inductively withdraw electrons and delocalize the negative charge, thereby stabilizing the carboxylate anion and increasing acidity. Electron-donating groups such as $-NH_2$ or $-OCH_3$ donate electrons and concentrate the negative charge, thereby destabilizing the carboxylate anion and decreasing acidity.

The relative acid strength among carboxylic acids depends on the <u>inductive effects</u> of the attached groups, and their proximity to the carboxyl. For example:

$CH_3CH_2-C(Cl)_2-COOH$ *is a stronger acid than* $CH_3CH_2-CH(Cl)-COOH$.

The reason for this is that chlorine, which is electronegative, withdraws electron density and stabilizes the carboxylate anion. Proximity is important, as:

$CH_3CH_2-C(Cl)_2-COOH$ *is a stronger acid than* $CH_3-C(Cl)_2-CH_2COOH$.

Thus the effect of halogen substitution decreases as the substituent moves further away from the carbonyl carbon atom (unsurprisingly, the effect of a charge decreases exponentially as distance increases; PHY 9.1).

8.1.1 Carboxylic Acid Formation

A carboxylic acid can be formed by reacting a Grignard reagent with carbon dioxide, or by reacting an aldehyde with $KMnO_4$ (*see* ORG 6.2.2). Carboxylic acids are also formed by reacting a nitrile (in which nitrogen shares a triple bond with a carbon) with aqueous acid.

Mechanisms to synthesize carboxylic acids:

- Oxidative cleavage of alkenes/alkynes gives carboxylic acids in the presence of oxidizing reagents such as $NaCr_2O_7$ or $KMnO_4$ or ozone.

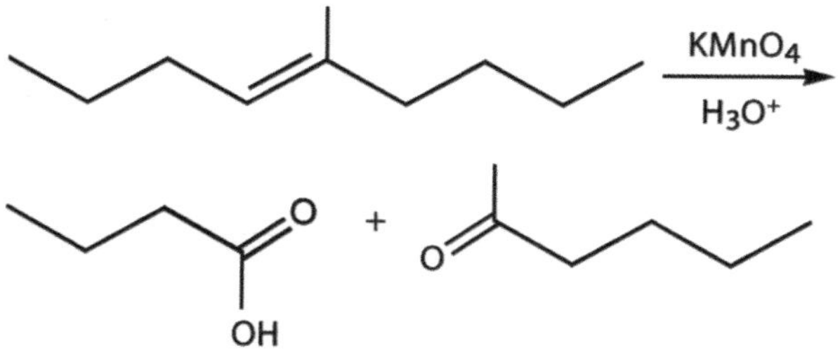

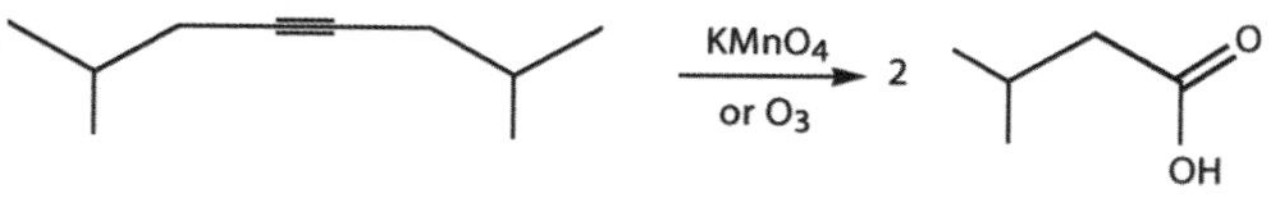

- Oxidation of primary alcohols and aldehydes gives carboxylic acids. Primary alcohols often react with an oxidant such as the Jones' reagent (CrO_3, H_2SO_4). Aldehydes often react with oxidants such as the Jones' reagent or Tollens' reagent $[Ag(NH_3)_2]^+$, also symbolized Ag_2O. Other

reagents include: $K_2Cr_2O_7/H_2SO_4$ or CrO_3/H_2SO_4 or $KMnO_4$.

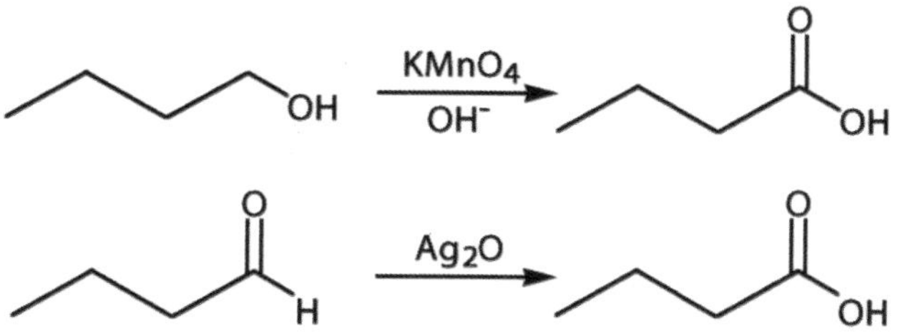

- Hydrolysis of nitriles, RCN, under either strong acid or base conditions can yield carboxylic acids and ammonia (or ammonium salts). Since cyanide anion CN^- is a good nucleophile in S_N2 reactions with primary and secondary alkyl halides, it allows the preparation of carboxylic acids from alkyl halides through cyanide displacement followed by hydrolysis of nitriles. Note that a nitrile hydrolysis reaction increases chain length by one carbon.

$$RCH_2X \xrightarrow{Na^{+-}CN} RCH_2C \equiv N$$

$$\xrightarrow{H_3O^+} RCH_2COOH + NH_3$$

- Carboxylation of Grignards or other organometallic reagents react with carbon dioxide CO_2 to form carboxylic acids. Alkyl halides react with metal magnesium to form organomagnesium halide, which then reacts with carbon dioxide in a nucleophilic addition mechanism. Protonation of the carboxylate ion forms the final carboxylic acid product. Note that the carboxylation of a Grignard reagent increases chain length by one carbon.

Grignard reagents are particularly useful in converting tertiary alkyl halides into carboxylic acids, which otherwise is very difficult.

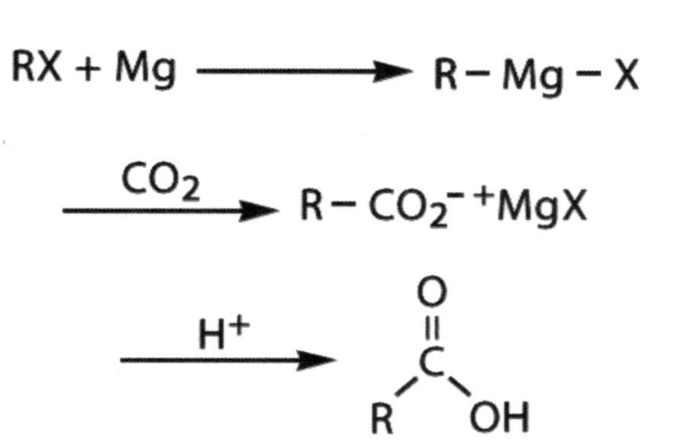

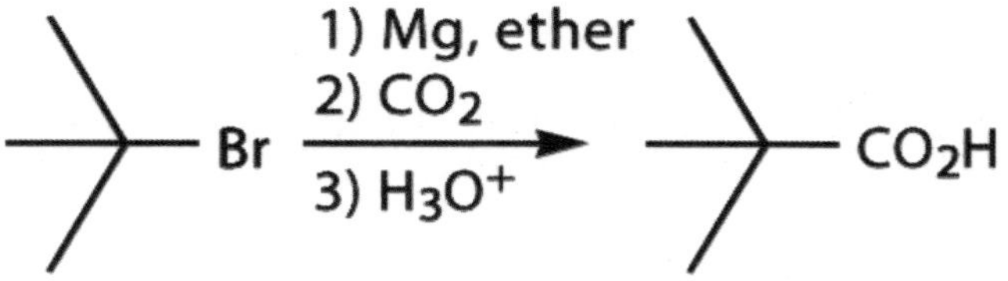

$$RX + Mg \longrightarrow R-Mg-X$$

$$\xrightarrow{CO_2} R-CO_2^- {}^+MgX$$

$$\xrightarrow{H^+} \underset{R}{\overset{O}{\underset{}{\|}}}\underset{OH}{C}$$

1) Mg, ether
2) CO_2
3) H_3O^+

8.2 Important Reactions of Carboxylic Acids

Carboxylic acids undergo nucleophilic substitution reactions (ORG 6.2.3) with many different nucleophiles, under a variety of conditions:

$$Nu^- + R-\overset{O}{\overset{\|}{C}}-OH \longrightarrow R-\overset{O}{\overset{\|}{C}}-Nu + OH^-$$

If the nucleophile is −OR, the resulting compound is an ester. If it is −NH_2, the resulting compound is an amide. If it is Cl from $SOCl_2$, or PCl_5, the resulting compound is an acid chloride.

The typical esterification reaction may be summarized:

$$R'O^*H + R-\overset{O}{\overset{\|}{C}}-OH$$
alcohol   acid

$$\longrightarrow R-\overset{O}{\overset{\|}{C}}-O^*R' + H_2O$$
ester

Notice that an asterix* was added to the oxygen of the alcohol so that you can tell where that oxygen ended up in the product (i.e. the ester). In the lab, instead of an asterix (!), an isotope (CHM 1.3; ORG 1.6) of oxygen is used as a tracer or label.

The <u>decarboxylation reaction</u> involves the loss of the carboxyl group as CO_2:

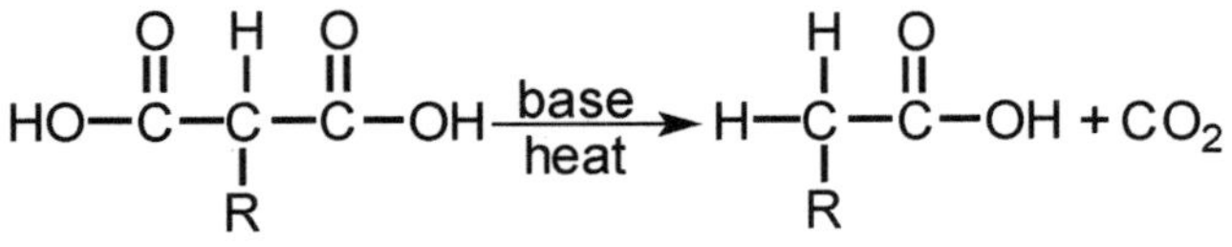

β – diacid

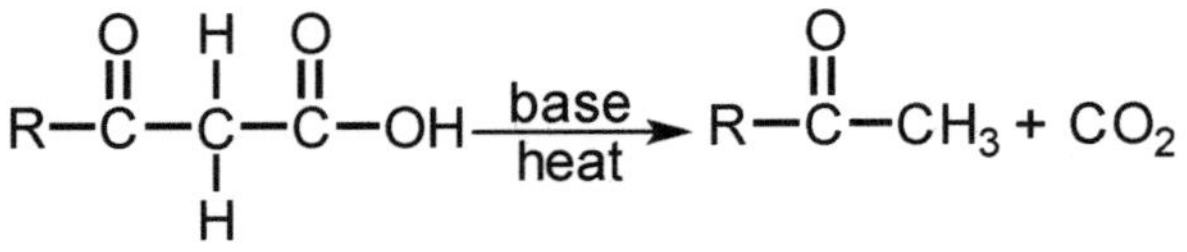

β – keto acid

This reaction is not important for most ordinary carboxylic acids. There are certain types of carboxylic acids that decarboxylate easily, mainly:

- Those which have a keto group at the β position, known as β-keto acids.
- Malonic acids and its derivatives (i.e. β-diacids: those with two carboxyl groups, separated by one carbon).
- Carbonic acid (CHM 1.5.1; ORG 8.1; BIO 12.4.1, 12.4.2) and its derivatives.

Carboxylic acids are reduced to alcohols with lithium aluminum hydride, $LiAlH_4$, or H_2/metals (see ORG 6.2.2).

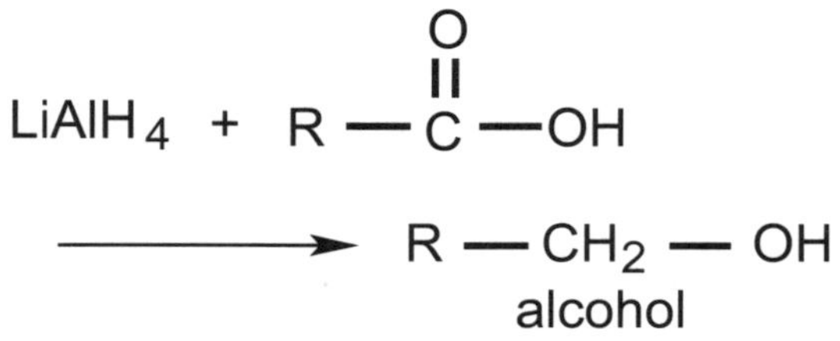

R — CH$_2$ — OH
alcohol

Sodium borohydride, $NaBH_4$, being a milder reducing agent, only reduces aldehydes and ketones. Carboxylic acids may also be converted to esters or amides first, and then reduced (ORG 9.2, 9.3, 9.4).

Go online to GAMSAT-prep.com for chapter review Q&A and forum.

CARBOXYLIC ACID DERIVATIVES
Chapter 9

Memorize	Understand	Not Required*
PAC nomenclature	* Mechanisms of reactions * Relative reactivity * Steric, inductive effects	* Knowledge beyond introductory-level (first year uni.) course

GAMSAT-Prep.com

Introduction

Carboxylic acid derivatives are a series of compounds that can be synthesized using carboxylic acids. For the GAMSAT, this includes acid chlorides, anhydrides, amides and esters.

Additional Resources

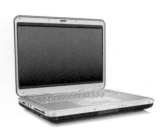

Free Online Q&A + Forum

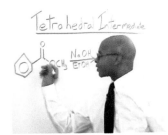

GAMSAT-prep.com Videos

Flashcards

Special Guest

* The real GAMSAT may have advanced level information presented (ie. in a passage) but previous knowledge of said information is not required to answer the questions that would follow. Practice ACER and GS practice GAMSATs can help you clarify this point.

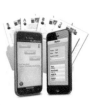

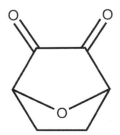

9.1 Acid Halides

The general structure of an acid halide is:

$$R - \underset{\underset{O}{\|}}{C} - X \qquad X = \text{Halide}$$

These are named by replacing the 'ic acid' of the parent carboxylic acid with the suffix 'yl halide.' For example:

$$CH_3CH_2CH_2 - \underset{\underset{O}{\|}}{C} - Br \qquad \text{Butanoyl bromide}$$

$$CH_3 - \underset{\underset{O}{\|}}{C} - Cl \qquad \begin{array}{l}\text{Acetyl chloride}\\\text{(ethanoyl chloride)}\end{array}$$

An "acyl" group (IUPAC name: alkanoyl) refers to the functional group RCO-.

Acid chlorides are synthesized by reacting the parent carboxylic acid with PCl_5 or $SOCl_2$. Acid chlorides react with $NaBH_4$ to form alcohols. This can be done in one or two steps. In one step, the acid chloride reacts with $NaBH_4$ to immediately form an alcohol. In two steps, the acid chloride can react first with $H_2/Pd/C$ to form a carboxylic acid; reaction of the carboxylic acid with $NaBH_4$ then produces an alcohol.

Acid halides can engage in nucleophilic reactions similar to carboxylic acids (see ORG 8.2); however, acid halides are more reactive (see ORG 9.6).

Acyl halides can be converted back to carboxylic acids through simple hydrolysis with H_2O. They can also be converted to esters by a reaction with alcohols. Lastly, acyl halides can be converted to amides ($RCONR_2$) by a reaction with amines.

9.1.1 Acid Anhydrides

The general structure of an acid anhydride is:

$$R - \underset{\underset{O}{\|}}{C} - O - \underset{\underset{O}{\|}}{C} - R$$

These are named by replacing the 'acid' of the parent carboxylic acid with the word 'anhydride.' For example:

$$CH_3 - \underset{\underset{O}{\|}}{C} - O - \underset{\underset{O}{\|}}{C} - CH_3$$

acetic anhydride
(ethanoic anhydride)

$$CH_3 - \underset{\underset{O}{\|}}{C} - O - \underset{\underset{O}{\|}}{C} - H$$

acetic formic anhydride
(ethanoic methanoic anhydride)

Anhydrides can be synthesized by the reaction of an acyl halide with a carboxylate salt and are a bit less reactive than acyl chlorides.

Both acid chlorides and acid anhydrides have boiling points comparable to esters of similar molecular weight.

9.2 Important Reactions of Carboxylic Acid Derivatives

- Nucleophilic acyl substitution reaction: Carboxylic acid derivatives undergo nucleophilic acyl substitution reactions in which a potential leaving group is substituted by the nucleophile, thereby generating a new carbonyl compound. Relative reactivity of carboxylic acid derivatives toward a nucleophilic acyl substitution reaction is amide < ester < acid anhydride < acid chloride. Note that it is possible to convert a more reactive carboxylic acid derivative to a less reactive one, but not the opposite.

- Synthesis of acid halides: Acid halides are synthesized from carboxylic acids by the reaction with thionyl chloride ($SOCl_2$), phosphorus trichloride (PCl_3) or phosphorus pentachloride (PCl_5). Reaction with phosphorus tribromide PBr_3 produces an acid bromide.

- Reactions of acid halides:

1. **Friedel-Crafts reaction:** A benzene ring attacks a carbocation electrophile -COR which is generated by the reaction with the $AlCl_3$ catalyst, yielding the final product Ar-COR.

2. **Conversion into acids:** Acid chlorides react with water to yield carboxylic acids. The attack of the nucleophile water followed by elimination of the chloride ion gives the product carboxylic acid and HCl.

3. **Conversion into esters:** Acid chlorides react with alcohol to yield esters. The same type of nucleophilic acyl substitution mechanism is observed here. The alkoxide ion attacks the acid chloride while chloride is displaced.

4. **Conversion into amides:** Acid chlorides react with ammonia or amines to yield amides. Both mono- and di-substituted amines react well with acid chlorides, but not tri-substituted amines. Two equivalents of ammonia or amine must be used, one reacting with the acid chloride while the other reacting with HCl to form the ammonium chloride salt.

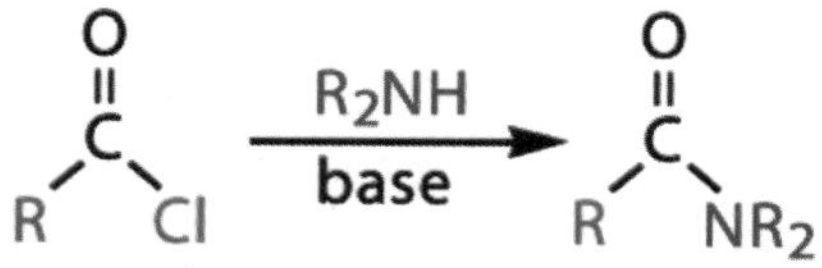

5. Conversion into alcohols: Acid chlorides are reduced by $LiAlH_4$ to yield primary alcohols. The reaction is a substitution reaction of -H for -Cl, which is then further reduced to yield the final product alcohol.

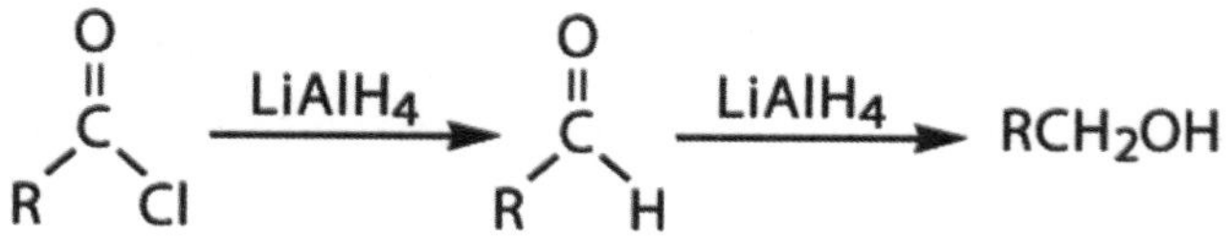

Acid chlorides react with Grignard reagents to yield tertiary alcohols. Two equivalents of the Grignard reagent attack the acid chloride yielding the final product, the tertiary alcohol.

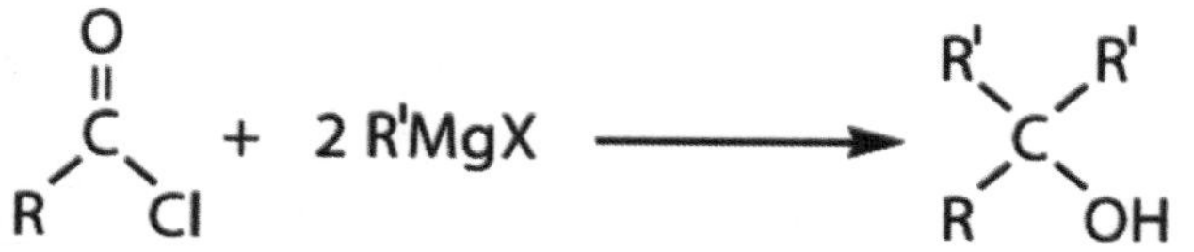

Acid chlorides also react with H_2 in the presence of Lindlar's catalyst ($Pd/BaSO_4$, quinoline) to yield an aldehyde intermediate which can then be further reduced to yield an alcohol.

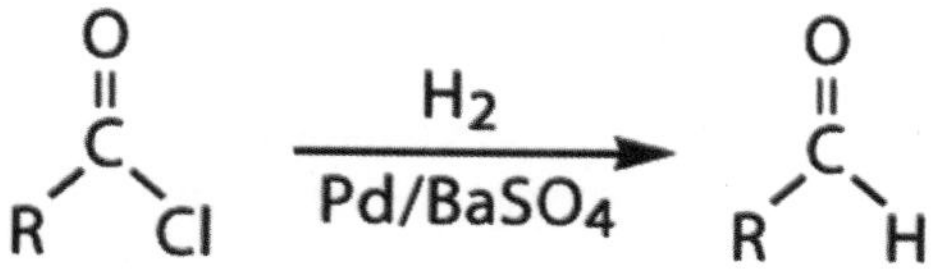

6. Synthesis of acid anhydrides: Acid anhydrides can be synthesized by a nucleophilic acyl substitution reaction of an acid chloride with a carboxylate anion.

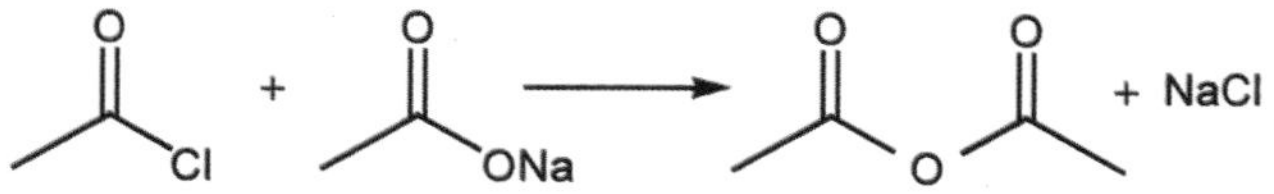

- **Reactions of acid anhydrides:** The chemistry of acid anhydrides is similar to that of acid chlorides. Since they are more stable due to resonance, acid anhydrides react more slowly.

1. Conversion into acids: Acid anhydrides react with water to yield carboxylic acids. The nucleophile in this reaction is water and the leaving group is a carboxylic acid.

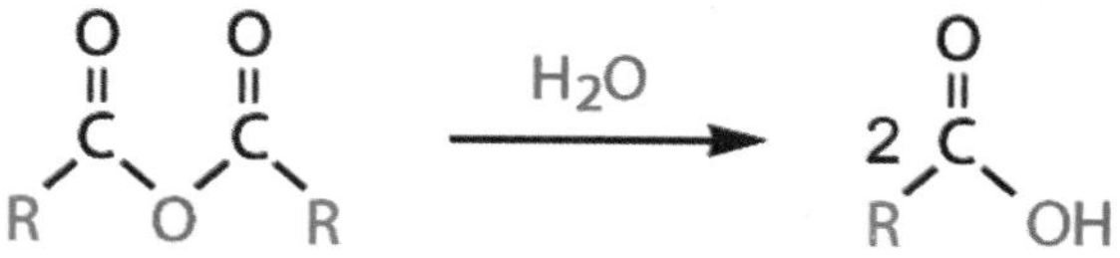

2. Conversion into esters: Acid anhydrides react with alcohols to form esters and acids as in the following example with ethanoic anhydride.

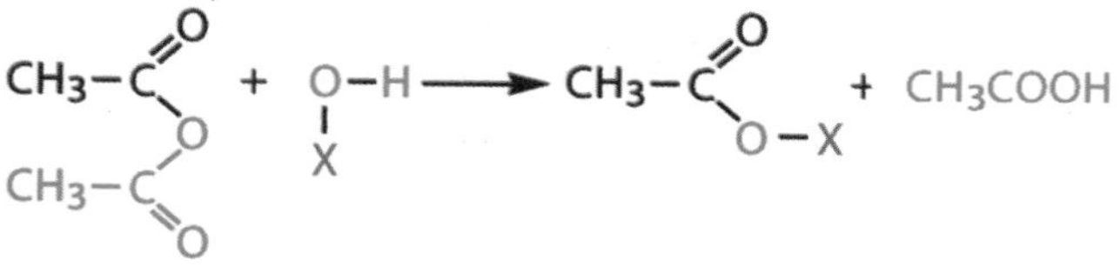

3. Conversion into amides: Ammonia (or an amine, ORG 11.1) attacks the acid anhydride, yielding an amide and the leaving group carboxylic acid, which is reacted with another molecule of ammonia to give the ammonium salt of the carboxylate anion.

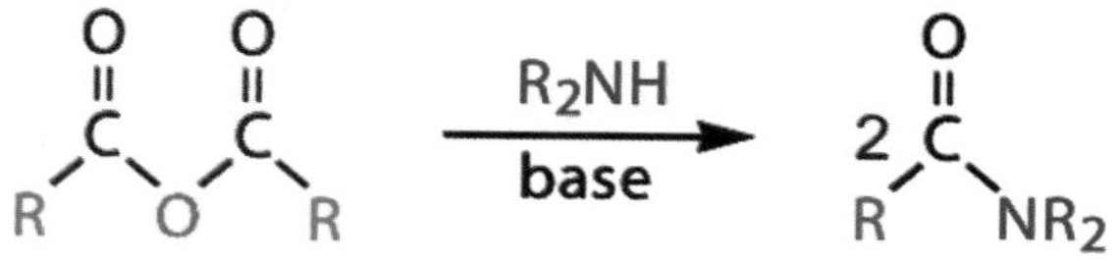

4. **Conversion into alcohols:** Acid anhydrides are reduced by LiAlH$_4$ to yield primary alcohols.

$$\underset{\substack{ROR}}{\overset{\substack{OO}}{C-O-C}} \xrightarrow{\text{[H]}} 2\,RCH_2OH$$

9.3 Amides

The general structure of an amide is:

$$R-\overset{\overset{\textstyle O}{\|}}{C}-NR'_2$$

These are named by replacing the '-ic (oic) acid' of the parent anhydride with the suffix '-amide.' If there are alkyl groups attached to the nitrogen, they are named as substituents, and designated by the letter N. For example:

$$CH_3-\overset{\overset{\textstyle O}{\|}}{C}-N\overset{\textstyle C_2H_5}{\underset{\textstyle C_2H_5}{}} \quad \text{N,N-diethylacetamide}$$

$$CH_3CH_2-\overset{\overset{\textstyle O}{\|}}{C}-NH_2 \quad \text{propanamide}$$

Both unsubstituted and monosubstituted amides form very strong intermolecular hydrogen bonds, and as a result, they have very high boiling and melting points. The boiling points of disubstituted amides are similar to those of aldehydes and ketones. Amides are essentially neutral (no acidity, as compared to carboxylic acids, and no basicity, as compared to amines).

Amides may be prepared by reacting carboxylic acids (or other carboxylic acid derivatives) with ammonia:

$$R-\overset{\overset{\textstyle O}{\|}}{C}-OH + NH_3 + heat \xrightarrow{-H_2O} R-\overset{\overset{\textstyle O}{\|}}{C}-NH_2$$

As well, amides undergo nucleophilic substitution reactions at the carbonyl carbon:

$$R-\overset{\overset{\textstyle O}{\|}}{C}-NH_2 + NuH \longrightarrow R-\overset{\overset{\textstyle O}{\|}}{C}-Nu + NH_3$$

Amides can be hydrolyzed to yield the parent carboxylic acid and amine. This reaction may take place under acidic or basic conditions:

$$\underset{\text{amide}}{R-\overset{\overset{\textstyle O}{\|}}{C}-NHR} + H_2O \xrightarrow{H^+} \underset{\text{acid}}{R-\overset{\overset{\textstyle O}{\|}}{C}-OH} + \underset{\text{amine}}{RNH_2}$$

$$\underset{\text{amide}}{R-\overset{\overset{\textstyle O}{\|}}{C}-NHR} + H_2O \xrightarrow{OH^-}$$

$$\underset{\text{carboxylate}}{R-\overset{\overset{\textstyle O}{\|}}{C}-O^-} + \underset{\text{amine}}{RNH_2} \xrightarrow{H^+} \underset{\text{acid}}{R-\overset{\overset{\textstyle O}{\|}}{C}-OH}$$

Amides can also form amines by reacting with $LiAlH_4$.

Amides can also be converted to primary amines with the loss of the carbonyl carbon. This is known as a <u>Hofmann rearrangement</u>:

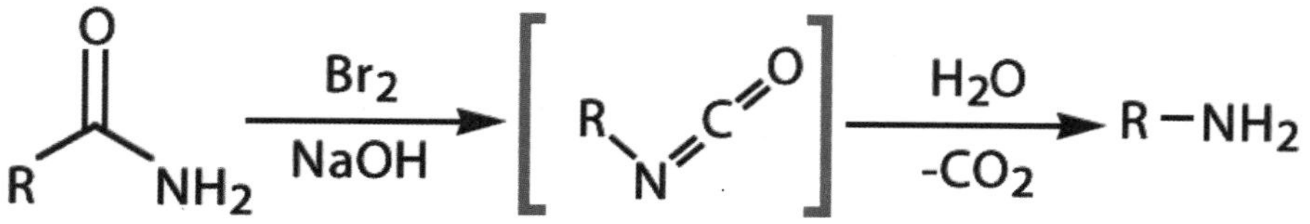

9.3.1 Important Reactions of Amides

Amides are much less reactive than acid chlorides, acid anhydrides or esters.

1. **Conversion into acids:** Amides react with water to yield carboxylic acids in acidic conditions or carboxylate anions in basic conditions.

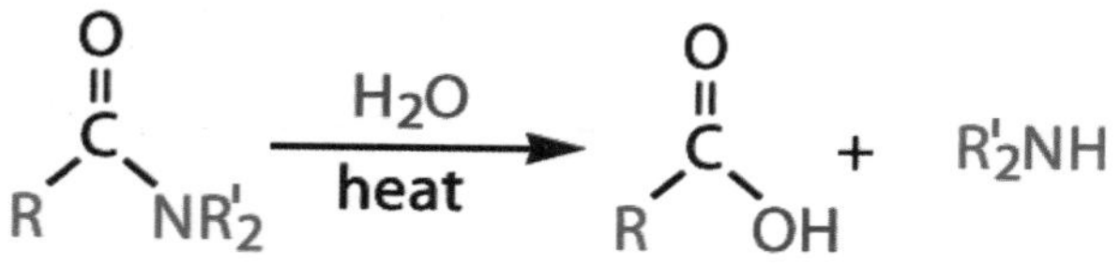

2. **Conversion into amines:** Amides can be reduced by $LiAlH_4$ to give amines. The net effect of this reaction is to convert an amide carbonyl group into a methylene group ($C=O \longrightarrow CH_2$).

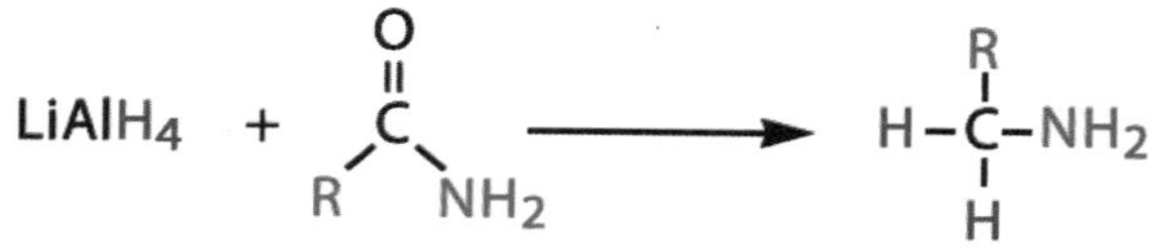

9.4 Esters

The general structure of an ester is:

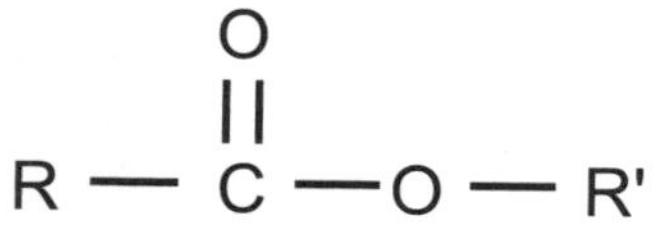

These are named by first citing the name of the alkyl group, followed by the parent acid, with the 'ic acid' replaced by 'ate.' For example:

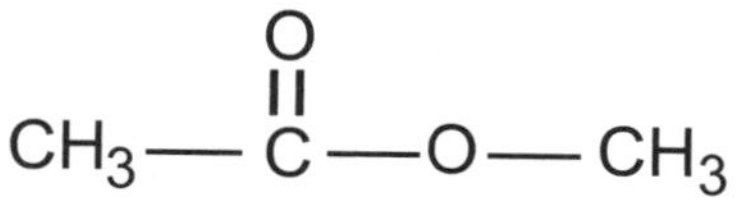

methyl acetate
(methyl ethanoate)

The boiling points of esters are lower than those of comparable acids or alcohols, and similar to comparable aldehydes and ketones, because they are polar compounds, without hydrogens to form hydrogen bonds. Esters with longer side chains (R-groups) are more nonpolar than esters with shorter side chains (R-groups). Esters usually have pleasing, fruity odors.

Esters may be synthesized by reacting carboxylic acids or their derivatives with alcohols under either basic or acidic conditions:

$$R'O^*H + R-\overset{\overset{\textstyle O}{\|}}{C}-OH \longrightarrow R-\overset{\overset{\textstyle O}{\|}}{C}-O^*R' + H_2O$$

alcohol   acid   ester

As well, esters undergo nucleophilic substitution reactions at the carbonyl carbon:

$$R-\overset{\overset{\textstyle O}{\|}}{C}-OR' + NuH \longrightarrow R-\overset{\overset{\textstyle O}{\|}}{C}-Nu + R'OH$$

Esters may also be hydrolyzed, to yield the parent carboxylic acid and alcohol. This reaction may take place under acidic or basic conditions.

$$R-\overset{\overset{\textstyle O}{\|}}{C}-O^*R' \;+\; H_2O \quad \overset{H^+}{\longrightarrow}$$

ester

$$R-\overset{\overset{\textstyle O}{\|}}{C}-OH \;+\; R'O^*H$$

acid   alcohol

Esters can be transformed from one ester into another by using alcohols as nucleophiles. This process is known as <u>transesterification</u>:

$$H_2C= \overset{\overset{\textstyle R^1}{|}}{\underset{\underset{\textstyle O}{\|}}{C}} -OR^2 \quad + \quad \overset{R^3}{\underset{R^4}{}}N-R^5-OH$$

$$\xrightarrow[-R^2OH]{catalyst}$$

$$H_2C= \overset{\overset{\textstyle R^1}{|}}{\underset{\underset{\textstyle O}{\|}}{C}} -O-R^5-N\overset{R^3}{\underset{R^4}{}}$$

Another reaction type involves the formation of ketones using Grignard reagents. The ketone formed is usually only temporary and is further reduced to a tertiary alcohol due to the reactive nature of the newly formed ketone:

$$CH_3-\overset{\overset{\textstyle O}{\|}}{C}-OC_2H_5 \xrightarrow{CH_3MgI} \left[CH_3-\overset{\overset{\textstyle OMgI}{|}}{\underset{\underset{\textstyle CH_3}{|}}{C}}-OC_2H_5 \right] \xrightarrow{-C_2H_5OMgI}$$

$$CH_3-C=O \atop CH_3$$

$$CH_3-\overset{\overset{\textstyle OH}{|}}{\underset{\underset{\textstyle CH_3}{|}}{C}}-CH_3 \xleftarrow{HOH} \left[CH_3-\overset{\overset{\textstyle OMgI}{|}}{\underset{\underset{\textstyle CH_3}{|}}{C}}-CH_3 \right] \xleftarrow{CH_3MgI}$$

2-methylpropan-2-ol
(*tert*-butanol)

The Ester Bunny

NB: The Ester Bunny is NOT GAMSAT material. In fact for you super-keeners: is the Ester Bunny a real ester? Find out in our Forum!

An important reaction of esters involves the combination of two ester molecules to form an acetoacetic ester (when two moles of ethyl acetate are combined). This is known as the <u>Claisen condensation</u> and is similar to the aldol condensation seen in ORG 7.2.4:

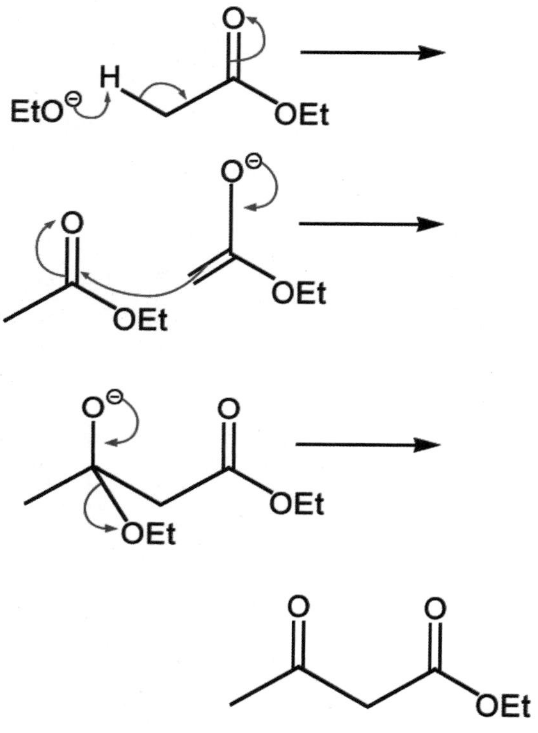

- <u>More reactions with esters</u>: Esters have similar chemistry to acid chlorides and acid anhydrides; however, they are less reactive toward nucleophilic substitution reactions.

1. **Conversion into amides:** Esters can react with ammonia or amines to give amides and an alcohol side product.

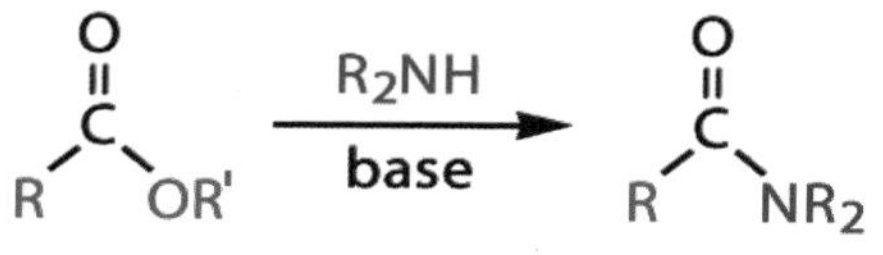

2. **Conversion into alcohols**: Esters can be easily reduced by $LiAlH_4$ to form primary alcohols. A hydride ion attacks the ester carbonyl carbon to form a tetrahedral intermediate. Loss of the alkoxide ion from the intermediate yields an aldehyde intermediate, which is further reduced by another hydride ion to give a primary alcohol final product.

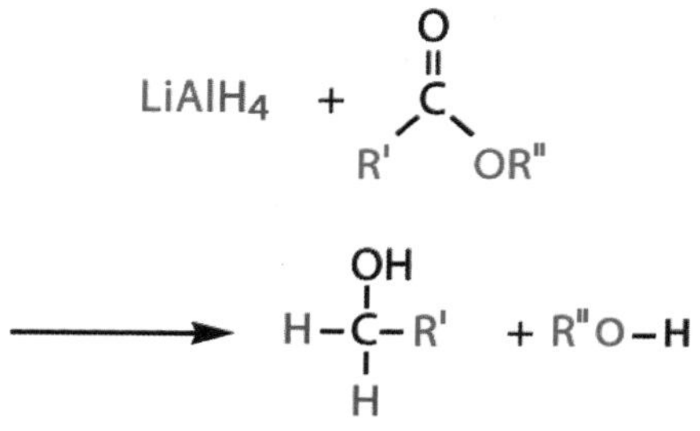

Esters can also be reduced to tertiary alcohols by reacting with a Grignard reagent (or alkyl lithium). Grignard reagents add to the ester carbonyl carbon to form ketone intermediates, which are further attacked by the next equivalent of the Grignard reagent. Thus two equivalents of the Grignard reagent (or alkyl lithium) are used to produce tertiary alcohols.

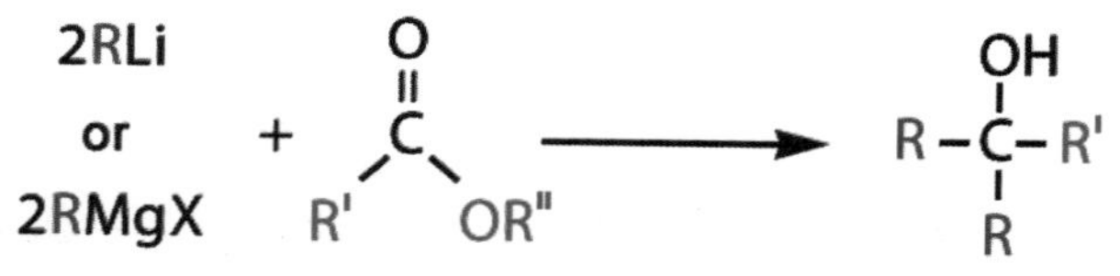

9.4.1 Fats, Glycerides and Saponification

A special class of esters is known as fats (i.e. mono-, di-, and triglycerides). These are biologically important molecules, and they are formed in the following reaction:

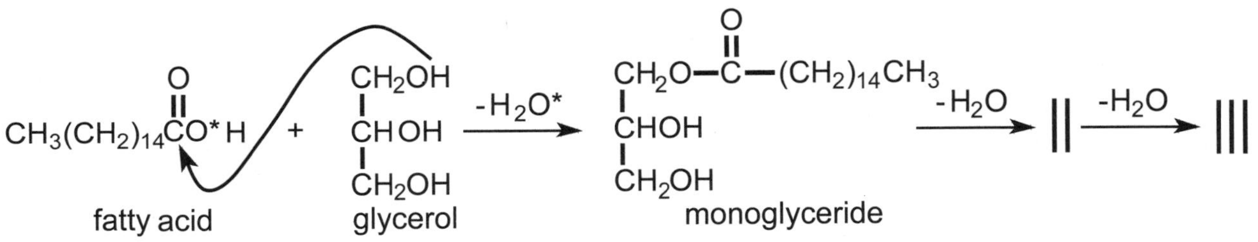

$$CH_3(CH_2)_{14}\overset{O}{\underset{}{C}}O^*H \quad + \quad \underset{\substack{| \\ CH_2OH \\ | \\ CHOH \\ | \\ CH_2OH}}{} \quad \xrightarrow{-H_2O^*} \quad \underset{\substack{| \\ CH_2O-\overset{O}{\underset{}{C}}-(CH_2)_{14}CH_3 \\ | \\ CHOH \\ | \\ CH_2OH}}{} \quad \xrightarrow{-H_2O} \; || \; \xrightarrow{-H_2O} \; |||$$

fatty acid   glycerol   monoglyceride

Fatty acids (= *long chain carboxylic acids*) are formed through the condensation of C2 units derived from acetate, and may be added to the monoglyceride formed in the above reaction, forming diglycerides, and triglycerides. Fats may be hydrolyzed by a base to the components glycerol and the salt of the fatty acids. The salts of long chain carboxylic acids are called <u>soaps</u>. Thus this process is called *saponification*:

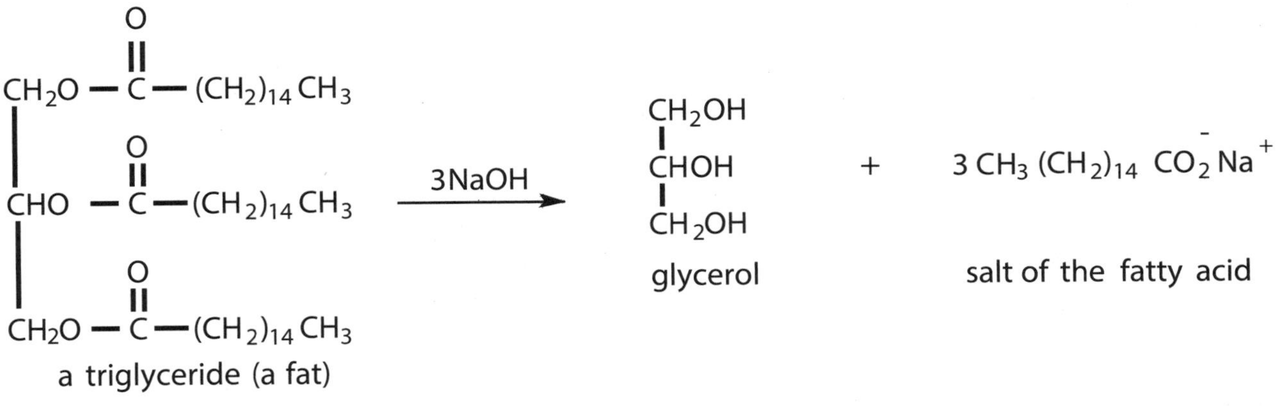

$$\underset{\text{a triglyceride (a fat)}}{\begin{array}{l} CH_2O-\overset{\overset{O}{||}}{C}-(CH_2)_{14}CH_3 \\ | \\ CHO-\overset{\overset{O}{||}}{C}-(CH_2)_{14}CH_3 \\ | \\ CH_2O-\overset{\overset{O}{||}}{C}-(CH_2)_{14}CH_3 \end{array}} \quad \xrightarrow{3NaOH} \quad \underset{\text{glycerol}}{\begin{array}{l} CH_2OH \\ | \\ CHOH \\ | \\ CH_2OH \end{array}} \quad + \quad \underset{\text{salt of the fatty acid}}{3\,CH_3(CH_2)_{14}\,CO_2^-\,Na^+}$$

9.5 β-Keto Acids

β-keto acids are carboxylic acids with a keto group (i.e. *ketone*) at the β position. Thus it is an acid with a carbonyl group one carbon removed from a carboxylic acid group.

Upon heating the carboxyl group can be readily removed as CO_2. This process is called *decarboxylation*. For example:

$$R-\overset{\overset{\displaystyle O}{\|}}{C}-CH_2-\overset{\overset{\displaystyle O}{\|}}{C}-OH \xrightarrow{\text{heat}} \overset{\overset{\displaystyle O}{\|}}{R C CH_3} \quad + \quad CO_2$$

β – keto acid   ketone

9.6 Relative Reactivity of Carboxylic Acid Derivatives

Any factors that make the carbonyl group more easily attacked by nucleophiles favor the nucleophilic acyl substitution reaction. In terms of nucleophilic substitution, generally, carboxylic acid derivatives are more reactive than comparable non-carboxylic acid derivatives. One important reason for the preceding is that the carbon in carboxylic acids is also attached to the electronegative oxygen atom of the carbonyl group; therefore, carbon is more δ^+, thus being more attractive to a nucleophile. Hence an acid chloride (R-COCl) is more reactive than a comparable alkyl chloride (R-Cl); an ester (R-COOR') is more reactive than a comparable ether (R-OR'); and an amide (R-CONH$_2$) is more reactive than a comparable amine (R-NH$_2$).

Amongst carboxylic acid derivatives, the car-bonyl reactivity in order from most to least reactive is:
acid chlorides > anhydrides >> esters
> acids > amides > nitriles

The reasons for this may be attributed to resonance effects and inductive effects. The resonance effect is the ability of the substituent to stabilize the carbocation intermediate by delocalization of electrons. The inductive effect is the substituent group, by virtue of its electronegativity, to pull electrons away increasing the partial positivity of the carbonyl carbon.

Within each carboxylic acid derivative, steric or bulk effects also play an important role. The less the steric hindrance (ORG 2.4, 6.2.3), the more access a nucleophile will have to attack the carbonyl carbon, and vice versa.

9.7 Phosphate Esters

Phosphoric acid derivatives have similar features to those of carboxylic acid derivatives. Phosphoric acid and mono- or di-phosphoric esters are acidic. Under acidic condition, these phosphoric esters can be converted to the parent acid H_3PO_4 and alcohols. To see the structure of phosphate esters, see ORG 12.5.

Go online to GAMSAT-prep.com for chapter review Q&A and forum.

ETHERS AND PHENOLS

Chapter 10

Memorize	Understand	Not Required*
sic nomenclature	* Ether synthesis, electrophilic aromatic substitution	* Knowledge beyond introductory-level (first year uni.) course

GAMSAT-Prep.com

Introduction

Ethers are composed of an oxygen atom connected to two alkyl or aryl groups of the general formula R–O–R'. A classic example is the solvent and anesthetic diethyl ether, often just called "ether." Phenol is a toxic, white crystalline solid with a sweet tarry odor often referred to as a "hospital smell"! Its chemical formula is C_6H_5OH and its structure is that of a hydroxyl group (-OH) bonded to a phenyl ring thus it is an aromatic compound.

Additional Resources

Free Online Q&A + Forum

GAMSAT-prep.com Videos

Flashcards

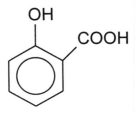

Special Guest

THE BIOLOGICAL SCIENCES ORG-115

* The real GAMSAT may have advanced level information presented (ie. in a passage) but previous knowledge of said information is not required to answer the questions that would follow. Practice ACER and GS practice GAMSATs can help you clarify this point.

10.1 Description and Nomenclature of Ethers

The general structure of an ether is R-O-R', where the R's may be either aromatic or aliphatic (= *non-aromatic hydrocarbon*). In the common system of nomenclature, the two groups on either side of the oxygen are named, followed by the word ether:

$$CH_3 — O — CH_3 \qquad CH_3 — O — \overset{\overset{\displaystyle CH_3}{|}}{CH}CH_3$$

dimethyl ether   methyl isopropyl ether

In the systematic system of nomenclature, the alkoxy (RO-) groups are always named as substituents (note that the shorter alkyl group becomes the alkoxy substituent):

$$CH_3{-}O{-}CH_3 \qquad CH_3{-}O{-}\overset{\overset{\displaystyle CH_3}{|}}{C}HCH_3$$

methoxy methane   methoxy isopropane

The boiling points of ethers are comparable to that of other hydrocarbons, which is regarded as relatively low temperatures when compared to alcohols. Ethers are more polar than other hydrocarbons, but are not capable of forming intermolecular hydrogen bonds (those between two ether molecules). Ethers are only slightly soluble in water. However, they can form intermolecular hydrogen bonds between the ether and the water molecules.

Ethers are <u>good solvents</u>, as the ether linkage is inert to many chemical reagents. Ethers are weak Lewis bases (CHM 3.4) and can be protonated to form positively charged conjugate acids (CHM 6.3). In the presence of a high concentration of a strong acid (especially HI or HBr), the ether linkage will be cleaved, to form an alcohol and an alkyl halide:

$$CH_3 — O — CH_3 + HI \longrightarrow$$
$$CH_3 — OH + CH_3 — I$$

10.1.1 Important Reactions of Ethers

- <u>Williamson ether synthesis</u>: A metal alkoxide can react with a primary alkyl halide to yield an ether in an S_N2 mechanism. The alkoxide, which is prepared by the reaction of an alcohol with a strong base (ORG 6.2.4), acts as a nucleophile and displaces the halide. Since primary halides work best in an S_N2 mechanism, asymmetrical ethers will be synthesized by the reaction between non-hindered halides and more hindered alkoxides. This reaction will not proceed with a hindered alkyl halide substrate:

$$Na^+\,{}^-OCH_3 + {}^{\delta+}CH_3 \text{-} I^{\delta-} \longrightarrow$$
$$CH_3 \text{-} O \text{-} CH_3 + Na^+I^-$$

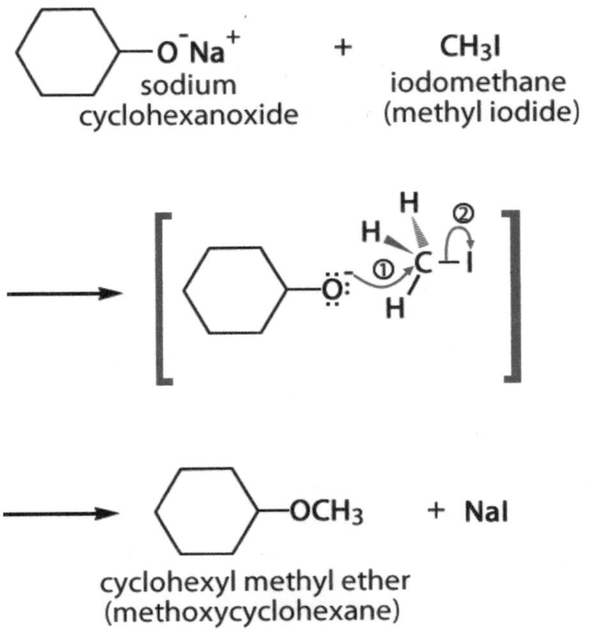
O⁻Na⁺
sodium cyclohexanoxide
+
CH3I
iodomethane (methyl iodide)
H
H
H
C
I
①
②
O
OCH3
+ NaI
cyclohexyl methyl ether (methoxycyclohexane)

In a variant of the Williamson ether synthesis, an alkoxide ion displaces a chloride atom within the same molecule. The precursor compounds are called halohydrins (ORG 4.2.1). For example, with 2-chloropropanol, an intramolecular epoxide formation reaction is possible creating the cyclic ether called oxirane (C_2H_4O). Note that oxirane is a three-membered cyclic ether (= *epoxide*).

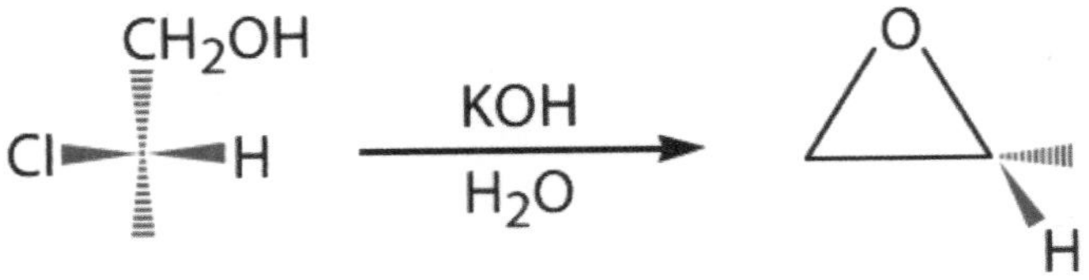
CH2OH
Cl
H
KOH
H2O
O
H

Cyclic ethers can also be prepared by reacting an alkene with m-CPBA (meta-chloroperoxybenzoic acid) which can also form an oxirane:

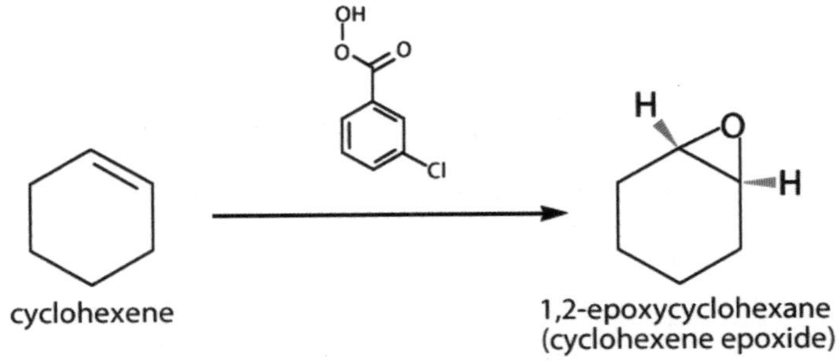
OH
O
O
Cl
H
O
H
cyclohexene
1,2-epoxycyclohexane (cyclohexene epoxide)

- Acidic Cleavage: Cleavage reactions of straight chain ethers takes place in the presence of HBr or HI (or even H_2SO_4) and is initiated by protonation of the ether oxygen.

Primary or secondary ethers react by an S_N2 mechanism in which I^- or Br^- attacks the protonated ether at the less hindered site. Tertiary, benzylic and allylic ethers react by an S_N1 or E1 mechanism because these substrates can produce stable intermediate carbocations. Please see the following mechanism:

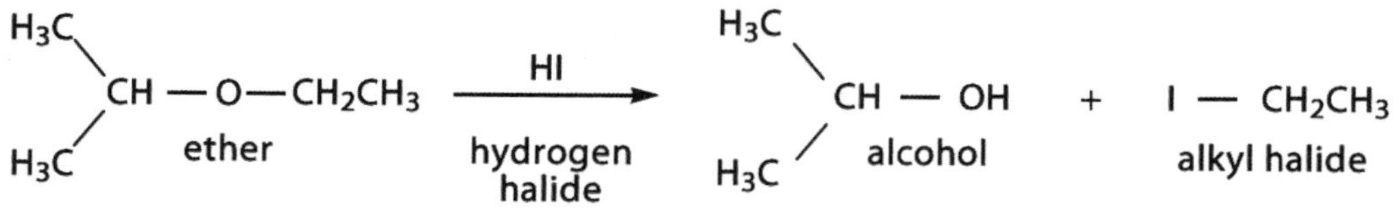

H₃C\
CH—O—CH₂CH₃ →(HI, hydrogen halide) H₃C\CH—OH (alcohol) + I—CH₂CH₃ (alkyl halide)

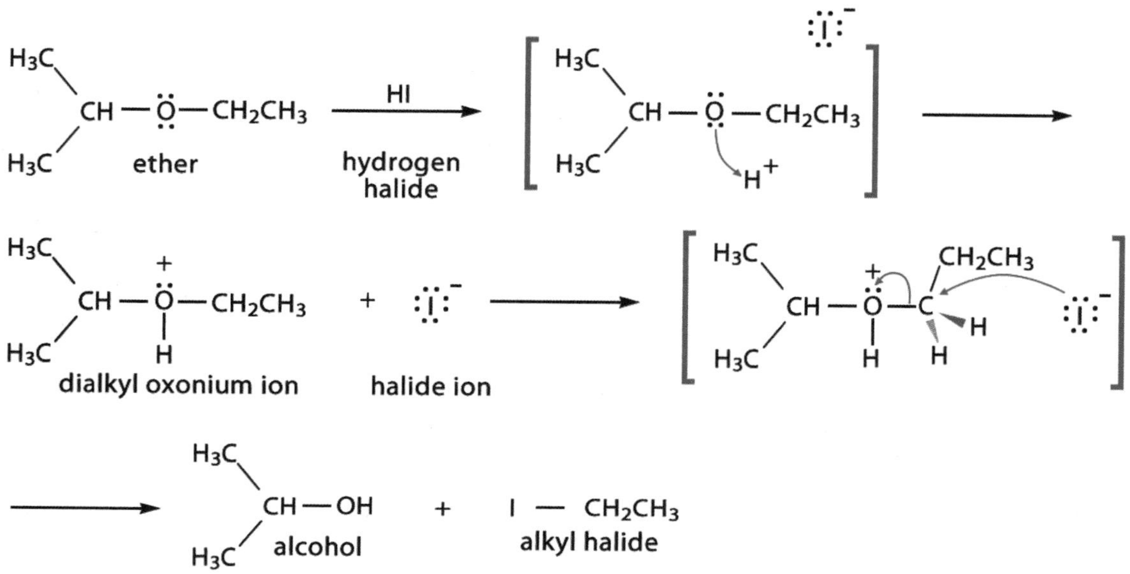

ether

10.2 Phenols

A phenol is a molecule consisting of a hydroxyl (–OH) group attached to a benzene (aromatic) ring (ORG 5.1). The following are some phenols and derivatives which are important to biochemistry, medicine and nature:

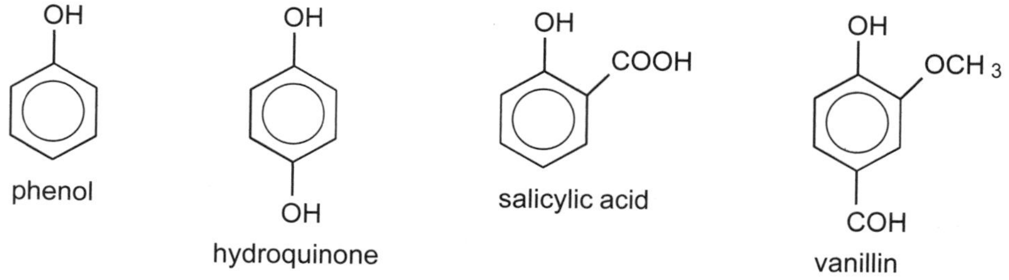

phenol

hydroquinone

salicylic acid

vanillin

Phenols are more acidic than their corresponding alcohols. This is due mainly to the electron withdrawing and resonance stabilization effects of the aromatic ring in the conjugate base anion (the phenoxide ion):

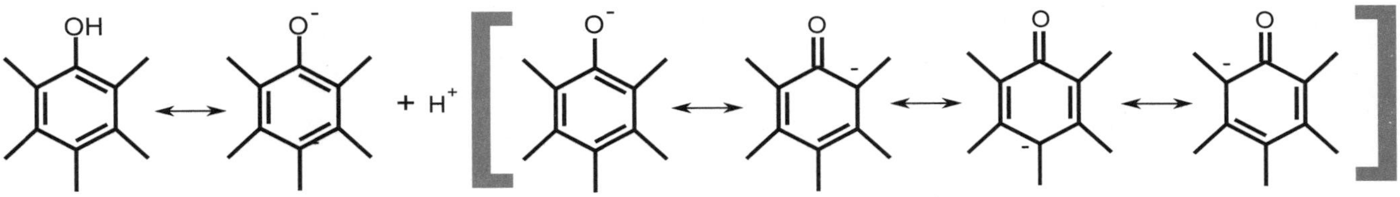

Substituent groups on the ring affect the acidity of phenols by both inductive effects (as with alcohols) and resonance effects. The resonance structures show that electron stabilizing (*withdrawing* or *meta directing*) groups at the ortho or para positions should increase the acidity of the phenol. Examples of these groups include the nitro group (−NO₂), −CN, −CO₂H, and the weakly deactivating o-p directors - the halogens. Destabilizing groups, such as alkyl groups, or other ortho-para directors, will make the compound less acidic. Phenols are ortho-para directors (see ORG Chapter 5).

Phenols can form hydrogen bonds, resulting in fairly high boiling points. Their solubility in water, however, is limited, because of the hydrophobic nature of the aromatic ring. Ortho phenols have lower boiling points than meta and para phenols, as they can form intramolecular hydrogen bonds. However, the para and even the ortho compounds can sometimes form intermolecular hydrogen bonds:

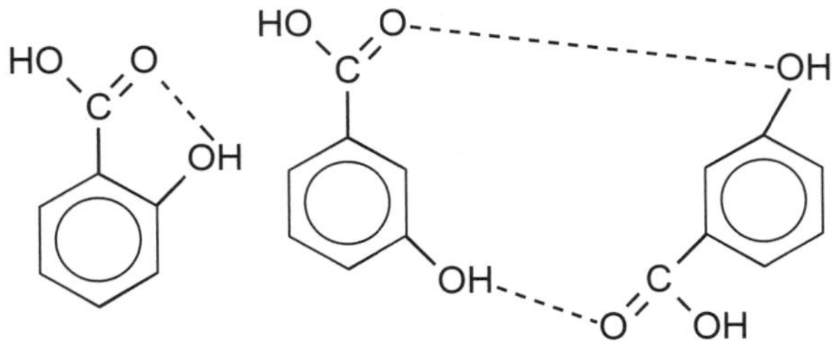

10.2.1 Electrophilic Aromatic Substitution for Phenols

The hydroxyl group is a powerful activating group and an ortho-para director in electrophilic substitutions. Thus phenols can brominate three times in bromine water as follows:

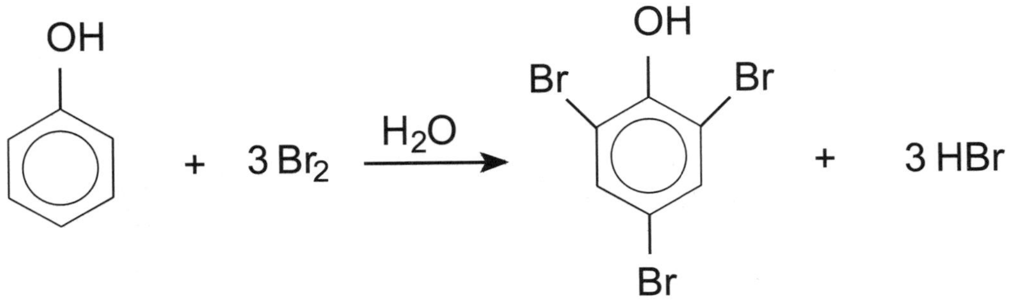

Go online to GAMSAT-prep.com for chapter review Q&A and forum.

AMINES

Chapter 11

Memorize	Understand	Not Required*
IUPAC nomenclature	* Effect of hydrogen bonds * Mechanisms of reactions * Trends in basicity * Resonance, delocalization of electrons	* Knowledge beyond introductory-level (first year uni.) course

GAMSAT-Prep.com

Introduction

Amines are compounds and functional groups that contain a basic nitrogen atom with a lone pair. Amines are derivatives of ammonia (NH_3), where one or more hydrogen atoms are replaced by organic substituents such as alkyl and aryl groups (consider reviewing the functional groups presented in ORG 1.6).

Additional Resources

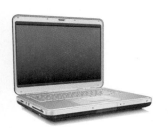

Free Online Q & A

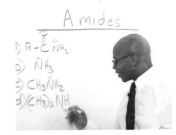

GAMSAT-prep.com Videos

Flashcards

Special Guest

* The real GAMSAT may have advanced level information presented (ie. in a passage) but previous knowledge of said information is not required to answer the questions that would follow. Practice ACER and GS practice GAMSATs can help you clarify this point.

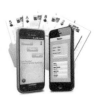

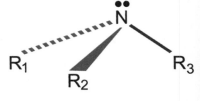

11.1 Description and Nomenclature

Organic compounds with a trivalent nitrogen atom bonded to one or more carbon atoms are called amines. These are organic derivatives of ammonia. They may be classified depending on the number of carbon atoms bonded to the nitrogen:

Primary Amine:	RNH_2
Secondary Amine:	R_2NH
Tertiary Amine:	R_3N
Quaternary Salt:	$R_4N^+ X^-$

In the common system of nomenclature, amines are named by adding the suffix '-amine' to the name of the alkyl group. In a secondary or tertiary amine, where there is more than one alkyl group, the groups are named as N-substituted derivatives of the larger group:

methyl ethyl isopropylamine

In the systematic system of nomenclature, amines are named analagous to alcohols, except the suffix '-amine' is used instead of the suffix '-ol'.

When amines are present with multiple asymmetric substituents, they are named by considering the largest group as the parent name and the other alkyl groups as N-substituents of the parent:

N, N-dimethyl-2-butanamine

The $-NH_2$ group is named as an amino substituent on a parent molecule when amines are present with more than one functional group:

4-aminobutanoic acid

The bonding in amines is similar to the bonding in ammonia. The nitrogen atom is sp^3 hybridized (ORG 1.1, 1.2, CHM 3.5). Primary, secondary and tertiary amines have a trigonal pyramidal shape (CHM 3.5). The C-N-C bond angle is approximately 108°. Quaternary amines have a tetrahedral shape and a normal tetrahedral bond angle of 109.5°.

With its tetrahedral geometry, amines with three different substituents are considered chiral. Such amines are analogous to chiral alkanes in that the nitrogen atom will possess four different substituents - considering the lone pair of electrons to be the fourth substituent. However, unlike chiral alkanes, chiral amines do not exist in two separate enantiomers. Pyramidal nitrogen inversion between the two enantiomeric forms occurs so rapidly at room temperature that the two forms cannot be isolated.

11.1.1 The Basicity of Amines

Along with the three attached groups, amines have an unbonded electron pair. Most of the chemistry of amines depends on this unbonded electron pair:

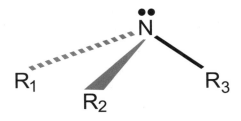

The electron pair is stabilized by the electron donating effects of alkyl groups. Thus the lone pair in tertiary amines is more stable than in secondary amines which, in turn, is more stable than in primary amines. As a result of this electron pair, amines are Lewis bases (see CHM 3.4), and good nucleophiles. In aqueous solution, amines are weak bases, and can accept a proton:

$$R_3N + H_2O \longrightarrow R_3NH^+ + OH^-$$

The ammonium cation in the preceding reaction is stabilized, once again, by the electron donating effects of the alkyl groups. Conversely, should the nitrogen be adjacent to a carbocation, the lone pair can stabilize the carbocation by delocalizing the charge.

The relative basicity of amines is determined by the following:

- If the free amine is stabilized relative to the cation, the amine is less basic.
- If the cation is stabilized relative to the free amine, the amine is more stable, thus the stronger base.

Groups that withdraw electron density (such as halides or aromatics) decrease the availability of the unbonded electron pair. Electron releasing groups (such as alkyl groups) increase the availability of the unbonded electron pair. The base strength then increases in the following series (where Ø represents a phenyl group):

$$NO_2-Ø-NH_2 < Ø-NH_2 < Ø-CH_2-NH_2 < NH_3$$
$$< CH_3-NH_2 < (CH_3)_2-N-H < (CH_3)_3-N$$

Note that a substituent attached to an aromatic ring can greatly affect the basicity of the amine. For example, electron withdrawing groups (i.e. $-NO_2$) withdraw electrons from the ring which, in turn, withdraws the lone electron pair (*delocalization*) from nitrogen. Thus the lone pair is less available to bond with a proton; consequently, it is a weaker base. The opposite occurs with an electron donating group, making the amine, relatively, a better base (see ORG Chapter 5).

11.1.2 More Properties of Amines

- The nitrogen atom can <u>hydrogen bond</u> (using its electron pair) to hydrogens attached to other N's or O's. It can also form hydrogen bonds from hydrogens attached to it with electron pairs of N, O, F or Cl:

$$-\overset{|}{\underset{|}{N}}-H\cdots\cdots O-H$$
$$\overset{H}{\underset{}{|}}$$

or
$$-\overset{|}{\underset{|}{N}}-\cdots\cdots\overset{H}{\underset{}{|}}$$
$$O-H$$

  Note that primary or secondary amines can hydrogen bond with each other, but tertiary amines cannot. This leads to boiling points which are higher than would be expected for compounds of similar molecular weight, like alkanes, but lower than similar alcohols or carboxylic acids. The hydrogen bonding also renders low weight amines soluble in water.

- A <u>dipole moment</u> is possible:

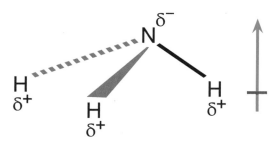

- The nitrogen in amines can contribute its lone pair electrons to activate a benzene ring. Thus amines are ortho-para directors.

- The <u>solubility of quaternary salts</u> decreases with increasing molecular weight. The quaternary structure has steric hindrance and the lone pair electrons on N is not available for H-bonding, thus their solubility is much less than other amines or even alkyl ammonium salts (i.e. $R-NH_3^+X^-$, $R_2-NH_2^+X^-$, $R_3-NH^+X^-$). Quaternary ammonium salts can be synthesized from ammonium hydroxides which are very strong bases.

$$(CH_3)_4N^+OH^- + HCl \longrightarrow (CH_3)_4N^+Cl^- + H_2O$$

Quaternary hydroxide   Quaternary salt

- **Amide formation** is an important reaction for protein synthesis. Primary and secondary amines will react with carboxylic acids and their derivatives to form *amides*:

$$R'NH_2 \quad + \quad R-\overset{\overset{\textstyle O}{\|}}{C}-OH$$

primary or secondary amines   acid

$$\longrightarrow \quad R-\overset{\overset{\textstyle O}{\|}}{C}-NHR' + H_2O$$

amide

Amides can engage in resonance such that the lone pair electrons on the nitrogen is delocalized. Thus amides are by far <u>less basic</u> than amines.

$$\left[R-\overset{\overset{\textstyle O}{\|}}{C}-NR_2 \longleftrightarrow R-\overset{\overset{\textstyle O^-}{|}}{C}=\overset{+}{N}R_2 \right]$$

As can be seen, the C–N bond has a partial double bond character. Thus there is restricted rotation about the C–N bond.

- **Alkylation** is another important reaction which involves amines with alkyl halides:

$$RCH_2Cl + R'NH_2 \longrightarrow RCH_2NH\,R' + HCl$$

$1°, 2°$ or $3°$ amine

Both amide formation and alkylation make use of the nucleophilic character of the electrons on nitrogen.

Thus ammonia or an alkyl amine reacts with an alkyl halide to yield an amine in an S_N2 mechanism. Ammonia produces a primary amine; a primary amine produces a secondary amine; a secondary amine produces a tertiary amine; and a tertiary amine produces a quaternary ammonium salt.

$$H-\overset{\overset{\textstyle R^1}{|}}{\underset{\underset{\textstyle R^2}{|}}{N}}\!\!: \quad + \quad R^3X$$

primary or   halogenoalkane
secondary amine

$$\longrightarrow \quad :\!\overset{\overset{\textstyle R^1}{|}}{\underset{\underset{\textstyle R^2}{|}}{N}}-R^3 \quad + \quad HX$$

alkyl-substituted amine   halogen acid
(secondary or tertiary)

Note: Standard notation for R dictates that when you see a subscript (i.e. 2), just like for other atoms or groups, it means that 2 R groups are present. This has a different meaning than a superscript 2 (ORG 1.6) which means that there is only 1 R group at that position but it is different from any other R group with a different superscript. You will also notice on this page: the R prime notation (R') indicating a single R group different from R without the prime symbol (ORG 1.6). Any of the above notations could be used during the GAMSAT.

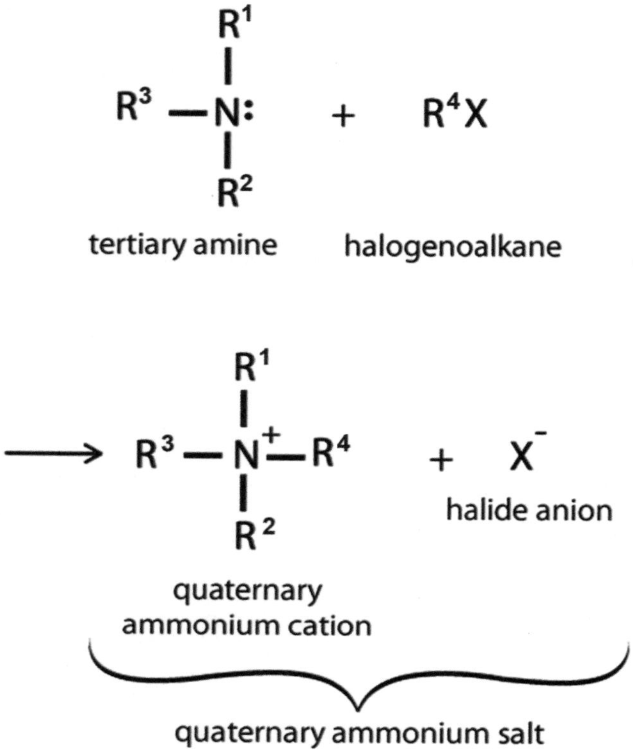

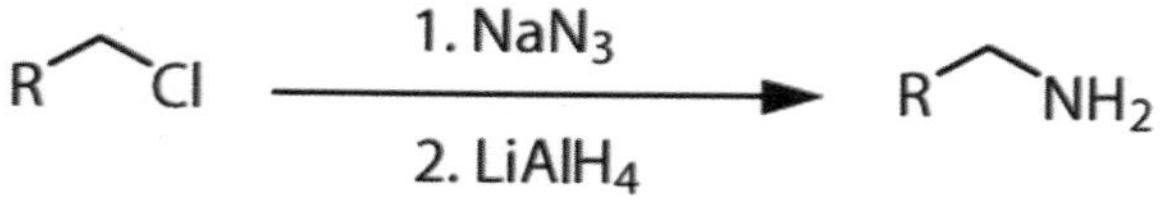

Gabriel amine synthesis occurs via a phthalimide ion displacing the halide from the alkyl halide followed by basic hydrolysis of the N-alkyl phthalimide yielding a primary amine.

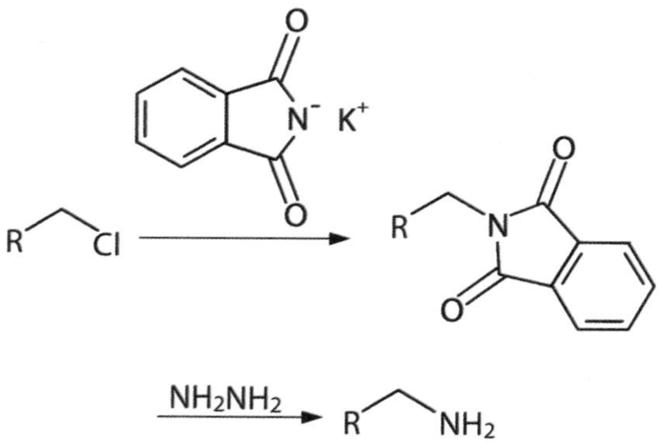

R^3 —N: + R^4X

tertiary amine   halogenoalkane

$\longrightarrow$ R^3 —$\overset{+}{N}$—R^4 + X^-

halide anion

quaternary
ammonium cation

quaternary ammonium salt

$$\xrightarrow{NH_2NH_2} R \diagdown NH_2$$

• **Reductive amination**: Amines can also be synthesized by reductive amination in which an aldehyde or ketone reacts with ammonia, a primary amine or a secondary amine to form a corresponding primary amine, secondary amine or tertiary amine.

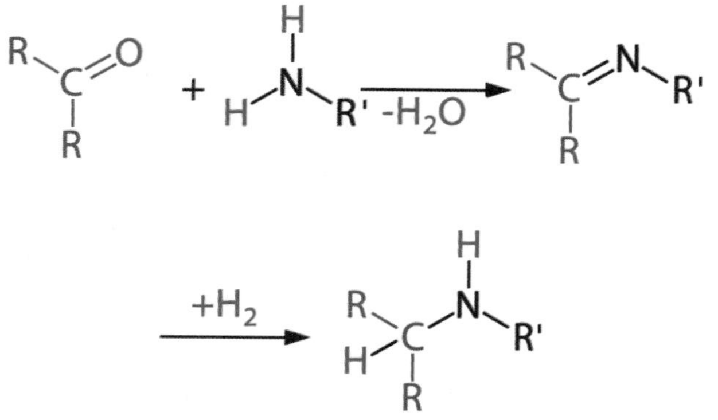

• **Gabriel synthesis:** Primary amines can also be obtained from azide synthesis and Gabriel synthesis in an S_N2 mechanism. The azide ion N_3^-, acting as a nucleophile, displaces the halide ion from the alkyl halide to form RN_3, which is then reduced by $LiAlH_4$ to form the desired primary amine.

$$R \diagdown Cl \xrightarrow[\text{2. } LiAlH_4]{\text{1. } NaN_3} R \diagdown NH_2$$

- **Reduction of nitriles**: Nitriles can be reduced by LiAlH$_4$ to produce primary amines. This offers a way to convert alkyl halides into primary amines with one more carbon atom.

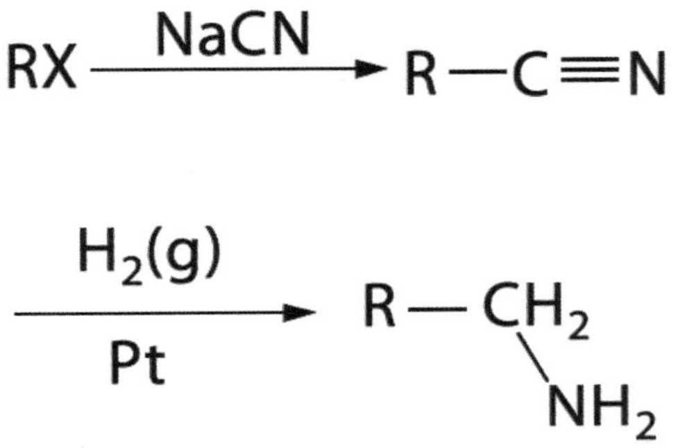

- **Reduction of amides**: Amides can also be reduced by LiAlH$_4$ to produce primary amines. Thus carboxylic acids can be converted into primary amines with the same number of carbon atoms.

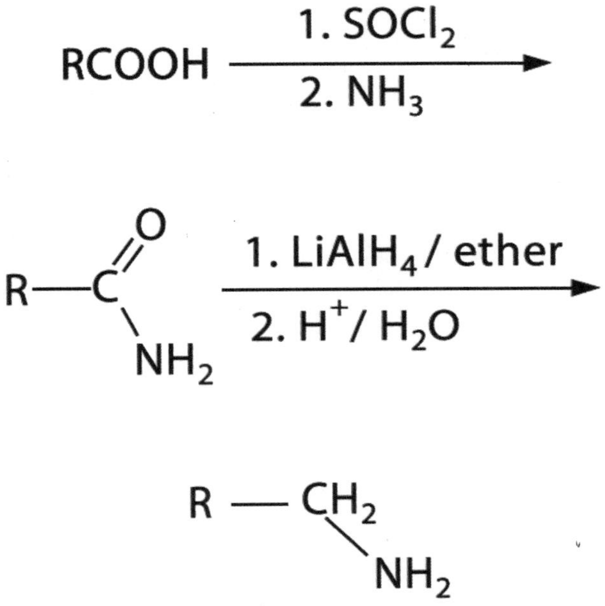

$$RX \xrightarrow{\text{NaCN}} R-C\equiv N$$

$$\xrightarrow[\text{Pt}]{H_2(g)} R-CH_2-NH_2$$

$$RCOOH \xrightarrow[\text{2. NH}_3]{\text{1. SOCl}_2}$$

$$R-\overset{\overset{\displaystyle O}{\|}}{C}-NH_2 \xrightarrow[\text{2. H}^+/\text{H}_2\text{O}]{\text{1. LiAlH}_4/\text{ether}}$$

$$R-CH_2-NH_2$$

Free Gold Standard GAMSAT Organic Chemistry Reactions Summary
Yes, it's online, it's free and it summarizes the most important reactions. You can find the link on the Members home page when you log into your gamsat-prep.com account or you can google it. You can choose to print the page and work through examples changing the different R groups to H's, secondary alkyl groups, aryl groups, etc. to see if you are really following what is happening and that you can name the products. Our Summary page also includes a free YouTube video by Dr. Ferdinand explaining each reaction. Each reaction is also cross-referenced (at the bottom of the page) to a specific section of this textbook for further reading should you wish.

Go online to GAMSAT-prep.com for chapter review Q&A and forum.

BIOLOGICAL MOLECULES

Chapter 12

Memorize	Understand	Not Required*
sic structures oelectric point equation efine: amphoteric, zwitterions	* Effect of H, S, hydrophobic bonds * Basic mechanisms of reactions * Effect of pH, isoelectric point * Protein structure * Different ways of drawing structures	* Knowledge beyond introductory-level (first year uni.) course * Memorizing all the names of amino acids * Detailed mech. specific to bio molecules

GAMSAT-Prep.com

Introduction

Biological molecules truly involve the chemistry of life. Such molecules include amino acids and proteins, carbohydrates (glucose, disaccharides, polysaccharides), lipids (triglycerides, steroids) and nucleic acids (DNA, RNA).

Additional Resources

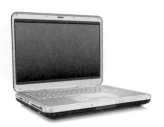

Free Online Q & A

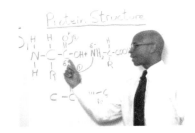

GAMSAT-prep.com Videos

Flashcards

Special Guest

* The real GAMSAT may have advanced level information presented (ie. in a passage) but previous knowledge of said information is not required to answer the questions that would follow. Practice ACER and GS practice GAMSATs can help you clarify this point.

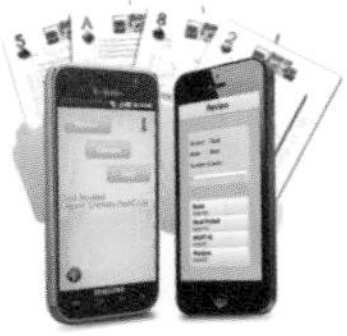

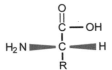

12.1 Amino Acids

Protein-building <u>amino acids</u> are molecules that contain a side chain (*R*), a carboxylic acid, and an amino group at the α carbon. Thus the general structure of α-amino acids is:

L - amino acid
"left-handed" isomer

D - amino acid
"right-handed" isomer

From your GAMSAT Organic Chemistry review, you should remember that the carbonyl carbon (C=O) in a carboxylic acid is carbon-1 (ORG 8.1), and the adjacent carbon (carbon-2) is the alpha position, carbon-3 is the beta position (ORG 7.1), and carbon-4 is thus the gamma position.

Amino acids may be named systematically as substituted carboxylic acids, however, there are 20 important α-amino acids that are known by common names. These are naturally occurring and they form the building blocks of most proteins found in humans. The following are a few examples of α-amino acids:

Glycine

Alanine

Serine

Aspartic acid

Note that the D/L system is commonly used for amino acid and carbohydrate chemistry. The reason is that naturally occurring amino acids have the same relative configuration, the <u>L-configuration</u>, while naturally occurring carbohydrates are nearly all <u>D-configuration</u>. However, the absolute configuration (i.e. R/S) depends on the priority assigned to the side group (*see ORG 2.3.1 for rules*).

The illustrations of the preceding amino acids are all in the L configuration and they also correspond to the S absolute stereochemistry (*except glycine which cannot be assigned any configuration since it is not chiral*).

The following mnemonic is helpful for determining the D/L isomeric form of an amino acid: the "CORN" rule. The substituents **CO**OH, **R**, **N**H$_2$, and H are arranged around the chiral center. Starting with H away from the viewer, if these groups are arranged clockwise around the chiral carbon, then it is the D-form. If counter-clockwise, it is the L-form. Of course, if hydrogen is pointing towards the viewer - like the structures on this page - then the pattern is reversed.

Also note that, except for glycine, the α-carbon of all amino acids are chiral indicating that there must be at least two different enantiomeric forms. Notice in the preceding illustrations that the alpha carbon in glycine is not bonded to 4 different substitutents since it is bonded to hydrogen twice; however, the alpha carbon in alanine, serine and aspartic acid has 4 different substituents in each case meaning that carbon is chiral. Notice that chirality of carbon hinges on its attachment to 4 different substituents (i.e. groups/ligands) and NOT necessarily 4 different atoms. A chiral carbon is sometimes referred to as a stereocenter or as a stereogenic or asymmetric carbon (ORG 2.2, 2.3).

Many important amino acids can play critical non-protein roles within the body. For example, glutamate and gamma-aminobutyric acid ("GABA", a non-standard gamma-amino acid) are, respectively, the main excitatory and inhibitory neurotransmitters in the human brain (BIO 5.1).

GABA: A gamma-amino acid.
Notice that the amino group is attached to the 3rd carbon from the carbonyl carbon (C=O).

Unless specified otherwise, the following sections will be exploring features of alpha-amino acids.

12.1.1 Hydrophilic vs. Hydrophobic

Different types of amino acids tend to be found in different areas of the proteins that they make up. Amino acids which are ionic and/or polar are hydrophilic, and tend to be found on the exterior of proteins (i.e. *exposed to water*). These include aspartic acid and its amide, glutamic acid and its amide, lysine, arginine and histidine. Certain other polar amino acids are found on either the interior or exterior of proteins. These include serine, threonine, and tyrosine. Hydrophobic ('water-fearing") amino acids which may be found on the interior of proteins include methionine, leucine, tryptophan, valine and phenylalanine. Hydrophobic molecules tend to cluster in aqueous solutions (= *hydrophobic bonding*). Alanine is a nonpolar amino acid which is unusual because it is less hydrophobic than most nonpolar amino acids. This is because its nonpolar side chain is very short.

Glycine is the smallest amino acid, and the only one that is not optically active. It is often found at the 'corners' of proteins. Alanine is small and, although hydrophobic, is found on the surface of proteins.

12.1.2 Acidic vs. Basic

Amino acids have both acid and basic components (= *amphoteric*). The amino acids with the R group containing an amino ($-NH_2$) group, are basic. The two basic amino acids are lysine and arginine. Amino acids with an R group containing a carboxyl ($-COOH$) group are acidic. The two acidic amino acids are aspartic acid and glutamic acid. One amino acid, histidine, may act as either an acid or a base, depending upon the pH of the resident solution. This makes histidine a very good physiologic buffer. The rest of the amino acids are considered to be neutral.

The basic $-NH_2$ group in an amino acid is present as an ammonium ion, $-NH_3^+$. The acidic carboxyl $-COOH$ group is present as a carboxylate ion, $-COO^-$. As a result, amino acids are <u>dipolar ions</u>, or *zwitterions*. In an aqueous solution, there is an equilibrium present between the dipolar, the anionic, and the cationic forms of the amino acid (see below; also note that the way amino acids are presented in ORG 12.1 is a simplification since, at any pH, some part of an amino acid will bear a charge due to the presence of both acidic and basic functional groups).

Therefore the charge on the amino acid will vary with the pH of the solution, and with the <u>isoelectric point</u>. This point is the pH where a given amino acid will be neutral (i.e. have no net charge). This isoelectric point is the average of the two pK_a values (CHM 6.1, 6.3) of an amino acid (*depending on the dissociated group*):

$$\text{isoelectric point} = pI = (pK_{a1} + pK_{a2})/2$$

Since this is a commonly tested GAMSAT concept, let's further summarize for the average amino acid: When in a relatively acidic solution, the amino acid is fully protonated and exists as a cation, that is, it has two protons available for dissociation, one from the carboxyl group and one from the amino group. When in a relatively basic solution, the amino acid is fully deprotonated and exists as an anion, that is, it has two proton accepting groups, the carboxyl group and the amino group.

At the isoelectric point (pI), although the amino acid is overall neutral, it is a dipolar zwitterion. This means that the carboxyl group is deprotonated forming a carboxylate anion, and the amino group is protonated forming an ammonium cation. At their pI, amino acids (and proteins) have minimum solubility in water or salt solutions and often precipitate out of solution. With no net charge, they tend to remain (and interact) together as opposed to when they have an overall, identical (repulsive) charge when interacting with a polar (e.g. water) or charged substance would be better.

$$H_3\overset{+}{N} - CH - CO_2H \xrightleftharpoons[H_3O^+]{} \quad H_3\overset{+}{N} - CH - CO_2^- \xrightleftharpoons[H_3O^+]{} \quad H_2N - CH - CO_2^-$$

CH_3	CH_3	CH_3
Acidic	Neutral	Basic

12.1.3 The 20 Alpha-Amino Acids

Approximately 500 amino acids are known - of these, only 22 are proteinogenic ("protein building") amino acids. Of these, 20 amino acids are known as "standard" and are found in human beings and other eukaryotes, and are encoded directly by the universal genetic code (BIO 3). The 2 exceptions are the "non-standard" pyrrolysine — found only in some methanogenic organisms but not humans — and selenocysteine which is present in humans and a wide range of other organisms.

Of the 20 standard amino acids, 9 are called "essential" for humans because they cannot be created from other compounds by the human body, and so must be taken in as food.

The following categorizes amino acids based on side chains, pK_a and charges at human, physiological pH (~7.4):

1. Nonpolar amino acids: R groups are hydrophobic and thus decrease solubility. These amino acids are usually found within the interior of the protein molecule.

2. Polar amino acids: R groups are hydrophilic and thus increase the solubility. These amino acids are usually found on the protein's surface.

3. Acidic amino acids: R groups contain an additional carboxyl group. These amino acids have a negative charge at physiological pH.

4. Basic amino acids: R groups contain an additional amine group. These amino acids have a positive charge at physiological pH. Note that asparagine and glutamine have amide side chains and are thus not considered basic (see ORG 9.3).

Table IV.A.1.1: Basic Nomenclature for Biological Molecules. The exception to the monomer/polymer rule is lipids since lipid base units are not generally considered monomers.

Building block	Polymerizes to form...	Chemical bonds	Macromolecule
Monomers	Dimer, trimer, tetramer, oligomers, etc.	Covalent* bonds	Polymer
Amino acids	Dipeptide, tripeptide, tetra/oligopeptide, etc	Peptide bonds	Polypeptide, protein (e.g. insulin, hemoglobin)
Monosaccharides ('simple sugars'**)	Disaccharide, tri/tetra/ oligosaccharide, etc.	Glycosidic bonds	Polysaccharide (e.g. starch, glycogen)
Nucleotides	Nucleotide dimer, tri/tetra/oligomer, etc.	Phosphodiester bonds	Polynucleotides, nucleic acids (e.g. DNA, RNA)

*There are exceptions. For example, in certain circumstances polypeptides are considered monomers and they may bond non-covalently to form dimers (i.e. higher orders of protein structure which will be discussed in following sections).

**Note that disaccharides are also sugars (i.e. sucrose is a glucose-fructose dimer known as 'table sugar'; lactose is a glucose-galactose dimer known as 'milk sugar').

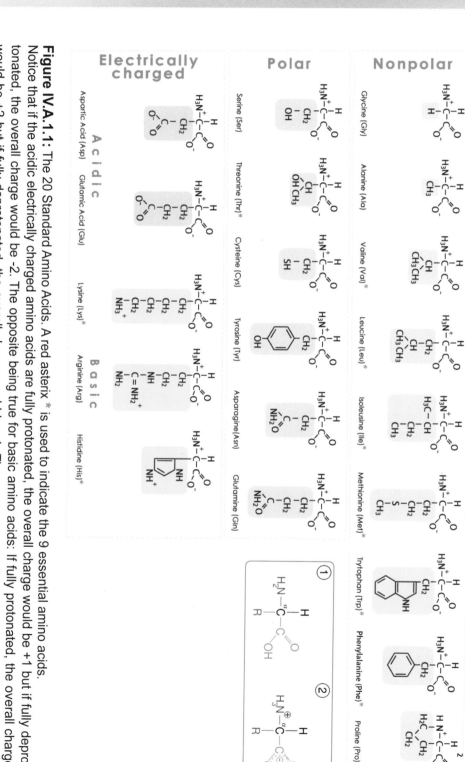

Figure IV.A.1.1: The 20 Standard Amino Acids. A red asterix * is used to indicate the 9 essential amino acids. Notice that if the acidic electrically charged amino acids are fully protonated, the overall charge would be -2. The opposite being true for basic amino acids: If fully protonated, the overall charge would be +1 but if fully deprotonated, the overall charge would be -1. These cases are different than for the average amino acid described at the end of section ORG 12.1.2. Skim through the names and structures of the 20 standard amino acids but please do not memorize.

Note the inset (in the red box) which shows the general structure for an amino acid in both the (1) un-ionized and (2) zwitterionic forms. For the latter, note the resonance stabilized carboxylate anion in red, the primary ammonium ion in blue, and the variable R group in green.

12.2 Proteins

12.2.1 General Principles

An oligopeptide consists of between 2 and 20 amino acids joined together by amide (peptide) bonds. Oligopeptides include dipeptides (2 amino acids), tripeptides (3), tetrapeptides (4), pentapeptides (5), etc. Polypeptides - generally regarded to be between the size of oligopeptides and proteins - are polymers of up to 100 or even 1000 α-amino acids (depending on the molecule and the reference). Proteins are long chain polypeptides which often form higher order structures. These peptide bonds are derived from the amino group of one amino acid, and the acid group of another. When a peptide bond is formed, a molecule of water is released (condensation = dehydration = water loss). The bond can be broken by adding water (hydrolysis = water lyses = water 'breaks apart' another molecule).

Since proteins are polymers of amino acids, they also have isoelectric points. Classification as to the acidity or basicity of a protein depends on the numbers of acidic and basic amino acids it contains. If there is an excess of acidic amino acids, the isoelectric point will be at a pH of less than 7. At pH = 7, these proteins will have a net negative charge. Similarly, those with an excess of basic amino acids will have an isoelectric point at a pH of greater than 7. Therefore, at pH = 7, these proteins will have a net positive charge. Proteins can be separated according to their isoelectric point on a polyacrylamide gel (electrophoresis; ORG 13). We will be discussing protein synthesis in Biology Chapter 3.

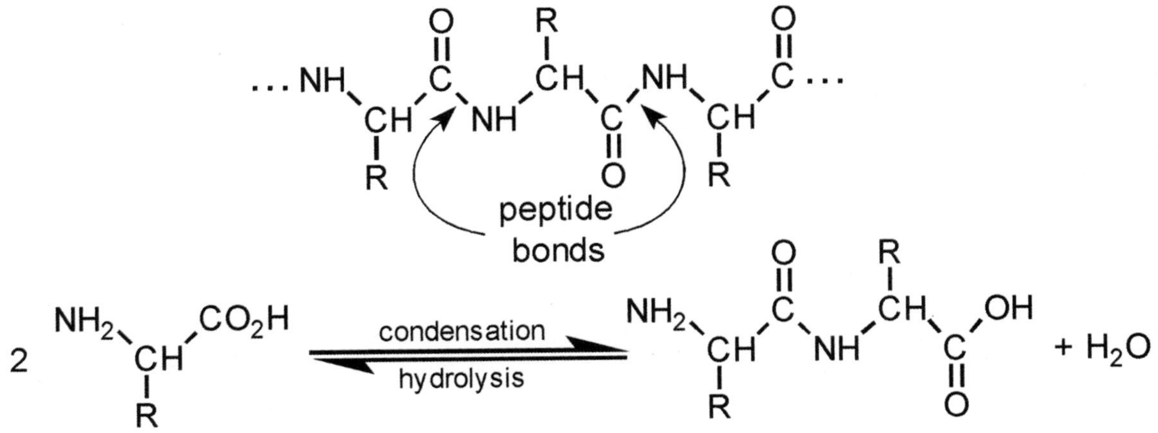

Figure IV.A.1.2: Condensation and hydrolysis. Note that the forward reaction shows 2 moles of amino acid producing a dipeptide and water. The dipeptide is composed of 2 amino acid 'residues' (i.e. what is left over once water is removed). By convention, the amino group (N-terminus) is on the left and the carboxyl group (C-terminus) is on the right.

Protein structure may be divided into primary, secondary, tertiary and quaternary structures. The <u>primary structure</u> is the sequence of amino acids as determined by the DNA and the location of covalent bonds (*including disulfide bonds*). This structure determines the higher order structures.

The primary structure is usually shown using 3-letter abbreviations for the amino acid residues as shown in Fig IV.A.1.1. By convention, the amino group (N-terminus) is on the left and the carboxyl group (C-terminus) on the right. For example, insulin (BIO 6.3.4) is composed of 51 amino acids in 2 chains. One chain has 30 amino acids, and the other has 21 amino acids with the following primary structure: GLY-ILE-VAL-GLU-GLN-CYS-CYS-THR-SER-ILE-CYS-SER-LEU-TYR-GLN-LEU-GLU-ASN-TYR-CYS-ASN.

The <u>secondary structure</u> is the orderly inter- or intramolecular *hydrogen bonding* of the protein chain. The resultant structure may be the more stable α-helix (e.g. keratin), or β-strands forming a β-pleated sheet (e.g. silk). Proline is an amino acid which cannot participate in the regular array of H-bonding in an α-helix. Proline disrupts the α-helix, thus it is usually found at the beginning or end of a molecule (i.e. hemoglobin).

The <u>tertiary structure</u> is the further folding of the protein molecule onto itself. This is the 3D shape (spatial organization) of an entire protein molecule. Protein folding is largely self-organising mainly based on the protein's primary structure. The tertiary structure is maintained by *noncovalent bonds* like hydrogen bonding, Van der Waals forces, hydrophobic bonding and electrostatic bonding (CHM 4.2). The resultant structure is a globular protein with a hydrophobic interior and hydrophilic exterior. Enzymes are classic examples of such a structure. In fact, enzyme activity often depends on tertiary structure.

The covalent bonding of cysteine (*disulfide bonds or bridge*) helps to stabilize the tertiary structure of proteins. Cysteine will form sulfur-sulfur covalent bonds with itself, producing *cystine*. For example, insulin is composed of 2 polypeptide chains, an A-chain and a B-chain (2 = a dimer), which are linked together by disulfide bonds.

$$2H_2N-CH-CO_2H \xrightarrow{-H_2}$$
$$CH_2SH$$
cysteine

cystine

The <u>quaternary structure</u> is when there are two or more protein chains bonded together by noncovalent bonds. For example, hemoglobin (BIO 7.5.1) consists of four polypeptide subunits (*globin*) held together by hydrophobic bonds forming a globular almost tetrahedryl arrangement.

The secondary, tertiary, and quaternary structures of a protein may be destroyed in a number of ways (= *denaturation*). For example, heating (cooking) can break hydrogen bonds. Altering the pH can protonate or deprotonate the molecule and interrupt ionic interactions. Reducing agents can break disulfide bonds. Depending on the conditions, denaturation may be reversible.

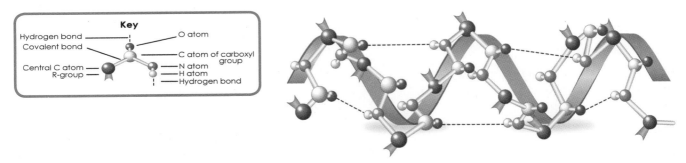

Figure IV.A.1.3: Secondary Structure: α-helix; note the peptide chain is coiled into a helical structure around a central axis. This helix is stabilized by hydrogen bonding between the N-H group and C=O group four residues away. A typical example with this secondary structure is keratin. Keratin is a fibrous, structural protein found in skin, hair and nails (BIO 13.2, 13.3.1). Seen in green above, a spiral ribbon can symbolize an α-helix.

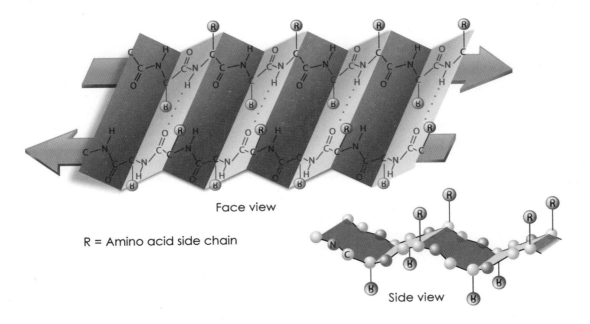

Figure IV.A.1.4: Secondary Structure: 2 β-strands (green arrows) forming a β-pleated sheet. Peptide chains lie alongside each other in a parallel manner. This structure is stabilized by hydrogen bonding between the N-H group on one β-strand and C=O group on another. A typical example with this secondary structure is produced by some insect larvae: the protein fiber "silk" which is mostly composed of fibroin.

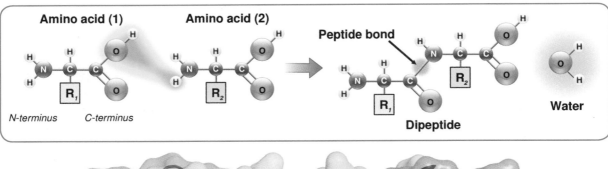

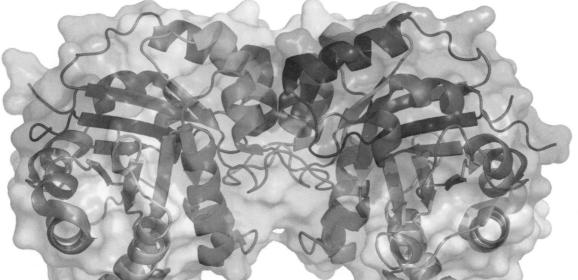

Figure IV.A.1.2: From the atoms that produce molecules - amino acids - which combine via peptide (= *amide*) bonds in a specific order (= **primary structure**), to the level of organization of these same molecules which conglomerate in a specified way based on the primary structure to produce higher-order structures resulting in the protein above. Approximately 250 amino acid residues combine to produce each of the 2 identical subunits (= *dimer*; notice the similarity between the left and right sides of the main image above). **Secondary structure:** The curled (helical, cylindrical, spiral) ribbons indicate α-helices. Arrows with thickness show the direction and twist of β-strands from amino to the carboxyl end forming parallel β-sheets. Aside from the preceding, note the strands (like rope or spaghetti) which can be coils, loops or turns relatively high in glycine (the smallest amino acid) and proline (with its unique, cyclic secondary amine R group). **Tertiary structure:** The overall 3D shape (globular structure), which is central to the function of the protein, can be seen - in part - as the 'surface contour' of the actual structure (based on a space-filling model). The 3D structure of each of the 2 subunits contains eight α-helices on the outside and eight parallel β-strands on the inside. In the illustration, the ribbon backbone of each subunit is colored in blue to red from N-terminus to C-terminus. **Quaternary structure:** 2 subunits (left-right in the image) forming a dimer held together by various noncovalent bonds.

The protein above is the enzyme (= catalyst) triose phosphate isomerase (TPI). TPI catalyzes a reaction in glycolysis (= the lysis or breakdown of glucose to produce energy, BIO 4.5) thus is essential for efficient energy production. TPI is a highly efficient enzyme, performing the reaction billions of times faster than it would occur naturally in solution. The reaction is so efficient that it is said to be 'catalytically perfect': It is limited only by the rate the substrate can diffuse into and out of the enzyme's active site.

Over the chapters to come, we will be exploring many of the specific functions of proteins. Suffice to say for now that proteins are involved in virtually every process within cells. Proteins include the enzymes that accelerate the rate of (= catalyze) biochemical reactions. Proteins also have both structural (cytoskeleton) and mechanical functions (muscle: actin and myosin). Other protein functions include cell signaling, immune responses, cell adhesion and the cell cycle. Proteins are a necessary component of our diets since we cannot synthesize all the amino acids we need and thus must obtain essential amino acids from food.

During the GAMSAT, it is likely that you will read passages that describe various methods in which proteins can be purified from other cellular components. These techniques include ultracentrifugation, precipitation, electrophoresis and chromatography (ORG 13). Protein structure and function are often studied using immunohistochemistry (BIO 1.5.1), nuclear magnetic resonance (NMR) and mass spectrometry (ORG 14).

12.3 Carbohydrates

12.3.1 Description and Nomenclature

In general, the names of most carbohydrates are recognizable by an -ose suffix. Carbohydrates are sugars and their derivatives. Formally they are 'carbon hydrates,' that is, they have the general formula $C_m(H_2O)_n$. Usually they are defined as polyhydroxy aldehydes and ketones, or substances that hydrolyze to yield polyhydroxy aldehydes and ketones. The basic units of carbohydrates are monosaccharides (sugars; see table in ORG 12.1.3).

There are two ways to classify sugars. One way is to classify the molecule based on the type of carbonyl group it contains: one with an aldehyde carbonyl group is an *aldose*; one with a ketone carbonyl group is a *ketose*. The second method of classification depends on the number of carbons in the molecule: those with 6 carbons are hexoses, with 5 carbons are pentoses, with 4 carbons are tetroses, and with 3 carbons are trioses. Sugars may exist in either the ring form, as hemiacetals, or in the straight chain form, as polyhydroxy aldehydes. *Pyranoses* are 6 carbon sugars in the ring form; *furanoses* are 5 carbon sugars in the ring form.

In the ring form, there is the possibility of α or β *anomers*. Anomers occur when 2 cyclic forms of the molecule differ in conformation only at the hemiacetal carbon (carbon 1). Generally, pyranoses take the 'chair' conformation, as it is very stable, with all (usually) hydroxyl groups at the equatorial position. *Epimers* are diastereomers that differ in the configuration of only one stereogenic center. For carbohydrates, epimers are 2 monosaccharides which differ in the conformation of one OH group.

To determine the number of possible optical isomers, one need only know the number of asymmetric carbons, normally 4 for hexoses and 3 for pentoses, designated as n. The number of optical isomers is then 2^n, where n is the number of asymmetric carbons (ORG 2.2.2).

Most of the naturally occurring aldoses have the D-configuration. Thus they have the same *relative* configuration as D-glyceraldehyde. The configuration (D or L) is *only* assigned to the highest numbered chiral carbon. The *absolute* configuration can be determined for any chiral carbon. For example, assessing its image (end of ORG 12.3.1), it can be determined that the absolute configuration of D-glyceraldehyde is the R-configuration.

Most carbohydrates contain one or more chiral carbons. For this reason, they are optically active. The names and structures of some common sugars are shown in Figure IV.A.1.5.

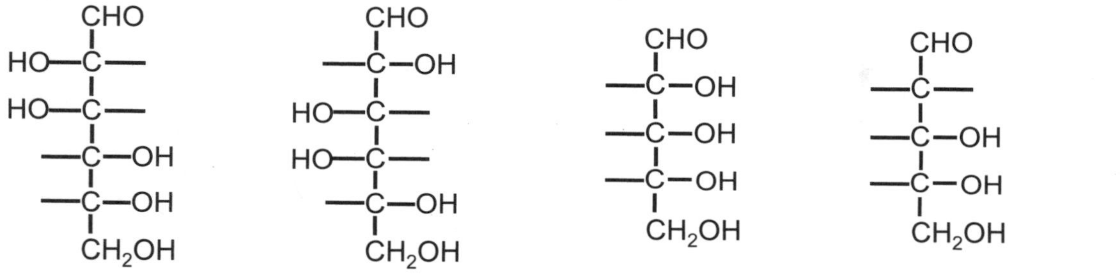

D - Mannose (C_2 epimer of glucose)

D - Galactose (C_4 epimer of glucose)

D - Ribose (in RNA)

2 - Deoxy - D - ribose (in DNA)

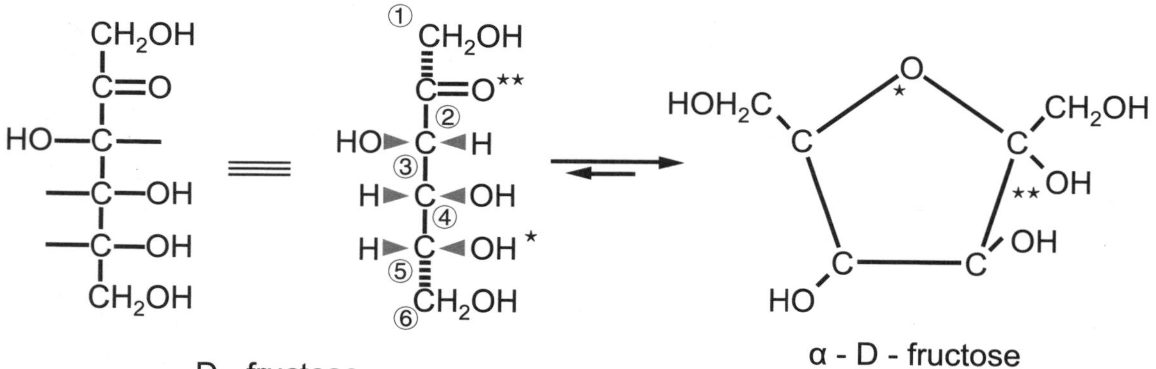

D - fructose (1,3,4,5,6-pentahydroxy-2-hexanone)

α - D - fructose (a furanose)

Figure IV.A.1.5 Part I: Names and configurations of common sugars. Notice that the asterix * and ** allow you to follow a specific oxygen atom. Following atoms through a reaction is a common GAMSAT-type question. An asterix, a prime symbol (') or a labelled isotope (ORG 1.6) are examples of techniques that may be used to identify the atom that you must follow. See ORG 12.3.2 for another example of a sugar 'folding' to become cyclic. Note that 3 parallel lines (≡) indicates: 'identical to'.

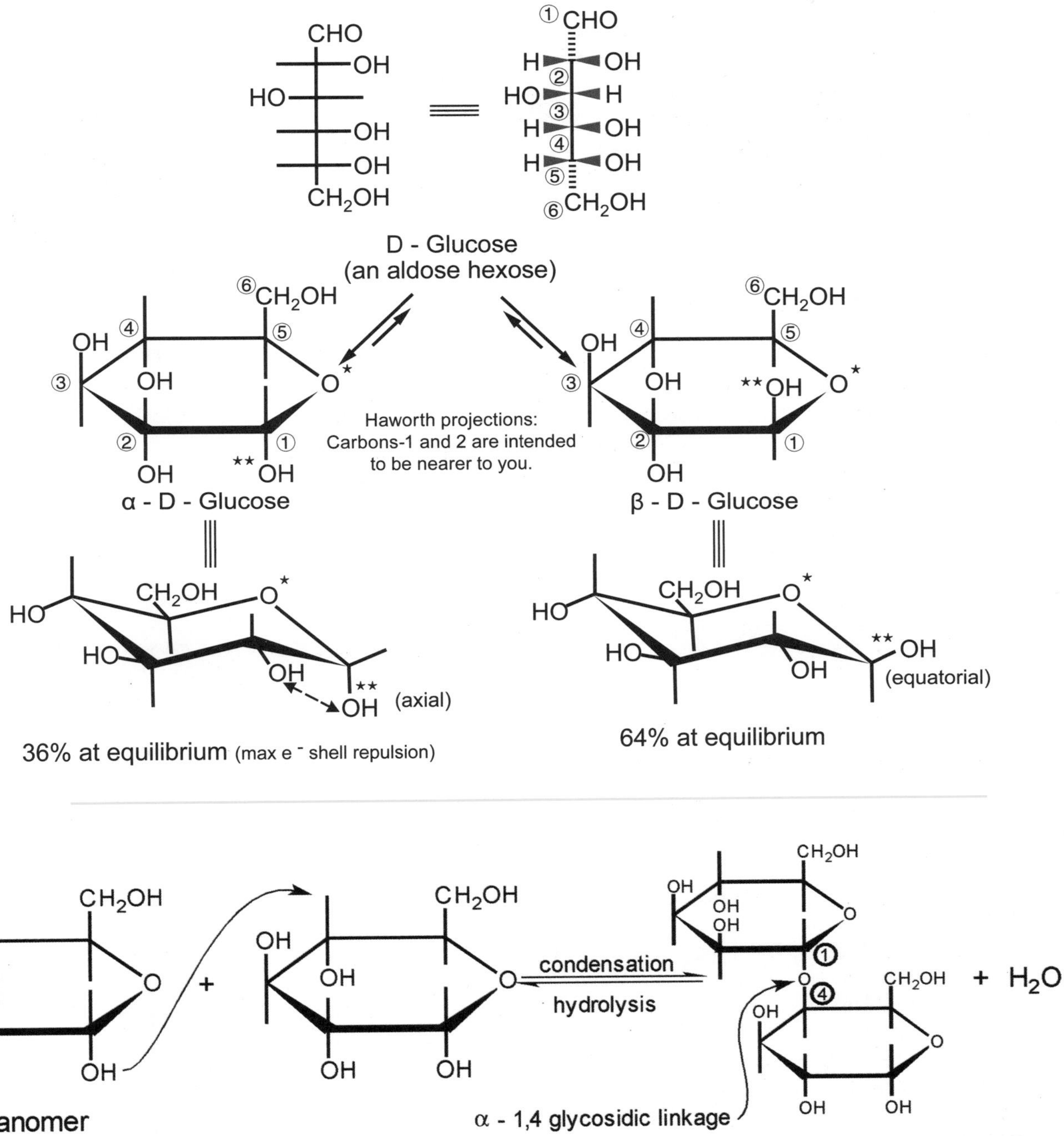
CHO
OH
HO
OH
OH
CH_2OH
D - Glucose
(an aldose hexose)
α - D - Glucose
β - D - Glucose
Haworth projections:
Carbons-1 and 2 are intended
to be nearer to you.
(axial)
(equatorial)
36% at equilibrium (max e⁻ shell repulsion)
64% at equilibrium
α anomer
condensation
hydrolysis
α - 1,4 glycosidic linkage
+ H_2O

Figure IV.A.1.5 Part II: Names, structures and configurations of common sugars. Though not by convention, H belongs to the end of all empty bonds in the diagrams above. Note the following equivalent positions for substituents with glucose as an example: Right on Fischer = down on Hawthorne = alpha configuration = axial in the chair confirmation, and the opposite if on the left for a Fischer projection. The images below the yellow line show 2 monosaccharides engaging in a glycosidic bond (= linkage) to form a disaccharide (ORG 12.3.2, ORG 12.1.3 table).

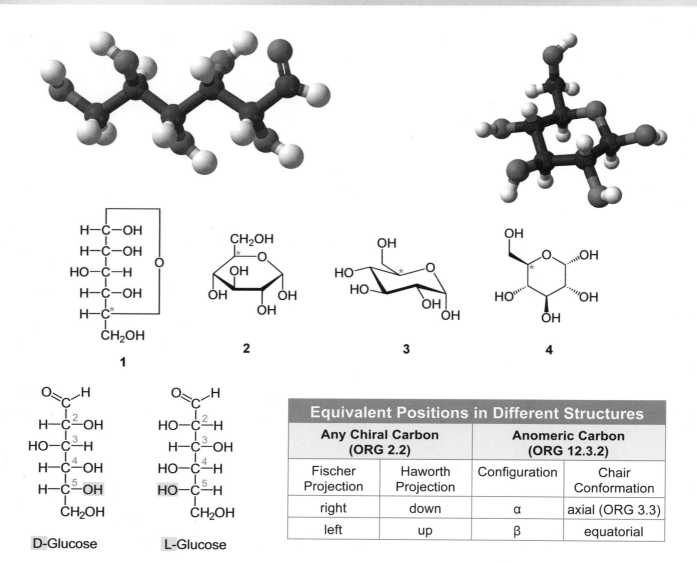

Equivalent Positions in Different Structures			
Any Chiral Carbon (ORG 2.2)		**Anomeric Carbon** (ORG 12.3.2)	
Fischer Projection	Haworth Projection	Configuration	Chair Conformation
right	down	α	axial (ORG 3.3)
left	up	β	equatorial

Figure IV.A.1.5 Part III: Different ways to represent glucose, $C_6H_{12}O_6$. The 3D ball-and-stick model of the linear D-glucose and the cyclic β-D-glucose (or more specifically, β-D-glucopyranose), are presented at the top where carbon is grey, oxygen is red, and hydrogen is white. The images in the middle row reflect 4 different illustrations of α-D-glucopyranose (1 carbon atom is followed with a red asterisk but, ideally, you should be able to identify the presence and orientation of each atom across all images on this page): (1) modified Fischer projection; (2) Haworth projection; (3) chair conformation; (4) structural formula showing the absolute stereochemistry. In the last row of images, notice that the carbon atoms numbered 2, 3, 4, and 5 each have four different groups attached to them, whereas carbon atoms 1 and 6 have only three different substituents each. Thus, there are four chiral carbon atoms in the linear form of glucose. The bottommost chiral carbon determines D/L: if OH is on the right, D; if on the left, L. The ring-closing reaction makes carbon C-1 chiral since its four bonds lead to -H, to -OH, to carbon C-2, and to the ring oxygen. Note that the information in the table above is not meant to be memorized. It should make sense after observing the structures carefully. Spatial reasoning with carbohydrates is helpful for ACER's Red Booklet 'GAMSAT Practice Questions', Unit 8, Q19-21. Go to the Video section of gamsat-prep.com for the worked solutions.

In the diagram that follows, you will notice a Fischer projection to the far left (*see* ORG 2.3.1). You will also find Fischer projections throughout this chapter since they are a common way to represent carbohydrates. Recall that the horizontal lines in a Fischer projection are projecting towards you.

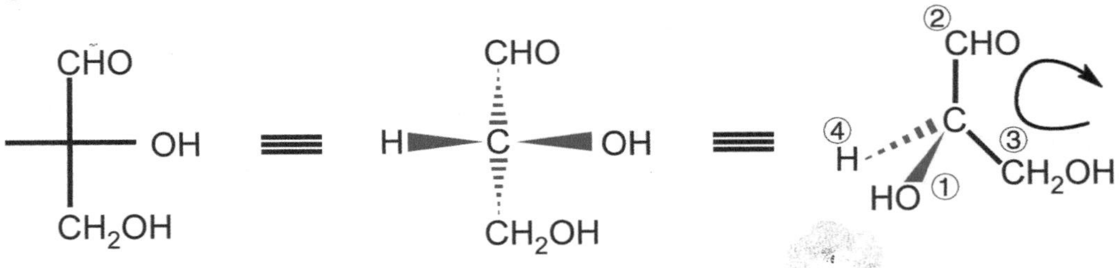

Fischer projection and 3D representation of D-glyceraldehyde, R-glyceraldehyde (*see* ORG 2.1, 2.2, 2.3 for rules). D/L can be determined by looking ONLY at the bottommost asymmetric (chiral) carbon in a Fischer projection: if the OH is on the right, D, on the left, L. Consider looking at the various sugars in this chapter to confirm that they are indeed in the D-configuration. For amino acids (see ORG 12.1), the amino group determines D/L.

12.3.2 Important Reactions of Carbohydrates

Hemiacetal Reaction

Monosaccharides can undergo an intra-molecular nucleophilic addition reaction to form cyclic hemiacetals (see ORG 7.2.2). For example, the hydroxyl group on C4 of ribose attacks the aldehyde group on C1 forming a five-membered ring called furanose.

Diastereomers differing in configuration at this newly formed chiral carbon (= C1 where the straight chain monosaccharide converted into a furanose or pyranose) are known as anomers. This newly chiral carbon, which used to be a carbonyl carbon, is known as the

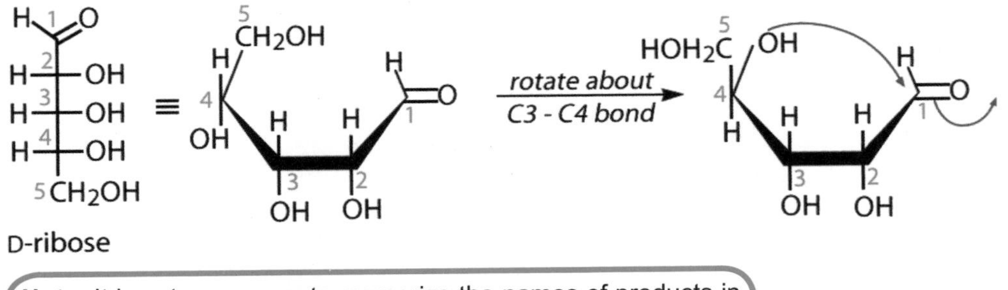

D-**ribose**

Note: It is not necessary to memorize the names of products in this section (ORG 12.3.2). However, you are expected to be able to follow what goes where. Of course during the real exam, there will be no color and it is unlikely that they would politely number all the carbons to make it easy for you to follow! ACER practice materials have several passages based on carbohydrates including the "Red" booklet ('GAMSAT Practice Questions') current units 8 (Q19-21) and 14 (Q36-39).

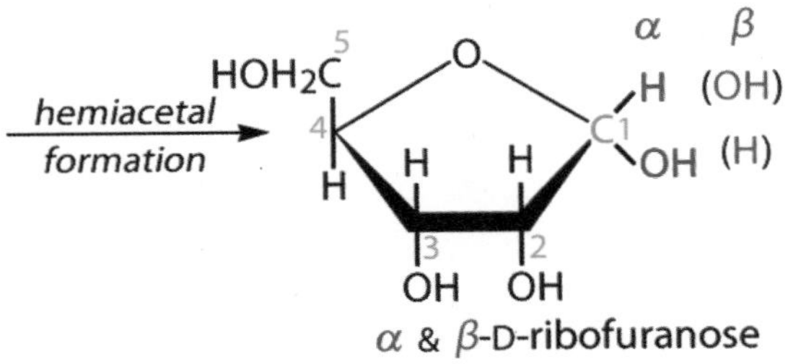

α & β-D-**ribofuranose**

anomeric center. When the OH group on C1 is *trans* to CH₂OH, it is called an α anomer. When the OH group on C1 is *cis* to CH₂OH, it is called a β anomer. {Mnemonic: α looks like an underwater fish, so the OH is down; β = birds so the OH is up.}

Mutarotation is the formation of both anomers into an equilibrium mixture when exposed to water.

Glycosidic Bonds

A disaccharide is a molecule made up of two monosaccharides, joined by a *glycosidic bond* between the hemiacetal carbon of one molecule, and the hydroxyl group of another. The glycosidic bond forms an α-1,4-glycosidic linkage if the reactant is an α anomer. A β-1,4-glycosidic linkage is formed if the reactant is a β anomer. When the bond is formed, one molecule of water is released (condensation). In order to break the bond, water must be added (hydrolysis). See Fig. IV.A.1.5 Part II for the preceding reactions and see below for common disaccharides and their component monomers.

- Sucrose (common sugar or table sugar) = glucose + fructose
- Lactose (milk sugar) = glucose + galactose
- Maltose (α-1,4 bond) = glucose + glucose
- Cellobiose (β-1,4 bond) = glucose + glucose

Ester Formation

Monosaccharides react with acid chloride or acid anhydride to form esters (see ORG 9.4, 9.4.1). All of the hydroxyl groups can be esterified.

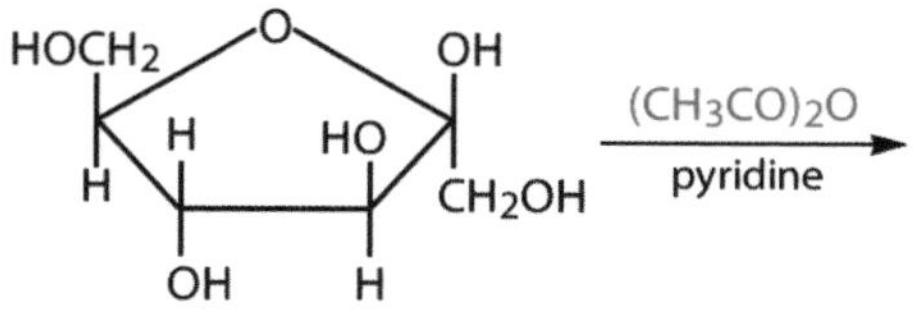

β-D-fructofuranose

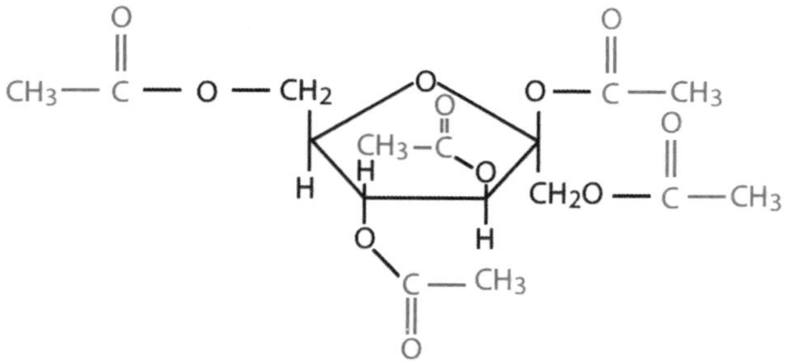

penta-O-acetyl-β-D-fructofuranoside

Ether Formation

Monosaccharides react with alkyl halide in the presence of silver oxide to form ethers. All of the hydroxyl groups are converted to -OR groups.

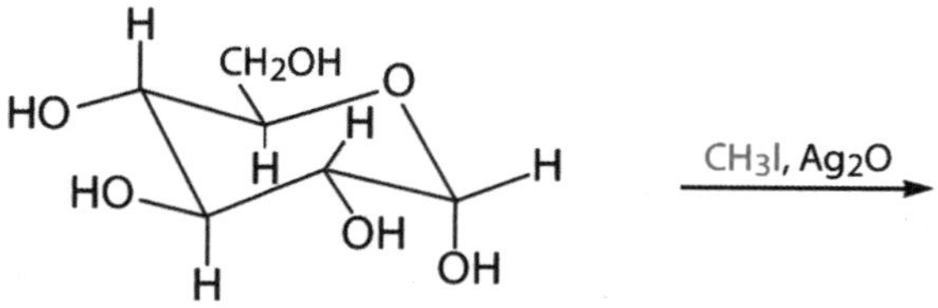

α-D-glucopyranose

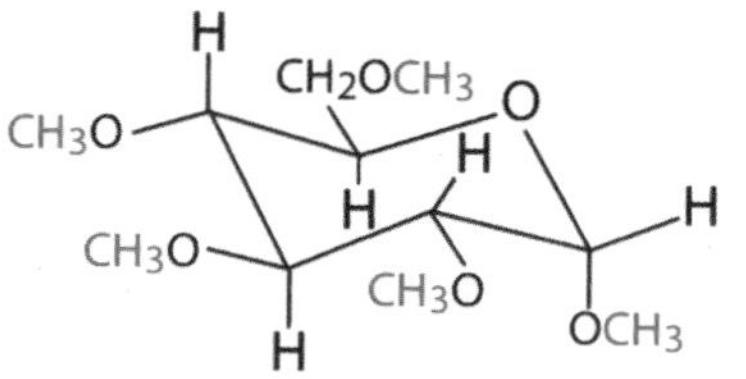

methyl-2, 3, 4, 6-tetra-O-methyl-α-D-glucopyranoside

ORGANIC CHEMISTRY

Ether synthesis can also proceed using alcohols (see ORG 10.1):

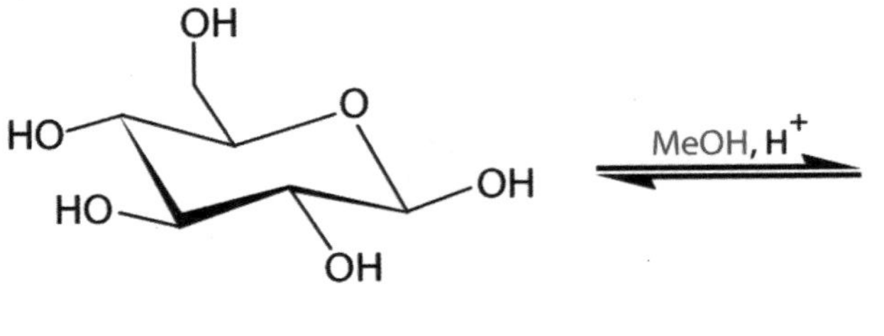

β-D-glucopyranose

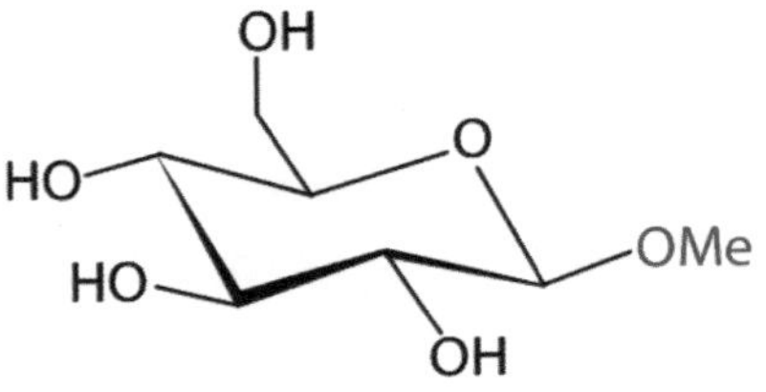

methyl-β-D-glucopyranoside

Reduction Reaction

Open chain monosaccharides are present in equilibrium between the aldehyde/ketone and the hemiacetal form. Therefore, monosaccharides can be reduced by $NaBH_4$ to form polyalcohols (see ORG 6.2.2).

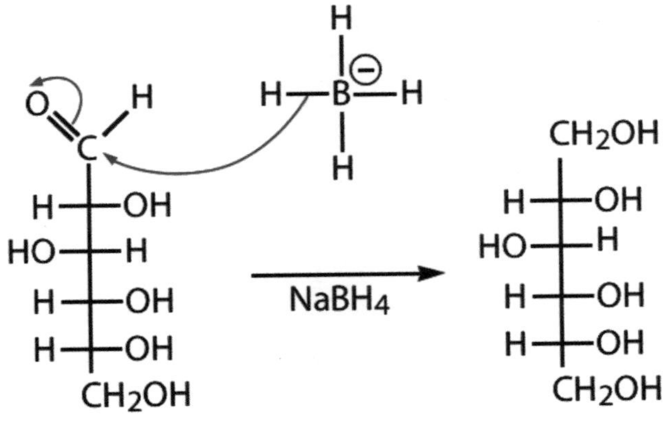

D-glucose   D-sorbitol

Oxidation Reaction

Again, the hemiacetal ring form is in equilibrium with the open chain aldehyde/ketone form. Aldoses can be oxidized by the Tollens' reagent $[Ag(NH_3)_2]^+$, Fehling's reagent $(Cu^{2+}/Na_2C_4H_4O_6)$, and Benedict's reagent $(Cu^{2+}/Na_3C_6H_5O_7)$ to yield carboxylic acids. If the Tollens' reagent is used, metallic silver is produced as a shiny mirror. If the Fehling's reagent or Benedict's reagent is used, cuprous oxide is produced as a reddish precipitate.

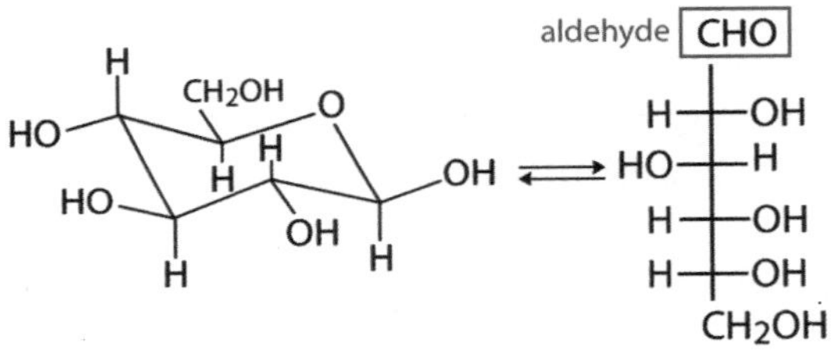

β-D-glucose   open-chain form

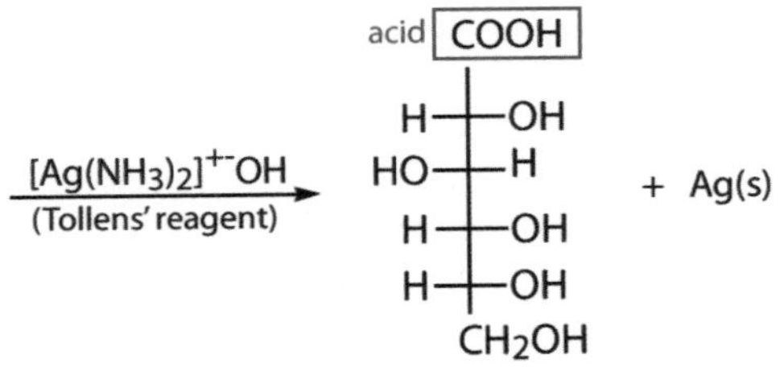

D-gluconic acid (+ side products)

Redox (reduction/oxidation) and chain extending GAMSAT questions are usually easily solved by noticing that the stereochemistry of groups that are not directly involved in the reaction remain unchanged. For these substituents, the integrity of the Fischer projection is intact (in other words, whether the H or OH is on the left or right of the structure does not change).

When aldoses are treated with bromine water, the aldehyde is oxidized to a carboxylic acid group, resulting in a product known as an *aldonic acid*:

CHO
H——OH
HO——H
H——OH
H——OH
CH$_2$OH   + Br$_2$ $\xrightarrow[\substack{CaCO_3 \\ pH\,5\text{-}6}]{H_2O}$

CO$_2$H
H——OH
HO——H
H——OH
H——OH
CH$_2$OH   + HBr

D-glucose
(an aldose)

D-Gluconic acid
(an aldonic acid)

Aldoses treated with dilute nitric acid will have both the primary alcohol and aldehyde groups oxidize to carboxylic acid groups, resulting in a product known as an *aldaric acid*:

CHO
H——OH
HO——H
H——OH
H——OH
CH$_2$OH $\xrightarrow[55\text{-}60^\circ]{HNO_3}$

CO$_2$H
H——OH
HO——H
H——OH
H——OH
CO$_2$H

D-glucose
(an aldose)

D-Glucaric acid
(an aldaric acid)

Reducing Sugars/Non-reducing Sugars

All aldoses are reducing sugars because they contain an aldehyde carbonyl group. Some ketoses such as fructose are reducing sugars as well. They can be isomerized through keto-enol tautomerization (ORG 7.1) to an aldose, which can be oxidized normally. Glycosides are non-reducing sugars because the acetal group cannot be hydrolyzed to aldehydes. Thus they do not react with the Tollens' reagent.

12.3.3 Polysaccharides

Polymers of many monosaccharides are called <u>polysaccharides</u>. As in disaccharides, they are joined by glycosidic linkages. They may be straight chains, or branched chains. Some common polysaccharides are:

- Starch (plant energy storage)
- Cellulose (plant structural component)
- Glycocalyx (associated with the plasma membrane)
- Glycogen (animal energy storage in the form of glucose)

- Chitin (structural component found in shells or arthropods)

Carbohydrates are the most abundant organic constituents of plants. They are the source of chemical energy in living organisms, and, in plants, they are used in making the support structures. Cellulose consists of $\beta(1\rightarrow4)$ linked D-glucose. Starch and glycogen are mostly $\alpha(1\rightarrow4)$ glycosidic linkages of D-glucose.

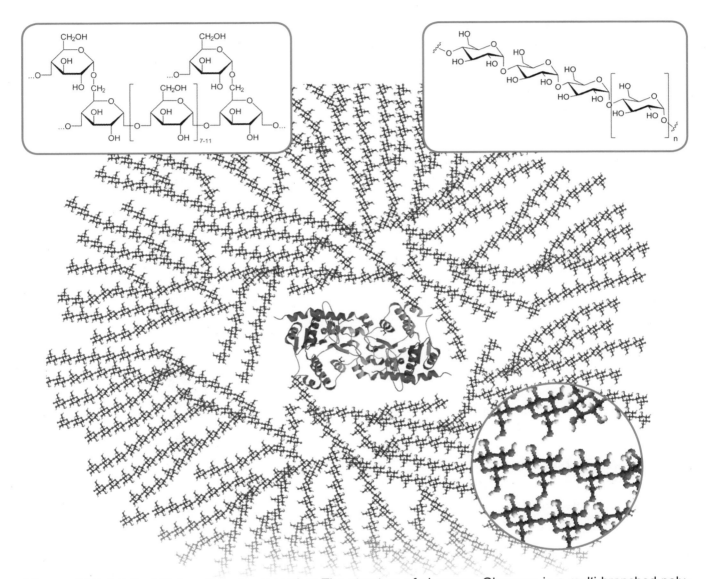

Figure IV.A.1.5 Part III A matter of perspective: The structure of glycogen. Glycogen is a multi-branched poly-saccharide of glucose that serves as a form of energy storage in animals, fungi, and bacteria. As humans, it is our main form of energy storage and it is found primarily in liver and muscle. In the left inset, repeating subunits (residues) of glucose can be seen as a linear chain (horizontally, note that '7-11' signifies 7 to 11 subunits) linked together by α(1→4) glycosidic bonds (that identical bonding pattern is also symbolized in the top right inset from a different perspective; you should be able to match carbons from the 2 insets). Branches are linked to the horizontal chains by α(1→6) glycosidic bonds (indicated by the vertical bonding in the left inset). The main image above is glycogen in a schematic 2D cross-sectional view (like cutting an orange down the middle and looking at one cut half). In the center is the core protein glycogenin and it is surrounded by chains and branches of glucose residues. The protein displays structural elements that we have already discussed (ORG 12.2.2), and the ball-and-stick model of the glucose polymer (magnified in the lower, right inset) follows the same rules we have seen before: O: red, C: grey, H: white. The entire globular granule may contain around 30 000 glucose residues. Central image: Häggström, Mikael (2014).

12.4 Lipids

Lipids are a class of organic molecules containing many different types of substances, such as fatty acids, fats, waxes, triacyl glycerols, terpenes and steroids. The main biological functions of lipids include storing energy, signaling and acting as structural components of cell membranes (BIO 1.1).

Lipids are relatively water-insoluble or nonpolar (e.g. oil floating on water). Lipids can be linear or cyclic in structure, and may or may not be aromatic. In general, the bulk of lipid structure is nonpolar or hydrophobic; however, often a part of their structure is polar or hydrophilic. This duality makes many lipids amphipathic (= amphiphilic) molecules (having both hydrophobic and hydrophilic portions).

Triacyl glycerols are oils and fats of either animal or plant origin. In general, fats are solid at room temperature, and oils are liquid at room temperature.

Triacyl glycerols are also commonly referred to as triglycerides (= triacylglycerides) and are, by definition, fatty acid triesters of the trihydroxy alcohol glycerol. {Note: "triacyl" refers to the presence of 3 acyl substituents (RCO-, ORG 9.1)}

$$\boxed{\text{Glycerol} + 3 \text{ Fatty acids} = \text{Triglyceride}}$$

The general structure of a triacyl glycerol is:

$$CH_2O-\overset{\displaystyle O}{\overset{\displaystyle \|}{C}}-R$$
$$CHO-\overset{\displaystyle O}{\overset{\displaystyle \|}{C}}-R'$$
$$CH_2O-\overset{\displaystyle O}{\overset{\displaystyle \|}{C}}-R''$$

The R groups may be the same or different, and are usually long chain alkyl groups. Upon hydrolysis of a triacyl glycerol, the products are three fatty acids and glycerol. The fatty acids may be saturated (= no multiple bonds, i.e. *palmitic acid*) or unsaturated (= containing double or triple bonds, i.e. *oleic acid*). Unsaturated fatty acids are usually in the cis configuration. Saturated fatty acids have a higher melting point than unsaturated fatty acids. Some common fatty acids are:

$$CH_3(CH_2)_{14}COOH$$
palmitic acid

$$CH_3(CH_2)_{16}COOH$$
stearic acid

$$CH_3(CH_2)_7 \underset{H}{\overset{}{C}} = \underset{H}{\overset{}{C}} (CH_2)_7CO_2H$$
oleic acid

The water is blue, the hydrophilic layer is purple and the hydrophobic area is orange-yellow.

$$\boxed{\begin{array}{c}\text{General formula for a saturated fatty acid} = \\ C_nH_{2n+1}COOH = CH_3(CH_2)_nCOOH\end{array}}$$

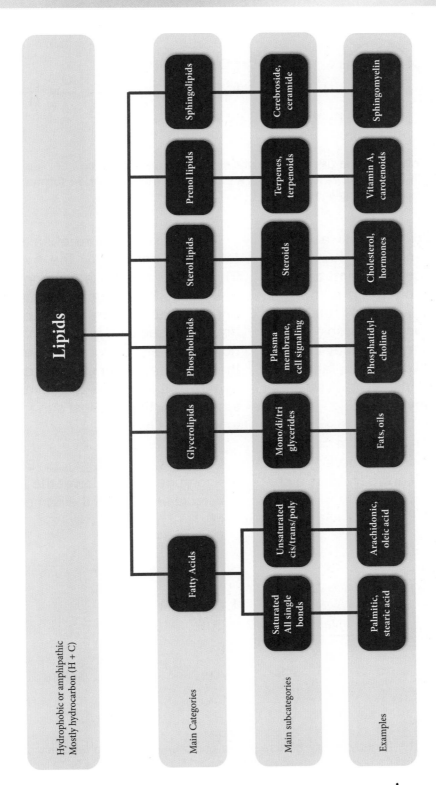

Figure A.1.6: Categories of lipids. Note that prostaglandins - hormone-like lipids - are derived from unsaturated fatty acids. Waxes, like oils and fats, are lipids. However, oils and fats are esters of glycerol whereas waxes may contain esters of carboxylic acids and long chain alcohols or combinations of long chain fatty acids and primary alcohols. The chart above is meant to give you an overview of lipids but please do not memorize.

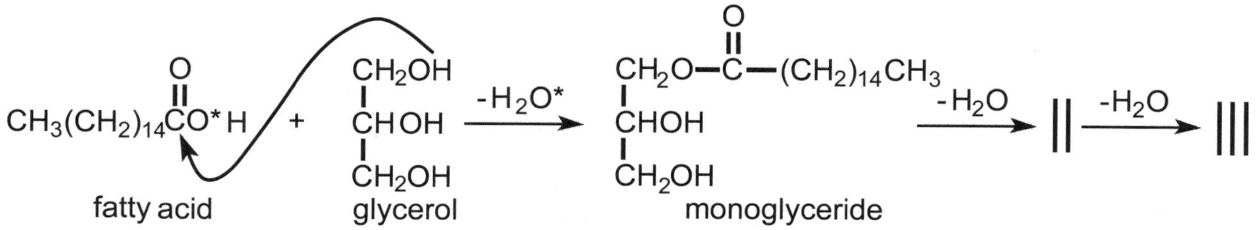

Biosynthesis of fats and oils. Fats and oils are a special class of esters (i.e. mono-, di-, and triglycerides). Fatty acids (= long chain carboxylic acids) may be added to the monoglyceride formed in the above reaction, forming diglycerides, and triglycerides.

"Essential" fatty acids are fatty acids that humans - and other animals - must ingest because the body requires them but cannot synthesize them. Only two are known in humans: alpha-linolenic acid and linoleic acid. Because they have multiple double bonds that begin near the methyl end, they are both known as polyunsaturated omega fatty acids (omega is the last letter of the Greek alphabet thus signifying the methyl end).

A wax is a simple ester of a fatty acid and a long-chain alcohol. In general, a wax, such as the wax in your ears, serves as a protective coating.

Soap is a mixture of salts of long chain fatty acids formed by the hydrolysis of fat. This process is called saponification. Soap possesses both a nonpolar hydrocarbon tail and a polar carboxylate head. When soaps are dispersed in aqueous solution, the long nonpolar tails are inside the sphere while the polar heads face outward. Recall that a sphere is the shape that minimizes surface tension (i.e. the smallest surface area relative to volume; CHM 4.2).

Soaps are surfactants (BIO 12.3). They are compounds that lower the surface tension of a liquid because of their amphipathic nature

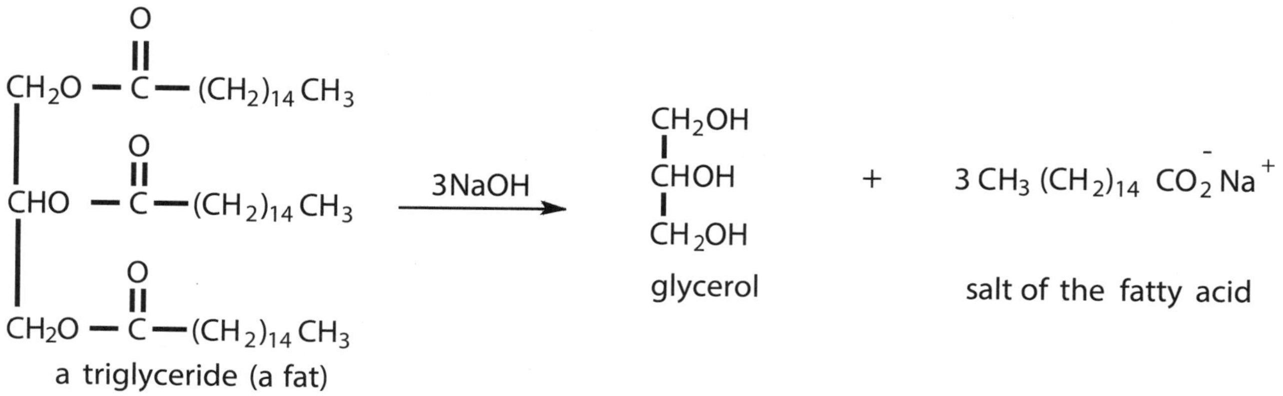

Saponification. Fats may be hydrolyzed by a base to the components glycerol and the salt of the fatty acids. The salts of long chain carboxylic acids are called soaps. Thus this process is called saponification.

(i.e. they contain both hydrophobic tails and hydrophilic heads; see BIO 1.1).

Of course, the cellular membrane is a lipid bilayer (Biology Chapter 1). The polar heads of the lipids align towards the aqueous environment, while the hydrophobic tails minimize their contact with water and tend to cluster together. Depending on the concentration of the lipid, this interaction may result in micelles (spherical), liposomes (spherical) or other lipid bilayers.

Micelles are closed lipid monolayers with a fatty acid core and polar surface. The main function of bile (BIO 9.4.1) is to facilitate the formation of micelles, which promotes the processing or emulsification of dietary fat and fat-soluble vitamins.

Liposomes are composed of a lipid bilayer separating an aqueous internal compartment from the bulk aqueous environment. Liposomes can be used as a vehicle for the administration of nutrients or pharmaceutical drugs.

The dual solubility nature of soap is why it removes oil or grease from skin or clothes. The soap forms a micelle that surrounds the nonpolar oil/grease in the nonpolar 'center' of the micelle. The polar end of the soap micelle is soluble in water, allowing the oil/grease to be removed during rinsing.

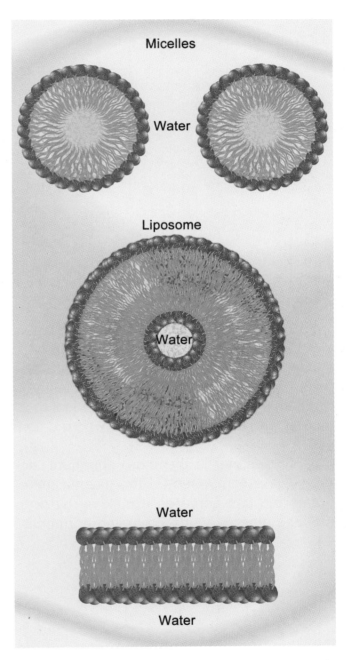

Figure IV.A.1.7. Amphipathic molecules arranged in micelles, a liposome and a bilipid layer.

12.4.1 Steroids

Steroids are a class of lipids which are derivatives of the basic ring structure:

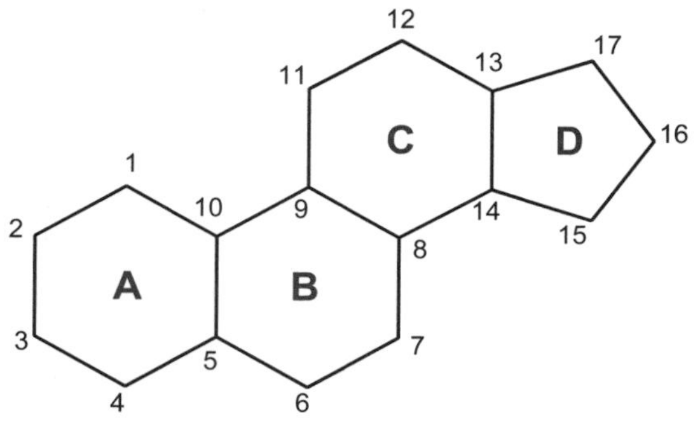

The IUPAC-recommended ring-lettering and the carbon atoms are numbered as shown. Many important substances are steroids, some examples include: cholesterol, D vitamins, bile acids, adrenocortical hormones, and male and female sex hormones.

Cholesterol is the most abundant steroid. It is a component of the plasma membrane and can serve as a building block to produce other steroids (including hormones)

and related molecules. Cholesterol comes from the diet, but may be synthesized by the liver if necessary.

The rate-limiting step in the production of steroids (= *steroidogenesis*) in humans is the conversion of cholesterol to pregnenolone, which is in the same family as progesterone. This occurs inside mitochondria (BIO 1.2.1) and serves as the precursor for all human steroids.

Since such a significant portion of a steroid contains hydrocarbons, which are hydrophobic, steroids can dissolve through the hydrophobic interior of a cell's plasma membrane (BIO 1.1, 6.3). Furthermore, steroid hormones contain polar side groups which allow the hormone to easily dissolve in water. Thus steroid hormones are well designed to be transported through the vascular space, to cross the plasma membranes of cells, and to have an effect either in the cell's cytosol or, as is usually the case, in the nucleus.

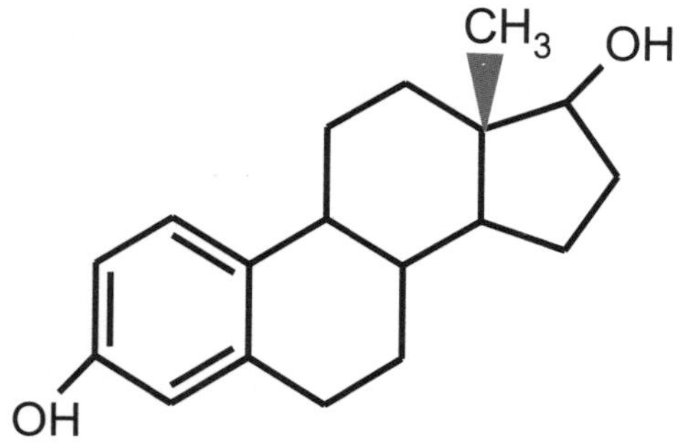

Estradiol
(an estrogen)

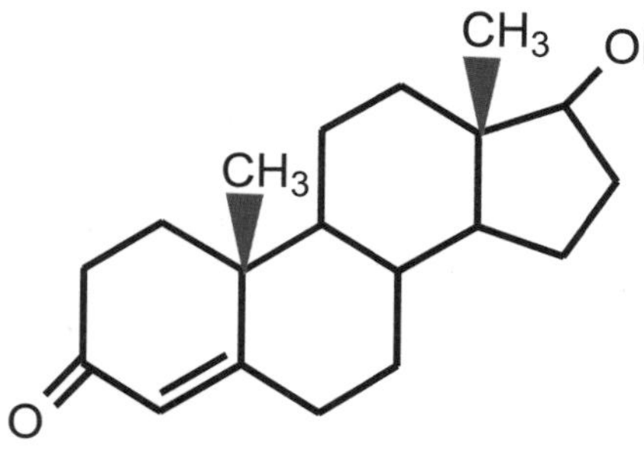

Testosterone
(an androgen)

Most biological molecules are proteins, followed by lipids. In fact, proteins and lipids by far dominate the biological molecules in the human body. Lipoproteins comprise unique biochemical assemblies (aggregates) containing both proteins and lipids, bound to the proteins, which allow lipids to move through hydrophilic intracellular and extracellular spaces. Many enzymes, structural proteins, transporters, antigens and toxins are lipoproteins.

Using electrophoresis and ultracentrifugation, lipoproteins can be classified according to size and density. Lipoproteins are larger and less dense when the fat to protein ratio is increased. Thus there are four major classes of plasma lipoproteins which enable lipids to be carried in the blood stream: (1) chylomicrons carry triglycerides from the intestines to the liver, to skeletal muscle, and to adipose tissue ("body fat"); (2) very low-density lipoproteins (VLDL) carry liver-synthesized triglycerides to adipose tissue; (3) low-density lipoproteins (LDL = "bad cholesterol") carry cholesterol from the liver to cells of the body; (4) and high-density lipoproteins (HDL = "good cholesterol") collect cholesterol from the body's tissues, and take it back to the liver.

12.5 Phosphorous in Biological Molecules

Phosphorous is an essential component of various biological molecules including adenosine triphosphate (ATP), phospholipids in cell membranes (BIO 1.1), and the nucleic acids which form DNA (BIO 1.2.2). Phosphorus can also form phosphoric acid (key to making the phosphate buffer in plasma; CHM 6.8), and several phosphate esters.

A phospholipid is produced from three ester linkages to glycerol. Phosphoric acid is ester linked to the terminal hydroxyl group and two fatty acids are ester linked to the two remaining hydroxyl groups of glycerol (see *Biology Section 1.1 for a schematic view of a phospholipid*).

ATP is critical for life since it transports chemical energy within cells. The components ADP and P_i (= *inorganic phosphate*) combine using the energy generated from a coupled reaction to produce ATP. We will be discussing

phosphoric acid   phosphate esters

the bioenergetics of ATP in Biology Chapter 4. The linkage between the phosphate groups are via *anhydride bonds*:

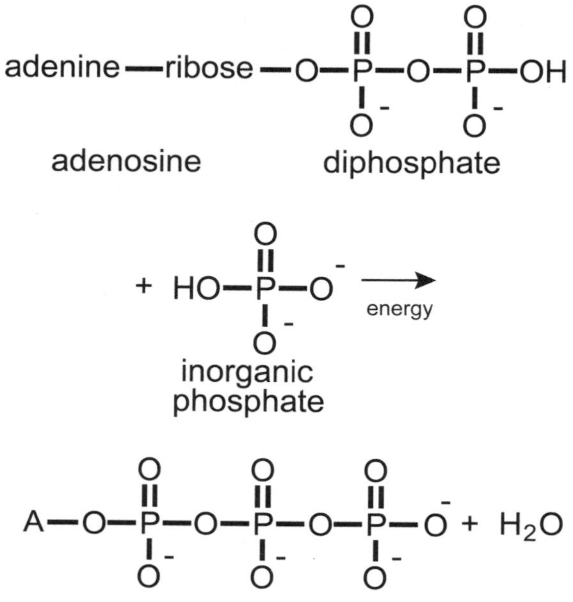

adenine —— ribose —— O —— $\overset{\displaystyle O}{\underset{\displaystyle O^-}{P}}$ —— O —— $\overset{\displaystyle O}{\underset{\displaystyle O^-}{P}}$ —— OH

adenosine   diphosphate

+ HO —— $\overset{\displaystyle O}{\underset{\displaystyle O^-}{P}}$ —— O$^-$ $\xrightarrow{\text{energy}}$

inorganic
phosphate

A —— O —— $\overset{\displaystyle O}{\underset{\displaystyle O^-}{P}}$ —— O —— $\overset{\displaystyle O}{\underset{\displaystyle O^-}{P}}$ —— O —— $\overset{\displaystyle O}{\underset{\displaystyle O^-}{P}}$ —— O$^-$ + H_2O

adenosine triphosphate, $C_{10}H_{16}N_5O_{13}P_3$

ATP is shown as shorthand above, the skeletal structure below, and the ball-and-stick model at the top of the next column with P: orange, O: red, N: blue, C: grey, H: white.

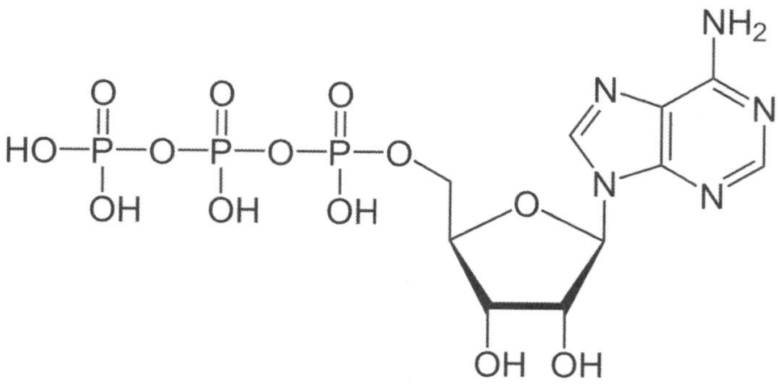

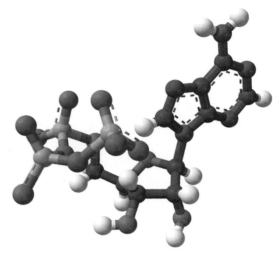

In DNA, the phosphate groups engage in two ester linkages creating phosphodiester bonds. It is the 5' phosphorylated position of one pentose ring which is linked to the 3' position of the next pentose ring (*see* BIO 1.2.2):

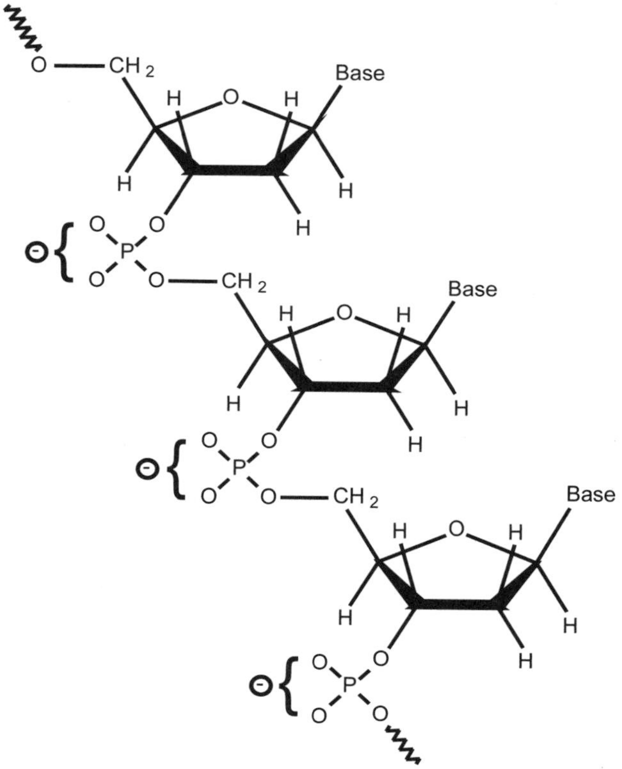

SEPARATIONS AND PURIFICATIONS
Chapter 13

Memorize	Understand	Not Required*
efinitions of the major techniques teractions between organic molecules	* Different phases in the various techniques * How to improve separation, purification * How to avoid overheating (distillation)	* Knowledge beyond introductory-level (first year uni.) course * Electrolysis, affinity purification * Refining, smelting

GAMSAT-Prep.com

Introduction ▮▮▮▮

Separation techniques are used to transform a mixture of substances into two or more distinct products. The separated products may be different in chemical properties or some physical property (i.e. size). Purification in organic chemistry is the physical separation of a chemical substance of interest from foreign or contaminating substances.

Additional Resources

Free Online Q & A

Flashcards

Special Guest

THE BIOLOGICAL SCIENCES ORG-157

* The real GAMSAT may have advanced level information presented (ie. in a passage) but previous knowledge of said information is not required to answer the questions that would follow. Practice ACER and GS practice GAMSATs can help you clarify this point.

Extraction is the process by which a solute is transferred (*extracted*) from one solvent and placed in another. This procedure is possible if the two solvents used cannot mix (= *immiscible*) and if the solute is more soluble in the solvent used for the extraction.

For example, consider the extraction of solute A which is dissolved in solvent X. We choose solvent Y for the extraction since solute A is highly soluble in it and because solvent Y is immiscible with solvent X. We now add solvent Y to the solution involving solute A and solvent X. The container is agitated. Solute A begins to dissolve in the solvent where it is most soluble, solvent Y. The container is left to stand, thus the two immiscible solvents separate. The phase containing solute A can now be removed.

In practice, solvent Y would be chosen such that it would be sufficiently easy to evaporate (= *volatile*) after the extraction so solute A can be easily recovered. Also, it is more efficient to perform several extractions using a small amount of solvent each time, rather than one extraction using a large amount of solvent.

The main purpose of filtration is to isolate a solid from a liquid. There are two basic types of filtration: gravity filtration and vacuum filtration. In gravity filtration the solution containing the substance of interest is poured through the filter paper with the solvent's own weight responsible for pulling it through. This is often done using a hot solvent to ensure that the product remains dissolved (e.g. filter used in a coffee maker).

In vacuum filtration the solvent is forced through the filter with a vacuum on the other side. This is helpful when it is necessary to isolate large quantities of solid.

Sublimation is a process which goes from a heated solid directly into the gas phase without passing through the intermediate liquid phase (CHM 4.3.1). Low pressure reduces the temperature required for sublimation. The substance in question is heated and then condensed on a cool surface ('cold finger'), leaving the non-volatile impurities behind.

Centrifugation is a separation process that involves the use of centrifugal forces for the sedimentation of mixtures. Particles settle at different rates depending on their size, viscosity, density and shape. Compounds of greater mass and density settle toward the bottom while compounds of lighter mass and density remain on top. This process is most useful in separating polymeric materials such as biological macromolecules.

Distillation is the process by which compounds are separated based on differences in boiling points. Compounds with a lower boiling point are preferably vaporized, condensed on a water cooler, and are separated from compounds with higher boiling points.

For instance, a classic example of simple distillation is the separation of salt from water. The solution is heated. Water will boil and vaporize at a far lower temperature than salt. Hence the water boils away leaving salt behind. Water vapor can now be condensed into pure liquid water (distilled water).

ORGANIC CHEMISTRY

As long as one compound is more volatile (CHM 4.4.2, 5.1.1), the distillation process is quite simple. If the difference between the two boiling points is low, it will be more difficult to separate the compounds by this method. Here are 3 standard ways to separate compounds using distillation:

1. **Simple distillation** is used to separate liquids whose boiling points differ by at least 25 °C and that boil below 150 °C. The composition of the distillate depends on the composition of the vapors at a given temperature and pressure.

2. **Vacuum distillation** is used to separate liquids whose boiling points differ by at least 25 °C and that boil above 150 °C. The vacuum environment prevents compounds from decomposition because the low pressure reduces the temperature required for distillation.

3. **Fractional distillation** is used to separate liquids whose boiling points are less than 25 °C apart. The repeated vaporization-condensation cycle of compounds will eventually yield vapors that contain a greater and greater proportion of the lower boiling point component.

The fractional distillation apparatus can include a column filled with glass beads which is placed between the distillation flask and the condenser (*see* Figure IV.B.13.0). The glass beads increase the surface area over which the less volatile compound can condense and drip back down to the distillation (distilling) flask below. The more volatile compound boils away and condenses. Thus the two compounds are separated.

The efficiency of the distillation process in producing a pure product is improved by repeating the distillation process, increasing the length of the fractionating column and avoiding overheating. Overheating may destroy the pure compounds or increase the percent of impurities. Some of the methods which are used to prevent overheating include boiling slowly, the use of boiling chips (= *ebulliator*, which makes bubbles) and the use of a vacuum which decreases the vapor pressure and thus the boiling point.

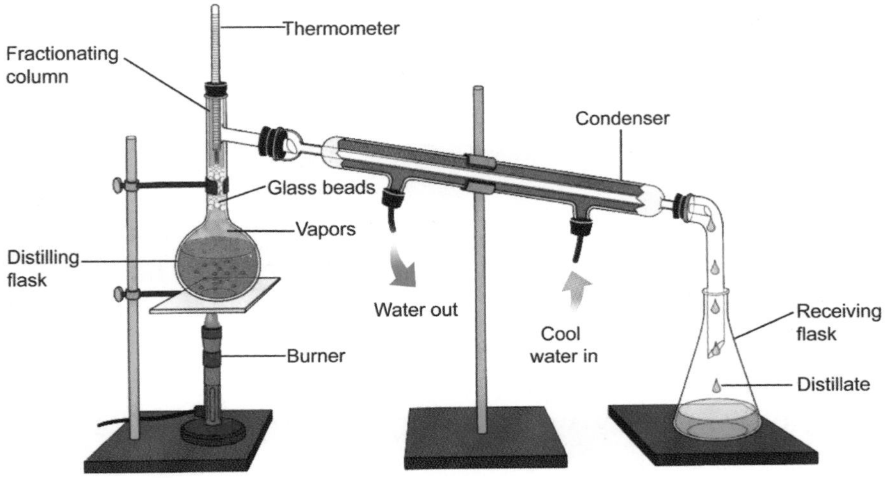

Figure IV.B.13.0: Standard fractional distillation apparatus heated with a Bunsen burner.

THE BIOLOGICAL SCIENCES ORG-159

13.2 Chromatography

Chromatography is the separation of a mixture of compounds by their distribution between two phases: one stationary and one moving. The mobile phase is run through the stationary phase. Different substances distribute themselves according to their relative affinities for the two phases. This causes the separation of the different compounds. Molecules are separated based on differences in polarity and molecular weight.

13.2.1 Gas-Liquid Chromatography

In gas-liquid chromatography, the *stationary phase* is a liquid absorbed to an inert solid. The liquid can be polyethylene glycol, squalene, or others, depending on the polarity of the substances being separated.

The mobile phase is a gas (i.e. He, N_2) which is unreactive both to the stationary phase and to the substances being separated. The sample being analyzed can be injected in the direction of gas flow into one end of a column packed with the stationary phase. As the sample migrates through the column, certain molecules will move faster than others. As mentioned the separation of the different types of molecules is dependent on size (*molecular weight*) and charge (*polarity*). Once the molecules reach the end of the column, special detectors signal their arrival.

13.2.2 Thin-Layer Chromatography

Thin-layer chromatography (TLC) is a solid-liquid technique, based on adsorptivity and solubility. The *stationary phase* is a type of finely divided polar material, usually silica gel or alumina, which is thinly coated onto a glass plate.

A mixture of compounds is placed on the stationary phase, either a thin layer of silica gel or alumina on a glass sheet. Silica gel is a very polar and hydrophobic substance. The mobile phase is usually of low polarity and moves by capillary action. Therefore, if silica gel is used as the stationary phase, nonpolar compounds move quickly while polar compounds have a strong interaction with the gel and are stuck tightly to it. In reverse-phase chromatography, the stationary phase is nonpolar and the mobile phase is polar; as a result, polar compounds move quickly while nonpolar compounds stick more tightly to the adsorbant.

There are several types of interactions that may occur between the organic molecules in the sample and the silica gel, in order from weakest to strongest (see CHM 3.4, 4.2):

- Van der Waals force (nonpolar molecules)
- Dipole-dipole interaction (polar molecules)
- Hydrogen bonding (hydroxylic compounds)
- Coordination (Lewis bases)

Molecules with functional groups with the greatest polarity will bind more strongly to the stationary phase and thus will not rise as high on the glass plate.

Organic molecules will also interact with the *mobile phase* (= a solvent), or *eluent* used in the process. The more polar the solvent, the more easily it will dissolve polar molecules. The mobile phase usually contains organic solvents like ethanol, benzene, chloroform, acetone, etc.

As a result of the interactions of the organic molecules with the stationary and moving phases, for any adsorbed compound there is a dynamic distribution equilibrium between these phases. The different molecules will rise to different heights on the plate. Their presence can be detected using special stains (i.e. pH indicators, $KMnO_4$) or uv light (*if the compound can fluoresce; PHY 12.6*).

Each spot from the TLC can be objectively assessed by its retardation factor (R_f) which is equal to the distance migrated over the total distance covered by the solvent.

$$R_f = \frac{\text{(distance traveled by sample)}}{\text{(distance traveled by solvent)}}$$

An Rf value will always be in the range 0 to 1; if the substance moves, it can only move in the direction of the solvent flow, and cannot move faster than the solvent. For example, if a particular substance in an unknown mixture travels 3.0 cm and the solvent front travels 5.0 cm, the retardation factor would be 3.0/5.0 = 0.6.

In the following diagram, what formula would you use to describe the Rf values of the blue and yellow dots, respectively?

Figure IV.B.13.1 Part I:
Thin-layer Chromatography.

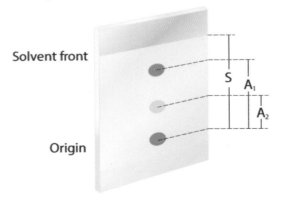

Figure IV.B.13.1 Part II: Calculating the retardation factor from the point of origin of the mixed sample from Fig. IV.B.13.1 Part I.

Using the equation provided, the retardation factors would be:

blue: $R_{f1} = A_1/S$; yellow: $R_{f2} = A_2/S$.

13.2.3 Paper chromatography: Conventional and 2D

Conventional, paper chromatography has been largely replaced by TLC. The former's mobile phase is a solution that travels up the stationary phase, due to capillary action. The mobile phase is generally an alcohol-solvent mixture, while the stationary phase is a strip of chromatography paper, also called a *chromatogram*.

A more useful variant is 2D (two-dimensional) chromatography. This technique involves using two solvents and rotating the paper 90° between trials. This is more helpful for separating complex mixtures of compounds having similar polarity, for example, amino acids. {Note: 2D chromatography is used in ACER's Green Booklet 'GAMSAT Practice Test', Unit 7, Q20-26. Go to the Video section of gamsat-prep.com for the worked solutions.}

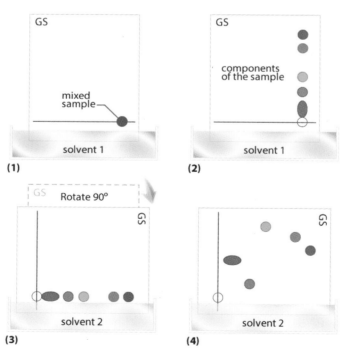

Figure IV.B.13.2: 2D Paper Chromatography. Regarding the 4 images: **(1)** a mixed sample can be placed in either the bottom left or bottom right corner to begin; **(2)** the initial chromatogram (conventional, 1D) is complete; **(3)** rotation into a different solvent; **(4)** the final 2D chromatogram is complete. R_f values can be calculated for each solvent separately and can provide unique information for each of the components of the sample in the illustration.

13.2.4 Column Chromatography

Column chromatography is similar to TLC in principle; however, column chromatography uses silica gel or alumina as an adsorbent in the form of a column rather than TLC which uses paper in a layer-like form. The solvent and compounds move down the column (by gravity) allowing much more separation. The solvent drips out into a waiting flask where fractions containing bands corresponding to the different compounds are collected. After the solvent has evaporated, the compounds can then be isolated. Often the desired compounds are proteins or nucleic acids for which several techniques exist:

1. Ion exchange chromatography – Beads coated with charged substances are placed in the column so that they will attract compounds with an opposing charge.
2. Size exclusion chromatography – The column contains beads with tiny pores which allow small substances to enter, leaving larger molecules to pass through the column faster.
3. Affinity chromatography – Columns are customized to bind a substance of interest (e.g. a receptor or antibody) which allows it to bind very tightly.

13.3 Gel Electrophoresis

Gel electrophoresis is an important method to separate biological macromolecules (i.e. protein and DNA) based on size and charge of molecules. Molecules are made to move through a gel which is placed in an electrophoresis chamber. When an electric current is applied, molecules move at different velocities. These molecules will move towards either the cathode or anode depending on their size and charge (**an**ions move towards the **an**ode while **cat**ions move towards the **cat**hode). The migration velocity is proportional to the net charge on the molecule and inversely proportional to a coefficient dependent on the size of the molecule. Highly charged, small molecules will move the quickest with size being the most important factor.

There are three main types of electrophoresis:

1. Agarose gel electrophoresis – Used to separate pieces of negatively charged nucleic acids based on their size.

2. SDS-polyacrylamide gel electrophoresis (SDS-PAGE) – Separates proteins on the basis of mass and not charge. The SDS (sodium dodecyl sulfate) binds to

proteins and creates a large negative charge such that the only variable effecting their movement is the frictional coefficient which is solely dependent on mass.

3. Isoelectric focusing – The isoelectric point is the pH at which the net charge of a protein is zero (ORG 12.1.2). A mixture of proteins can be separated by placing them in an electric field with a pH gradient. The proteins will lose their charge and come to a stop when the pH is equal to their isoelectric point.

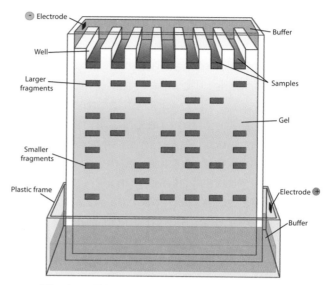

Figure IV.B.13.3: Gel Electrophoresis.

13.4 Recrystallization

Recrystallization is a useful purification technique. A solid organic compound with some impurity is dissolved in a hot solvent, and then the solvent is slowly cooled to allow the pure compound to reform or *recrystallize*, while leaving the impurities behind in the solvent. This is possible because the impurities do not normally fit within the crystal structure of the compound.

In choosing a solvent, solubility data (e.g. K_{sp} at various temperatures, etc.) regarding both the compound to be purified and the impurities should be known. The data should be analyzed such that the solvent would:

• have the capability to dissolve alot of the compound (to be purified) at or near the boiling point of the solvent, while being able to dissolve little of the compound at room temperature. As well, the impurities should be soluble in the cold solvent.

• have a low boiling point, so as to be easily removed from the solid in a drying process.

• not react with the solid.

Go online to GAMSAT-prep.com for chapter review Q&A and forum.

SPECTROSCOPY

Chapter 14

Memorize	Understand	Not Required*
•thing	* Basic theory: IR spect., NMR, mass spectrometry * Very basic spectrum (graph) analysis	* Knowledge beyond introductory-level (first year uni.) course * Interpreting the results of spectroscopy without first being given clues or being reminded of the rules.

GAMSAT-Prep.com

Introduction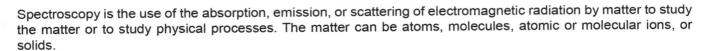

Spectroscopy is the use of the absorption, emission, or scattering of electromagnetic radiation by matter to study the matter or to study physical processes. The matter can be atoms, molecules, atomic or molecular ions, or solids.

Consider the hundreds of molecules and dozens of functional groups that we have already seen in this textbook. Spectroscopy can provide evidence for which atoms compose those molecules, and how those atoms are arranged in those molecules.

Additional Resources

Free Online Q & A

GAMSAT-prep.com Videos

Flashcards

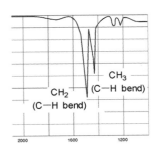

Special Guest

14.1 IR Spectroscopy

In an <u>infrared spectrometer</u>, a beam of infrared (IR) radiation is passed through a sample. The spectrometer will then analyze the amount of radiation transmitted (= *% transmittance*) through the sample as the incident radiation is varied. Ultimately, a plot results as a graph showing the transmittance or absorption (*the inverse of transmittance*) versus the frequency or wavelength of the incident radiation or the wavenumber (= the reciprocal of the wavelength). IR spectroscopy is best used for the identification of functional groups.

The location of an IR absorption band (*or peak*) can be specified in *frequency units* by its wavenumber, measured in cm^{-1}. As the wave number decreases, the wavelength increases, thus the energy decreases (this can be determined using two physics equations which we have already seen, PHY 7.1.2, 9.2.4: $v = \lambda f$ and $E = hf$). A schematic representation of the IR spectrum of octane is:

Electromagnetic radiation consists of discrete units of energy called *quanta* or *photons* (PHY 7.1.3, 11.1). All organic compounds are capable of absorbing many types of electromagnetic energy. The absorption of energy leads to an increase in the amplitude of intramolecular rotations and vibrations.

<u>Intramolecular rotations</u> are the rotations of a molecule about its center of gravity. The difference in rotational energy levels is inversely proportional to the moment of inertia of a molecule. Rotational energy is quantized and gives rise to absorption spectra in the <u>microwave region</u> of the electromagnetic spectrum.

<u>Intramolecular vibrations</u> are the bending and stretching motions of bonds within a molecule. The relative spacing between vibrational energy levels increases with the increasing strength of an intramolecular bond. Vibrational energy is quantized and gives rise

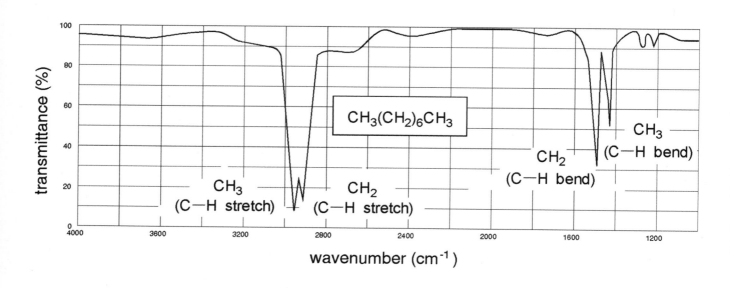

to absorption spectra in the <u>infrared region</u> of the electromagnetic spectrum.

Thus there are two types of bond vibration: stretching and bending. That is, after exposure to the IR radiation the bonds stretch and bend (*or contract*) to a greater degree once energy is absorbed. In general, bending vibrations will occur at lower frequencies (higher wavelengths) than stretching vibrations of the same groups. So, as seen in the sample spectra for octane, each group will have two characteristic peaks, one due to stretching, and one due to bending.

Different functional groups will have transmittances at characteristic wave numbers, which is why IR spectroscopy is useful. Some examples (*approximate values*) of characteristic absorbances are shown in the table.

By looking at the characteristic transmittances of a compound's spectrum, it is possible to identify the functional groups present in the molecule.

Symmetrical molecules or molecules composed of the same atoms do not exhibit

Group	Frequency Range (cm^{-1})
Alkyl (C–H)	2850 – 2960
Alkene (C=C)	1620 – 1680
Alkyne (C≡C)	2100 – 2260
Alcohol (O–H)	3200 – 3650
Benzene (Ar–H)	3030
Carbonyl (C=O)	1630 – 1780
▶ Aldehyde	1680 – 1750
▶ Ketone	1735 – 1750
▶ Carboxylic Acid	1710 – 1780
▶ Amide	1630 – 1690
Amine (N–H)	3300 – 3500
Nitriles (C≡N)	2220 – 2260

a change in dipole moment under IR radiation and thus absorptions do not show up in IR spectra.

Most introductory level courses require students to memorize at least the absorbances for, arguably, the two most important functional groups at the introductory level: carbonyl (around 1700) and alcohol (around 3300). Knowing these 2 benchmarks may be helpful but there is no evidence that even these 2 values are required knowledge for the GAMSAT.

14.2 Proton NMR Spectroscopy

<u>Nuclear Magnetic Resonance (NMR) spectroscopy</u> can be used to examine the environments of the hydrogen atoms in a molecule. In fact, using a (*proton*) NMR or

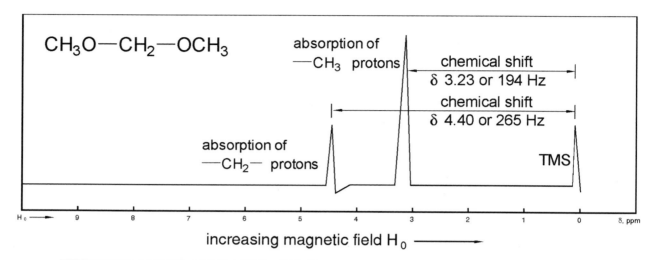

CH$_3$O—CH$_2$—OCH$_3$

absorption of
—CH$_3$ protons

chemical shift
δ 3.23 or 194 Hz

chemical shift
δ 4.40 or 265 Hz

absorption of
—CH$_2$— protons

TMS

H$_0$ ⟶   9   8   7   6   5   4   3   2   1   0 δ, ppm

increasing magnetic field H$_0$ ⟶

^{1}HNMR, one can determine both the number and types of hydrogens in a molecule. The basis of this stems from the magnetic properties of the hydrogen nucleus (proton). Similar to electrons, the hydrogen proton has a nuclear spin, able to take either of two values. These values are designated as +1/2 and −1/2. As a result of this spin, the nucleus will respond to a magnetic field by being oriented in the direction of the field. NMR spectrometers measure the absorption of energy by the hydrogen nuclei in an organic compound.

A schematic representation of an NMR spectrum, that of dimethoxymethane is shown in the diagram above.

The small peak at the right is that of TMS, tetramethylsilane, shown here:

CH$_3$
|
CH$_3$ — Si — CH$_3$
|
CH$_3$

This compound is added to the sample to be used as a reference, or standard. It is volatile, inert and absorbs at a higher field than most other organic chemicals.

The position of a peak relative to the standard is referred to as its *chemical shift*. Since NMR spectroscopy differentiates between types of protons, each type will have a different chemical shift, as shown. Protons in the same environment, like the three hydrogens in −CH$_3$, are called *equivalent protons*.

Dimethoxymethane is a symmetric molecule, thus the protons on either methyl group are equivalent. So, in the example above, the absorption of −CH$_3$ protons occurs at one peak (*a singlet*) 3.23 ppm downfield from TMS. In most organic molecules, the range of absorption will be in the 0−10 ppm (= *parts per million*) range.

The area under each peak is directly related to the number of protons contributing to it, and thus may be used to determine the

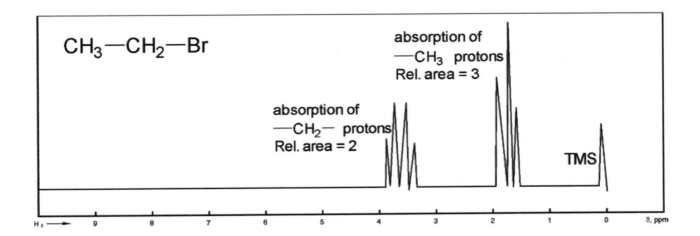

relative number of protons in the molecule. Accurate measurements of the area under the two peaks in the NMR of dimethoxymethane yield the ratio 1:3 which represents the relative number of hydrogens (i.e. $1:3 = 2:6$).

Let us now examine a schematic representation of the NMR spectrum of ethyl bromide shown in the diagram above.

It is obvious that something is different. Looking at the molecule, one can see that there are two different types of protons (*either far from Br or near to Br*). However, there are more than two signals in the spectrum. As such, the NMR signal for each group is said to be split. This type of splitting is called <u>spin-spin splitting</u> (= *spin-spin coupling*) and is caused by the presence of neighboring protons (*protons on an adjacent or vicinal carbon*) that are not equivalent to the proton in question. Note that protons that are farther than two carbons apart do not exhibit a coupling effect.

The number of lines in the splitting pattern for a given set of equivalent protons depends on the number of adjacent protons according to the following rule: if there are n equivalent protons in adjacent positions, a proton NMR signal is split into $n + 1$ lines.

Therefore the NMR spectrum for ethyl bromide can be interpreted thus:

- There are two groups of lines (*two split peaks*), therefore there are two different environments for protons.

- The relative areas under each peak is 2:3, which represents the relative number of hydrogens in the molecule.

- There are 4 splits (*quartet*) in the peak which has relatively two hydrogens ($-CH_2$). Thus the number of adjacent hydrogens is $n + 1 = 4$; therefore, there are 3 hydrogens on the carbon adjacent to $-CH_2$.

- There are 3 splits (*triplet*) in the peak which has relatively three hydrogens ($-CH_3$).

Thus the number of adjacent hydrogens is $n + 1 = 3$; therefore, there are 2 hydrogens on the carbon adjacent to $-CH_3$.

The relative areas under each peak may be expressed in three ways: (i) the information may simply be provided to you (*too easy!*); (ii) the integers may be written above the signals (= *integration integers*, i.e. 2, 3 in the previous example); or (iii) a step-like *integration curve* above the signals where the relative height of each step equals the relative number of hydrogens.

14.2.1 Deuterium Exchange

Deuterium, the hydrogen isotope ^2H or D (PHY 12.2), can be used to identify substances with readily exchangeable or acidic hydrogens. Rather than H_2O, D_2O is used to identify the chemical exchange:

$$ROH + DOD \rightleftharpoons ROD + HOD$$

The previous signal due to the acidic $-O\boxed{H}$ would now disappear. However, if excess D_2O is used, a signal as a result of HOD may be observed.

Solvents may also be involved in exchange phenomena. The solvents carbon tetrachloride (CCl_4) and deuteriochloroform ($CDCl_3$) can also engage in exchange-induced decoupling of acidic hydrogens (usu. in alcohols).

14.2.2 ^{13}C NMR

The main difference between the proton NMR and ^{13}C NMR is that most carbon 13 signals occur $0-200$ δ downfield from the carbon peak of TMS. There is also very little coupling between carbon atoms as only 1.1% of carbon atoms are ^{13}C. There is coupling between carbon atoms and their adjacent protons which are directly attached to them. This coupling of one bond is similar to the three bond coupling exhibited by proton NMR.

Signals will be split into a triplet with an area of 1:2:1 when a carbon atom is attached to two protons. Another unique feature of ^{13}C NMR is a phenomenon called spin decoupling where a spectrum of singlets can be recorded - each corresponding to a singular carbon atom. This allows one to accurately determine the number of different carbons in their respective chemical environments as well as the number of adjacent hydrogens (spin-coupled only).

To remind yourself of the isotopes deuterium and carbon-13, consider reviewing PHY 12.2.

14.3 Mass Spectrometry

Mass spectrometry (the former expression "mass spectroscopy" is discouraged), unlike other forms of NMR we have seen, destroys the sample during its analysis. The analysis is carried out using a beam of electrons which ionize the sample and a detector to measure the number of particles that are deflected due to the presence of a magnetic field. The reflected particle is usually an unstable species which decomposes rapidly into a cationic fragment and a radical fragment.

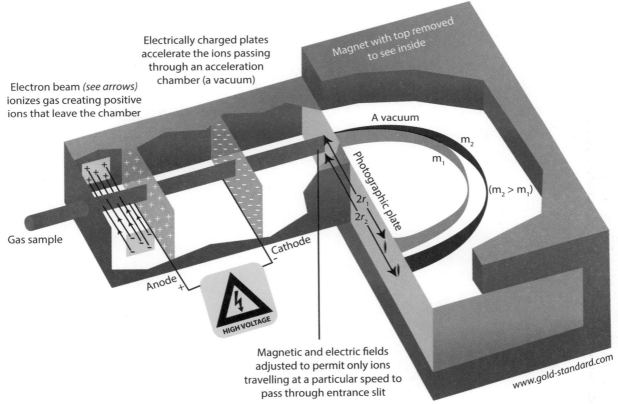

Electrically charged plates accelerate the ions passing through an acceleration chamber (a vacuum)

Electron beam *(see arrows)* ionizes gas creating positive ions that leave the chamber

Magnet with top removed to see inside

A vacuum

m_2

m_1

$(m_2 > m_1)$

Photographic plate

$2r_1$

$2r_2$

Gas sample

Cathode

Anode +

HIGH VOLTAGE

Magnetic and electric fields adjusted to permit only ions travelling at a particular speed to pass through entrance slit

www.gold-standard.com

Figure IV.B.14.1: Diagrammatic representation of a mass spectrometer. Electrons stream out (beam) from a heated cathode (negatively charged orange plate) towards the anode (positively charged orange plate) thus bombarding the gas creating cations. The cations are accelerated by a high voltage electric field. Magnetic and electric fields are adjusted to permit only ions traveling at a particular speed to pass through the entrance slit (i.e. to pass through the slit between the acceleration chamber and the magnetic chamber). Notice that the heavier particles are less deviated (more inertia; PHY 4.2) and thus have a larger diameter (= 2r) from the slit to the photographic plate. ACER's GAMSAT "Red" Booklet (GAMSAT Practice Questions, currently Unit 15) has a series of questions based on the mass spectrometer requiring an integration of concepts including electromagnetic fields (PHY 9.1, 9.2) and, because of the path of the ions in the magnetic chamber, circular motion (PHY 3.3). (adapted from chemeddl.org)

Since there are many ways in which the particle can decompose, a typical mass spectrum is often composed of numerous lines, with each one corresponding to a specific mass/charge ratio (m/z, sometimes symbolized as m/e or m/q). It is important to note that only cations are deflected by the magnetic field, thus only cations will appear on the spectrum which plots m/z (x-axis) vs. the abundance of the cationic fragments (y-axis). See the figure provided.

The tallest peak represents the most common ion and is also referred to as the base peak. The molecular weight can be obtained not from the base peak but rather from the peak with the highest m/z ratio, 129 in this case. This is called the parent ion peak and is designated by M+. By looking at the fragmentation pattern we can ascertain information regarding the compound's structure, something that IR spectroscopy is incapable of achieving. Note that if the charge on the ion has a magnitude of 1 (which is usually the case) then the magnitude on the x axis is simply the mass (i.e. m/z = m/1 = m = atomic mass units = amu; PHY 12.2, CHM 1.3).

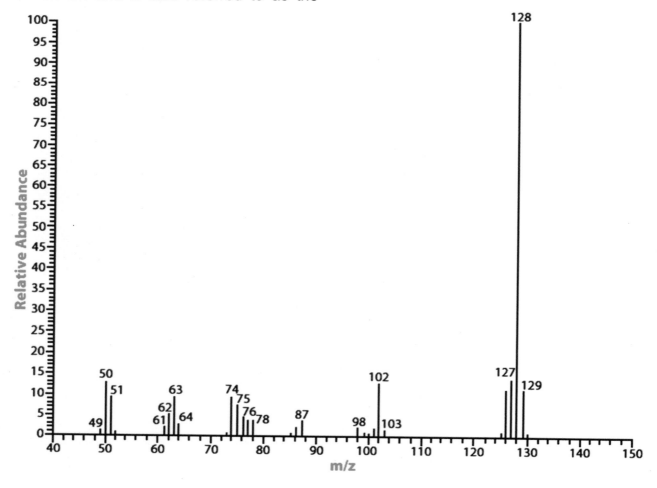

If IR, NMR or 'mass spec.' show up on the GAMSAT, you will be reminded of the rules to apply prior to the questions (i.e. there is no need to commit the rules to memory). Ideally, moving forward, you would not focus on re-reading chapters. Rather, the bulk of your GAMSAT Organic Chemistry preparation should include affirming basic nomenclature, geometric reasoning (following substituents, bonds, etc.), applying rules (Diels-Alder, Hückel's, separations, spectroscopy), reviewing Gold Notes, GAMSAT videos, and of course, 'practice, practice, practice'!

Go online to GAMSAT-prep.com for chapter review Q&A and forum.

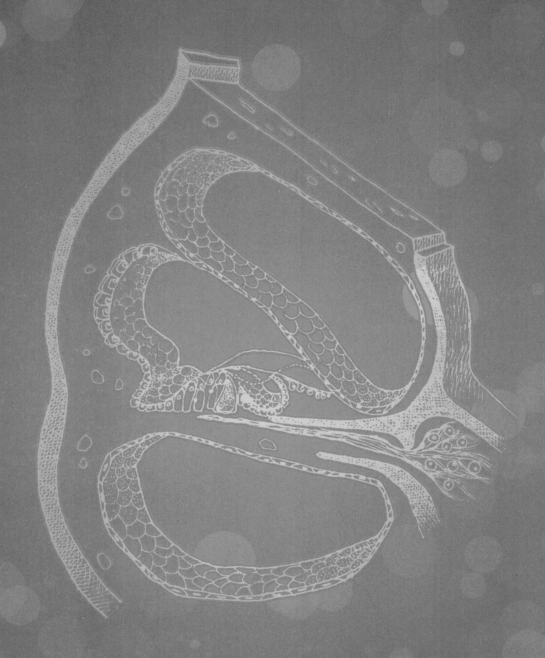

GAMSAT-Prep.com

BIOLOGY
PART IV.A: BIOLOGICAL SCIENCES

IMPORTANT: Before doing your science survey for the GAMSAT, be sure you have read the Preface, Introduction and Part II, Chapter 2. The beginning of each science chapter provides guidelines as to what you should Memorize, Understand and what is Not Required. These are guides to get you a top score without getting lost in the details. Our guides have been determined from an analysis of all ACER materials plus student surveys. Additionally, the original owner of this book gets a full year access to many online features described in the Preface and Introduction including an online Forum where each chapter can be discussed.

GENERALIZED EUKARYOTIC CELL
Chapter 1

Memorize	Understand	Not Required*
ructure/function: cell/components	* Intro level college info	* Advanced level college info
omponents and function: cytoskeleton	* Membrane transport	* Molecular bio., detailed mechanisms
NA structure and function	* Hyper/hypotonic solutions	* Plant cells, chloroplasts
ransmission of genetic information	* Saturation kinetics: graphs	* Experiments in genetics
itosis, events of the cell cycle	* Unique features of eukaryotes	* Specify polymerases or such details
	* Basics: Cell junctions, microscopy	

GAMSAT-Prep.com

Introduction

Cells are the basic organizational unit of living organisms. They are contained by a plasma membrane and/or cell wall. Eukaryotic cells (*eu* = true; *karyote* refers to nucleus) are cells with a true nucleus found in all multicellular and nonbacterial unicellular organisms including animal, fungal and plant cells. The nucleus contains genetic information, DNA, which can divide into 2 cells by mitosis.

Get ready to waste some time! Glad to have your attention! Our experience is that most students 'overstudy' Biology and underperform in Biology when they see the types of questions that are asked on the GAMSAT. Please do not get trapped in details. We'll guide you as much as we can but in the end, it's up to you: color-coded table of contents, yellow highlighter, underline, online practice questions, etc. For now, enjoy the story that you are expected to be exposed to for the GAMSAT, but generally the content will likely be more helpful to you in medical school.

Additional Resources

Free Online Q&A + Forum

Video: Online or DVD

Flashcards

Special Guest

* The real GAMSAT may have advanced level information presented (ie. in a passage) but previous knowledge of said information is not required to answer the questions that would follow. Practice ACER and GS practice GAMSATs can help you clarify this point.

1.1 Plasma Membrane: Structure and Functions

The plasma membrane is a semiperme-able barrier that defines the outer perimeter of the cell. It is composed of lipids (fats) and protein. The membrane is dynamic, selective, active, and fluid. It contains phospholipids which are amphipathic molecules. They are amphipathic because their tail end contains fatty acids which are insoluble in water (*hydrophobic*), the opposite end contains a charged phosphate head which is soluble in water (*hydrophilic*). The plasma membrane contains two layers or "leaflets" of phospholipids thus it is called a bilipid layer. Unlike eukaryotic membranes, prokaryotic membranes do not contain steroids such as cholesterol.

The Fluid Mosaic Model tells us that the hydrophilic heads project to the outside and the hydrophobic tails project towards the inside of the membrane. Further, these phospholipids are fluid - thus they move freely from place to place in the membrane. Fluidity of the membrane increases with increased temperature and with decreased saturation of fatty acyl tails. Fluidity of the membrane decreases with decreased temperature, increased saturation of fatty acyl tails and increase in the membrane's cholesterol content. The structures of these and other biological molecules were discussed in Organic Chemistry Chapter 12.

Glycolipids are limited to the extracellular aspect of the membrane or outer leaflet. The carbohydrate portion of glycolipids extends from the outer leaflet into the extracellular space and forms part of the glycocalyx. "Glycocalyx" is the sugar coat on the outer surface of the outer leaflet of plasma membrane. It consists of oligosaccharide linked to

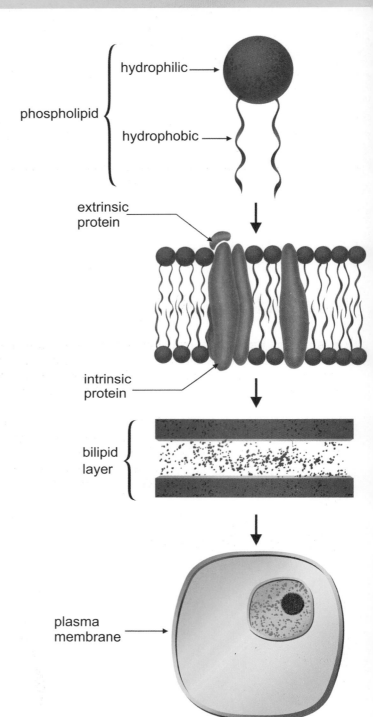

Figure IV.A.1.1: Structure of the plasma membrane. Note that: hydro = water, phobic = fearing, philic = loving

protein or lipids of the plasma membrane. The glycocalyx aids in attachment of some cells, facilitates cell recognition, helps bind antigen and antigen-presenting cells to the cell surface. Distributed throughout the membrane is a <u>mosaic</u> of proteins with limited mobility.

Proteins can be found associated with the outside of the membrane (<u>ex</u>trinsic or peripheral) or may be found spanning the membrane (<u>in</u>trinsic or integral). Integral proteins are dissolved in the lipid bilayer. Transmembrane proteins contain hydrophilic and hydrophobic amino acids and cross the entire plasma membrane. Most transmembrane proteins are glycoproteins. They usually function as membrane receptors and transport proteins.

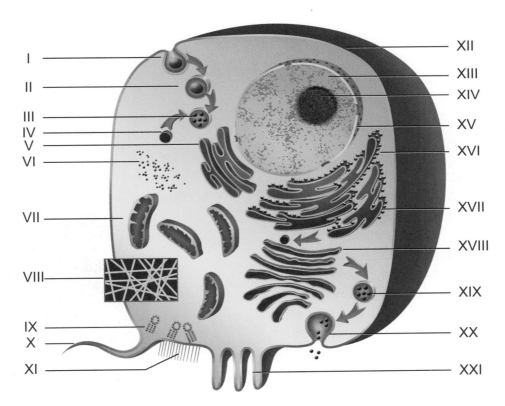

Figure IV.A.1.2: The generalized eukaryotic cell

I	endocytosis	VIII	cytoskeleton (further magnified)	XV	nuclear envelope
II	endocytotic vesicle	IX	basal body (magnified)	XVI	cytosol
III	secondary lysosome	X	flagellum	XVII	rough endoplasmic reticulum
IV	primary lysosome	XI	cilia	XVIII	Golgi apparatus
V	smooth endoplasmic reticulum	XII	plasma membrane	XIX	exocytotic vesicle
VI	free ribosomes	XIII	nucleus	XX	exocytosis
VII	mitochondrion	XIV	nucleolus	XXI	microvillus

Peripheral proteins do not extend into the lipid bilayer but can temporarily adhere to either side of the plasma membrane. They bond to phospholipid groups or integral proteins of the membrane via noncovalent interactions. Common functions include regulatory protein subunits of ion channels or transmembrane receptors, associations with the cytoskeleton and extracellular matrix, and as part of the intracellular second messenger system.

The plasma membrane is semipermeable. In other words, it is permeable to small uncharged substances which can freely diffuse across the membrane (i.e. O_2, CO_2, urea). The eukaryotic plasma membrane does not have pores, as pores would destroy the barrier function. On the other hand, it is relatively impermeable to charged or large substances which may require transport proteins to cross the membrane (i.e. ions, amino acids, sugars) or cannot cross the membrane at all (i.e. protein hormones, intracellular enzymes). Substances which can cross the membrane may do so by simple diffusion, carrier-mediated transport, or by endo/exocytosis.

1.1.1 Simple Diffusion

Simple diffusion is the spontaneous spreading of a substance going from an area of higher concentration to an area of lower concentration (i.e. a concentration gradient exists). Gradients can be of a chemical or electrical nature. A chemical gradient arises as a result of an unequal distribution of molecules and is often called a concentration gradient. In a chemical (or concentration) gradient, there is a higher concentration of molecules in one area than there is in another area, and molecules tend to diffuse from areas of high concentration to areas of lower concentration.

An electrical gradient arises as a result of an unequal distribution of charge. In an electrical gradient, there is a higher concentration of charged molecules in one area than in another (this is independent of

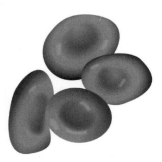

Figure IV.A.1.2.1a: Isotonic Solution.
The fluid bathing the cell (i.e. red blood cell or RBC in this case; see BIO 7.5) contains the same concentration of solute as the cell's inside or cytoplasm. When a cell is placed in an isotonic solution, the water diffuses into and out of the cell at the same rate.

the concentration of all molecules in the area). Molecules tend to move from areas of higher concentration of charge to areas of lower concentration of charge.

Figure IV.A.1.2.1b: Hypertonic Solution.
Here the fluid bathing the RBC contains a high concentration of solute relative to the cell's cytoplasm. When a cell is placed in a hypertonic solution, the water diffuses out of the cell, causing the cell to shrivel (crenation).

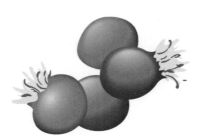

Figure IV.A.1.2.1c: Hypotonic Solution.
Here the surrounding fluid has a low concentration of solute relative to the cell's cytoplasm. When a cell is placed in a hypotonic solution, the water diffuses into the cell, causing the cell to swell and possibly rupture (lyse).

Osmosis is the diffusion of water across a semipermeable membrane moving from an area of higher water concentration (i.e. lower solute concentration = hypotonic) to an area of lower water concentration (i.e. higher solute concentration = hypertonic). The hydrostatic pressure needed to oppose the movement of water is called the osmotic pressure. Thus, an isotonic solution (i.e. the concentration of sol-ute on both sides of the membrane is equal), would have an osmotic pressure of zero.

{Memory guide: notice that the "O" in hyp-O-tonic looks like a swollen cell. The O is also a circle which makes you think of the word "around." So IF the environment is hypOtonic AROUND the cell, then fluid rushes in and the cell swells like the letter O}.

1.1.2 Carrier-mediated Transport

Amino acids, sugars and other solutes need to reversibly bind to proteins (carriers) in the membrane in order to get across. Because there are a limited amount of carriers, if the concentration of solute is too high, the carriers would be saturated, thus the rate of crossing the membrane would level off (= saturation kinetics).

The two carrier-mediated transport systems are:

(i) facilitated transport where the carrier helps a solute diffuse across a membrane it could not otherwise penetrate. Facilitated diffusion occurs via ion channels or carrier proteins and transport molecules down a concentration of electrochemical gradient. Ions and large molecules are therefore able to cross the membrane that would otherwise be impermeable to them.

ii) active transport where energy (i.e. ATP) is used to transport solutes against their

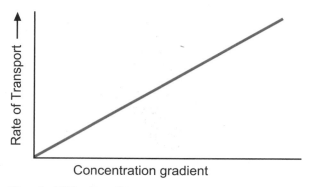

Simple Diffusion: the greater the concentration gradient, the greater the rate of transport across the plasma membrane.

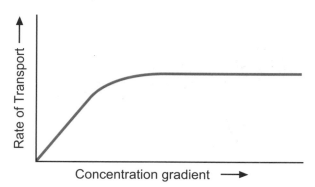

Carrier-mediated Transport: increasing the concentration gradient increases the rate of transport up to a maximum rate, at which point all membrane carriers are saturated.

Figure IV.A.1.3: Simple diffusion versus Carrier-mediated transport.

concentration gradients. The Na$^+$-K$^+$ exchange pump uses ATP to actively pump Na$^+$ to where its concentration is highest (outside the cell) and K$^+$ is brought within the cell where its concentration is highest (see Neural Cells and Tissues, BIO 5.1.1).

1.1.3 Endo/Exocytosis

Endocytosis is the process by which the cell membrane actually invaginates, pinches off and is released intracellularly (endocytotic vesicle). If a solid particle was ingested by the cell (i.e. a bacterium), it is called phagocytosis. If fluid was ingested, it is pinocytosis.

The receptor-mediated endocytosis of ligands (e.g. low density lipoprotein, transferrin, growth factors, antibodies, etc.) are mediated by clathrin-coated vesicles (CCVs). CCVs are found in virtually all cells and form areas in the plasma membrane termed clathrin-coated pits. Caveolae are the most common reported non-clathrin-coated plasma membrane buds, which exist on the surface

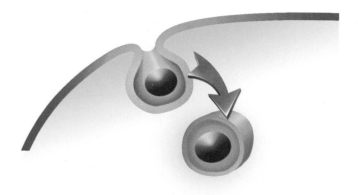

Figure IV.A.1.4: Endocytosis.

of many, but not all cell types. They consist of the cholesterol-binding protein caveolin with a bilayer enriched in cholesterol and glycolipids.

Exocytosis is, essentially, the reverse process. The cell directs an intracellular vesicle to fuse with the plasma membrane thus releasing its contents to the exterior (i.e. neurotransmitters, pancreatic enzymes, cell membrane proteins/lipids, etc.).

The transient vesicle fusion with the cell membrane forms a structure shaped like a pore (= *porosome*). Thus porosomes are cup-shaped structures where vesicles dock in the process of fusion and secretion. Porosomes contain many different types of protein including chloride and calcium channels, actin, and SNARE proteins that mediate the docking and fusion of vesicles with the cell membrane. The primary role of SNARE proteins is to mediate vesicle fusion through

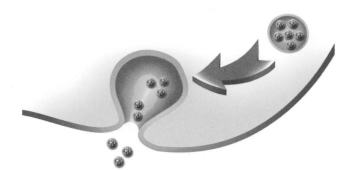

Figure IV.A.1.5: Exocytosis.

full fusion exocytosis or open and close exocytosis. The former is where the vesicle collapses fully into the plasma membrane; in the latter, the vesicle docks transiently with the membrane (= "kiss-and-run") and is recycled (i.e. in the synaptic terminal; BIO 1.5.1, 5.1).

1.2 The Interior of a Eukaryotic Cell

Cytoplasm is the interior of the cell. It refers to all cell components enclosed by the cell's membrane which includes the cytosol, the cytoskeleton, and the membrane bound organelles. Transport within the cytoplasm occurs by cyclosis (circular motion of cyto-plasm around the cell).

Cytosol is the solution which bathes the organelles and contains numerous solutes like amino acids, sugars, proteins, etc.

Cytoskeleton extends throughout the entire cell and has particular importance in shape and intracellular transportation. The cytoskeleton also makes extracellular com-

plexes with other proteins forming a matrix so that cells can "stick" together. This is called cellular adhesion.

The components of the cytoskeleton in increasing order of size are: microfilaments, intermediate filaments, and microtubules. Microfilaments are important for cell movement and contraction (i.e. actin and myosin. See Contractile Cells and Tissues, BIO 5.2). Microfilaments, also known as actin filaments, are composed of actin monomer (G actin) linked into a double helix. They display polarity (= having distinct and opposite poles), with polymerization and depolymerization occuring preferentially at the barbed end [also called the plus (+) end which is where ATP is bound to G actin; BIO 5.2]. Microfilaments squeeze the membrane together in phagocytosis and cytokinesis. They are also important for muscle contraction and microvilli movement.

Intermediate filaments and microtubules extend along axons and dendrites of neurons acting like railroad tracks, so organelles or protein particles can shuttle to or from the cell body. Microtubules also form:

(i) the core of cilia and flagella (see the 9 doublet + 2 structure in BIO 1.5);
(ii) the mitotic spindles which we shall soon discuss; and
(iii) centrioles.

A flagellum is an organelle of locomotion found in sperm and bacteria. Eukaryotic flagella are made from microtubule configurations while prokaryotic flagella are thin strands of a single protein called flagellin. Thus, eukaryotic flagella move in a whip-like motion while prokaryotic flagella rotate. Cilia are hair-like vibrating organelles which can be used to move particles along the surface of the cell (e.g., in the fallopian tubes cilia can help the egg move toward the uterus). Microtubules are composed of tubulin subunits. They display polarity, with polymerization and depolymerization occuring preferentially at the plus end where GTP is bound to the tubulin subunit. Microtubules are involved in flagella and cilia construction, and the spindle apparatus. Centrioles are cylinder-shaped complexes of microtubules associated with the mitotic spindle (MTOC, see later). At the

base of flagella and cilia, two centrioles can be found at right angles to each other: this is called a basal body.

Microvilli are regularly arranged finger-like projections with a core of cytoplasm (see BIO 9.5). They are commonly found in the small intestine where they help to increase the absorptive and digestive surfaces (= brush border).

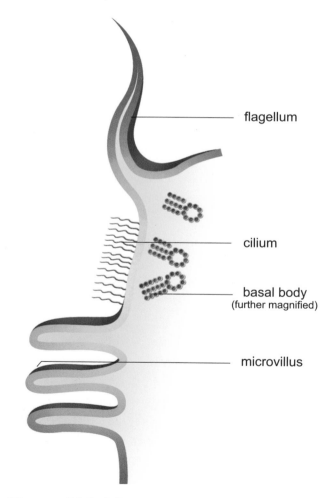

flagellum

cilium

basal body
(further magnified)

microvillus

Figure IV.A.1.6: Cytoskeletal elements and the plasma membrane. The core of cilia and flagella is composed of 9 doublet or pairs of microtubules with another *doublet* in the center (= *axoneme*; see BIO 1.5).

1.2.1 Membrane Bound Organelles

Mitochondrion: The Power House

Mitochondria produce energy (i.e. ATP) for the cell through aerobic respiration (BIO 4.4). It is a double membraned organelle whose inner membrane has shelf-like folds which are called cristae. The matrix, the fluid within the inner membrane, contains the enzymes for the Krebs cycle and circular DNA. The latter is the only cellular DNA found outside of the nucleus with the exception of chloroplasts (= the organelle capable of photosynthesis, the conversion of light into chemical energy, in plant cells). There are numerous mitochondria in muscle cells. Mitochondria synthesize ATP via the Krebs cycle via oxidation of glucose, amino acids or fatty acids (BIO 4.4-4.10).

Mitochondria have their own DNA and ribosomes and replicate independently from eukaryotic cells. However, most proteins used in mitochondria are coded by nuclear DNA, not mitochondrial DNA (BIO 15.6.1).

Figure IV.A.1.7: Mitochondria.

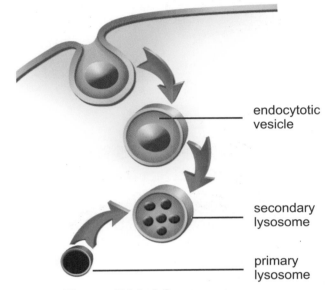

endocytotic vesicle

secondary lysosome

primary lysosome

Figure IV.A.1.8: Heterolysis.

Lysosomes: Suicide Sacs

In a diseased cell, lysosomes may release their powerful acid hydrolases to digest away the cell (autolysis). In normal cells, a primary (normal) lysosome can fuse with an endocytotic vesicle to form a secondary lysosome where the phagocytosed particle (i.e. a bacterium) can be digested. This is called heterolysis. There are numerous lysosomes in phagocytic cells of the immune system (i.e. macrophages, neutrophils; BIO 7.5).

Endoplasmic Reticulum: Synthesis Center

The endoplasmic reticulum (ER) is an interconnected membraned system resembling flattened sacs and extends from the cell membrane to the nuclear membrane.

rough ER

smooth ER

Figure IV.A.1.9: The endoplasmic reticulum.

There are two kinds: (i) dotted with ribosomes on its surface which is called rough ER and (ii) without ribosomes which is smooth ER.

The ribosomes are composed of ribosomal RNA (rRNA) and numerous proteins. It may exist freely in the cytosol or bound to the rough ER or outer nuclear membrane. The ribosome is a site where mRNA is translated into protein.

Rough ER is important in protein synthesis and is abundant in cells synthesizing secretory proteins. It is associated with the synthesis of secretory protein, plasma membrane protein, and lysosomal protein. Smooth ER is abundant in cells synthesizing steroids, triglycerides and cholesterol. It is associated with the synthesis and transport of lipids such as steroid hormone and detoxification of a variety of chemicals. It is also common in skeletal muscle cells involving

muscle contraction and relaxation. It is a factor in phospholipid and fatty acid synthesis and metabolism.

Golgi Apparatus: The Export Department

The Golgi apparatus forms a stack of smooth membranous sacs or *cisternae* that function in protein modification, such as the addition of polysaccharides (i.e. glycosylation). The Golgi also packages secretory proteins in membrane bound vesicles which can be exocytosed.

The Golgi apparatus has a distinct polarity with one end being the "cis" face and the other being "trans". The cis face lies close to a separate vesicular-tubular cluster (VTC) also referred to as the ER-Golgi intermediate compartment (ERGIC) which is an organelle. The ERGIC mediates trafficking between the ER and Golgi complex, facilitating the sorting of 'cargo'. The medial (middle) compartment of the Golgi lies between the cis and trans faces. The trans face is oriented towards vacuoles

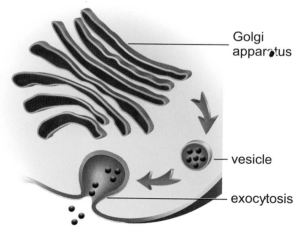

Golgi apparatus

vesicle

exocytosis

Figure IV.A.1.10: Golgi apparatus.

and secretory granules. The trans Golgi network separates from the trans face and sorts proteins for their final destination.

An abundant amount of rER and Golgi is found in cells which produce and secrete protein. For example, *B-cells* of the immune system which secrete antibodies, *acinar cells* in the pancreas which secrete digestive enzymes into the intestines, and *goblet cells* of the intestine which secrete mucus into the lumen.

Peroxisomes (Microbodies)

Peroxisomes are membrane bound organelles that contain enzymes whose functions include oxidative deamination of amino acids, oxidation of long chain fatty acids and synthesis of cholesterol.

The name "*perox*isome" comes from the fact that it is an organelle with enzymes that can transfer hydrogen from various substrates to oxygen, producing and then degrading hydrogen *perox*ide (H_2O_2).

The Nucleus

The nucleus is surrounded by a double membrane called the nuclear envelope. Throughout the membrane are nuclear pores which selectively allow the transportation of large particles to and from the nucleus. The nucleus is responsible for protein synthesis in the cytoplasm via ribosomal RNA (rRNA), messenger RNA (mRNA), and transfer RNA (tRNA).

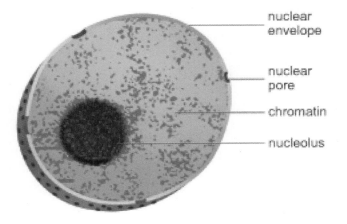

Figure IV.A.1.11: The nucleus.

DNA can be found within the nucleus as chromatin (DNA complexed to proteins like *histones*) or as chromosomes which are more clearly visible in a light microscope. The nucleolus is not membrane bound. It contains mostly ribosomal RNA and protein as well as the DNA necessary to synthesize ribosomal RNA.

The nucleolus is associated with the synthesis of ribosomal RNA (rRNA) and its assembly into ribosome precursors.

Chromosomes are basically extensively folded chromatin maintained by histone proteins. Each chromosome is composed of DNA and associated proteins, forming a nucleosome, the basic structural unit of chromatin. Chromatin exists as heterochromatin and euchromatin. Heterochromatin is a transcriptionally inactive form of chromatin while euchromatin is a transcriptionally active form of chromatin. Chromatin is responsible for RNA synthesis.

1.2.2 DNA: The Cell's Architect

Deoxyribonucleic Acid (DNA) and ribonucleic acid (RNA) are essential components in constructing the proteins which act as the cytoskeleton, enzymes, membrane channels, antibodies, etc. It is the DNA which contains the genetic information of the cell.

DNA and RNA are both important nucleic acids. Nucleotides are the subunits which attach in sequence or in other words polymerize via phosphodiester bonds to form nucleic acids. A nucleotide (also called a *nucleoside phosphate*) is composed of a five carbon sugar, a nitrogen base, and an inorganic phosphate.

The sugar in RNA is ribose but for DNA an oxygen atom is missing in the second position of the sugar thus it is 2-deoxyribose.

There are two categories of nitrogen bases: *purines* and *pyrimidines*. The purines have two rings and include adenine (A) and guanine (G). The pyrimidines contain one ring and include thymine (T), cytosine (C), and uracil (U).

DNA contains the following four bases: adenine, guanine, thymine, and cytosine. RNA contains the same bases except uracil is substituted for thymine.

Watson and Crick's model of DNA has allowed us to get insight into what takes shape as the nucleotides polymerize to form this special nucleic acid. The result is a double *helical* or *stranded* structure.

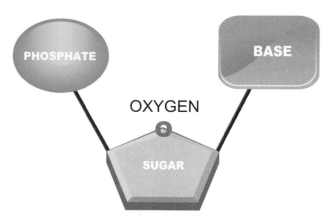

Figure IV.A.1.12: Nucleotide.

The DNA double helix is composed of two complementary and anti-parallel DNA strands held together by hydrogen bonds between base pairing A-T and G-C.

DNA is made from deoxyribose while RNA is made from ribose. DNA is double stranded while RNA is single stranded. DNA contains thymine while RNA contains uracil.

The backbone of each helix is the 2-deoxyribose phosphates. The nitrogen bases project to the center of the double helix in order to hydrogen bond with each other (imagine the double helix as a winding staircase: each stair would represent a pair of bases binding to keep the shape of the double helix intact).

There is specificity in the binding of the bases: one purine binds one pyrimidine. In fact, adenine only binds thymine (through two hydrogen bonds) and guanine only binds cytosine (through three hydrogen bonds).

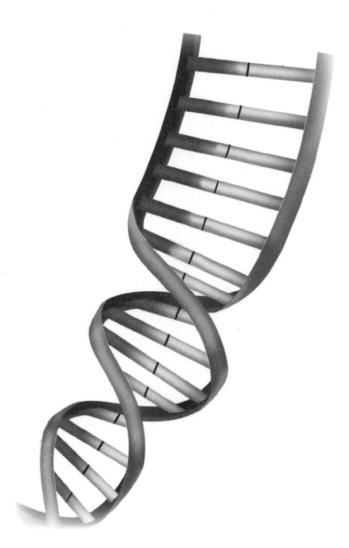

enzymes including DNA polymerase, and the parent strand as a template. The preceding is termed "DNA Synthesis" and occurs in the S stage of interphase during the cell cycle.

Each nucleotide has a hydroxyl or phosphate group at the 3rd and 5th carbons designated the 3' and 5' positions (see ORG 12.3.2, 12.5). Phosphodiester bonds can be formed between a free 3' hydroxyl group and a free 5' phosphate group. Thus the DNA strand has *polarity* since one end of the molecule will have a free 3' hydroxyl while the other terminal nucleotide will have a free 5' phosphate group. Polymerization of the two strands occurs in opposite directions (= *antiparallel*). In other words, one strand runs in the 5' - 3' direction, while its partner runs in the 3' - 5' direction.

DNA replication is semi-discontinuous. DNA polymerase can only synthesize DNA in the 5' to 3' direction. As a result of the anti-parallel nature of DNA, the 5' - 3' strand is replicated continuously (the *leading strand*), while the 3' - 5' strand is replicated discontinuously (the *lagging strand*) in the reverse direction. The short, newly synthesized DNA fragments that are formed on the lagging strand are called *Okazaki fragments*. DNA synthesis begins at a specific site called the replication origin (*replicon*) and proceeds in both directions. Eukaryotic chromosomes contain multiple origins while prokaryotic chromosomes contain a single origin. The parental strand is always read in the 3' - 5' direction and the daughter strand is always synthesized in the 5' - 3' direction.

The more the H-bonds (i.e. the more G-C), the more stable the helix will be.

The *replication* (duplication) of DNA is semi-conservative: each strand of the double helix can serve as a template to generate a complementary strand. Thus for each double helix there is one parent strand (*old*) and one daughter strand (*new*). The latter is synthesized using one nucleotide at a time,

Previous knowledge of recombinant DNA techniques, restriction enzymes, hybridization, DNA repair mechanisms, etc., is not normally required for the GAMSAT. However, because these topics do occasionally show up on the exam, they are discussed here and in BIO 2.2.1 and BIO 15.7. The following is an overview regarding DNA repair.

Because of environmental factors including chemicals and UV radiation, any one of the trillions of cells in our bodies may undergo as many as 1 million individual molecular "injuries" per day. Structural damage to DNA may result and could have many effects such as inducing mutation. Thus our DNA repair system is constantly active as it responds to damage in DNA structure.

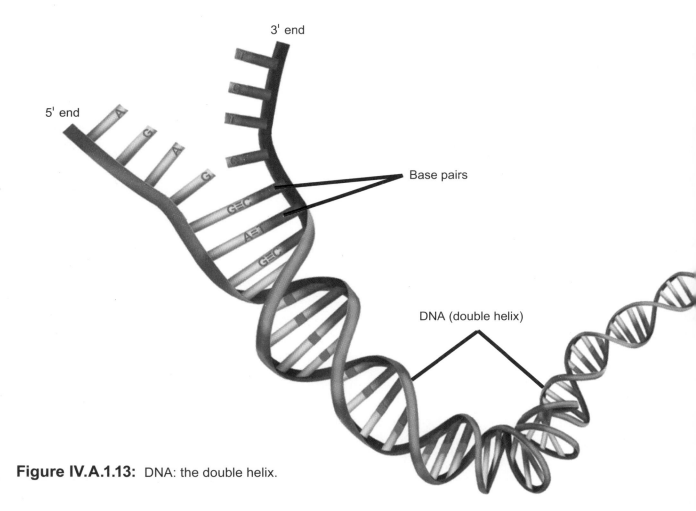

Figure IV.A.1.13: DNA: the double helix.

A cell that has accumulated a large amount of DNA damage, or one that no longer effectively repairs damage to its DNA, can: (1) become permanently dormant; (2) exhibit unregulated cell division which could lead to cancer; (3) succumb to cell suicide, also known as *apoptosis* or programmed cell death.

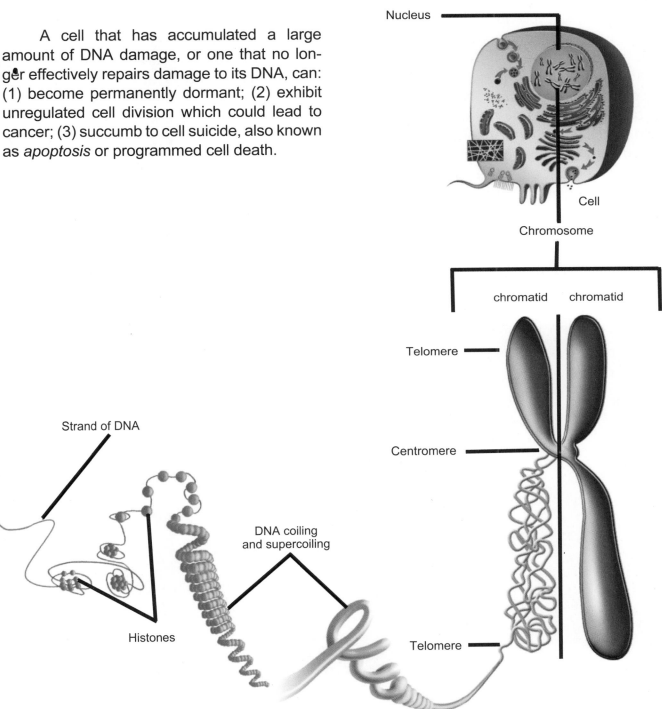

Nucleus

Cell

Chromosome

chromatid   chromatid

Telomere

Centromere

Strand of DNA

DNA coiling and supercoiling

Histones

Telomere

1.3 The Cell Cycle

The cell cycle is a period of approximately 18 - 22 hours during which the cell can synthesize new DNA and partition the DNA equally; thus the cell can divide. Mitosis involves nuclear division (*karyokinesis*) which is usually followed by cell division (*cytokinesis*). Mitosis and cytokinesis together define the mitotic (M) phase of the cell cycle - the division of the mother cell into two daughter cells, genetically identical to each other and to their parent cell. The cell cycle is divided into a number of phases: interphase (G_1, S, G_2) and mitosis (prophase, metaphase, anaphase and telophase).

The cell cycle is temporarily suspended in resting cells. These cells stay in the G_0 state but may reenter the cell cycle and start to divide again. The cell cycle is permanently suspended in non-dividing differentiated cells such as cardiac muscle cells.

Interphase occupies about 90% of the cell cycle. During interphase, the cell prepares for DNA synthesis (G_1), synthesizes or replicates DNA (S) resulting in duplication of chromosomes, and ultimately begins preparing for mitosis (G_2). During interphase, the DNA is not folded and the individual chromosomes are not visible. Also, centrioles grow to maturity, RNA and protein for mitosis are synthesized. Mitosis begins with prophase.

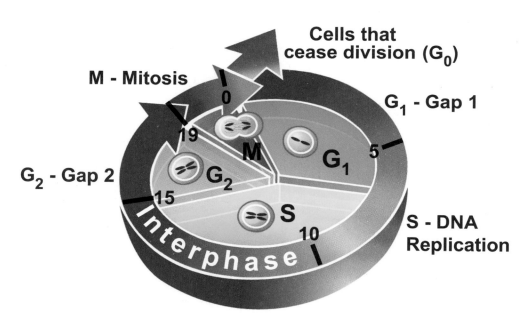

Figure IV.A.1.14: The cell cycle.

The numbers represent time in hours. Note how mitosis (M) represents the shortest period of the cycle.

Figure IV.A.1.15: Prophase.

<u>Prophase</u>: pairs of centrioles migrate away from each other while microtubules appear in between forming a spindle. Other microtubules emanating from the centrioles give a radiating star-like appearance; thus they are called asters. Therefore, centrioles form the core of the Microtubule Organizing Centers (MTOC). The MTOC is a structure found in eukaryotic cells from which microtubules emerge and associated with the protein tubulin.

Simultaneously, the diffuse nuclear chromatin condenses into the visible chromosomes which consist of two sister chromatids - each being identical copies of each other. Each chromatid consists of a complete double stranded DNA helix. The area of constriction where the two chromatids are attached is the *centromere*. Kinetochores develop at the centromere region and function as MTOC. Just as centromere refers to the center, *telomere* refers to the ends of the chromosome (note: as cells divide and we age, telomeres progressively shorten). Ultimately, the nuclear envelope disappears at the end of prophase.

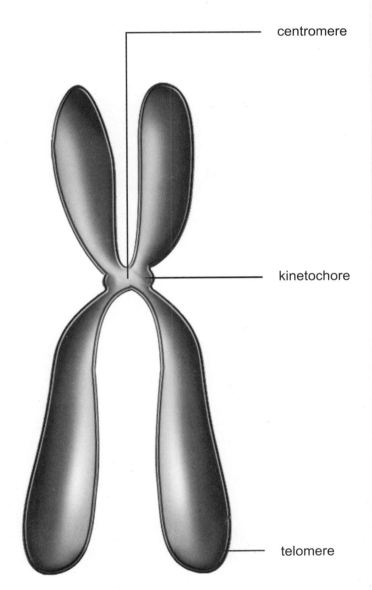

centromere

kinetochore

telomere

Figure IV.A.1.16: Chromosome Anatomy. Each chromosome has two arms separated by the centromere, labeled p (the shorter, named for 'petit' meaning 'small') and q (the longer of the two). The telomeres contain repetitive nucleotide sequences which protect the end of the chromosome. Over time, due to each cell division, the telomeres become shorter.

Figure IV.A.1.17: Metaphase.

Figure IV.A.1.19: Telophase.

<u>Metaphase</u>: centromeres line up along the equatorial plate. At or near the centromeres are the *kinetochores* which are proteins that face the spindle poles (asters). Microtubules, from the spindle, attach to the kinetochores of each chromosome.

<u>Anaphase</u>: sister chromatids are pulled apart such that each migrates to opposite poles being guided by spindle microtubules. At the end of anaphase, a cleavage furrow forms around the cell due to contraction of actin filaments called the contractile ring.

<u>Telophase</u>: new membranes form around the daughter nuclei; nucleoli reappear; the chromosomes uncoil and become less distinct (decondense). At the end of telophase, the cleavage furrow becomes deepened, facilitating the division of cytoplasm into two new daughter cells - each with a nucleus and organelles.

Finally, *cytokinesis* (cell separation) occurs. The cell cycle continues with the next interphase. {Mnemonic for the sequence of phases: P. MATI}

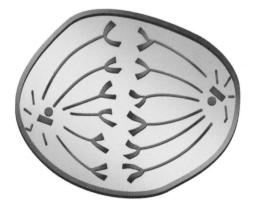

Figure IV.A.1.18: Anaphase.

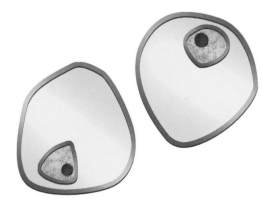

Figure IV.A.1.20: Interphase.

1.4 Cell Junctions

Multicellular organisms (i.e. animals) have cell junctions or intercellular bridges. They are especially abundant in epithelial tissues and serve as points of contact between cells and/or the extracellular matrix (BIO 4.3, 4.4). The multiprotein complex that comprise cell junctions can also build up the barrier around epithelial cells (*paracellular*) and control paracellular transport.

The molecules responsible for creating cell junctions include various cell adhesion molecules (CAMs). CAMs help cells stick to each other and to their surroundings. There are four main types: selectins, cadherins, integrins, and the immunoglobulin superfamily.

> You are expected to have been exposed to these topics but please do not try to memorize details: BIO 1.4.1, 1.5, 1.5.1.

1.4.1 Types of Cell Junctions

There are three major types of cell junctions in vertebrates:

1. **Anchoring junctions**: (note: "adherens" means "to adhere to"): (i) <u>Adherens junctions</u>, AKA "belt desmosome" because they can appear as bands encircling the cell (= zonula adherens); they link to the actin cytoskeleton; (ii) <u>desmosomes</u>, AKA macula (= "spot") adherens analogous to spot welding. Desmosomes include cell adhesion proteins like cadherins which can bind intermediate filaments and provide mechanical support and stability; and (iii) <u>hemidesmosomes</u> ("hemi" = "half"), whereas desmosomes link two cells together, hemidesmosomes attach one cell to the extracellular matrix (usually anchoring the 'bottom' or basal aspect of the epithelial cell or keratinocyte to the basement membrane; see Fig. IV.A.1.21 and BIO 5.3).

2. **Communicating junctions**: <u>Gap junctions</u> which are narrow tunnels which allow the free passage of small molecules and ions. One gap junction channel is composed of two connexons (or hemichannels) which connect across the intercellular space.

3. **Occluding junctions**: <u>Tight junctions</u>, AKA zonula occludens, as suggested by the name, are a junctional complex that join together forming a virtually impermeable barrier to fluid. These associate with different peripheral membrane proteins located on the intracellular side of the plasma membrane which anchor the strands to the actin component of the cytoskeleton. Thus, tight junctions join together the cytoskeletons of adjacent cells. Often tight junctions form narrow belts that circumferentially surround the upper part of the lateral (i.e. "side") surfaces of adjacent epithelial cells.

Invertebrates have several other types of specific junctions; for example, the septate junction which is analogous to the tight junction in vertebrates.

In multicellular plants, the structural functions of cell junctions are instead provided for by cell walls. The analogues of communicating cell junctions in plants are called plasmodesmata.

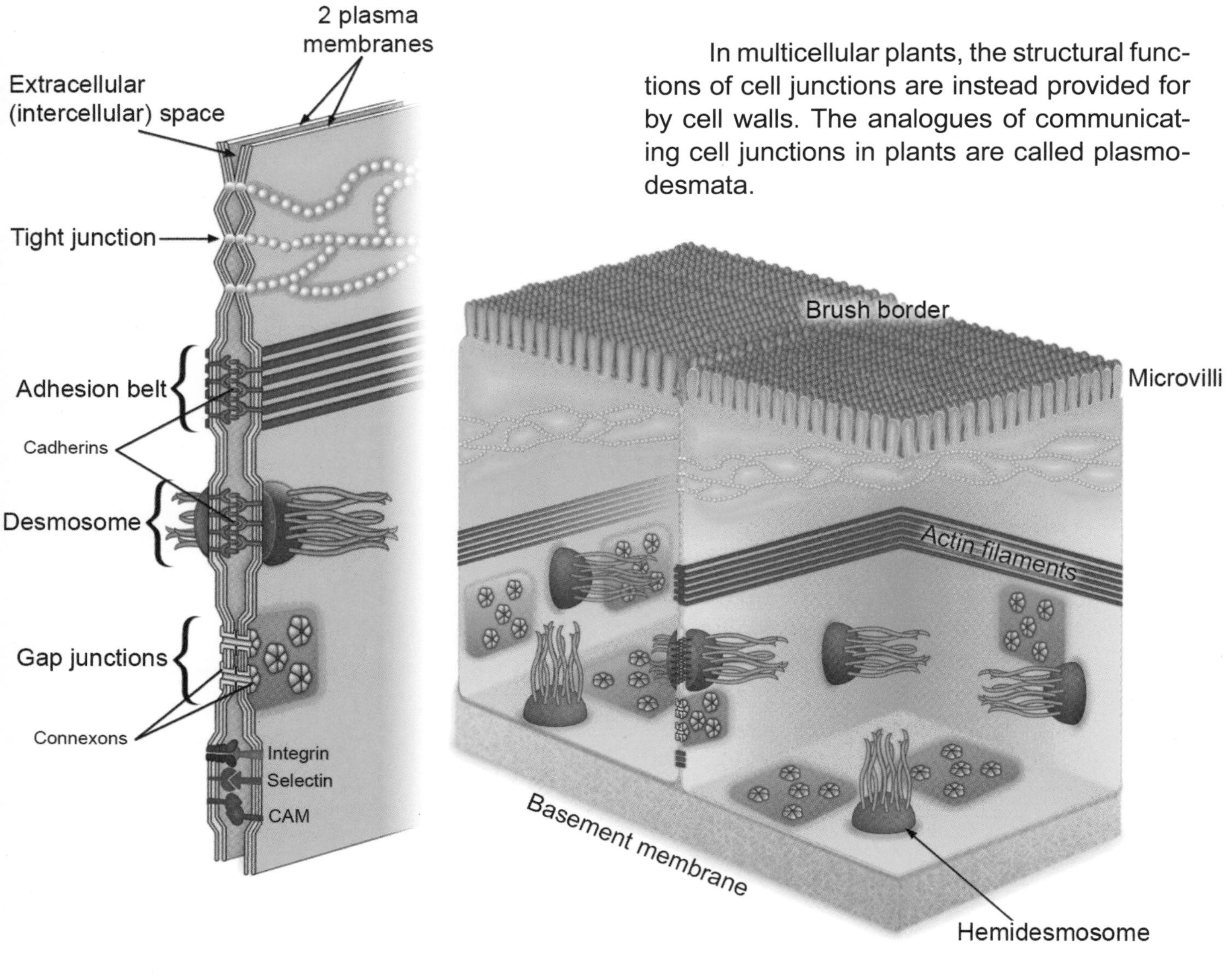

2 plasma membranes

Extracellular (intercellular) space

Tight junction

Adhesion belt

Cadherins

Desmosome

Gap junctions

Connexons

Integrin
Selectin
CAM

Brush border

Microvilli

Actin filaments

Basement membrane

Hemidesmosome

Figure IV.A.1.21: Various cell junctions in epithelia with microvilli at the surface (brush border, BIO 9.5).

1.5 Microscopy

A natural question about cells would be: if they are so small, how do we know what the inside of a cell really looks like? The story begins with the instrument used to produce magnified images of objects too small to be seen by the naked eye: the microscope.

Let us compare the basic principles of two popular methods of microscopy utilized by the vast majority of molecular biology research scientists: (1) the optical or light microscope; and (2) the electron microscope (the transmission electron microscope or TEM and the scanning electron microscope or SEM).

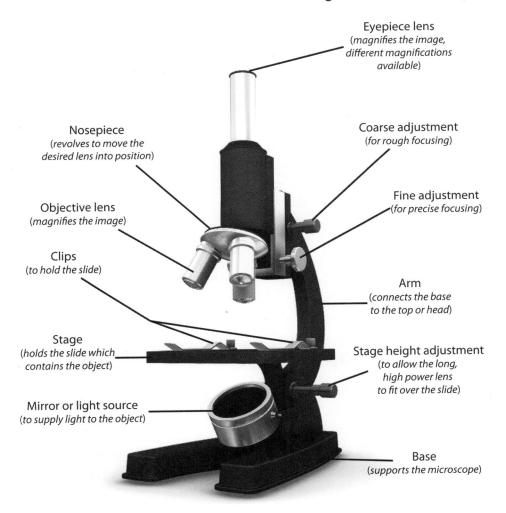

Eyepiece lens
(*magnifies the image, different magnifications available*)

Nosepiece
(*revolves to move the desired lens into position*)

Coarse adjustment
(*for rough focusing*)

Fine adjustment
(*for precise focusing*)

Objective lens
(*magnifies the image*)

Clips
(*to hold the slide*)

Arm
(*connects the base to the top or head*)

Stage
(*holds the slide which contains the object*)

Stage height adjustment
(*to allow the long, high power lens to fit over the slide*)

Mirror or light source
(*to supply light to the object*)

Base
(*supports the microscope*)

Figure IV.A.1.21: Compound light microscope. Typical magnification for the eyepiece is 10x and for the objective: 10x, 40x or 100x.

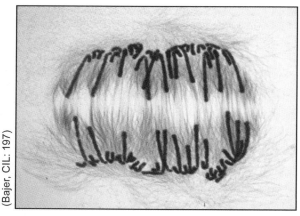

(Bajer, CIL: 197)

Figure IV.A.1.22: Light microscope image of a cell from the endosperm (= tissue in the seed) of an African lily. Staining shows microtubules in red and chromosomes in blue during late anaphase (BIO 1.3).

Light microscopy involves the use of an external or internal light source. The light first passes through the *iris* which controls the amount of light reaching the specimen. The light then passes through a *condenser* which is a lens that focuses the light beam through the specimen before it ultimately meets the *objective lens* which magnifies the image depending on your chosen magnification factor. Two terms you should be familiar with are *magnification* (how much bigger the image appears) and *resolution* (the ability to distinguish between two points on an image).

Magnification (PHY 11.3, 11.5) is the ratio between the apparent size of an object (or its size in an image) and its true size, and thus it is a dimensionless number usually followed by the letter "x". A compound microscope uses multiple lenses to collect light from the sample or specimen (this lens is the objective with a magnification of up to 100x), and then a separate set of lenses to focus the light into the

eye or camera (the eyepiece, magnification up to 10x). So the total magnification can be 100 x 10 = 1000 times the size of the specimen (1000x makes a 100 nanometer object visible).

Light microscopes enjoy their popularity thanks to their relative low cost and ease of use. A very important feature is that they can be used to view live specimens. Their shortfall is that the magnification is limited.

Common Units of Length in Biology
For details on units, see GM 2.1.2, 2.1.3

- m = meter(s)
- cm = centimeter(s) (1 cm = 10^{-2} m)
- mm = millimeter(s) (1 mm = 10^{-3} m)
- μm = micrometer(s) (1 μm = 10^{-6} m)
     NOT micron or μ
- nm = nanometer(s) (1 nm = 10^{-9} m)
- Å = angstrom(s) (1 Å = 10^{-10} m)
- pm = picometer(s) (1 pm = 10^{-12} m)

The term "micron" is no longer in technical use.

Electron microscopy is less commonly used due to its high price and associated scarcity. It also cannot observe live organisms as a vacuum is required and the specimen is flooded with electrons. All images being produced are in black and white though color is sometimes added to the raw images. Its primary advantage lies in the fact that it is possible to achieve a magnification up to 10,000,000x and it is the obvious choice when a high level of detail is required using an extremely small specimen. In fact, an object as tiny as a small fraction of a nanometer becomes visible with an incredible 50 picometer resolution. TEM shows the interior of the cell while SEM shows the surface of the specimen.

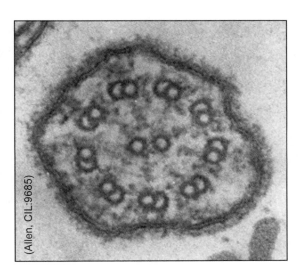

(Allen, CIL:9685)

Figure IV.A.1.23: TEM of the cross section of a cilium (BIO 1.2) showing an axoneme consisting of 9 doublet and 2 central microtubules (= 9x2 + 2). Each doublet is composed of 2 subfibers: a complete A subfiber with dynein and an attached B subfiber. Eukaryotic flagella are also 9x2 + 2.

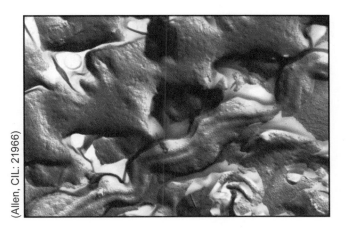

(Allen, CIL: 21966)

Figure IV.A.1.24: TEM freeze fracture of the plasma membrane which is cleaved between the acyl tails of membrane phospholipids (BIO 1.1; ORG 12.4), leaving a monolayer on each half of the specimen. The "E" face is the inner face of the outer lipid monolayer. The complementary surface is the "P" face (the inner surface of the inner leaflet of the bilayer shown above). The 2 large ribbons are intrinsic proteins.

1.5.1 Fluorescent Microscopy and Immunofluorescence

Lastly, you should be familiar with <u>fluorescent microscopy</u> which is commonly used to identify cellular components (organelles, cytoskeleton, etc.) and microbes with a high degree of specificity and color. The fluorescent microscope makes use of a special filter that only permits certain radiation wavelengths that matches the fluorescing material being analyzed. It is an optical microscope and very similar to the light microscope except that a highly intensive light source is used to excite a fluorescent species in the sample of interest.

<u>Immunofluorescence</u> is a technique that uses the specificity of the antibody-antigen interaction (BIO 8.2) to target fluorescent dyes to specific molecules in a cell. Immunofluorescence can be used on tissue sections, cultured cell lines or individual cells. This can be called *immunostaining*, or specifically, *immunohistochemistry* where the location of the antibodies can be seen using fluorophores (= a fluorescent chemical that can re-emit light upon light excitation; PHY 12.5, 12.6).

There are two classes of immunofluorescence: direct (= primary) and indirect (= secondary).

<u>Direct immunofluorescence</u> uses a single antibody linked to a fluorophore. The antibody binds to the target molecule (antigen),

and the fluorophore attached to the antibody can be detected with a microscope. This technique is cheaper, faster but less sensitive than indirect immunofluorescence.

Indirect immunofluorescence uses two antibodies: (1) the unlabeled first, or primary, antibody binds the antigen; and (2) the secondary antibody, which carries the fluorophore and recognizes the primary antibody and binds to it.

Photobleaching is the photochemical destruction of a dye or a fluorophore. Thus the fluorescent molecules are sometimes destroyed by the light exposure necessary to stimulate them into fluorescing. On the other hand, photobleaching can be fine tuned to improve the signal-to-noise ratio (like seeing the tree from the forest). Photobleaching can also be used to study the motion of molecules (i.e. FRAP).

Immunofluorescence samples can be seen through a simple fluorescent microscope (*epifluorescence*) or through the more complex *confocal* microscope.

A confocal microscope is a state-of-the-art fluorescent microscope which uses a laser as the light source. The confocal microscope is used in FRAP, fluorescence recovery after photobleaching, which is an optical technique used to "view" the movement of proteins or molecules. FRAP is capable of quantifying the 2D diffusion of a thin film of molecules containing fluorescently labeled probes, or to examine single cells. FRAP has had many uses including: studies of cell membrane diffusion and protein binding; determining if axonal transport is retrograde or anterograde, meaning towards or away from the neuron's cell body (soma), respectively.

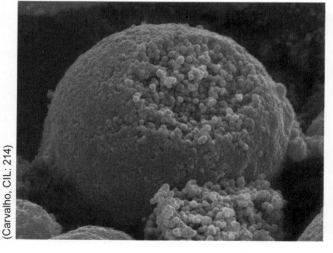

(Carvalho, CIL: 214)

Figure IV.A.1.25: SEM colorized image of a neuron's presynaptic terminal (BIO 5.1) that has been broken open to reveal the synaptic vesicles (orange and blue) beneath the cell membrane.

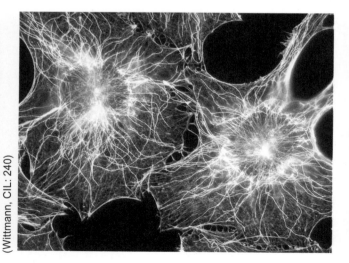

(Wittmann, CIL: 240)

Figure IV.A.1.26: Fluorescence microscopy of two interphase cells with immunofluorescence labeling of actin filaments (purple), microtubules (yellow), and nuclei (green).

Go online to GAMSAT-prep.com for additional chapter review Q&A and forum.

THE BIOLOGICAL SCIENCES BIO-27

MICROBIOLOGY

Chapter 2

Memorize

uctures, functions, life cycles
neralized viral life cycle
sic categories of bacteria
uation for bacterial doubling
fferences, similtarities

Understand

* Eukaryotes vs. Prokaryotes
* General aspects of life cycles
* Gen. aspects of genetics/reproduction
* Calculation of exponential growth
* Scientific method

Not Required*

* Advanced level college info
* Evolutionary history, habitats
* Taxonomic (scientific) classification
* Role in infectious diseases

GAMSAT-Prep.com

Introduction

Microbiology is the study of microscopic organisms including viruses, bacteria and fungi. It is important to be able to focus on the differences and similarities between these microorganisms and the generalized eukaryotic cell you have just studied.

Additional Resources

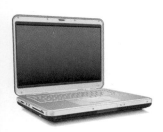

Free Online Q&A + Forum

Video: Online or DVD

Flashcards

Special Guest

* The real GAMSAT may have advanced level information presented (ie. in a passage) but previous knowledge of said information is not required to answer the questions that would follow. Practice ACER and GS practice GAMSATs can help you clarify this point.

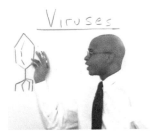

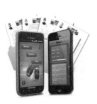

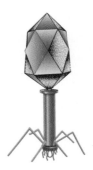

2.1 Viruses

Unlike cells, viruses are too small to be seen directly with a light microscope. Viruses infect all types of organisms, from animals and plants to bacteria and archaea (BIO 2.2). Only a very basic and general understanding of viruses is required for the GAMSAT.

Viruses are obligate intracellular para-sites; in other words, in order to replicate their genetic material and thus multiply, they must gain access to the inside of a cell. Replication of a virus takes place when the virus takes control of the host cell's synthetic machinery. Viruses are often considered non-living for several reasons:

(i) they do not grow by increasing in size

(ii) they cannot carry out independent metabolism

(iii) they do not respond to external stimuli

(iv) they have no cellular structure.

The genetic material for viruses may be either DNA or RNA, never both. Viruses do not have organelles or ribosomes. The nucleic acid core is encapsulated by a protein coat (capsid) which together forms the head region in some viruses. The tail region helps to anchor the virus to a cell. An extracellular viral particle is called a *virion*.

Figure IV.A.2.1: A virus.

Viruses are much smaller than prokaryotic cells (i.e. bacteria) which, in turn, are much smaller than eukaryotes (i.e. animal cells, fungi). A virus which infects bacteria is called a <u>bacteriophage</u> or simply a <u>phage</u>.

The life cycle of viruses has many variants; the following represents the main themes for GAMSAT purposes. A virus attaches to a specific receptor on a cell. Some viruses may now enter the cell; others, as in the diagram, will simply inject their nucleic acid. Either way, viral molecules induce the metabolic machinery of the host cell to produce more viruses.

The new viral particles may now exit the cell by lysing (bursting). This is also a feature of many bacteria. The preceding is deemed <u>lytic</u> or virulent. Some virus lie latent for long periods of time without lysing the host and its genome becomes incorporated by genetic recombination into the host's chromosome. Therefore, whenever the host replicates, the viral genome is also replicated. These are called <u>lysogenic</u> or temperate viruses. Eventually, at some point, the virus may become activated and lyse the host cell.

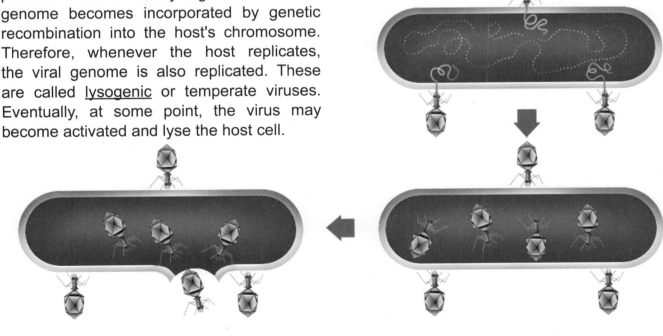

Figure IV.A.2.2: Lytic viral life cycle in a rod shaped bacterium (bacilli).

2.1.1 Retroviruses

A retrovirus uses RNA as its genetic material. It is called a retrovirus because of an enzyme (reverse transcriptase) that gives these viruses the unique ability of transcribing RNA (their RNA) into DNA (see Biology Chapter 3 for the central dogma regarding protein synthesis). The retroviral DNA can then integrate into the chromosomal DNA of the host cell to be expressed there. The human immunodeficiency virus (HIV), the cause of AIDS, is a retrovirus.

Retroviruses are used, in genetics, to deliver DNA to a cell (= a vector); in medicine, they are used for gene therapy.

2.2 Prokaryotes

Prokaryotes (= pre-nucleus) are organisms without a membrane bound nucleus which includes 2 types of organisms: bacteria (= Eubacteria) and archaea (= bacteria-like organisms that live in extreme environments). For the purposes of the GAMSAT, we will focus on bacteria. They are haploid and have a long circular strand of DNA in a region called the nucleoid.

The nucleoid is a region in a bacterium that contains DNA but is not surrounded by a nuclear membrane. Because bacterial DNA is not surrounded by a nuclear membrane, transcription and translation can occur at the same time, that is, protein synthesis can begin while mRNA is being produced. Bacteria also have smaller circular DNA called plasmid, which is extra chromosomal genetic element that can replicate independently of the bacterial chromosome and helps to confer resistance to antibiotics.

Bacteria do not have mitochondria, Golgi apparatus, lysosomes, nor endoplasmic reticulum. Instead, metabolic processes can

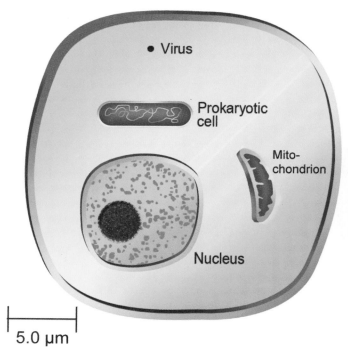

Typical eukaryotic cell

Figure IV.A.2.3

Comparing the size of a typical eukaryote, prokaryote and virus. Note that both the prokaryote and mitochondrion are similar in size and both contain circular DNA suggesting an evolutionary link.

be carried out in the cytoplasm or associated with bacterial membranes. Bacteria have ribosomes (smaller than eukaryotes), plasma membrane, and a cell wall. The cell wall, made of peptidoglycans, helps to prevent the hypertonic bacterium from bursting. Some bacteria have a slimy polysaccharide mucoid-like capsule on the outer surface for protection.

Bacteria can achieve movement with their flagella. Bacterial flagella are helical filaments, each with a rotary motor at its base which can turn clockwise or counterclockwise.

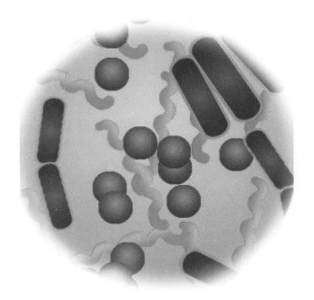

Figure IV.A.2.5
Schematic representation of bacteria colored for the purpose of identification: cocci (spherical, green), bacilli (cylindrical, purple) and spirilli (helical, orange).

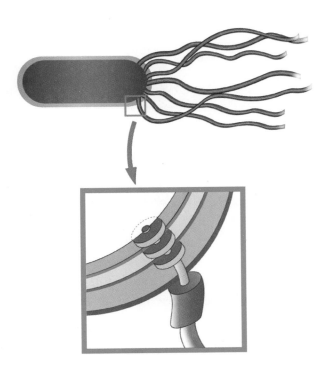

Figure IV.A.2.4
Schematic representation of the basis for flagellar propulsion. The flagellum, similar to a flexible hook, is anchored to the membrane and cell wall by a series of protein rings forming a motor. Powered by the flow of protons, the motor can rotate the flagellum more than 100 revolutions per second.

The form and rotary engine of flagella are maintained by proteins (i.e. flagellin) which interact with the plasma membrane and the basal body (BIO 1.2). Power is generated by a proton motive force similar to the proton pump in metabolism (Biology, Chapter 4).

Bacteria also have short, hairlike filaments called pili (also called fimbriae) arising from the bacterial cell wall. These pili are much shorter than flagella. Common pili can serve as adherence factors which promote binding of bacteria to host cells. Sex pili, encoded by a self-transmissible plasmid, are involved in transferring of DNA from one bacterium to another via conjugation.

Bacteria are partially classified according to their shapes: <u>cocci</u> which are spheri-

Prokaryotic Cells	Eukaryotic Cells
Small cells (1-10 μm)	Larger cells (10-100 μm)
Always unicellular	Often multicellular
No nuclei or any membrane-bound organelles, such as mitochondria	Always have nuclei and other membrane-bound organelles
DNA is circular, without proteins	DNA is linear and associated with proteins to form chromatin
Ribosomes are small (70S)	Ribosomes are large (80S)
No cytoskeleton	Always has a cytoskeleton
Motility by rigid rotating flagellum made of flagellin)	Motility by flexible waving cilia or flagellae (made of tubulin)
Cell division is by binary fission	Cell division is by mitosis or meiosis
Reproduction is always asexual	Reproduction is asexual or sexual
Great variety of metabolic pathways	Common metabolic pathways

Table IV.A.2.1: Summary of the differences between prokaryotic and eukaryotic cells.

cal or sometimes elliptical; bacilli which are rod shaped or cylindrical (Fig. IV.A.2.2 in BIO 2.1 showed phages attacking a bacillus bacterium); spirilli which are helical or spiral. They are also classified according to whether or not their cell wall reacts to a special dye called a Gram stain; thus they are gram-positive if they retain the stain and gram-negative if they do not.

Most bacteria engage in a form of asexual reproduction called binary fission. Two identical DNA molecules migrate to opposite ends of a cell as a transverse wall forms, dividing the cell in two. The cells can now separate and enlarge to the original size. Under ideal conditions, a bacterium can undergo fission every 10-20 minutes producing over 10^{30} progeny in a day and a half. If resources are unlimited, exponential growth would be expected. The doubling time of bacterial populations can be calculated as follows:

$$b = B \times 2^n$$

where b is the number of bacteria at the end of the time interval, B is the number of bacteria at the beginning of the time interval and n is the number of generations. Thus if we start with 2 bacteria and follow for 3 generations then we get:

$$b = B \times 2^n = 2 \times 2^3 = 2 \times 8 = 16$$
bacteria after 3 generations.

{Note: bacterial doubling time is a relatively popular question type.}

Bacteria do not produce gametes nor zygotes, nor do they undergo meiosis; however, four forms of genetic recombination do occur: <u>transduction</u>, <u>transformation</u>, <u>conjugation</u> and <u>transposon insertion</u>.

In transduction, fragments of bacterial chromosome accidentally become packaged into virus during a viral infection. These viruses may then infect another bacterium. A piece of bacterial DNA that the virus is accidentally carrying will be injected and incorporated into the host chromosome if there is homology between the newly injected piece of DNA and the recipient bacterial genome.

In transformation, a foreign chromosome fragment (plasmid) is released from one bacterium during cell lysis and enters into another bacterium. The DNA can then become incorporated into the recipient's genome if there is homology between the newly incorporated genome and the recipient one.

In conjugation, DNA is transferred directly by cell-to-cell contact formed by a conjugation bridge called the sex pilus. For conjugation to occur, one bacterium must

have the sex factor called F plasmid. Bacteria that carry F plasmids are called F^+ cells. During conjugation, a F^+ cell replicates its F factor and will pass its F plasmid to an F^- cell, converting it to an F^+ cell. This type of exchange is the major mechanism for transfer of antibiotic resistance.

In transposon insertion, mobile genetic elements called transposons move from one position to another in a bacterial chromosome or between different molecules of DNA without having DNA homology.

Most bacteria cannot synthesize their own food and thus depend on other organisms for it; such a bacterium is heterotrophic. Most heterotrophic bacteria obtain their food from dead organic matter; this is called saprophytic. Some bacteria are autotrophic meaning they can synthesize organic compounds from simple inorganic substances. Thus some are photosynthetic producing carbohydrate and releasing oxygen, while others are chemoautotrophic obtaining energy via chemical reactions including the oxidation of iron, sulfur, nitrogen, or hydrogen gas.

Bacteria can be either aerobic or anaerobic. The former refers to metabolism in the presence of oxygen and the latter in the absence of oxygen (i.e. fermentation).

Based on variations in the oxygen requirement, bacteria are divided into four types:

1) Obligate aerobes: require oxygen for growth

2) Facultative anaerobes: are aerobic; however, can grow in the absence of oxygen by undergoing fermentation

3) Aerotolerant anaerobes: use fermentation for energy; however, can tolerate low amounts of oxygen

4) Obligate anaerobes: are anaerobic, can be damaged by oxygen

Symbiosis generally refers to close and often long term interactions between different biological species. Bacteria have various symbiotic relationships with, for example, humans. These include mutualism (both benefit: GI tract bacteria, BIO 9.5), parasitism (parasite benefits over the host: tuberculosis, appendicitis) and commensalism (one benefits and the other is not significantly harmed or benefited: some skin bacteria).

2.2.1 Operons

E. coli is a gram-negative, rod-shaped intestinal bacterium with DNA sequences called *operons* that direct biosynthetic pathways. Operons are composed of:

1. A repressor which can bind to an operator and prevent gene expression by blocking RNA polymerase. However, in the presence of an inducer, a repressor will be bound to the inducer instead, forming an inducer-repressor complex. This complex cannot bind to an operator and thus gene expression is permitted.

2. A promoter which is a sequence of DNA where RNA polymerase attaches to begin transcription.

3. Operators which can block the action of RNA polymerase if there is a repressor present.

4. A regulator which codes for the synthesis of a repressor that can bind to the operator and block gene transcription.

5. Structural genes that code for several related enzymes that are responsible for production of a specific end product.

The *lac operon* controls the breakdown of lactose and is the simplest way of illustrating how gene regulation in bacteria works. In the lac operon system there is an active repressor that binds to the operator. In this scenario RNA polymerase is unable to transcribe the structural genes necessary to control the uptake and subsequent breakdown of lactose. When the repressor is inactivated (in the presence of lactose) the RNA polymerase is now able to transcribe the genes that code for the required enzymes. These enzymes are said to be *inducible* as it is the lactose that is required to turn on the operon.

Lac Operon

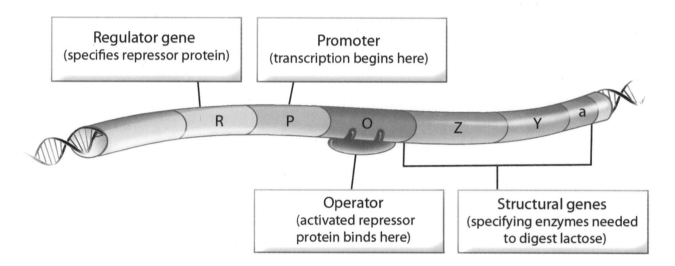

Regulator gene
(specifies repressor protein)

Promoter
(transcription begins here)

R   P   O   Z   Y   a

Operator
(activated repressor
protein binds here)

Structural genes
(specifying enzymes needed
to digest lactose)

2.3 Fungi

Fungi are eukaryotic (= true nucleus) organisms which absorb their food through their chitinous cell walls. They may either be unicellular (i.e. yeast) or filamentous (i.e. mushrooms, molds) with individual filaments called hyphae which collectively form a mycelium. Fungal cell membranes contain ergosterol rather than cholesterol found in cell membranes of other eukaryotes.

Fungi often reproduce asexually. In molds, spores can be produced and then liberated from outside of a sporangium; or, as in yeast, a simple asexual budding process may be used. Sexual reproduction can involve the fusion of opposite mating types to produce asci (singular: ascus), basidia (singular: basidium), or zygotes. All of the three preceding diploid structures must undergo meiosis to produce haploid spores. If resources are unlimited, exponential growth would be expected.

Fungi are relatively important for humans as a source of disease and a decomposer of both food and dead organic matter. On the lighter side, they also serve as food (mushrooms, truffles), for alcohol and food production (cheese molds, bread yeast) and they have given us the breakthrough antibiotic, penicillin (from penicillium molds).

2.4 Vectors

A vector can be a person, animal or microorganism that carries and transmits an infectious organism (i.e. bacteria, viruses, etc.) into another living organism. Examples: the mosquito is a vector for malaria; bats are vectors for rabies and a SARS-like virus.

2.5 The Scientific Method

The scientific method could be used in conjunction with any GAMSAT Biology experiment but microbiology is most common.

The point of the experiment is to test your ability to read scientific material, understand what is being tested, and determine if the hypothesis has been proved, refuted or neither. When a hypothesis survives rigorous testing, it graduates to a *theory*.

Observation, formulation of a theory, and testing of a theory by additional observation is called the scientific method. In biology, a key aspect to evaluate the validity of a trial or experiment is the presence of a *control group*. Generally, treatment is withheld from the control group but given to the *experimental group*.

First we will make an observation and then use deductive reasoning to create an appropriate hypothesis which will result in an experimental design. Consider the following: trees grow well in the sunlight. Hypothesis: exposure to light is directly related to tree growth. Experiment: two groups of trees are grown in similar conditions except one group (*experimental*) is exposed to light while the other group (*control*) is not exposed to light. Growth is carefully measured and the two groups are compared. Note that tree growth (*dependent variable*) is dependent on light (*independent variable*).

There are experiments where it is important to expose the control group to some factor different from the factor given to the experimental group (= *positive control*); as opposed to not giving the control group any exposure at all (= *negative control*). Exposure for a control group is used in medicine and dentistry because of the "Placebo Effect."

Experiments have shown that giving a person a pill that contains no biologically active material will cure many illnesses in up to 30% of individuals. Thus if Drug X is developed using a traditional control group, and the "efficacy" is estimated at 32%, it may be that the drug is no more effective than a sugar pill! In this case, the control group must be exposed to an unmedicated preparation to negate the Placebo Effect. To be believable the experiment must be well-grounded in evidence (= *valid,* based on the scientific method) and then one must be able to reproduce the results.

2.5.1 The Experiment

A lab in Sydney reports 15% cell death when maximally stimulating the APO-1 receptor. In order to appropriately interpret the results, it must first be compared to:

A. data from other labs.

B. the attrition rate of other cell types.

C. the actual number of APO-1 cells dying in the tissue culture.

D. the rate of cell death without stimulation of APO-1.

• The experiment: stimulating a specific receptor on cells led to a 15% rate of cell death.

• Treatment is the stimulation of a receptor.

• The control (group without treatment): under the same conditions, do not stimulate the receptor (choice D.).

Choice C. does not answer the question. Choices A. and B. are most relevant if the initial data is shown to be significant. To prove that the data is significant or valid, one must first compare to a control group (choice D.).

Go online to GAMSAT-prep.com for additional chapter review Q&A and forum.

THE BIOLOGICAL SCIENCES BIO-39

PROTEIN SYNTHESIS

Chapter 3

Memorize	Understand	Not Required*
e genetic code (triplet) ntral Dogma: DNA ➡ RNA ➡ protein finitions: mRNA, tRNA, rRNA don-anticodon relationship tiation, elongation and termination	* Mechanism of transcription * Mechanism of translation * Roles of mRNA, tRNA, rRNA * Role and structure of ribosomes * One-gene–one-enzyme hypothesis * The biosynthetic pathway	* Advanced level college info * Splicosomes, heterphil nuclear RNA * Inhibitory, signal peptides * Specific post translation changes * Memorizing the ribosomal subunits in Svedberg units * Memorizing stop or start codons

GAMSAT-Prep.com

Introduction

Protein synthesis is the creation of proteins using DNA and RNA. Individual amino acids are connected to each other in peptide linkages in a specific order given by the sequence of nucleotides in DNA. Thus the process occurs through a precise interplay directed by the genetic code and involving mRNA, tRNA and amino acids - all in an environment provided by a ribosome. The "one-gene–one-enzyme hypothesis" and its relation to biosynthetic pathways comprise rather regular GAMSAT questions.

Additional Resources

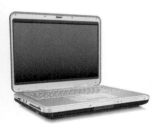

Free Online Q&A + Forum

Video: Online or DVD

Flashcards

Special Guest

* The real GAMSAT may have advanced level information presented (ie. in a passage) but previous knowledge of said information is not required to answer the questions that would follow. Practice ACER and GS practice GAMSATs can help you clarify this point.

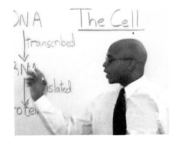

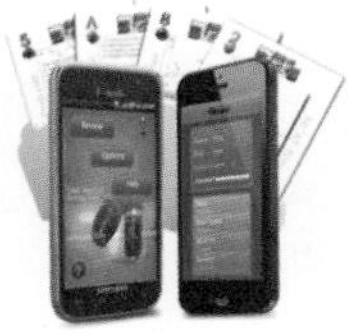

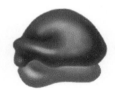

Building Proteins

Proteins (which comprise many hormones, enzymes, antibodies, etc.) are long chains formed by peptide bonds between combinations of twenty amino acid subunits. Each amino acid is encoded in a sequence of three nucleotides (a triplet code = the *genetic code*). A gene is a conglomeration of such codes and thus is a section of DNA which encodes for a protein (or a polypeptide which is exactly like a protein but much smaller).

DNA Transcription

The information in DNA is rewritten (transcribed) into a messenger composed of RNA (= mRNA); the reaction is catalyzed by the enzyme RNA polymerase. The newly synthesized mRNA is elongated in the 5′ to 3′ direction. It carries the complement of a DNA sequence.

Transcription can be summarized in 4 or 5 steps for prokaryotes or eukaryotes, respectively:

1. RNA polymerase moves the transcription bubble, a stretch of unpaired nucleotides, by breaking the hydrogen bonds between complementary nucleotides (see BIO 1.2.2 for nucleoside phosphates - nucleotides - and the binding of nitrogen bases).

2. RNA polymerase adds matching RNA nucleotides that are paired with complementary DNA bases.

3. The extension of the RNA sugar-phosphate backbone is catalyzed by RNA polymerase.

4. Hydrogen bonds of the untwisted RNA +

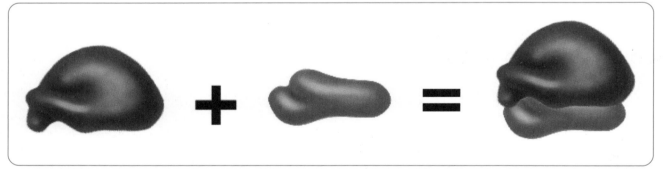

Figure IV.A.3.1: A ribosome provides the environment for protein synthesis. Ribosomes are composed of a large and a small subunit. The unit of measurement used is called the "Svedberg unit" (S) which is a measure of the rate of sedimentation in a centrifuge as opposed to a direct measurement of size. For this reason, fragment names do not add up (70S is made of 50S and 30S). Prokaryotes have 70S ribosomes, each comprised of a small (30S) and a large (50S) subunit. Eukaryotes have 80S ribosomes, each comprised of a small (40S) and large (60S) subunit. The ribosomes found in chloroplasts and mitochondria of eukaryotes also consist of large and small subunits bound together with proteins into one 70S ribosome. These organelles are believed to be descendants of bacteria ("Endosymbiotic theory") thus their ribosomes are similar to those of bacteria (see BIO 16.6.3).

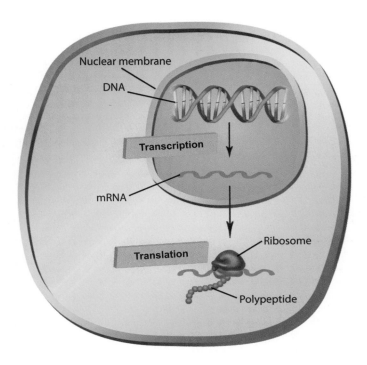

Figure IV.A.3.2: The central dogma of protein synthesis.

DNA helix break, freeing the newly synthesized RNA strand.

5. If the cell has a nucleus, the RNA is further processed [addition of a 5′ cap and a 3′ poly(A) tail] and then exits through the nuclear pore to the cytoplasm.

The mRNA synthesis in eukaryotes begins with the binding of RNA polymerase at a specific DNA sequence known as promoters. Elongation continues until the RNA polymerase reaches a termination signal. The initially formed primary mRNA transcript, also called pre-mRNA, contains regions called introns that are not expressed in the synthesized protein.The introns are removed and the regions that are expressed (exons) are spliced together to form the final functional mRNA molecule. {EXons EXpressed; INtrons IN the garbage!}

Post-transcriptional processing of mRNA occurs in the nucleus. Even before transcription is completed, a 7-methylguanosine cap is added to the 5′ end of the growing mRNA serving as attachment site for protein synthesis and protection against degradation. The 3′ end is added with a poly(A) tail consisting of 20 to 250 adenylate residues as protection. Of course, "A" refers to adenine and the nucleotide is thus adenosine monophosphate or AMP (BIO 1.2.2, ORG 12.5) which *polymerizes* to create the tail of residues. The mes-

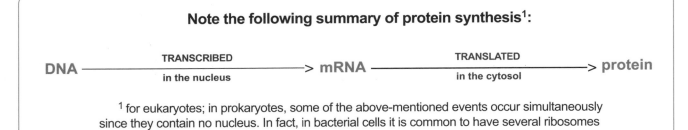

Note the following summary of protein synthesis[1]:

DNA ————— TRANSCRIBED / in the nucleus ————> mRNA ————— TRANSLATED / in the cytosol ————> protein

[1] for eukaryotes; in prokaryotes, some of the above-mentioned events occur simultaneously since they contain no nucleus. In fact, in bacterial cells it is common to have several ribosomes working in parallel on a single mRNA, forming what is called polyribosomes or polysome.

senger then leaves the nucleus with the information necessary to make a protein.

RNA Translation

The mRNA is constantly produced and degraded, which is the main method through which cells regulate the amount of a particular protein they synthesize. It attaches to a small subunit of a ribosome which will then attach to a larger ribosomal subunit thus creating a full ribosome. A ribosome is composed of a complex of protein and ribosomal RNA (= rRNA). The rRNA is the most abundant of all RNA types.

Floating in the cytoplasm is yet another form of RNA; this RNA specializes in taking amino acids and transfering them onto other amino acids when contained within the environment of the ribosome. More specifically, this transfer RNA (tRNA) molecule can be charged with a specific amino acid by aminoacyl-tRNA synthetase enzyme, bring the amino acid to the environment of ribosome, recognize the triplet code (= codon) on mRNA via its own triplet code anticodon, which is a three nucleotide sequence on tRNA that recognizes the complementary codon

in mRNA; and finally, tRNA can transfer its amino acid onto the preceding one thus elongating the polypeptide chain. In a way, tRNA translates the code that mRNA carries into a sequence of amino acids which can produce a protein.

Translation of mRNA into a protein involves three stages: initiation, elongation and termination. The direction of synthesis of the protein chain proceeds from the amino end/terminus to the carboxyl end/terminus. Synthesis begins when the ribosome scans the mRNA until it binds to a start codon (AUG), which specifies the amino acid methionine. During elongation, a peptide bond is formed between the existing amino acid in the protein chain and the incoming amino acid. Following peptide bond formation, the ribosome shifts by one codon in the 5′ to 3′ direction along mRNA and the uncharged tRNA is expelled and the peptidyl-tRNA grows by one amino acid. Protein synthesis terminates when the ribosome binds to one of the three mRNA termination codons (UAA, UAG or UGA; notice the similarity with the DNA stop codons in Table IV.A.3.1 except that U replaces T in this RNA molecule).

The 20 Amino Acids	The 64 DNA Codons
Alanine	GCT, GCC, GCA, GCG
Arginine	CGT, CGC, CGA, CGG, AGA, AGG
Asparagine	AAT, AAC
Aspartic acid	GAT, GAC
Cysteine	TGT, TGC
Glutamic acid	GAA, GAG
Glutamine	CAA, CAG
Glycine	GGT, GGC, GGA, GGG
Histidine	CAT, CAC
Isoleucine	ATT, ATC, ATA
Leucine	CTT, CTC, CTA, CTG, TTA, TTG
Lysine	AAA, AAG
Methionine	ATG
Phenylalanine	TTT, TTC
Proline	CCT, CCC, CCA, CCG
Serine	TCT, TCC, TCA, TCG, AGT, AGC
Threonine	ACT, ACC, ACA, ACG
Tyrosine	TAT, TAC
Tryptophan	TGG
Valine	GTT, GTC, GTA, GTG
Stop codons	TAA, TAG, TGA

Table IV.A.3.1: The 20 standard amino acids. Do not memorize.

The 20 standard amino acids are encoded by the genetic code of 64 codons. Notice that since there are 4 bases (A, T, G, C), if there were only two bases per codon, then only 16 amino acids could be coded for ($4^2=16$). However, since at least 21 codes are required (20 amino acids plus a stop codon) and the next largest number of bases is three, then 4^3 gives 64 possible codons, meaning that some degeneracy exists.

Degeneracy is the redundancy of the genetic code. Degeneracy occurs because there are more codons than encodable amino acids. This makes the genetic code more tolerant to point mutations (BIO 15.5). For example, in theory, fourfold degenerate codons can tolerate any point mutation at the third position (see valine, alanine, glycine, etc. in Table IV.A.3.1 and notice that any 3rd base codes for the same amino acid). The structure of amino acids will be discussed in ORG 12.1.

A nonsense mutation is a point mutation (BIO 15.5) in a sequence of DNA that results in a premature stop codon (UAA, UAG, UGA), or a nonsense codon in the transcribed mRNA. Either way, an incomplete, and usually nonfunctional protein is the result. A missense mutation is a point mutation where a single nucleotide is changed to cause substitution of a different amino acid. Some genetic disorders (i.e. thalassemia) result from nonsense mutations.

Protein made on free ribosomes in the cytoplasm may be used for intracellular

purposes (i.e. enzymes for glycolysis, etc.). Whereas proteins made on rER ribosomes are usually modified by both rER and the Golgi apparatus en route to the plasma membrane or exocytosis (i.e. antibodies, intestinal enzymes, etc.).

Key Points

Note the following: i) the various kinds of RNA are single stranded molecules which are produced using DNA as a template; ii) hormones can have a potent regulatory effect on protein synthesis (esp. enzymes); iii) allosteric enzymes (= proteins with two different configurations - each with different biological

DNA	Coding Strand (codons)	5′ → → ------ T T C ------ → → 3′
	Template Strand (anticodons)	3′ ← ← ------ A A G ------ ← ← 5′
mRNA	The Message (codons)	5′ → → ------ U U C ------ → → 3′
tRNA	The Transfer (anticodons)	3′ ← ← A A G ← ← 5′
Protein	Amino Acid	**N-terminus** → → Phenylalanine → → **C-terminus**

Table IV.A.3.2. DNA, RNA and protein strands with directions of synthesis. For both DNA and RNA, strands are synthesized from the **5′** ends → → to the **3′** ends. Protein chains are synthesized from the **N-terminus** → → to the **C-terminus**. Color code: the **old** end is **cold blue**; the **new** end is **red hot** where new residues are added. As shown in the table, mRNA is synthesized complementary and antiparallel to the **template strand (anticodons)** of DNA, so the resulting mRNA consists of codons corresponding to those in the coding strand of DNA. The **anticodons of tRNA** read each three-base mRNA codon and thus transfers the corresponding **amino acid** to the growing **polypeptide chain** or **protein** according to the genetic code.

properties) are important regulators of transcription; iv) there are many protein factors which trigger specific events in the <u>initiation</u> (using a start codon, AUG), <u>elongation</u> and <u>termination</u> (using a stop codon) of the synthesis of a protein; v) one end of the protein has an amine group (-NH$_2$, which projects from the first amino acid), while the other end has a carboxylic acid group (-COOH, which projects from the last amino acid). {Amino acids and protein structure will be explored in ORG 12.1 and 12.2}

Note that the free amine group end, the start of the protein, is also referred to as: N-terminus, amino-terminus, NH$_2$-terminus, N-terminal end or amine-terminus. The free carboxylic acid end, which is the end of the protein, is also referred to as: C-terminus, carboxyl-terminus, carboxy-terminus, C-terminal tail, C-terminal end, or COOH-terminus.

Differences in translation between prokaryotes and eukaryotes:

1) Ribosomes: in prokaryotes it is 70S, in eukaryotes it is 80S

2) Start codon: the start codon AUG specifies formyl-methionine [f-Met] in prokaryotes, in eukaryotes it is methionine

Location of translation: in prokaryotes translation occurs at the same compartment and same time as transcription, in eukaryotes transcription occurs in the nucleus while translation occurs in the cytosol.

Because of the incredible variety of organisms that use the genetic code, it was thought to be a *truly* 'universal' code but that is not quite accurate. Variant codes have evolved. For example, protein synthesis in human mitochondria relies on a genetic code that differs from the standard genetic code.

Furthermore, not all genetic information is stored using the genetic code. DNA also has regulatory sequences, chromosomal structural areas and other non-coding DNA that can contribute greatly to phenotype. Such elements operate under sets of rules that are different from the codon-to-amino acid standard underlying the genetic code.

3.1 One Gene, One Enzyme, and the Biosynthetic Pathway

Duchenne muscular dystrophy (DMD) is a disease caused by a mutation in the DNA (X-linked recessive mutation; BIO 15.3). DMD patients have a mutation in the gene coding for the protein dystrophin. This protein connects the cytoskeleton to the extracellular matrix (thus through the plasma membrane) in muscle cells and appears to stabilize the muscle during contraction. Without dystrophin, the plasma membrane ruptures during muscle contraction and degeneration of the muscle tissue occurs (most DMD patients become wheelchair-dependent early in life). One gene, one protein and we can see how it is expressed in the organism (phenotype; BIO 15.1).

Experiments done in the 1940s, that would later give birth to Molecular Biology, used the bread mold *Neurospora* (a fungus; BIO 2.3) to conclude the following:

- Molecules are synthesized in a series of steps (= biosynthetic pathway, or, more generally: metabolic pathway)
- Each step is catalyzed by a unique enzyme (of course, enzymes are proteins)

- Each enzyme is specified by a unique gene ("one gene, one enzyme").

As we will see in Chapter 4, in a metabolic pathway, a principal chemical is modified by a series of chemical reactions. Enzymes catalyze these reactions. Because of the many chemicals (= "metabolites") that may be involved, metabolic pathways can be complex. Consider the following straightforward synthetic pathway (Int = Intermediate):

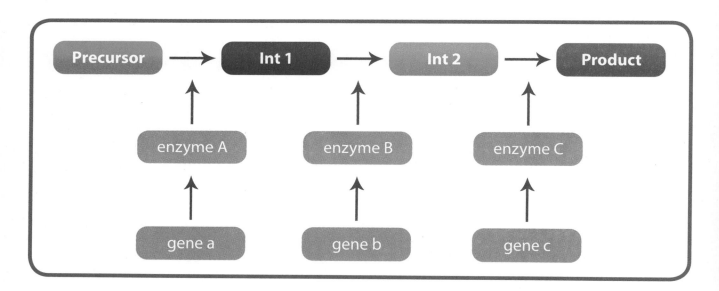

Consider the following questions:

1. Imagine that there was a mutation (or inactivation) in gene c, would any Product be produced? Would you expect the intermediates to be produced? Would their concentrations go up or down?

2. What would be the consequences of a mutation in gene b?

3. What happens if we add Intermediate 1 or Intermediate 2 to the media of a gene b mutation? Would either case result in Product? {Note: "media" is plural and refers to a growth medium or culture medium which is a liquid or gel designed to support the growth of cells}

Consider your answers before continuing. You can expect questions like this on the real exam.

1. If there is a mutation at gene c then enzyme C is blocked (i.e. it is either not being produced or it is not functioning normally) which means the Product would not be produced and we would expect Intermediate 2 to increase in concentration (imagine a production line where one worker stops working but there continues to be items arriving at their desk, the result is accumulation at that point and non-production beyond that point).

2. A mutation at gene b stops the function of enzyme B thus the production of Intermediate 2 is blocked thus no Product is formed. Intermediate 1 begins to accumulate.

3. Adding Intermediate 1 just leads to its accumulation since we are presented with one way arrows so the reaction can only move forward but it is blocked because of the gene b mutation [had the arrows been double sided, which is quite normal in nature, then Le Chat-elier's principle (CHM 9.9) would suggest that Precursor would be produced because of the stress of increasing Intermediate 1].

However, if Intermediate 2 is added to the media with the gene b mutation, since gene c is not mutated, the Product will be formed. Being beyond the 'blockage' caused by enzyme B dysfunction, the medium supplemented with Intermediate 2 bypasses the problem and is able to produce Product because there are no issues with gene c.

It should be noted that the one gene-one enzyme hypothesis predated the understanding of the genetic code and our modern understanding of enzymes – many of which are composed of multiple polypeptides (ORG 12.2), each of which is coded for by one gene. Thus "one gene-one polypeptide" would be more accurate but even so, remains incomplete because of more recent discoveries outside the scope of this exam.

Peptide: The result of the moon pulling on the Pepsi. ;)

At the time of publication, the preceding information would be helpful to solve ACER GAMSAT Red Booklet Unit 16, and Blue Booklet Unit 17, and somewhat helpful for Purple Booklet questions 87 and 88. In other words, the reasoning may be helpful during the real exam.

Go online to GAMSAT-prep.com for additional chapter review Q&A and forum.

ENZYMES AND CELLULAR METABOLISM
Chapter 4

Memorize	Understand	Not Required*
ine: catabolism, anabolism, vation energy ine: metabolism, active/ steric sites	* Feedback, competitive, non-competitive inhibition * Krebs cycle, electron transport chain: main features * Metabolism: carbohydrates (glucose), fats and proteins	* Advanced level college info * Photosynthesis, gluconeogenesis, fatty acid oxidation * Knowing the deficiencies in the theoretical yield (36 ATP) calculation

GAMSAT-Prep.com

Introduction

Cells require energy to grow, reproduce, maintain structure, respond to the environment, etc. Biochemical reactions and other energy producing processes that occur in cells, including cellular metabolism, are regulated in part by enzymes. GAMSAT tests almost always include multiple questions exploring your understanding of a cycle or biochemical mechanism with or without negative or positive feedback. The questions do not center on your memorizing details but rather having an understanding of how the presented cycle functions or how it can be stimulated or inhibited.The end of Chapter 6 will focus on feedback loops with respect to hormones. Metabolism can be complex and it forms a story that you should be familiar with but that you should not spend time trying to memorize for the GAMSAT.

Additional Resources

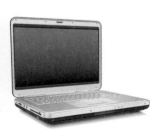

Free Online Q&A + Forum

Video: Online or DVD

Flashcards

Special Guest

* The real GAMSAT may have advanced level information presented (ie. in a passage) but previous knowledge of said information is not required to answer the questions that would follow. Practice ACER and GS practice GAMSATs can help you clarify this point.

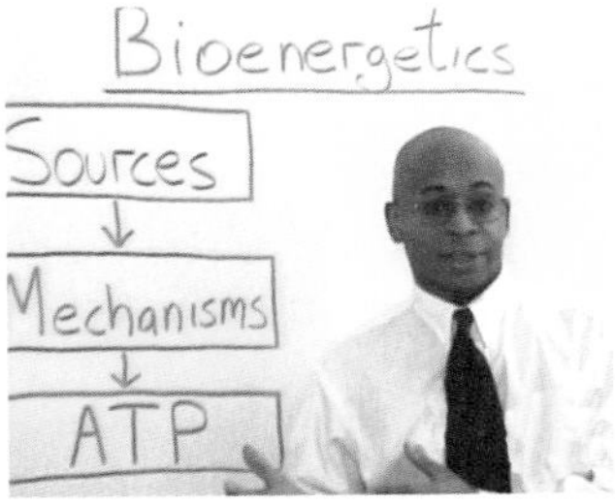

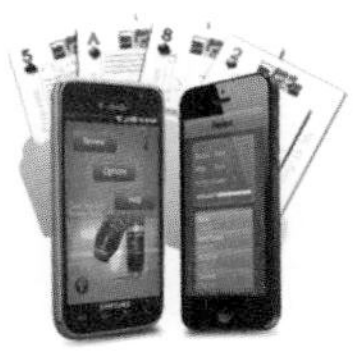

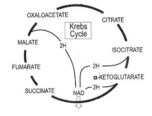

4.1 Overview

In an organism or an individual many biochemical reactions take place. All these biochemical reactions are collectively termed metabolism. In general, metabolism can be broadly divided into two main categories. They are:

(a) Catabolism which is the breakdown of macromolecules (larger molecules) such as glycogen to micromolecules (smaller molecules) such as glucose.

(b) Anabolism which is the building up of macromolecules such as protein using micromolecules such as amino acids.

As we all know, chemical reactions in general involve great energy exchanges when they occur. Similarly most catabolic and anabolic reactions would involve massive amounts of energy if they were to occur in vitro (outside the cell). However, all these reactions could be carried out within an environment of less free energy exchange, using molecules called enzymes.

What is an enzyme?

An enzyme is a protein catalyst. A protein is a large polypeptide made up of amino acid subunits. A catalyst is a substance that alters the rate of a chemical reaction without itself being permanently changed into another compound. A catalyst accelerates a reaction by decreasing the free energy of activation (see diagrams in CHM 9.5, 9.7).

Enzymes fall into two general categories:

(a) Simple proteins which contain only amino acids like the digestive enzymes ribonuclease, trypsin and chymotrypsin.

(b) Complex proteins which contain amino acids and a non-amino acid cofactor. Thus the complete enzyme is called a holoenzyme and it is made up of a protein portion (apoenzyme) and a cofactor.

> Holoenzyme = Apoenzyme + Cofactor.

A metal may serve as a cofactor. Zinc, for example, is a cofactor for the enzymes carbonic anhydrase and carboxypeptidase. An organic molecule such as pyridoxal phosphate or biotin may serve as a cofactor. Cofactors such as biotin, which are covalently linked to the enzyme are called prosthetic groups or ligands.

In addition to their enormous catalytic power which accelerates reaction rates, enzymes exhibit exquisite specificity in the types of reactions that each catalyzes as well as specificity for the substrates upon which they act. Their specificity is linked to the concept of an active site. An active site is a cluster of amino acids within the tertiary (i.e. 3-dimensional) configuration of the enzyme where the actual catalytic event occurs. The active site is often similar to a pocket or groove with properties (chemical or structural) that accommodate the intended substrate with high specificity.

Examples of such specificity are as follows: Phosphofructokinase catalyzes a reaction between ATP and fructose-6-phosphate. The enzyme does not catalyze a reaction between other nucleoside triphosphates. It is worth mentioning the specificity of trypsin and chymotrypsin though both of them are proteolytic (i.e. they degrade or hydrolyse proteins). Trypsin catalyzes the hydrolysis of peptides and proteins only on the carboxyl side of polypeptidic amino acids lysine and arginine. Chymotrypsin catalyzes the hydrolysis of peptides and proteins on the carboxyl side of polypeptidic amino acids phenylalanine, tyrosine and tryptophan. The degree of specificity described in the previous examples originally led to the **Lock and Key Model** which has been generally replaced by the **Induced Fit Hypothesis**. While the former suggests that the spatial structure of the active site of an enzyme fits exactly that of the substrate, the latter is more widely accepted and describes a greater flexibility at the active site and a conformational change in the enzyme to strengthen binding to the substrate.

4.2 Enzyme Kinetics and Inhibition

There is an increase in reaction velocity (= reaction rate) with an increase in the concentration of substrate. At increasingly higher substrate concentrations the increase in activity is progressively smaller. From this, it could be inferred that enzymes exhibit saturation kinetics. The mechanism of the preceding lies largely with saturation of the enzyme's active sites. As substrate concentration increases, more and more enzymes are converted to the substrate bound enzyme complex until all the enzyme active sites are bound to substrate. After this point, further increase in substrate concentration will not increase reaction rate.

Enzyme inhibitors are classified as: competitive inhibitor, noncompetitive inhibitor and irreversible inhibitor. In <u>competitive inhibition</u>, the inhibitor and the substrate are analogues that compete for binding to the active site, forming an unreactive enzyme-inhibitor complex. However, at higher substrate concentration, the inhibition can be reversed. In <u>noncompetitive inhibition</u>, the inhibitor can bind to the enzyme at a site different from the active site where the substrate binds to, thus forming either an unreactive enzyme-inhibitor complex or enzyme-substrate-inhibitor complex. However, a higher substrate concentration does not reverse the inhibition. In <u>irreversible inhibition</u>, the inhibitor binds permanently to the enzyme and inactivates it (e.g. heavy metals, aspirin, organophosphates). The effects caused by irreversible inhibitors are only overcome by synthesis of new enzyme.

4.3 Regulation of Enzyme Activity

The activity of enzymes in the cell is subject to a variety of regulatory mechanisms. The amount of enzyme can be altered by increasing or decreasing its synthesis or degradation. Enzyme induction refers to an enhancement of its synthesis. Repression refers to a decrease in its biosynthesis.

Enzyme activity can also be altered by covalent modification. Phosphorylation of specific serine residues by protein kinases increases or decreases catalytic activity depending upon the enzyme. Proteolytic cleavage of proenzymes (e.g., chymotrypsinogen, trypsinogen, protease and clotting factors) converts an inactive form to an active form (e.g., chymotrypsin, trypsin, etc.).

Enzyme activity can be greatly influenced by its environment (esp. pH and temperature). For example, most enzymes exhibit optimal activity at a pH in the range 6.5 to 7.5. However, pepsin (an enzyme found in the stomach) has an optimum pH

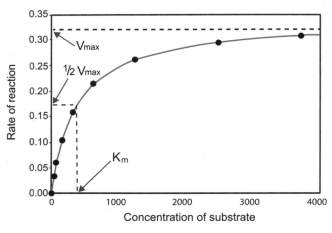

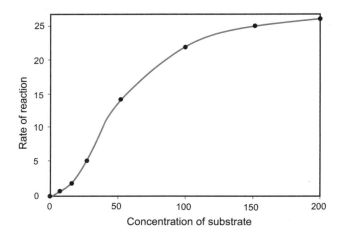

Michaelis-Menten Kinetics: Enzymes with single-substrate mechanisms usually follow the Michaelis-Menten model, in which the plot of velocity vs. substrate concentration [S] produces a rectangular hyperbola. Initially, the reaction rate [V] increases as substrate concentration [S] increases over a range of substrate concentration. However, as [S] gets higher, the enzyme becomes saturated with substrate and eventually the reaction rate [V] reaches maximum velocity V_{max} when the enzyme is fully saturated with substrate. Compare the diagram above with the curve of carrier-mediated transport (i.e. showing saturation kinetics) for solutes crossing the plasma membrane in BIO 1.1.2. The K_m is the substrate concentration at which an enzyme-catalyzed reaction occurs at half its maximal velocity, $V_{max}/2$. K_m is called the Michaelis constant. Each enzyme has a unique K_m value.

Non-Michaelis-Menten Kinetics: Some enzymes with multiple-substrate mechanisms exhibit the non-Michaelis-Menten model, in which the plot of velocity vs. substrate concentration [S] produces a sigmoid curve. This characterizes cooperative binding of substrate to the active site, which means that the binding of one substrate to one subunit affects the binding of subsequent substrate molecules to other subunits. This behavior is most common in multimeric enzymes with several active sites. Positive cooperativity occurs when binding of the first substrate increases the affinity of the other active sites for the following substrates. Negative cooperativity occurs when binding of the first substrate decreases the affinity of the other active site for the following substrates.

Fig. IV. A. 4.1 Enzyme Kinetic Curve Plot.

of ~ 2.0. Thus it cannot function adequately at a higher pH (i.e. in the small intestine). Likewise, enzymes function at an optimal temperature. When the temperature is lowered, kinetic energy decreases and thus the rate of reaction decreases. If the temperature is raised too much then the enzyme may become denatured and thus non-functional.

Enzyme activity can also be modified by an *allosteric* mechanism which involves binding to a site other than the active site. Isocitrate dehydrogenase is an enzyme in the Krebs Tricarboxylic Acid Cycle, which is activated by ADP. ADP is not a substrate or substrate analogue. It is postulated to bind a site *distinct* from the active site called the *allosteric site.* Positive effectors stabilize the more active form of enzyme and enhance enzyme activity while negative effectors stabilize the less active form of enzyme and inhibit enzyme activity.

Some enzymes fail to behave by simple saturation kinetics. In such cases a phenomenon called positive cooperativity is explained in which binding of one substrate or ligand shifts the enzyme from the less active form to the more active form and makes it easier for the second substrate to bind. Instead of a hyperbolic curve of velocity vs. substrate concentration [S] that many enzymes follow, sigmoid curve of velocity vs. [S] characterizes cooperativity (i.e. see the Enzyme Kinetic Curve Plot in this section as well as hemoglobin and myoglobin, BIO 7.5.1).

4.4 Bioenergetics

Biological species must transform energy into readily available sources in order to survive. ATP (adenosine triphosphate) is the body's most important short term energy storage molecule. It can be produced by the breakdown or oxidation of protein, lipids (i.e. fat) or carbohydrates (esp. glucose). If the body is no longer ingesting sources of energy it can access its own stores: glucose is stored in the liver as glycogen, lipids are stored throughout the body as fat, and ultimately, muscle can be catabolized to release protein (esp. amino acids).

We will be examining four key processes that can lead to the production of ATP: glycolysis, Krebs Citric Acid Cycle, the electron transport chain (ETC), and oxidative phosphorylation. Figure IV.A.4.2 is a schematic summary.

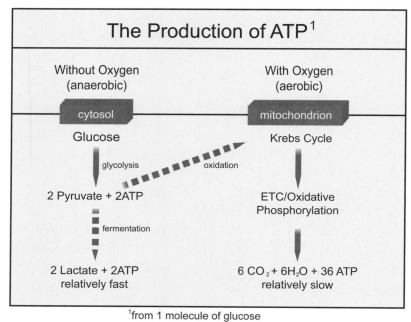

Figure IV.A.4.2: Summary of ATP production.

4.5 Glycolysis

The initial steps in the catabolism or *lysis* of D-glucose constitute the Embden - Meyerhof glyco*lytic* pathway. This pathway can occur in the absence of oxygen (anaerobic). The enzymes for glycolysis are present in all human cells and are located in the cytosol. The overall reaction can be depicted as follows (ADP: adenosine diphosphate, NAD: nicotinamide adenine dinucleotide, P_i: inorganic phosphate):

$$\text{Glucose} + 2\text{ADP} + 2\ \text{NAD}^+ + 2P_i \longrightarrow 2\text{Pyruvate} + 2\text{ATP} + 2\text{NADH} + 2\text{H}^+$$

The first step in glycolysis involves the phosphorylation of glucose by ATP. The enzyme that catalyzes this irreversible reaction is either hexokinase or glucokinase. Phosphohexose isomerase then catalyzes the conversion of glucose-6-phosphate to fructose-6-phosphate. Phosphofructokinase (PFK) catalyzes the second phosphorylation. It is an irreversible reaction. This reaction also utilizes 1 ATP. This step, which produces fructose-1,6-diphosphate, is said to be the rate limiting or pacemaker step in glycolysis. Aldolase then catalyzes the cleavage of fructose-1,6-diphosphate to glyceraldehyde-

3-phosphate and dihydroxyacetone phosphate (= 2 triose phosphates). Triose phosphate isomerase catalyzes the interconversion of the two preceding compounds. Glyceraldehyde-3-phosphate dehydrogenase mediates a reaction between the designated triose, NAD^+ and P_i to yield 1,3-diphosphoglycerate.

Next, phosphoglycerate kinase catalyzes the reaction of the latter, an energy rich compound, with ADP to yield ATP and phosphoglycerate. This reaction generates 2 ATP per glucose molecule. Phosphoglycerate mutase catalyzes the transfer of the phosphoryl group to carbon two to yield 2-phosphoglycerate. Enolase catalyzes a dehydration reaction to yield phosphoenolpyruvate and water. The enzyme enolase is inhibited by fluoride at high, nonphysiological concentrations. This is why blood samples that are drawn for estimation of glucose are added to fluoride to inhibit glycolysis. Phosphoenolpyruvate is then acted upon by pyruvate kinase to yield pyruvate which is a three carbon compound and 2 ATP.

NADH produced in glycolysis must regenerate NAD^+ so that glycolysis can continue. Under **aerobic** conditions (i.e. in the presence of oxygen) pyruvate is converted to Acetyl CoA which will enter the Krebs Cycle followed by oxidative phosphorylation producing a total of 38 ATP per molecule of glucose (i.e. 2 pyruvate). Electrons from NADH are transferred to the electron transfer chain located on the inside of the inner mitochondrial membrane and thus NADH produced during glycolysis in the cytosol is converted back to NAD^+.

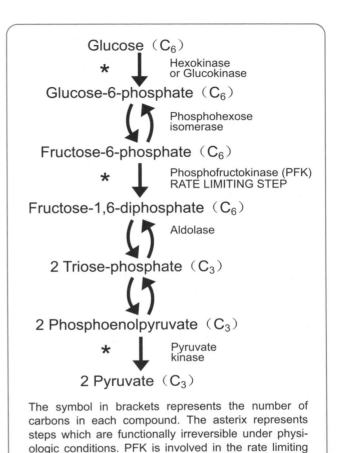

The symbol in brackets represents the number of carbons in each compound. The asterix represents steps which are functionally irreversible under physiologic conditions. PFK is involved in the rate limiting step which is activated by ADP and inhibited by ATP.

Figure IV.A.4.3: Summary of glycolysis.

Under **anaerobic conditions**, pyruvate is quickly reduced by NADH to lactic acid using the enzyme lactate dehydrogenase and NAD^+ is regenerated. A net of only 2 ATP is produced per molecule of glucose (this process is called *fermentation*).

Oxygen Debt: after running a 100m dash you may find yourself gasping for air even if you have completely ceased activity. This is because during the race you could not get an adequate amount of oxygen to your muscles and your muscles needed energy quickly; thus the anaerobic pathway was used. The lactic acid which built up during the race will require you to *pay back* a certain amount of oxygen in order to oxidize lactate to pyruvate and continue along the more energy efficient aerobic pathway.

4.6 Glycolysis: A Negative Perspective

An interesting way to summarize the main events of glycolysis is to follow the fate of the phosphate group which contains a negative charge. Note that *kinases* and *phosphatases* are enzymes that can add or subtract phosphate groups, respectively.

The first event in glycolysis is the phosphorylation of glucose. Thus glucose becomes negatively charged which prevents it from leaking out of the cell. Then glucose-6-phosphate becomes its isomer (= *same* molecular formula, *different* structure) fructose-6-phosphate which is further phosphorylated to fructose-1,6-diphosphate. Imagine that this six carbon sugar (*fructose*) now contains two large negatively charged ligands which repel each other! The six carbon sugar (*hexose*) sensibly breaks into two three-carbon compounds (*triose phosphates*).

A triose phosphate is ultimately converted to 1,3-diphosphoglycerate which is clearly an unstable compound (i.e. *two negative phosphate groups*). Thus it transfers a high energy phosphate group onto ADP to produce ATP. When ATP is produced from a substrate (i.e. 1,3-diphosphoglycerate), the reaction is called *substrate level phosphorylation*.

A closer look at ATP and glycolysis: from one molecule of glucose, 2 molecules of pyruvate are obtained. During the glycolytic reaction, 2 ATP are used (one used in the phosphorylation of glucose to glucose 6-phosphate and one used in the phosphorylation of fructose 6-phosphate to fructose 1,6-bisphosphate) and 4 ATP are generated (two in the conversion of 1,3-bisphophoglycerate to 3-phosphoglycerate and two in the conversion of phosphoenolpyruvate to pyruvate).

4.7 Krebs Citric Acid Cycle

Aerobic conditions: for further breakdown of pyruvate it has to enter the mitochondria where a series of reactions will cleave the molecule to water and carbon dioxide. All these reactions (which were discovered by Hans. A. Krebs) are collectively known as the Tricarboxylic Acid Cycle (TCA) or Krebs Citric Acid Cycle. Not only carbohydrates but also lipids and proteins use the TCA for channelling their metabolic pathways. This is why

TCA is often called the final common pathway of metabolism.

The glycolysis of glucose (C_6) produces 2 pyruvate (C_3) which in turn produces 2 CO_2 and 2 acetyl CoA (C_2). Pyruvate is oxidized to acetyl CoA and CO_2 by the pyruvate dehydrogenase complex (PDC). The PDC is a complex of 3 enzymes located in the mitochondria of eukaryotic cells (and of course, in the cytosol of prokaryotes). This step is also known as the *link reaction* or *transition step* since it links glycolysis and the TCA cycle.

The catabolism of both glucose and fatty acids yield acetyl CoA. Metabolism of amino acids yields acetyl CoA or actual intermediates of the TCA Cycle. The Citric Acid Cycle provides a pathway for the oxidation of acetyl CoA. The pathway includes eight discrete steps. Seven of the enzyme activities are found in the mitochondrial matrix; the eighth (succinate dehydrogenase) is associated with the Electron Transport Chain (ETC) within the inner mitochondrial membrane.

The following includes key points to remember about the TCA Cycle: i) glucose → 2 acetyl CoA → 2 turns around the TCA Cycle; ii) 2 CO_2 per turn is generated as a waste product which will eventually be blown off in the lungs; iii) one GTP (guanosine triphosphate) per turn is produced by substrate level phosphorylation; one GTP is equivalent to one ATP (*GTP + ADP → GDP + ATP*); iv) *reducing equivalents* are <u>hydrogens</u> which are carried by NAD^+ (→ $NADH + H^+$) three times per turn and FAD (→ $FADH_2$) once per turn; v) for each molecule of glucose, 2 pyruvates are produced and oxidized to acetyl CoA in the "fed" state (as opposed to the "fasting" state). The acetyl CoA then enters the TCA cycle, yielding 3 NADH, 1 $FADH_2$, and 1 GTP per acetyl CoA. These reducing equivalents will eventually be oxidized to produce ATP (*oxidative phosphorylation*) and eventually produce H_2O as a waste product (the last step in the ETC); vi) the hydrogens (*H*) which are reducing equivalents are not protons (*H^+*) - quite the contrary! Often the reducing equivalents are simply called electrons.

4.8 Oxidative Phosphorylation

The term oxidative phosphorylation refers to reactions associated with oxygen consumption and the phosphorylation of ADP to yield ATP. The synthesis of ATP is coupled to the flow of electrons from NADH and $FADH_2$ to O_2 in the electron transport chain. Oxidative phosphorylation is associated with an Electron Transport Chain or Respiratory Chain which is found in the inner mitochondrial membrane of eukaryotes. A similar process occurs within the plasma membrane of prokaryotes such as *E.coli*.

The importance of oxidative phosphorylation is that it accounts for the reoxidation of reducing equivalents generated in the reac-

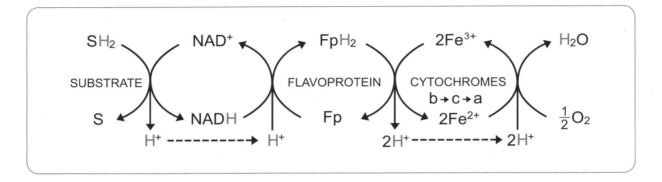

Figure IV.A.4.4: Transport of reducing equivalents through the respiratory chain. Examples of substrates (S) which provide reductants are isocitrate, malate, etc. Cytochromes contain iron (Fe).

tions of the Krebs Cycle as well as in glycolysis. This process accounts for the preponderance of ATP production in humans. The electron flow from NADH and $FADH_2$ to oxygen by a series of carrier molecules located in the inner mitochondrial membrane (IMM) provides energy to pump hydrogens from the mitochondrial matrix to the intermembrane space against the proton electrochemical gradient. The proton motive force then drives the movement of hydrogen back into the matrix thus providing the energy for ATP synthesis by ATP synthase. A schematic summary is in Figure IV.A.4.4.

The term *chemiosmosis* refers to the movement of protons across the IMM (a selectively permeable membrane) down their electrochemical gradient using the kinetic energy to phosphorylate ADP making ATP. The generation of ATP by chemiosmosis occurs in chloroplasts and mitochondria as well as in some bacteria.

4.9 Electron Transport Chain (ETC)

The following are the components of the ETC: iron - sulphur proteins, cytochromes c, b, a and coenzyme Q or *ubiquinone*. The respiratory chain proceeds from NAD specific dehydrogenases through flavoprotein, ubiquinone, then cytochromes and ultimately molecular oxygen. Reducing equivalents can enter the chain at two locations. Electrons from NADH are transferred to NADH dehydrogenase. In reactions involving iron - sulphur proteins electrons are transferred to coenzyme Q; protons are translocated from the mitochondrial matrix to the exterior of the inner membrane during this process. This creates a proton gradient, which is coupled to the production of ATP by ATP synthase.

Electrons entering from succinate dehydrogenase ($FADH_2$) are donated directly to coenzyme Q. Electrons are transported from reduced coenzyme Q to cytochrome b and then cytochrome c. Electrons are then carried by cytochrome c to cytochrome a.

Cytochrome a is also known as *cytochrome oxidase*. It catalyzes the reaction of electrons and protons with molecular oxygen to produce water. Cyanide and carbon monoxide are powerful inhibitors of cytochrome oxidase.

4.10 Summary of Energy Production

Note the following: i) 1 NADH produces 3 ATP molecules while 1 $FADH_2$ produces only 2 ATP; ii) there is a cost of 2 ATP to get the two molecules of NADH generated in the cytoplasm (see the preceding point # 2.) to enter the mitochondrion, thus the *net yield for eukaryotes is 36 ATP.*

The efficiency of ATP production is far from 100%. Energy is lost from the system

primarily in the form of heat. Under standard conditions, less than 40% of the energy generated from the complete oxidation of glucose is converted to the production of ATP. As a comparison, a gasoline engine fairs much worse with an efficiency rating generally less than 30%. Further inefficiencies reduce the net theoretical yield in the (non-GAMSAT!) real world.

Process of reaction	ATP yield
1. Glycolysis (Glucose → 2 Pyruvate)	2
2. Glycolysis (2NADH from glyceraldehyde-3-phosphate dehydrogenase)	6
3. Pyruvate dehydrogenase (2NADH)	6
4. Isocitrate dehydrogenase (2NADH)	6
5. Alpha-ketoglutarate dehydrogenase (2NADH)	6
6. Succinate thiokinase (2GTP)	2
7. Succinate dehydrogenase (2$FADH_2$)	4
8. Malate dehydrogenase (2NADH)	6
TOTAL	38 ATP yield per hexose.

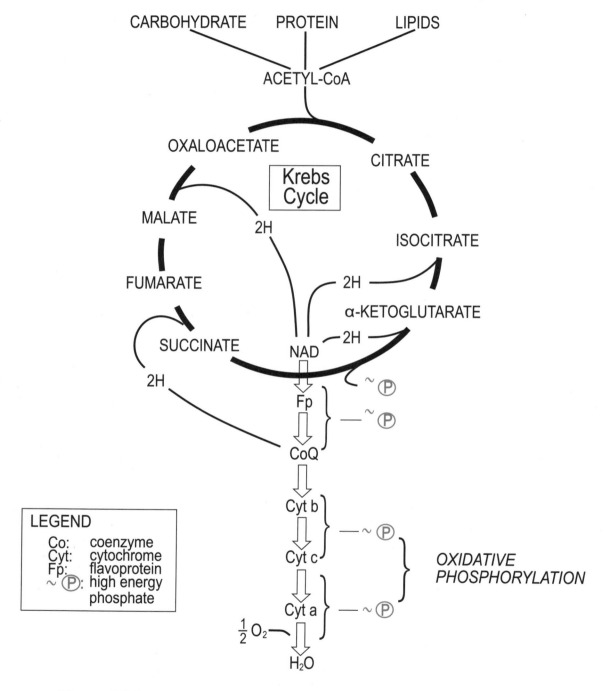

Figure IV.A.4.5: Summary of the Krebs Cycle and the Electron Transport Chain.
Note: Acetyl CoA can be the product of carbohydrate, protein, or lipid metabolism. Thick black arrows represent the Krebs Cycle while white arrows represent the Electron Transport Chain. High energy phosphate groups are transferred from ADP to produce ATP. Ultimately, oxygen accepts electrons and hydrogen from Cyt a to produce water.

Go online to GAMSAT-prep.com for additional chapter review Q&A and forum.

Memorize	Understand	Not Required*
ron: basic structure and function sons for the membrane potential	* Resting potential: electrochemical gradient/action potential, graph * Excitatory and inhibitory nerve fibers: summation, frequency of firing * Organization of contractile elements: actin and myosin filaments * Cross bridges, sliding filament model; calcium regulation of contraction	* Advanced level college info * Memorizing details about epithelial cells, connective tissue

GAMSAT-Prep.com

Introduction ▥▥▥▥

To build a living organism, with all the various tissues and organs, cells must specialize. Communication among cells and organs, movement, protection and support are achieved to a great degree by neurons, muscle cells, epithelial cells and the cells of connective tissue, respectively.

Additional Resources

Free Online Q&A + Forum

Video: Online or DVD

Flashcards

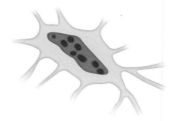

Special Guest

* The real GAMSAT may have advanced level information presented (ie. in a passage) but previous knowledge of said information is not required to answer the questions that would follow. Practice ACER and GS practice GAMSATs can help you clarify this point.

The brain, spinal cord and peripheral nervous system are composed of nerve tissue. The basic cell types of nerve tissue is the *neuron* and the *glial cell*. Glial cells support and protect neurons and participate in neural activity, nutrition and defense processes. Neurons (= nerve cells) represent the functional unit of the nervous system. They conduct and transmit nerve impulses.

Neurons can be classified based on the shape or *morphology*. Unipolar neurons possess a single process. Bipolar neurons possess a single axon and a single dendrite. Multipolar neurons possess a single axon and more than one dendrite and are the most common type. Pseudounipolar neurons possess a single process that subsequently branches out into an axon and dendrite (note that in biology "pseudo" means "false"). Neurons can also be classified based on function. Sensory neurons receive stimuli from the environment and conduct impulses to the CNS. Motor neurons conduct impulses from the CNS to other neurons, muscles or glands. Interneurons connect other neurons and regulate transmitting signal between neurons.

Each neuron consists of a nerve cell body (*perikaryon or soma*), and its processes, which usually include multiple *dendrites* and a single *axon*. The cell body of a typical neuron contains a nucleus, *Nissl* material which is rough endoplasmic reticulum, free ribosomes, Golgi apparatus, mitochondria, many neurotubules, neurofilaments and pigment inclusions. The cell processes of neurons occur as axons and dendrites.

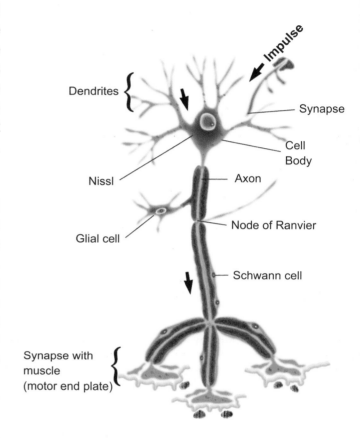

Figure IV.A.5.1: A neuron and other cells of nerve tissue, showing the neuromuscular junction, or motor end plate.

Dendrites contain most of the components of the cell, whereas axons contain major structures found in dendrites except for the Nissl material and Golgi apparatus. As a rule, dendrites receive stimuli from sensory cells, axons, or other neurons and conduct these impulses to the cell body of neurons and ultimately through to the axon. Axons are long cellular processes that conduct impulses away from the cell body of neurons. These originate from the axon hillock, a specialized region that contains many microtubules and neurofilaments. At the synaptic (terminal) ends of axons, the presynaptic process contains vesicles from which are elaborated excitatory or inhibitory substances.

Unmyelinated fibers in peripheral nerves lie in grooves on the surface of the neurolemma (= plasma membrane) of a type of glial cell (*Schwann cell*). **Myelinated** peripheral neurons are invested by numerous layers of plasma membrane of Schwann cells or oligodendrocytes that constitute a *myelin sheath*, which allows axons to conduct impulses faster. The myelin sheath is produced by oligodendrocytes in the CNS and by Schwann cells in the PNS. In junctional areas between adjacent Schwann cells or oligodendrocytes there is a lack of myelin. These junctional areas along the myelinated process constitute the nodes of Ranvier.

The neurons of the nervous system are arranged so that each neuron stimulates or inhibits other neurons and these in turn may stimulate or inhibit others until the functions of the nervous system are performed. The area between a neuron and the successive cell (i.e. another neuron, muscle fiber or gland) is called a *synapse*. Synapses can be classified as either a chemical synapse or an electrical synapse. A chemical synapse involves the release of a neurotransmitter by the presynaptic cell which then diffuses across the synapse and can act on the postsynaptic cell to generate an action potential. Signal transmission is delayed due to the time required for diffusion of the neurotransmitter across the synapse onto the membrane of the postsynaptic cell. An electrical synapse involves the movement of ions from one neuron to another via gap junctions (BIO 1.4.1). Signal transmission is immediate. Electrical synapses are often found in neural systems that require the fastest possible response, such as defensive reflexes.

When a neuron makes a synapse with muscle, it is called a *motor end plate* (see Fig. IV.A.5.1). The terminal endings of the nerve filament that synapse with the next cell are called presynaptic terminals, synaptic knobs, or more commonly - synaptic boutons. The postsynaptic terminal is the membrane part of another neuron or muscle or gland that is receiving the impulse. The synaptic cleft is the narrow space between the presynaptic and postsynaptic membrane.

At the synapse there is no physical contact between the two cells. The space between the dendrite of one neuron and the axon of another neuron is called the synaptic cleft and it measures about 200 - 300 angstroms (1 angstrom = 10^{-10} m) in a chemical synapse and about a tenth of that distance in an electrical synapse. The mediators in a chemical synapse, known as neurotransmitters, are housed in the presynaptic terminal and are exocytosed in response to an increase in intracellular Ca^{2+} concentration. The mediators or transmitters diffuse through the synaptic cleft when an impulse reaches the terminal and bind to receptors in the postsynaptic membrane. This transmitter substance may either excite the *postsynaptic* neuron or inhibit it. They are therefore called either excitatory or inhibitory transmitters (examples include *acetylcholine* and *GABA*, respectively).

5.1.1 The Membrane Potential

A membrane or resting potential (V_m) occurs across the plasma membranes of all cells. In large nerve and muscle cells this potential amounts to about 70 millivolts with positivity outside the cell membrane and negativity inside ($V_m = -70$ mV). The development of this potential occurs as follows: every cell membrane contains a $Na^+ - K^+$ ATPase that pumps each ion to where its concentration is highest. The concentration of K^+ is higher inside the neuron and the concentration of Na^+ is higher outside; therefore, Na^+ is pumped to the outside of the cell and K^+ to the inside. However, more Na^+ is pumped outward than K^+ inward ($3Na^+$ per $2K^+$). Also, the membrane is relatively permeable to K^+ so that it can leak out of the cell with relative ease. Therefore, the net effect is a loss of positive charges from inside the membrane and a gain of positive charges on the outside. The resulting membrane potential is the basis of all conduction of impulses by nerve and muscle fibers.

5.1.2 Action Potential

The action potential is a sequence of changes in the electric potential that occurs within a small fraction of a second when a nerve or muscle membrane impulse spreads over the surface of the cell. An excitatory stimulus on a postsynaptic neuron depolarizes the membrane and makes the membrane potential less negative. Once the membrane potential reaches a critical threshold, the voltage-gated Na^+ channels become fully open, permitting the inward flow of Na^+ into the cell. The membrane potential is at the critical threshold when it is in a state where an action potential is inevitable. As a result, the positive sodium ions on the outside of the membrane now flow rapidly to the more negative interior. Therefore, the membrane potential suddenly becomes reversed with positivity on the inside and negativity on the outside. This state is called *depolarization* and is caused by an inward Na^+ current.

Depolarization also leads to the inactivation of the Na^+ channel and slowly opens the K^+ channel. The combined effect of the two preceding events repolarizes the membrane back to its resting potential. This is called *repolarization*. In fact, the neuron may shoot past the resting membrane potential and become even more negative, and this is called hyperpolarization. The depolarized nerve goes on depolarizing the adjacent nerve membrane in a wavy manner which is called an impulse. In other words, an impulse is a wave of depolarization. Different axons can propagate impulses at different speeds. The increasing diameter of a nerve fiber or degree of myelination results in a faster impulse. The impulse is fastest in myelinated fibers since the wave of depolarization "jumps" from node to node of Ranvier: this is called *saltatory* conduction because an action potential can be generated only at nodes of Ranvier.

Immediately following an action potential, the neuron will pass through three stages in the following order: a) it can no longer elicit

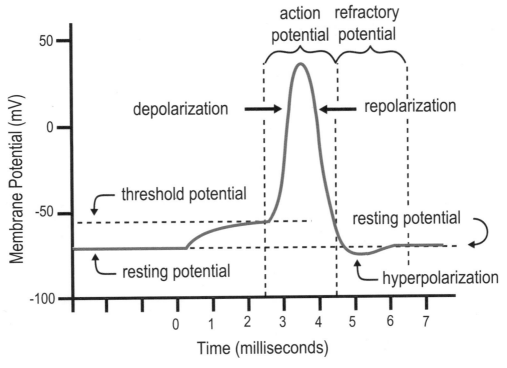

Figure IV.A.5.2: Action potential.

another action potential no matter how large the stimulus is = *absolute refractory period*; b) it can elicit another action potential only if a larger than usual stimulus is provided = *relative refractory period*; c) it returns to its original resting potential and thus can depolarize as easily as it originally did.

The action potential is an all-or-none event. The magnitude or strength of the action potential is not graded according to the strength of the stimulus. It occurs with the same magnitude each time it occurs, or it does not occur at all.

5.1.3 Action Potential: A Positive Perspective

To better understand the action potential it is useful to take a closer look at what occurs to the positive ions Na$^+$ and K$^+$. To begin with, there are protein channels in the plasma membrane that act like gates which guard the passage of specific ions. Some gates open or close in response to V_m and are thus called *voltage gated channels*.

Once a threshold potential is reached, the voltage gated Na^+ channels open allowing the permeability or *conductance* of Na^+ to increase. The Na^+ ions can now diffuse across their chemical gradient: from an area of high concentration (*outside the membrane*) to an area of low concentration (*inside the membrane*). The Na^+ ions will also diffuse across their electrical gradient: from an area of relative positivity (*outside the membrane*) to an area of relative negativity (*inside the membrane*). Thus the inside becomes positive and the membrane is depolarized. Repolarization occurs as the Na^+ channels close and the voltage gated K^+ channels open. As K^+ conductance increases to the outside (where K^+ concentration is lowest), the membrane repolarizes to once again become relatively negative on the inside.

5.2 Contractile Cells and Tissues

There are three types of muscle tissue: smooth, skeletal and cardiac. All three types are composed of muscle cells (fibers) that contain myofibrils possessing contractile filaments of actin and myosin.

Smooth muscle:- Smooth muscle cells are spindle shaped and are organized chiefly into sheets or bands of smooth muscle tissue. They contain a single nucleus and actively divide and regenerate. This tissue is found in blood vessels and other tubular visceral structures (i.e. intestines). Smooth muscles contain both actin and myosin filaments but actin predominates. The filaments are not organized into patterns that give cross striations as in cardiac and skeletal muscle. Filaments course obliquely in the cells and attach to the plasma membrane. Contraction of smooth muscle is involuntary and is innervated by the autonomic nervous system.

Skeletal muscle:- Skeletal muscle fibers are characterized by their peripherally located multiple nuclei and striated myofibrils. Myofibrils are longitudinally arranged bundles of thick and thin myofilaments. Myofilaments are composed of thick and thin filaments present in an alternating arrangement responsible for the cross-striation pattern. The striations in a sarcomere consists of an A-band (dark), which contains both thin and thick filaments. These are bordered toward the Z-lines by I-bands (light), which contain thin filaments only. The mid-region of the A-band contains an H-band (light), which contains thick filaments only and is bisected by an M-line. The Z lines are dense regions bisecting each I-band and anchor the thin filaments. The filaments interdigitate and are cross-bridged in the A-band with myosin filaments forming a hexagonal pattern of one myosin filament surrounded by six actin filaments. In the contraction of a muscle fiber,

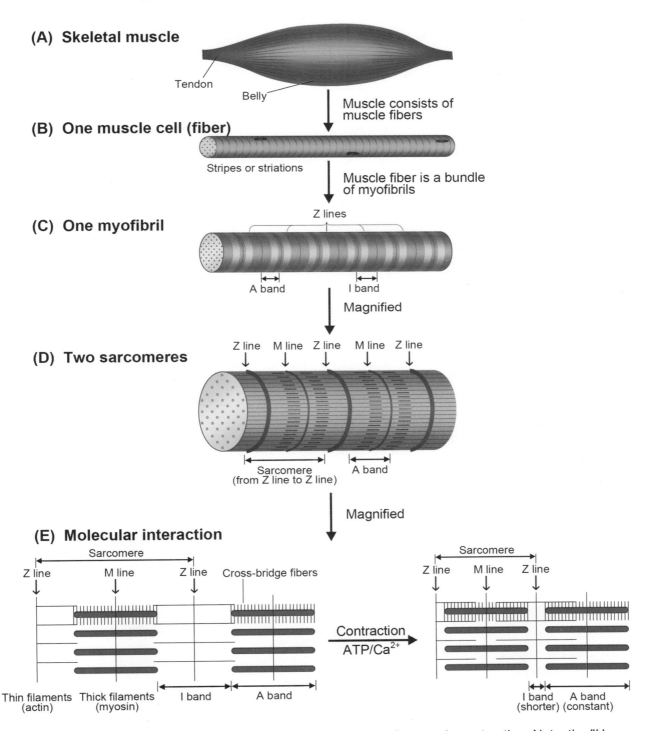

Figure IV.A.5.3: A schematic view of the molecular basis for muscle contraction. Note: the "H zone" is the central portion of an A band and is characterized by the presence of myosin filaments.

thick and thin filaments do not shorten but increase their overlap. The actin filaments of the I-bands move more deeply into the A-band, resulting in a shortening of the H-band and the I-bands as Z disks are brought closer. However, the A-band remains constant in length. {Mnemonic: "HI" bands shorten}

Each skeletal muscle fiber is invested with a sarcolemma (= plasmalemma = plasma membrane) that extends into the fiber as numerous small transverse tubes called T-tubules. These tubules ring the myofibrils at the A-I junction and are bounded on each side by terminal cisternae of the endoplasmic (sarcoplasmic) reticulum. The T-tubules, together with a pair of terminal cisternae form a triad. The triad helps to provide a uniform contraction throughout the muscle cell as it provides channels for ions to flow freely and helps to propagate action potentials. There are thousands of triads per skeletal muscle fiber.

The sarcoplasmic reticulum is a modified endoplasmic reticulum that regulates muscle contraction by either transporting Ca^{2+} into storage (muscle relaxation) or releasing Ca^{2+} during excitation-contraction coupling (muscle contraction).

The thick filaments within a myofibril are composed of about 250 myosin molecules arranged in an antiparallel fashion and some associated proteins. The myosin molecule is composed of two identical heavy chains and two pairs of light chain. The heavy chain consists of two "heads" and one "tail". The head contains an actin binding site which is involved

in muscle contraction. The thin filaments within a myofibril are composed of actin and to a lesser degree two smaller proteins: *troponin and tropomyosin*. An action potential in the muscle cell membrane initiates depolarization of the T tubules, which causes the nearby sarcoplasmic reticulum to release its Ca^{2+} ions and thus an increase in intracellular $[Ca^{2+}]$. Calcium then attaches to a subunit of troponin resulting in the movement of tropomyosin and the uncovering of the active sites for the attachment of actin to the cross bridging heads of myosin. Due to this attachment, ATP in the myosin head hydrolyses, producing energy, Pi and ADP which results in a bending of the myosin head and a pulling of the actin filament into the A-band. These actin-myosin bridges detach again when myosin binds a new ATP molecule and attaches to a new site on actin toward the plus end as long as Ca^{2+} is bound to troponin. Finally, relaxation of muscle occurs when Ca^{2+} is sequestered by the sarcoplasmic reticulum. Thus calcium is pumped out of the cytoplasm and calcium levels return to normal, tropomyosin again binds to actin, preventing myosin from binding.

There are three interesting consequences to the preceding:

i) neither actin nor myosin change length during muscle contraction; rather, shortening of the muscle fiber occurs as the filaments slide over each other increasing the area of overlap.

ii) initially a dead person is very stiff (*rigor mortis*) since they can no longer produce the ATP necessary to detach the actin-myosin bridges thus their muscles remain locked in position.

iii) Ca^{2+} is a critical ion both for muscle contraction and for transmitter release from presynaptic neurons.

Cardiac muscle:- Cardiac muscle contains striations and myofibrils that are similar to those of skeletal muscle. Contraction of cardiac muscle is involuntary and is innervated by the autonomic nervous system. It differs from skeletal muscle in several major ways. Cardiac muscle fibers branch and contain centrally located nuclei (characteristically, one nucleus per cell) and large numbers of mitochondria. Individual cardiac muscle cells are attached to each other at their ends by *intercalated* disks. These disks contain several types of membrane junctional complexes, the most important of which is the *gap junction* (BIO 1.4.1). Cardiac muscle cells do not regenerate: injury to cardiac muscle is repaired by fibrous connective tissue.

The gap junction electrically couples one cell to its neighbor (= *syncytium*) so that electric depolarization is propagated throughout the heart by cell-to-cell contact rather than by nerve innervation to each cell. The sarcoplasmic reticulum - T-tubule system is arranged differently in cardiac muscle than in skeletal muscle. In cardiac muscle each T-tubule enters at the Z-line and forms a diad with only one terminal cisterna of sarcoplasmic reticulum.

5.3 Epithelial Cells and Tissues

Epithelia have the following characteristics:

1. they cover all body surfaces (i.e. skin, organs, etc.)
2. they are the principal tissues of glands
3. their cells are anchored by a nonliving layer (= the basement membrane)
4. they lack blood vessels and are thus nourished by diffusion.

Epithelial tissues are classified according to the characteristics of their cells. Tissues with elongated cells are called *columnar*, those with thin flattened cells are *squamous*, and those with cube-like cells are *cuboidal*. They are further classified as **simple** if they have a single layer of cells and **stratified** if they have multiple layers of cells. As examples of the classification, skin is composed of a stratified squamous epithelium while various glands (i.e. thyroid, salivary, etc.) contain a simple cuboidal epithelium. The former epithelium serves to protect against microorganisms, loss of water or heat, while the latter epithelium functions to secrete glandular products.

5.4 Connective Cells and Tissues

Connective tissue connects and joins other body tissue and parts. It also carries substances for processing, nutrition, and waste release. Connective tissue is characterized by the presence of relatively few cells surrounded by an extensive network of extracellular matrix, consisting of ground substance, extracellular fluid, and fibers.

The adult connective tissues are: connective tissue proper, cartilage, bone and blood (see *The Circulatory System*, section 7.5). Connective tissue proper is further classified into loose connective tissue, dense connective tissue, elastic tissue, reticular tissue and adipose tissue.

5.4.1 Loose Connective Tissue

Loose connective tissue is found in the superficial fascia. It is generally considered as the *packaging material* of the body, in part, because it frequently envelopes muscles. Fascia - usually a clear or white sheet (or band) of fibrous connective tissue - helps to bind skin to underlying organs, to fill spaces between muscles, etc. Loose connective tissue contains most of the cell types and all the fiber types found in the other connective tissues. The most common cell types are the fibroblast, macrophage, adipose cell, mast cell, plasma cell and wandering cells from the blood (which include several types of white blood cells).

Fibroblasts are the predominant cell type in connective tissue proper and have the capability to differentiate into other types of cells under certain conditions.

Macrophages are part of the *reticuloendothelial system* (tissue which predominately destroys foreign particles). They are responsible for phagocytosing foreign bodies and assisting the immune response. They possess large lysosomes containing digestive enzymes which are necessary for the digestion of phagocytosed materials. Mast cells reside mostly along blood vessels and contain granules which include *heparin* and *histamine*. Heparin is a compound which prevents blood clotting and histamine is associated with allergic reactions. Mast cells mediate type I hypersensitivity.

Plasma cells are part of the immune system in that they produce circulatory antibodies (BIO 7.5, 8.2). They contain extensive amounts of rough endoplasmic reticulum (rER).

Adipose cells are found in varying quantities, when they predominate, the tissue is called adipose (fat) tissue.

Fibers are long protein polymers present in different types of connective tissue. Common types of fibers include collagen fiber, reticular fiber and elastic fiber.

Collagen fibers are usually found in bundles and provide **strength** to the tissue. Many different types of collagen fibers are identified on the basis of their molecular structure. Of the five most common types, collagen type I is the most abundant, being found in dermis, bone, dentine, tendons, organ capsules, fascia and sclera. Type II is located in hyaline and elastic cartilage. Type III is probably the collagenous component of reticular fibers. Type IV is found in a specific part (*the basal lamina*) of basement membranes. Type V is a component of placental basement membranes. **Reticular fibers** are smaller, more delicate fibers that form the basic framework of reticular connective tissue. **Elastic fibers** branch and provide elasticity and support to connective tissue.

Ground substance is the gelatinous material that fills most of the space between the cells and the fibers. It is composed of acid mucopolysaccharides and structural glycoproteins and its properties are important in determining the permeability and consistency of the connective tissue.

5.4.2 Dense Connective Tissue

Dense irregular connective tissue is found in the dermis, periosteum, perichondrium and capsules of some organs. All of the fiber types are present, but collagenous fibers predominate. Dense regular connective tissue occurs as aponeuroses, ligaments and tendons. In most ligaments and tendons collagenous fibers are most prevalent and are oriented parallel to each other. Fibroblasts are practically the only cell type present.

5.4.3 Cartilage

Cartilage is composed of chondrocytes (= cartilage cells) embedded in an intercellular (= extracellular) matrix, consisting of fibers and an amorphous firm ground substance. In cases of injury, cartilage repairs slowly since it has no direct blood supply. Three types of cartilage are distinguished on the basis of the amount of ground substance and the relative abundance of collagenous and elastic fibers. They are hyaline, elastic and fibrous cartilage.

Hyaline Cartilage is found as costal (rib) cartilage, articular cartilage and cartilage of the nose, larynx, trachea and bronchi. The extracellular matrix consists primarily of collagenous fibers and a ground substance rich in chondromucoprotein, a copolymer of a protein and chondroitin sulphates.

Elastic Cartilage is found in the pinna of the ear, auditory tube and epiglottis, and some laryngeal cartilage. Elastic fibers predominate and thus provide greater flexibility. Calcification of this type of cartilage is rare.

Fibrous Cartilage occurs in the anchorage of tendons and ligaments, in intervertebral disks, in the symphysis pubis, and in some interarticular disks and in some ligaments. Chondrocytes occur singly or in rows between large bundles of collagenous fibers. Compared with hyaline cartilage, only small amounts of hyaline matrix surround the chondrocytes of fibrous cartilage.

5.4.4 Bone

Bone tissue consists of three **cell types** and a calcified **extracellular matrix** that contains organic and inorganic components. The three cell types are: *osteoblasts* which synthesize the organic components of the matrix (osteoid) and become embedded in lacunae; *osteocytes* which are mature bone cells entrapped in their own lacunae within the matrix and maintain communication with each other via gap junctions; and *osteoclasts* which are large multinucleated cells functioning in resorption and remodeling of bone.

The organic matrix consists of dense collagenous fibers (primarily type I collagen) which is important in providing flexibility and tensile strength to bone. The inorganic component is responsible for the *rigidity* of the bone and is composed chiefly of calcium phosphate and calcium carbonate with small amounts of magnesium, fluoride, hydroxide, sulphate and hydroxyapatite.

Compact bone contains <u>haversian systems</u> (osteons), interstitial lamellae and circumferential lamellae. The Haversian system is the structural unit for bone and each osteon consists of a central Haversian canal surrounded by a number of concentric deposits of bony matrix called lamellae. Haversian systems consist of extensively branching haversian canals that are oriented chiefly longitudinally in long bones. Each canal contains blood vessels and is surrounded by 8 to 15 concentric lamellae and osteocytes.

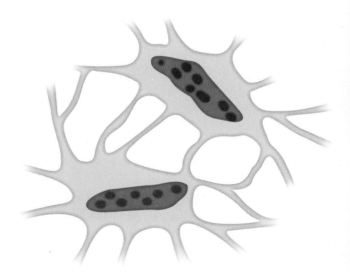

Figure IV.A.5.4: Osteocytes.

Nutrients from blood vessels in the haversian canals pass through canaliculi and lacunae to reach all osteocytes in the system. Volkmann's canals traverse the bone transversely and interconnect the haversian systems. They enter through the outer circumferential lamellae and carry blood vessels and nerves which are continuous with those of the haversian canals and the periosteum. The periosteum is the connective tissue layer which envelopes bone. The endosteum is the connective tissue layer which lines the marrow cavities and supplies osteoprogenitor cells and osteoblasts for bone formation.

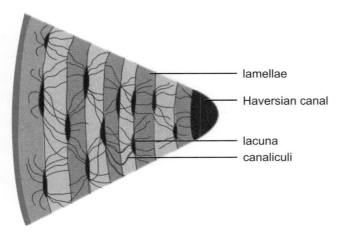

Figure IV.A.5.5: Schematic drawing of part of a haversian system.

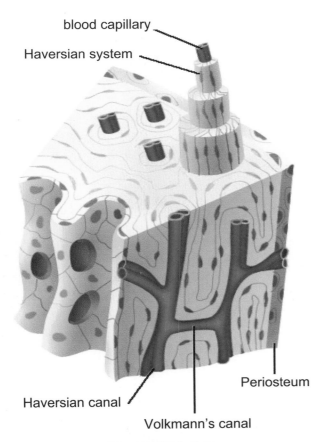

Figure IV.A.5.6
Schematic drawing of the wall of a long bone.

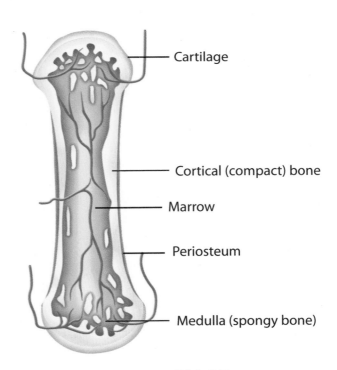

Figure IV.A.5.7
Schematic drawing of adult bone structure.

Bones are supplied by a loop of blood vessels that enter from the periosteal region, penetrate the cortical bone, and enter the medulla before returning to the periphery of the bone. Long bones are specifically supplied by arteries which pass to the marrow through diaphyseal, metaphyseal and epiphyseal arteries (for bone structure, see BIO 11.3.1).

Bone undergoes extensive remodelling, and harvesian systems may break down or be resorbed in order that calcium can be made available to other parts of the body. Bone resorption occurs by osteocytes engaging in osteolysis or by osteoclastic activity.

NERVOUS AND ENDOCRINE SYSTEMS
Chapter 6

Memorize	Understand	Not Required*
ous system: basic structure, major tions c sensory reception and processing ne: endocrine gland, hormone	* Organization of the nervous system; sensor and effector neurons * Feedback loop, reflex arc: role of spinal cord, brain * Endocrine system: specific chemical control at cell, tissue, and organ level * Cellular mechanisms of hormone action, transport of hormones * Integration with nervous system: feedback control	* Advanced level college info * Memorizing all cranial nerves * Details regarding ear, eye: structure and function * Details regarding endocrine glands: names

GAMSAT-Prep.com

Introduction

The nervous and endocrine systems are composed of a network of highly specialized cells that can communicate information about an organism's surroundings and itself. Thus together, these two systems can process incoming information and then regulate and coordinate responses in other parts of the body.

Additional Resources

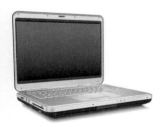

Free Online Q&A + Forum

Video: Online or DVD

Flashcards

Special Guest

* The real GAMSAT may have advanced level information presented (ie. in a passage) but previous knowledge of said information is not required to answer the questions that would follow. Practice ACER and GS practice GAMSATs can help you clarify this point.

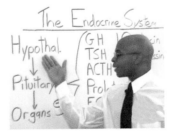

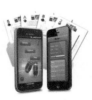

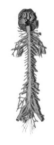

The role of the nervous system is to control and coordinate body activities in a rapid and precise mode of action. The nervous system is composed of central and peripheral nervous systems.

The **central nervous system** (CNS) is enclosed within the cranium (skull) and vertebral (spinal) canal and consists respectively of the brain and spinal cord. The **peripheral nervous system** (PNS) is outside the bony encasement and is composed of peripheral nerves, which are branches or continuations of the spinal or cranial nerves. The PNS can be divided into the **somatic nervous system** and the **autonomic nervous system** which are *anatomically* a portion of both the central and peripheral nervous systems.

The somatic nervous system contains sensory fibers that bring information back to the CNS and motor fibers that innervate skeletal muscles. The autonomic nervous system (ANS) contains motor fibers that innervate smooth muscle, cardiac muscle and glands. The ANS is then divided into *sympathetic* and *parasympathetic* divisions, which generally act against each other. The sympathetic division acts to prepare the body for an emergency situation (fight or flight) while the parasympathetic division acts to conserve energy and restore the body to resting level (rest and digest).

As a rule, a collection of nerve cell bodies in the CNS is called a *nucleus* and outside the CNS it is called a *ganglion*. Neurons that carry information from the environment to the brain or spinal cord are called *afferent neurons*. Neurons that carry motor commands from the brain or spinal cord to the different parts of body are called *efferent neurons*. Neurons that connect sensory and motor neurons in neural pathways are called *interneurons*.

The spinal cord is a long cylindrical structure whose hollow core is called the *central canal*. The central canal is surrounded by a gray matter which is in turn surrounded by a white matter (the reverse is true for the brain: outer gray matter and inner white matter). Basically, the gray matter consists of the cell bodies of neurons whereas the white matter consists of the nerve fibers (axons and dendrites). There are 31 pairs of spinal nerves each leaving the spinal cord at various levels: 8 cervical (neck), 12 thoracic (chest), 5 lumbar (abdomen), 5 sacral and 1 coccygeal (these latter 6 are from the pelvic region). The lower end of the spinal cord is cone shaped and is called the *conus medullaris*.

The brain can be divided into three main regions: the forebrain which contains the telencephalon and the diencephalon; the midbrain; and the hindbrain which contains the cerebellum, the pons and the medulla. The **brain stem** includes the latter two structures and the midbrain.

The telencephalon is the **cerebral hemispheres** (cerebrum) which contain an outer surface (cortex) of gray matter. Its function is in higher order processes (i.e. learning, memory, emotions, voluntary motor activity, processing sensory input, etc.). For

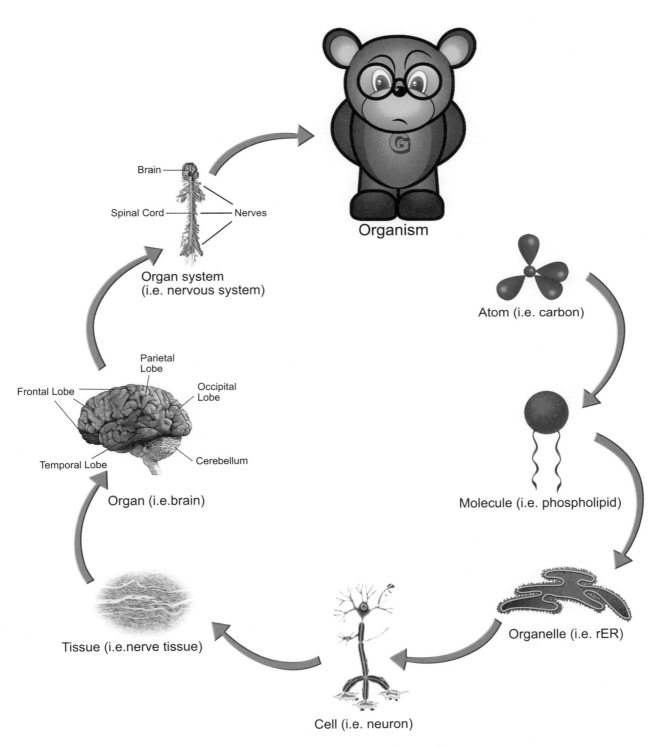

Figure IV.A.6.0: Levels of organization.

most people, the left hemisphere specializes in language, while the right hemisphere specializes in patterns and spatial relationships.

Each hemisphere is subdivided into four lobes: *occipital* which receives input from the optic nerve for vision; *temporal* which receives auditory signals for hearing; *parietal* which receives somatosensory information from the opposite side of the body (= heat, cold, touch, pain, and the sense of body movement); and *frontal* which is involved in problem solving and controls voluntary movements for the opposite side of the body.

The diencephalon contains the **thalamus** which is a relay center for sensory input, and the **hypothalamus** which is crucial for homeostatic controls (heart rate, body temperature, thirst, sex drive, hunger, etc.). Protruding from its base and greatly influenced by the hypothalamus is the **pituitary** which is an endocrine gland. The limbic system, which functions to produce emotions, is composed of the diencephalon and deep structures of the cerebrum (esp. basal ganglia).

The midbrain is a relay center for visual and auditory input and also regulated motor function.

The hindbrain consists of the cerebellum, the pons and the medulla. The cerebellum plays an important role in coordination and the control of muscle tone. The pons acts as a relay center between the cerebral cortex and the cerebellum. The medulla controls many vital functions such as breathing, heart rate, arteriole blood pressure, etc.

There are 12 pairs of cranial nerves which emerge from the base of the brain (esp. the brain stem): *olfactory* (I) for smell; *optic* (II) for vision; *oculomotor* (III), *trochlear* (IV) and *abducens* (VI) for eye movements; *trigeminal* (V) for motor (i.e. *mastication* which is chewing) and sensory activities (i.e. pain, temperature, and pressure for the head and face); *facial* (VII) for taste (sensory) and facial expression (motor); *vestibulo-cochlear* (VIII) for the senses of equilibrium (vestibular branch) and hearing (cochlear branch); *glosso-pharyngeal* (IX) for taste and swallowing; *vagus* (X) for speech, swallowing, slowing the heart rate, and many sensory and motor innervations to smooth muscles of the viscera (internal organs) of the thorax and abdomen; *accessory* (XI) for head rotation and shoulder movement; and *hypoglossal* (XII) for tongue movement.

Both the brain and the spinal cord are surrounded by three membranes (= meninges). The outermost covering is called the dura mater, the innermost is called the pia mater (which is in direct contact with nervous tissue), while the middle layer is called the arachnoid mater. {DAP = **d**ura - **a**rachnoid - **p**ia, repectively, from out to in}.

6.1.1 The Sensory Receptors

The sensory receptors include any type of nerve ending in the body that can be stimulated by some physical or chemical stimulus either outside or within the body. These receptors include the rods and cones of the eye, the cochlear nerve endings of the ear, the taste endings of the mouth, the olfactory endings in the nose, sensory nerve endings in the skin, etc. Afferent neurons carry sense signals to the central nervous system.

6.1.2 The Effector Receptors

These include every organ that can be stimulated by nerve impulses. An important effector system is skeletal muscle. Smooth muscles of the body and the glandular cells are among the important effector organs. Efferent neurons carry motor signals from the CNS to effector receptors. {The term "effector" in biology refers to an organ, cell or molecule that *acts* in response to a stimulus (cause-effect).}

6.1.3 Reflex Arc

One basic means by which the nervous system controls the functions in the body is the reflex arc, in which a stimulus excites a receptor, appropriate impulses are transmitted into the CNS where various nervous reactions take place, and then appropriate effector impulses are transmitted to an effector organ to cause a reflex effect (i.e. removal of one's hand from a hot object, the knee-jerk reflex, etc.). The preceding can be processed at the level of the spinal cord.

Example of knee-jerk reflex: tapping on the patellar tendon causes the thigh muscle (quadriceps) to stretch. The stretching of muscle stimulates the afferent fibers, which synapse on the motoneuron (= motor neuron; BIO 5.1) in the spinal cord. The activation of the motoneuron causes contraction of the muscle that was stretched. This contraction makes the lower leg extend.

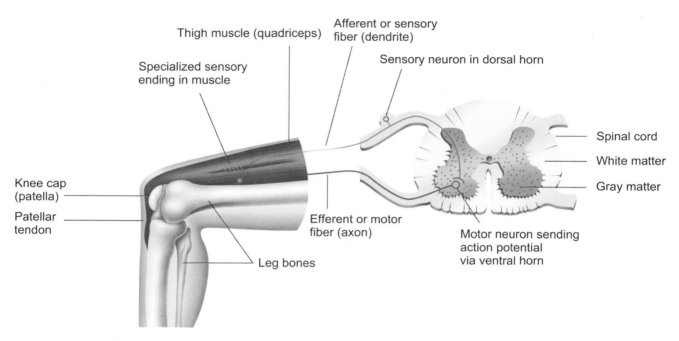

Figure IV.A.6.1: Schematic representation of the basis of the knee jerk reflex.

6.1.4 Autonomic Nervous System

While the Somatic Nervous System controls voluntary activities (i.e. innervates skeletal muscle), the Autonomic Nervous System (ANS) controls involuntary activities. The ANS consists of two components which often antagonize each other: the sympathetic and parasympathetic nervous systems.

The **Sympathetic Nervous System** originates in neurons located in the lateral horns of the gray matter of the spinal cord. Nerve fibers pass by way of anterior (ventral) nerve roots first into the spinal nerves and then immediately into the sympathetic chain. From here fiber pathways are transmitted to all portions of the body, especially to the

different visceral organs and to the blood vessels.

The sympathetic nervous system uses norepinephrine as its primary neurotransmitter. This division of the nervous system is crucial in the "fight, fright or flight" responses (i.e. pupillary dilation, increase in breathing, blood pressure and heart rate, increase of blood flow to skeletal muscle, decrease of visceral function, etc.).

Parasympathetic Nervous System: The parasympathetic fibers pass mainly through the *vagus nerves*, though a few fibers pass through several of the other cranial nerves and through the anterior roots of the sacral segments of the spinal cord. Parasympathetic fibers do not spread as extensively through the body as do sympathetic fibers, but they do innervate some of the thoracic and abdominal organs, as well as the pupillary sphincter and ciliary muscles of the eye and the salivary glands.

The parasympathetic nervous system uses acetylcholine as its primary neurotransmitter. This division of the nervous system is crucial for vegetative responses (i.e. pupillary constriction, decrease in breathing, blood pressure and heart rate, increase in blood flow to the gastro-intestinal tract, etc.).

6.1.5 Autonomic Nerve Fibers

The nerve fibers from the ANS are primarily motor fibers. Unlike the motor pathways of the somatic nervous system, which usually include a single neuron between the CNS and an effector, those of the ANS involve *two* neurons. The first neuron has its cell body in the brain or spinal cord but its axon (= *preganglionic fiber*) extends outside of the CNS. The axon enters adjacent sympathetic chain ganglia, where they synapse with the cell body of a second neuron or travel up or down the chain to synapse with that of a remote second neuron (*recall: a ganglion is a collection of nerve cell bodies outside the CNS*). The axon of the second neuron (= *postganglionic fiber*) extends to a visceral effector.

The sympathetic ganglia form chains which, for example, may extend longitudinally along each side of the vertebral column. Conversely, the parasympathetic ganglia are located *near* or *within* various visceral organs (i.e. bladder, intestine, etc.) thus requiring relatively short postganglionic fibers. Therefore, sympathetic nerve fibers are characterized by short preganglionic fibers and long post-

ganglionic fibers while parasympathetic nerve fibers are characterized by long preganglionic fibers and short postganglionic fibers.

Both divisions of the ANS secrete *acetylcholine* from their preganglionic fibers. Most sympathetic postganglionic fibers secrete *norepinephrine* (= nor*adren*alin), and for this reason they are called **adren**ergic fibers. The parasympathetic postganglionic fibers secrete acetyl**choline** and are called **cholinergic fibers.**

There are two types of acetylcholine receptors (AChR) that bind acetylcholine and transmit its signal: muscarinic AChRs and nicotinic AChRs, which are named after the agonists muscarine and nicotine, respectively. The two receptors are functionally different, the muscarinic type is a G-protein coupled receptor that mediates a slow metabolic response via second messenger cascades (involving cAMP), while the nicotinic type is a ligand-gated ionotropic channel that mediates a fast synaptic transmission of the neurotransmitter (no use of second messengers).

6.2 Sensory Reception and Processing

Each modality of sensation is detected by a particular nerve ending. The most common nerve ending is the free nerve ending. Different types of free nerve endings result in different types of sensations such as pain, warmth, pressure, touch, etc. In addition to free nerve endings, skin contains a number of specialized endings that are adapted to respond to some specific type of physical stimulus.

Sensory endings deep in the body are capable of detecting proprioceptive sensations such as joint receptors, which detect the degree of angulation of a joint, Golgi tendon organs which detect the degree of tension in the tendons, and muscle spindles which detect the degree of stretch of a muscle fiber (see diagram of reflex with muscle spindle in BIO 6.1.2).

6.2.1 Olfaction

Olfaction (the sense of smell) is perceived by the brain following the stimulation of the olfactory epithelium located in the nostrils. The olfactory epithelium contain large numbers of neurons with chemoreceptors called olfactory cells which are responsible for the detection of different types of smell. Odorant molecules bind to the receptors located on the cilia of olfactory receptor neurons and produce a depolarizing receptor potential. Once the depolarization passes threshold, an action potential is generated and is conducted into CNS. It is believed that there might be seven or more primary sensations of smell which combine to give various types of smell that we perceive in life.

6.2.2 Taste

Taste buds in combination with olfaction give humans the taste sensation. Taste buds are primarily located on the surface of the tongue with smaller numbers found in the roof of the mouth and the walls of the pharynx (throat). Taste buds contain chemoreceptors which are activated once the chemical is dissolved in saliva which is secreted by the salivary glands. Contrary to olfactory receptor cells, taste receptors are not true neurons: they are chemical receptors only.

Four different types of taste buds are known to exist, each of these responding principally to saltiness, sweetness, sourness and bitterness.

When a stimulus is received by either a taste bud or an olfactory cell for the second time, the intensity of the response is diminished. This is called sensory *adaptation*.

6.2.3 Ears: Structure and Function

Ears function in both hearing and balance. It consists of three parts: the *external ear* which receives sound waves; the air-filled *middle ear* which transmits and amplifies sound waves; and the fluid-filled *inner ear* which transduces sound waves into nerve impulse. The vestibular organ, located in the inner ear, is responsible for equilibrium.

The external ear is composed of the external cartilaginous portion, the pinna or *auricle*, and the external auditory meatus or canal. The external auditory meatus connects the auricle and the middle ear or *tympanic cavity*. The tympanic cavity is bordered on the outside by the tympanic membrane, and inside the air-filled cavity are the auditory ossicles - the *malleus* (hammer), *incus* (anvil), and *stapes* (stirrup). The stapes is held by ligaments to a part of inner ear called the *oval window*. The auditory ossicles function in amplifying the sound vibration and transmitting it from the tympanic membrane to the oval window.

The inner ear or *labyrinth* consists of an osseous (= bony) labyrinth containing a membranous labyrinth. The bony labyrinth houses the semicircular canals, the cochlea and the vestibule. The semicircular canals contain the semicircular ducts of the membranous labyrinth, which can detect angular acceleration. The vestibule contains the saccule and utricle, which are sac-like thin connective tissue lined by vestibular hair cells which are responsible for the detection of linear acceleration. Together, the semicircular canals and the vestibule, known as the vestibular system,

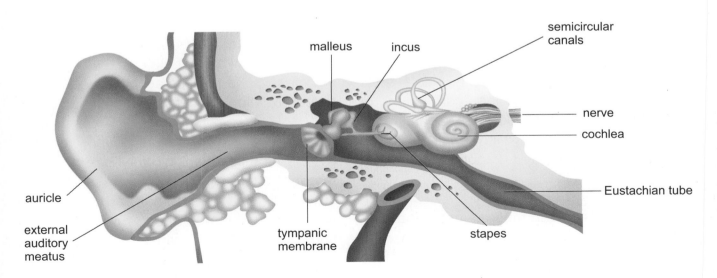

Figure IV.A.6.2: Structure of the external, middle and inner ear.

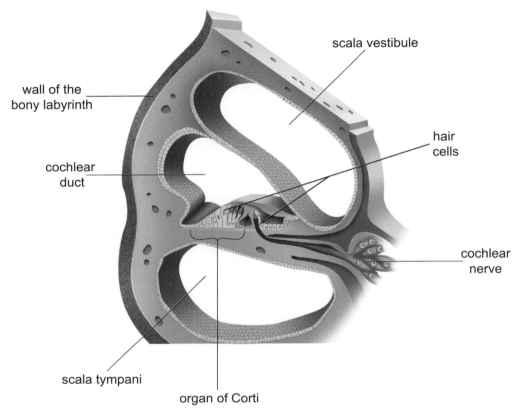

wall of the
bony labyrinth

scala vestibule

hair
cells

cochlear
duct

cochlear
nerve

scala tympani

organ of Corti

Figure IV.A.6.3: Cross-section of the cochlea.

are responsible for detection of linear and angular acceleration of the head. The cochlea is divided into three spaces: the scala vestibule, scala tympani and the scala media, or cochlear duct. The cochlear duct contains the spiral organ of Corti, which functions in the reception of sound and responds to different sound frequencies.

The eustachian tube connects the middle ear to the pharynx. This tube is important in maintaining equal pressure on both sides of the tympanic membrane. During ascent in an airplane, there is a decrease in cabin air pressure, leading to a relative increase in the pressure of the middle ear. Swallowing or yawning opens the eustachian tube allowing an equalization of pressure in the middle ear.

Mechanism of hearing: Sound is caused by the compression of waves that travel through the air. Each compression wave is funneled by the external ear to strike the tympanic membrane (ear drum). Thus the sound vibrations are transmitted through the osseous system which consists of three tiny bones (the malleus, incus, and stapes) into the cochlea at the oval window. Movement of the stapes at the oval window causes disturbance in the lymph of cochlea and stimulates the hair cells found in the basilar membrane which is called the *organ of Corti*. Bending of the hair cells causes depolarization of the basilar membrane. From here the auditory nerves carry the impulses to the auditory area of the brain (*temporal lobe*) where it is interpreted as sound.

6.2.4 Vision: Eye Structure and Function

The eyeball consists of three layers: i) an outer fibrous tunic composed of the sclera and cornea; ii) a vascular coat (uvea) of choroid, the ciliary body and iris; and iii) the retina formed of pigment and sensory (nervous) layers. The anterior chamber lies between the cornea anteriorly (in front) and the iris and pupil posteriorly (behind); the posterior chamber lies between the iris anteriorly and the ciliary processes and the lens posteriorly.

The transparent cornea constitutes the anterior one sixth of the eye and receives light from external environment. The sclera forms

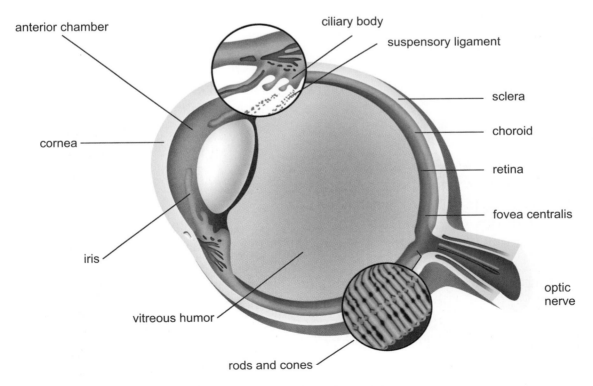

Figure IV.A.6.4: Structure of the eye.

the posterior five sixths of the fibrous tunic and is composed of dense fibrous connective tissue. The choroid layer consists of vascular loose connective tissue. The ciliary body is an anterior expansion of the choroid that encircles the lens. The lens can focus light on the retina by the contraction or relaxation of muscles in the ciliary body which transmit tension along suspensory ligaments to the lens.

Contraction of the ciliary muscle makes the lens become more convex, thereby allowing the eye to focus on nearby objects. Relaxation of the ciliary muscle allows the eye to focus on far objects. The iris separates the anterior and the posterior chamber and forms an aperture called the "pupil" whose diameter is continually adjusted by the pupillary muscles. This helps to control the intensity of light impinging on the retina.

The retina is divisible into ten layers. Layers two to five contain the rod and cone receptors of the light pathway.

Rods and Cones: The light sensitive receptors (*photoreceptors*) of the retina are millions of minute cells called rods and cones. The rods (*"night vision"*) distinguish only the black and white aspects of an image and are sensitive to light of low intensity (*"high sensitivity"*). The cones (*"day vision"*) are capable of distinguishing three colors: red, green and blue and are sensitive to light of high intensity (*"low sensitivity"*). From different combinations of these three colors, all colors can be seen.

Photoreceptors contain photosensitive pigments. For example, rods contain the membrane protein *rhodopsin* which is covalently linked to a form of vitamin A. Light causes an isomerization of *retinal* (an aldehyde form of vitamin A) which can affect Na^+ channels in a manner as to start an action potential.

The central portion of the retina which is called the fovea centralis has only cones, which allows this portion to have very sharp vision, while the peripheral areas, which contain progressively more and more rods, have progressively more diffuse vision. Since acuity and color vision are mediated by the same cells (cones), visual acuity is much better in bright light than dim light.

Each point of the retina connects with a discrete point in the visual cortex which is in the back of the brain (i.e. the occipital lobe). The image that is formed on the retina is upside down and reversed from left to right. This information leaves the eye via the optic nerve en route to the visual cortex which corrects the image.

Defects of vision

1. Myopia (short-sighted or nearsighted): In this condition, an image is formed in front of the retina because the lens converges light too much since the eyeballs are long. A diverging (concave) lens helps focus the image on the retina and it is used for the correction of myopia.

2. Hyperopia (long-sighted or farsighted): In this condition, an image is formed behind the retina since the eyeballs are too short. A converging (convex) lens helps focus the image on the retina.

3. Astigmatism: In this condition, the curvatures of either the cornea or the lens are different at different angles. A cylindrical lens helps to improve this condition.

4. Presbyopia: This condition is characterized by the inability to focus (especially objects which are closer). This condition, which is often seen in the elderly, is corrected by using a converging lens.

6.3 Endocrine Systems

The endocrine system is the set of glands, tissues and cells that secrete hormones directly into circulatory system (ductless). The hormones are transported by the blood system, sometimes bound to plasma proteins, en route to having an effect on the cells of a target organ. Thus hormones control many of the body's functions by acting - predominantly - in one of the following major ways:

1. By controlling transport of substances through cell membranes

2. By controlling the activity of some of the specific genes, which in turn determine the formation of specific enzymes

3. By controlling directly some metabolic systems of cells.

Steroid hormones can diffuse across the plasma membrane and bind to specific receptors in the cytosol or nucleus, thus forming a direct intracellular effect (i.e. on DNA; ORG 12.4.1). Non-steroid hormones do not diffuse across the membrane. They tend to bind plasma membrane receptors, which leads to the production of a second messenger.

Secondary messengers are a component of signal transduction cascades which amplify the strength of a signal (i.e. hormone, growth factors, neurotransmitter, etc.). Examples include cyclic AMP (cAMP), phosphoinositol, cyclic GMP and arachidonic acid systems.

In all four cases, a hormone (= the primary messenger or *agonist*) binds the receptor exposing a binding site for a G-protein (the *transducer*). The G-protein, named for its ability to exchange GDP on its alpha subunit for a GTP (BIO 4.4-4.10), is bound to the inner membrane. Once the exchange for GTP takes place, the alpha subunit of the G-protein transducer breaks free from the beta and gamma subunits, all parts remaining membrane-bound. The alpha subunit is now free to move along the inner membrane and eventually contacts another membrane-bound protein - the *primary effector*.

The primary effector has an action which creates a signal that can diffuse within the cell. This signal is the *secondary messenger*.

Calcium ions are important intracellular messengers which can regulate calmodulin and are responsible for many important physiological functions, such as in muscle contraction (BIO 5.2). The enzyme phospholipase C (primary effector) produces diacylglycerol and inositol trisphosphate (secondary messenger), which increases calcium ion (secondary effector) membrane permeability. Active G-protein can also open calcium channels. The other product of phospholipase C, diacylglycerol (secondary messenger), activates

protein kinase C (secondary effector), which assists in the activation of cAMP (another second messenger).

The agonist epinephrine (hormone, BIO 6.1.3) can bind a receptor activating the transducer (G-protein) and using a primary effector (adenylyl cyclase) produces a secondary messenger (cAMP) which, in turn, brings about target cell responses that are recognized as the hormone's actions.

Of the following hormones, if there is no mention as to its chemical nature, then it is a non-steroidal hormone (i.e. protein, polypeptide, etc.).

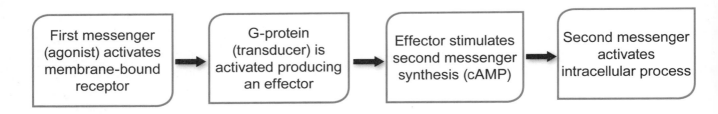

6.3.1 Pituitary Hormones

The **pituitary gland** secretes hormones that regulate a wide variety of functions in the body. This gland is divided into two major divisions: the anterior and the posterior pituitary gland. Six hormones are secreted by the anterior pituitary gland whereas two hormones are secreted by the posterior gland. The **hypothalamus** influences the secretion of hormones from both parts of the pituitary in different ways: i) it secretes specific *releas-*

ing factors into special blood vessels (a *portal system* called hypothalamic-hypophysial portal system) which carries these factors (hormones) that affect the cells in the anterior pituitary by either stimulating or inhibiting the release of anterior pituitary hormones; ii) the hypothalamus contains neurosecretory cell bodies that synthesize, package and transport their products (esp. the two hormones oxytocin and ADH) down the axons directly into the posterior pituitary where they can be released into circulation.

The hormones secreted by the anterior pituitary gland are as follows:

1. Growth hormone (GH)
2. Thyroid Stimulating Hormone (TSH)
3. Adrenocorticotropic hormone (ACTH)
4. Prolactin
5. Follicle Stimulating Hormone (FSH) or Interstitial Cell Stimulating Hormone (ICSH)
6. Luteinizing Hormone (LH)

[N.B. these latter two hormones will be discussed in the section on Reproduction, see BIO 14.2, 14.3]

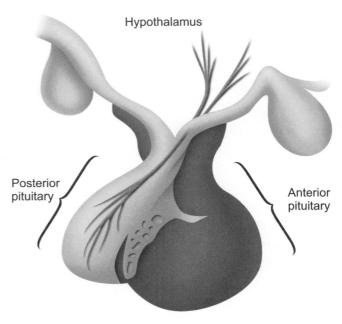

Figure IV.A.6.5: The pituitary gland.

Growth Hormone causes growth of the body. It causes enlargement and proliferation of cells in all parts of the body. Ultimately, the epiphyses of the long bones unite with the shaft of the bones (BIO 11.3.1). After adolescence, growth hormone continues to be secreted lower than the pre-adolescent rate. Though most of the growth in the body stops at this stage, the metabolic roles of the growth hormone continue such as the enhancement of protein synthesis and lean body mass, increasing blood glucose concentration, increasing lipolysis, etc.

Abnormal increase in the secretion of growth hormone at a young age results in a condition called gigantism, while a reduction in the production of growth hormone leads to dwarfism. Abnormal increase in the secretion of growth hormone in adults results

in a condition called acromegaly, a disorder characterized by a disproportionate bone enlargement, especially in the face, hands and feet.

Thyroid Stimulating Hormone stimulates the thyroid gland. The hormones produced by the thyroid gland (*thyroxine:* T_4, *triiodothyronine:* T_3) contain four and three iodine atoms, respectively. They increase the basal metabolic rate of the body (BMR). Therefore, indirectly, TSH increases the overall rate of metabolism of the body.

Adrenocorticotropic hormone strongly stimulates the production of cortisol by the adrenal cortex, and it also stimulates the production of the other adrenocortical hormones, but to a lesser extent.

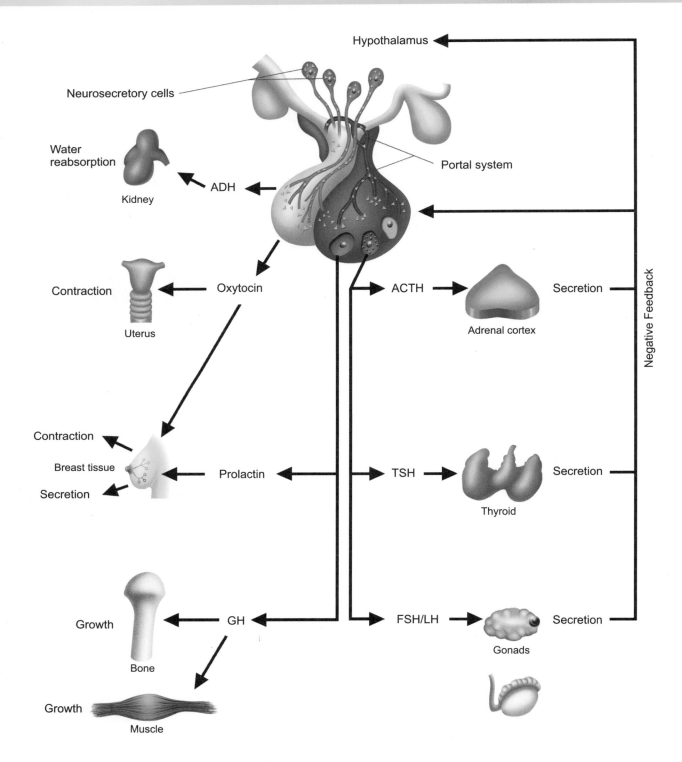

Figure IV.A.6.6: Pituitary hormones and their target organs.

Prolactin plays an important role in the development of the breast during pregnancy and promotes milk production in the breast. In addition, a high level of prolactin can inhibit ovulation.

Antidiuretic hormone (ADH) is synthesized by neurosecretory cells in the hypothalamus and then travels down the axons to the posterior pituitary for secretion. Antidiuretic hormone enhances the rate of water reabsorption from the renal tubules leading to the concentration of urine (BIO 10.3). ADH also constricts the arterioles and causes a rise in arterial pressure and hence it is also called *vasopressin*.

Similar to ADH, *oxytocin* originates in the hypothalamus and then travels down the axons to the posterior pituitary for secretion. Oxytocin causes contraction of the uterus and, to a lesser extent, the other smooth muscles of the body. It also stimulates the myoepithelial cells of the breast in a manner that makes the milk flow into the ducts. This is termed milk ejection or milk *let-down*.

6.3.2 Adrenocortical Hormones

On the top of each kidney lies an adrenal gland which contains an inner region (*medulla*) and an outer region (*cortex*). The adrenal cortex secretes three different types of steroid hormones that are similar chemically but vary widely in a physiological manner.

These are:

1. Mineralocorticoids - e.g., Aldosterone
2. Glucocorticoids - e.g., Cortisol, Cortisone
3. Sex Hormones e.g., Androgens, Estrogens

Mineralocorticoids - Aldosterone

The mineralocorticoids influence the electrolyte balance of the body. Aldosterone is a mineralocorticoid which is secreted and then enhances sodium transport from the renal tubules into the peritubular fluids, and at the same time enhances potassium transport from the peritubular fluids into the tubules. In other words, aldosterone causes conservation of sodium in the body and excretion of potassium in the urine. As a result of sodium retention, there is an increased passive reabsorption of chloride ions and water from the tubules. Overproduction of aldosterone will result in excessive retention of fluid, which leads to hypertension.

Glucocorticoids - Cortisol

Several different glucocorticoids are secreted by the adrenal cortex, but almost all of the glucocorticoid activity is caused by cortisol, also called hydrocortisone. Glucocorticoids affect the metabolism of carbohydrates, proteins and lipids. It causes an increase in the blood concentration of glucose by stimulation of gluconeogenesis (generation of glucose from non-carbohydrate carbon substrates). It causes degradation of proteins and causes increased use of fat for energy. Long term use of glucocorticoids suppresses the immune system. It also has an anti-inflammatory effect by inhibiting the release of inflammatory mediators.

Sex hormones

Androgens (i.e. testosterone) are the masculinizing hormones in the body. They are responsible for the development of the secondary sexual characteristics in a male (i.e. increased body hair). On the contrary estrogens have a feminizing effect in the body and they are responsible for the development of the secondary sexual characteristics in a female (i.e. breast development). The proceeding hormones supplement secretions from the gonads which will be discussed later (see "*Reproduction*"; BIO 14.2, 14.3).

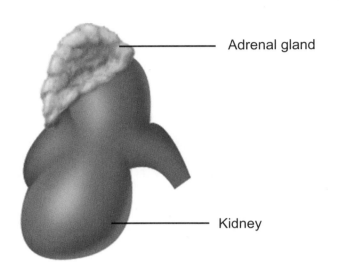

Figure IV.A.6.7: The adrenal gland sits on top of the kidney.

The Adrenal Medulla

The adrenal medulla synthesizes epinephrine (= *adrenaline*) and norepinephrine which: i) are non-steroidal stimulants of the sympathetic nervous system; ii) raise blood glucose concentrations; iii) increase heart rate and blood pressure; iv) increase blood supply to the brain, heart and skeletal muscle; and v) decrease blood supply to the skin, digestive system and renal system.

6.3.3 Thyroid Hormones

The thyroid gland is located anteriorly in the neck and is composed of follicles lined with thyroid glandular cells. These cells secrete a glycoprotein called thyroglobulin. The tyrosine residue of thyroglobulin then reacts with iodine forming mono-iodotyrosine (MIT) and di-iodotyrosine (DIT). When two molecules of DIT combine, thyroxine (T_4) is formed. When one molecule of DIT and one molecule of MIT combine, tri-iodothyronine (T_3) is formed. The rate of synthesis of thyroid hormone is influenced by TSH from the pituitary.

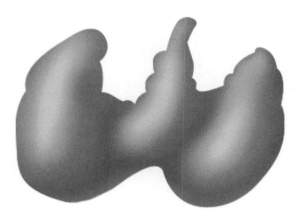

Figure IV.A.6.8: The thyroid gland.

Once thyroid hormones have been released into the blood stream they combine with several different plasma proteins. Then they are released into the cells from the blood stream. They play a vital role in maturation of CNS as thyroid hormone deficiency leads to irreversible mental retardation. They increase heart rate, ventilation rate and O_2 consumption. They also increase the size and numbers of mitochondria and these in turn increase the rate of production of ATP, which is a factor that promotes cellular metabolism; glycogenolysis and gluconeogenesis both increase; lipolysis increases; and protein synthesis also increases. The overall effect of thyroid hormone on metabolism is catabolic.

Hyperthyroidism is an excess of thyroid hormone secretion above that needed for normal function. Basically, an increased rate of metabolism throughout the body is observed. Other symptoms include fast heart rate and respiratory rate, weight loss, sweating, tremor, and protruding eyes.

Hypothyroidism is an inadequate amount of thyroid hormone secreted into the blood stream. Generally it slows down the metabolic rate and enhances the collection of mucinous fluid in the tissue spaces, creating an edematous (fluid filled) state called myxedema. Other symptoms include slowed heart rate and respiratory rate, weight gain, cold intolerance, fatigue, and mental slowness.

The thyroid and parathyroid glands affect blood calcium concentration in different ways. The thyroid produces *calcitonin* which inhibits osteoclast activity and stimulates osteoblasts to form bone tissue; thus blood $[Ca^{2+}]$ decreases. The parathyroid glands produce parathormone (= parathyroid hormone = PTH), which stimulates osteoclasts to break down bone, thus raising $[Ca^{2+}]$ and $[PO_4^{3-}]$ in the blood (BIO 5.4.4).

6.3.4 Pancreatic Hormones

The pancreas contains clusters of cells (= *islets of Langerhans*) closely associated with blood vessels. The islets of Langerhans, which perform the endocrine function of the pancreas, contain alpha cells that secrete *glucagon* and beta cells that secrete *insulin*. Glucagon increases blood glucose concentration by promoting the following events in the liver: the conversion of glycogen to glucose (*glycogenolysis*) and the production of glucose from amino acids (*gluconeogenesis*). Insulin decreases blood glucose by increasing cellular uptake of glucose, promoting glycogen formation and decreasing gluconeogenesis. A deficiency in insulin or insensitivity to insulin results in *diabetes mellitus*.

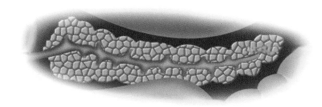

Figure IV.A.6.9: The pancreas.

6.3.5 Kidney Hormones

The kidney produces and secretes *renin*, *erythropoietin* and it helps in the activation of vitamin D. Renin is an enzyme that catalyzes the conversion of angiotensinogen to angiotensin I. Angiotensin I is then converted to angiotensin II by angiotensin-converting enzyme (ACE). Angiotensin II acts on the adrenal cortex to increase the synthesis and release of aldosterone, which increases Na^+ reabsorption, and causes vasoconstriction of arterioles leading to an increase in both blood volume and blood pressure. Erythropoietin increases the production of *erythrocytes* by acting on red bone marrow.

Vitamin D is a steroid which is critical for the proper absorption of calcium from the small intestine; thus it is essential for the normal growth and development of bone and teeth. Vitamin D can either be ingested or produced from a precursor by the activity of ultraviolet light on skin cells. It must be further activated in the liver and kidney by hydroxylation.

6.3.6 A Negative Feedback Loop

In order to maintain the internal environment of the body in equilibrium (= *homeostasis*), our hormones engage in various negative feedback loops. Negative feedback is self-limiting: a hormone produces biologic actions that, in turn, directly or indirectly inhibit further secretion of that hormone.

For example, if the body is exposed to extreme cold, the hypothalamus will activate systems to conserve heat (see *Skin as an Organ System*, BIO 13.1) and to produce heat. Heat production can be attained by increasing the basal metabolic rate. To achieve this, the hypothalamus secretes a releasing factor (thyrotropin releasing factor - TRF) which stimulates the anterior pituitary to secrete TSH. Thus the thyroid gland is stimulated to secrete the thyroid hormones.

Body temperature begins to return to normal. The high levels of circulating thyroid hormones begin to *inhibit* the production of TRF and TSH (= *negative feedback*) which in turn ensures the reduction in the levels of the thyroid hormones. Thus homeostasis is maintained.

6.3.7 A Positive Feedback Loop

As opposed to negative feedback, a positive feedback loop is where the body senses a change and activates mechanisms that accelerate or increase that change. Occasionally this may help homeostasis by working in conjunction with a larger negative feedback loop, but unfortunately it often produces the opposite effect and can be life-threatening.

An example of a beneficial positive feedback loop is seen in childbirth, where stretching of the uterus triggers the secretion of oxytocin (BIO 6.3.1), which stimulates uterine contractions and speeds up labor. Of course, once the baby is out of the mother's body, the loop is broken.

Often, however, positive feedback produces the very opposite of homeostasis: a rapid loss of internal stability with potentially fatal consequences. For example, most human deaths from SARS and the bird flu (H5N1) epidemic were caused by a "cytokine storm" which is a positive feedback loop between immune cells and cytokines (signalling molecules similar to hormones). Thus, in many cases, it is the body's exaggerated response to infection that is the cause of death rather than the direct action of the original infecting agent. Many diseases involve dangerous positive feedback loops.

Go online to GAMSAT-prep.com for additional chapter review Q&A and forum.

THE CIRCULATORY SYSTEM
Chapter 7

Memorize	Understand	Not Required*
and lymphatic systems: basic ctures and functions	* Circ: structure/function; 4 chambered heart: systolic/diastolic pressure	* Advanced level college info
position of blood, lymph, purpose of ⯈h nodes	* Oxygen transport; hemoglobin, oxygen content/affinity	* Memorizing names of small to medium arteries, veins
production and destruction; spleen, ⯈ marrow	* Substances transported by blood, lymph	* Memorizing Starling's equation
	* Source of lymph: diffusion from capillaries by differential pressure	

GAMSAT-Prep.com

Introduction ▌▌▌▌

The circulatory system is concerned with the movement of nutrients, gases and wastes to and from cells. The circulatory or cardiovascular system (closed) distributes blood while the lymphatic system (open) distributes lymph.

Additional Resources

Free Online Q&A + Forum

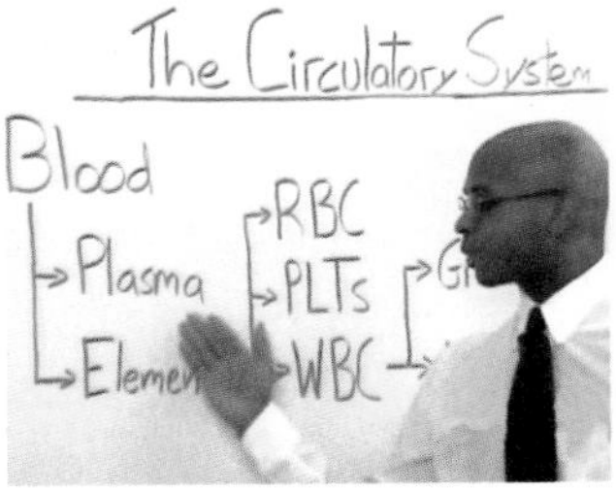

Video: Online or DVD

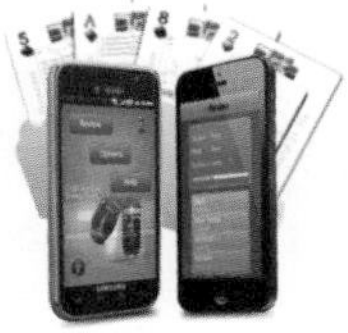

Flashcards

Special Guest

7.1 Generalities

The circulatory system is composed of the heart, blood, and blood vessels. The heart (which acts like a pump) and its blood vessels (which act like a closed system of ducts) are called the *cardiovascular system* which moves the blood throughout the body.

The following represents some important functions of blood within the circulatory system.

* It transports:

- hormones from endocrine glands to target tissues
- molecules and cells which are components of the immune system

- nutrients from the digestive tract (usu. to the liver)
- oxygen from the respiratory system to body cells
- waste from the body cells to the respiratory and excretory systems.

* It aids in temperature control (*thermoregulation*) by:

- distributing heat from skeletal muscle and other active organs to the rest of the body
- being directed to or away from the skin depending on whether or not the body wants to release or conserve heat, respectively.

7.2 The Heart

The heart is a muscular, cone-shaped organ about the size of a fist. The heart is composed of connective tissue (BIO 5.4) and cardiac muscle (BIO 5.2) which includes a region that generates electrical signals (see BIO 11.2 for SA node). The heart contains four chambers: two thick muscular walled *ventricles* and two thinner walled *atria*. An inner wall or *septum* separates the heart (and therefore the preceding chambers) into left and right sides. The atria contract or *pump* blood more or less simultaneously and so do the ventricles.

Deoxygenated blood returning to the heart from all body tissues except the lungs (= *systemic circulation*) enters the right atrium

through large veins (= *venae cavae*). The blood is then pumped into the right ventricle through the tricuspid valve (which is one of many one-way valves in the cardiovascular system). Next the blood is pumped to the lungs (= *pulmonary circulation*) through semilunar valves (pulmonary valves) and pulmonary arteries {remember: blood in underline{ar}teries goes underline{a}way from the heart}.

The blood loses CO_2 and is **oxygenated** in the lungs and returns through pulmonary veins to the left atrium. Now the blood is pumped through the mitral (= bicuspid) valve into the largest chamber of the heart: the left ventricle. This ventricle's task is to return

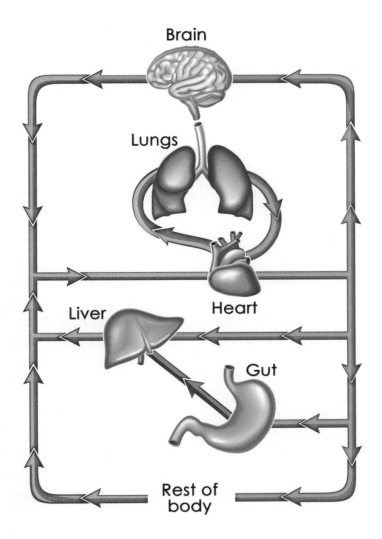

Brain

Lungs

Liver

Heart

Gut

Rest of body

Figure IV.A.7.0: Overview of vascular anatomy.

The vascular anatomy of the human body or for an individual organ is comprised of both in-series and in-parallel vascular components. Blood leaves the heart through the aorta (high in oxygen, red in color) from which it is distributed to major organs by large arteries, each of which originates from the aorta. Therefore, these major distributing arteries are in parallel with each other. Thus the circulations of the head, arms, gastrointestinal systems, kidneys, and legs are all parallel circulations. There are some exceptions, notably the gastrointestinal (gut) and hepatic (liver) circulations, which are partly in series because the venous drainage from the intestines become the hepatic portal vein which supplies most of the blood flow to the liver. Vessels transporting from one capillary bed to another are called portal veins (besides the liver, note the portal system in the anterior pituitary, BIO 6.3.1).

blood into the systemic circulation by pumping into a huge artery: the *aorta* (its valve is the aortic valve).

The mitral (= <u>bi</u>cuspid = <u>2</u> leaflets) and tricuspid (<u>tri</u> = <u>3</u> leaflets) valves are prevented from everting into the atria by strong fibrous cords (*chordae tendineae*) which are attached to small mounds of muscle (*papillary muscles*) in their respective ventricles. A major cause of heart murmurs is the inadequate functioning of these valves.

7.3 Blood Vessels

Blood vessels include arteries, arterioles, capillaries, venules and veins. Whereas arteries tend to have thick, smooth muscular walls and contain blood at high pressure, veins have thinner walls and low blood pressure. However, veins contain the highest proportion of blood in the cardiovascular system (about 2/3rds). The wall of a blood vessel is composed of an outer <u>adventitia</u>, an inner <u>intima</u> and a *m*iddle *m*uscle layer, the <u>media</u>.

Oxygenated blood entering the systemic circulation must get to all the body's tissues. The aorta must divide into smaller and smaller arteries (small artery = **arteriole**) in order to get to the level of the capillary which i) is the smallest blood vessel; ii) often forms branching networks called *capillary beds*; and iii) is the level at which the exchange of wastes and gases (i.e. O_2 and CO_2) occurs by diffusion.

In the next step in circulation, the newly deoxygenated blood enters very small veins (= **venules**) and then into larger and larger veins until the blood enters the venae cavae and then the right atrium. There are two venae cavae: one drains blood from the upper body while the other drains blood from the lower body (*superior* and *inferior* venae cavae, respectively).

Since the walls of veins are thin and somewhat floppy, they are often located in muscles. Thus movement of the leg squeezes the veins, which pushes the blood through 1-way bicuspid valves toward the heart. This is referred to as the *muscle pump*.

<u>Coronary arteries</u> branch off the aorta to supply the heart muscle.

Systemic Circulation   **Pulmonary Circulation**

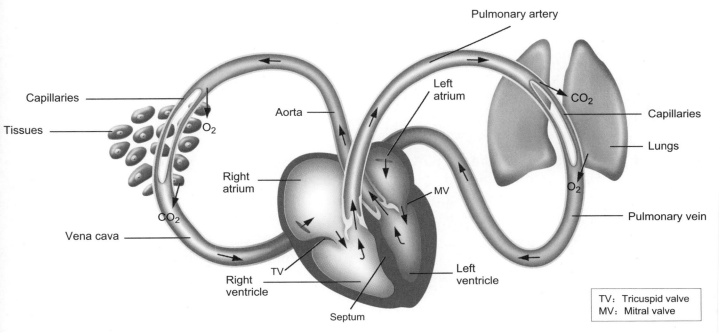

Figure IV.A.7.1: Schematic representation of the circulatory system.

Systemic circulation: transports blood from the left ventricle into the aorta then to all parts of the body and then returns to the right atrium from the superior and inferior venae cavae. *Pulmonary circulation:* transports blood from the right ventricle into pulmonary arteries to the lungs for exchange of oxygen and carbon dioxide and returns blood to the left atrium from pulmonary veins.

7.4 Blood Pressure

Blood pressure is the force exerted by the blood against the inner walls of blood vessels (esp. arteries). Maximum arterial pressure is measured when the ventricle contracts and blood is pumped into the arterial system (= *systolic pressure*). Minimal arterial pressure is measured when the ventricle is relaxed and blood is returned to the heart via veins (= *diastolic pressure*). Pulse pressure is the difference between the systolic pressure and the diastolic pressure. Blood pressure is usually measured in the brachial artery in the arm. A pressure of 120/80 signifies a systolic pressure of 120 mmHg and a diastolic pressure of 80 mmHg. The *pulse pressure* is the difference (i.e. 40 mmHg).

Peripheral resistance is essentially the result of arterioles and capillaries which resist the flow of blood from arteries to veins (the narrower the vessel, the higher the resistance). Arterioles are the site of the highest resistance in the cardiovascular system. An increase in peripheral resistance causes a rise in blood pressure. As blood travels down the systemic circulation, blood pressure decreases progressively due to the peripheral resistance to blood flow.

7.5 Blood Composition

Blood contains plasma (55%) and *formed elements* (45%). Plasma is a straw colored liquid which is mostly composed of water (92%), electrolytes, and the following plasma proteins:

* **Albumin** which is important in maintaining the osmotic pressure and helps to transport many substances in the blood

* **Globulins** which include both transport proteins and the proteins which form antibodies

* **Fibrinogen** which polymerizes to form the insoluble protein *fibrin* which is essential for normal blood clotting. If you take away fibrinogen and some other clotting factors from plasma you will be left with a fluid called *serum*.

The formed elements of the blood originate from precursors in the bone marrow which produce the following for the circulatory system: 99% red blood cells (= *erythrocytes*), then there are platelets (= *thrombocytes*), and white blood cells (= *leukocytes*). Red blood cells (RBCs) are biconcave cells without nuclei (*anucleate*) that circulate for 110-120 days before their components are recycled by macrophages. Interestingly, mature RBCs do not possess most organelles such as mitochondria, Golgi nor ER because RBCs are packed with hemoglobin. The primary function of hemoglobin is the transport of O_2 and CO_2 to and from tissue.

Platelets are cytoplasmic fragments of large bone marrow cells (*megakaryocytes*) which are involved in blood clotting by adhering to the collagen of injured vessels, releasing mediators which cause blood vessels to constrict (= *vasoconstriction*), etc.

Calcium ions (Ca^{2+}) are also important in blood clotting because they help in signaling platelets to aggregate.

White blood cells help in the defense against infection; they are divided into *granulocytes* and *agranulocytes* depending on whether or not the cell does or does not contain granules, respectively.

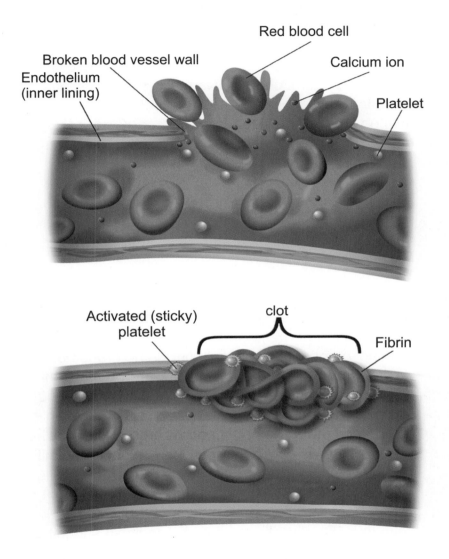

Figure IV.A.7.1.1: Schematic representation of blood clotting.

Granulocytes (= *polymorphonuclear leukocytes*) possess varying number of azurophilic (burgundy when stained) granules and are divided into: i) neutrophils which are the first white blood cells to respond to infection, they are important in controlling bacterial infection by phagocytosis - killing and digesting bacteria - and are the main cellular constituent of pus; ii) eosinophils which, like neutrophils, are phagocytic and also participate in allergic reactions and the destruction of parasites; iii) basophils which can release both anticoagulants (heparin) and substances important in hypersensitivity reactions (histamine).

Agranulocytes (= *mononuclear leuko-cytes*)) lack specific granules and are divided into: i) *lymphocytes* which are vital to the immune system (see *Immune System*, chapter 8); and monocytes (often called *phago-cytes* or *macrophages* when they are outside of the circulatory system) which can phagocytose large particles.

The hematocrit measures how much space (volume) in the blood is occupied by red blood cells and is expressed as a percentage. Normal hematocrit in adults is about 45%.

{*See* BIO 15.2 *for ABO Blood Types*}

7.5.1 Hemoglobin

Each red blood cell carries hundreds of molecules of a substance which is responsible for their red color: **hemoglobin**. Hemoglobin (Hb) is a complex of *heme*, which is an iron-containing porphyrin ring, and *globin*, which is a tetrameric (= has 4 subunits) protein consisting of two α-subunits and two β-subunits. The iron from the heme group is normally in its reduced state (Fe^{2+}); however, in the presence of O_2, it can be oxidized to Fe^{3+}.

In the lungs, oxygen concentration or *partial pressure* is high, thus O_2 dissolves in the blood; oxygen can then quickly and reversibly combine with the iron in Hb forming bright red *oxyhemoglobin*. The binding of oxygen to hemoglobin is cooperative. In other words, each oxygen that binds to Hb facilitates the binding of the next oxygen. Consequently, the dissociation curve for oxyhemoglobin is sigmoidal as a result of the change in affinity of hemoglobin as each O_2 successively binds to the globin subunit (see BIO 4.3).

Examine Figure IV.A.7.2 carefully. Notice that at a PO_2 of 100 mmHg (e.g. arterial blood), the percentage of saturation of hemoglobin is almost 100%, which means all four heme groups on the four hemoglobin subunits are bound with O_2. At a PO_2 of 40 mmHg (e.g. venous blood), the percentage of saturation of hemoglobin is about 75%, which means three of the four heme groups on the four hemoglobin subunits are bound with O_2. At a PO_2 of 27 mmHg, the percentage of saturation of hemoglobin is only 50%, which means half of the four heme groups on the four hemoglobin subunits are bound with O_2. The partial pressure of oxygen (PO_2) at 50% saturation is called P50.

The curve can: (i) shift to the left which means that for a given PO_2 in the tissue capillary there is decreased unloading (release) of oxygen and that the affinity of hemoglobin for O_2 is increased; or (ii) shift to the right which means that for a given PO_2 in the tissue capillary there is increased

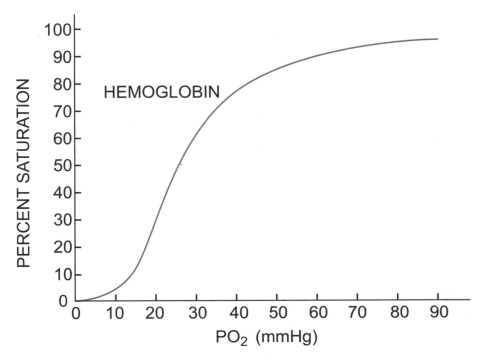

Figure IV.A.7.2: Oxygen dissociation curve: percent O_2 saturation versus O_2 partial pressure.

unloading of oxygen and that the affinity of hemoglobin for O_2 is decreased. The latter occurs when the tissue (i.e. muscle) is very active and thus requires more oxygen.

Thus a right shift occurs when the muscle is hot (↑ temperature during exercise), acid (↓ pH due to lactic acid produced in exercising muscle, see BIO 4.4. and 4.5), hypercarbic (↑CO_2 as during exercise, tissue produces more CO_2, see BIO 4.4. and 12.4.1), or contains high levels of organic phosphates (esp. increased synthesis of 2,3 DPG in red blood cells as a means to adapt to chronic hypoxemia).

In the body tissues where the partial pressure of O_2 is low and CO_2 is high, O_2 is released and CO_2 combines with the protein component of Hb forming the darker colored *carbaminohemoglobin* (also called: deoxyhemoglobin). The red color of muscle is due to a different heme-containing protein concentrated in muscle called myoglobin. Myoglobin is a monomeric protein containing one heme prosthetic group. The O_2 binding curve for myoglobin is hyperbolic, which means that it lacks cooperativity.

7.5.2 Capillaries: A Closer Look

Capillary fluid movement can occur as a result of two processes: diffusion (dominant role) and filtration (secondary role but critical for the proper function of organs, especially the kidney; BIO 10.3). Osmotic pressure (BIO 1.1.1, CHM 5.1.3) due to proteins in blood plasma is sometimes called colloid osmotic pressure or oncotic pressure. The Starling equation is an equation that describes the role of hydrostatic and oncotic forces (= Starling forces) in the movement of fluid across capillary membranes as a result of filtration.

When blood enters the arteriole end of a capillary, it is still under pressure produced by the contraction of the ventricle. As a result of this pressure, a substantial amount of water (hydrostatic) and some plasma proteins filter through the walls of the capillaries into the tissue space. This fluid, called interstitial fluid (BIO 7.6), is simply blood plasma minus most of the proteins.

Interstitial fluid bathes the cells in the tissue space and substances in it can enter the cells by diffusion (mostly) or active transport. Substances, like carbon dioxide, can diffuse out of cells and into the interstitial fluid.

Near the venous end of a capillary, the blood pressure is greatly reduced. Here another force comes into play. Although the composition of interstitial fluid is similar to that of blood plasma, it contains a smaller con-centration of proteins than plasma and thus a somewhat greater concentration of water.

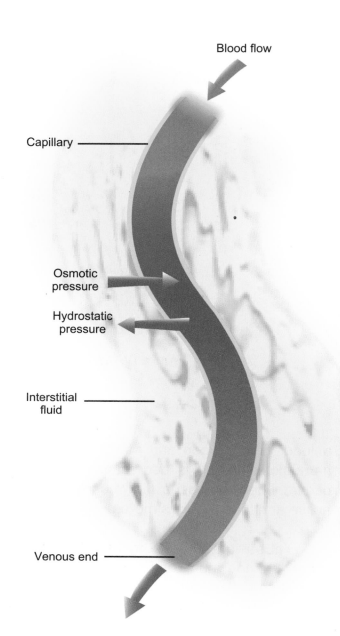

Figure IV.A.7.2b: Circulation at the level of the capillary. The exchange of water, oxygen, carbon dioxide, and many other nutrient and waste chemical substances between blood and surrounding tissues occurs at the level of the capillary.

This difference sets up an osmotic pressure. Although the osmotic pressure is small, it is greater than the blood pressure at the venous end of the capillary. Thus the fluid reenters the capillary here.

To summarize: when the blood pressure is greater than the osmotic pressure, filtration is favored and fluid tends to move out of the capillary; when the blood pressure is less than the osmotic pressure, reabsorption is favored and fluid tends to enter into the capillary.

7.6 The Lymphatic System

Body fluids can exist in blood vessels (intravascular), in cells (intracellular) or in a 3rd space which is intercellular (between cells) or extracellular (outside cells). Such fluids are called <u>interstitial fluids</u>. The **lymphatic system** is a network of vessels which can circulate fluid from the 3rd space to the cardiovascular system.

Aided by osmotic pressure, interstitial fluids enter the lymphatic system via small closed-ended tubes called *lymphatic capillaries* (in the small intestine they are called *lacteals*). Once the fluid enters it is called **lymph**. The lymph continues to flow into larger and larger vessels propelled by muscular contraction (esp. skeletal) and one-way valves. Then the lymph will usually pass through *lymph nodes* and then into a large vessel (esp. *the thoracic duct*) which drains into one of the large veins which eventually leads to the right atrium.

Lymph functions in important ways. Most protein molecules which leak out of blood capillaries are returned to the bloodstream by lymph. Also, microorganisms which invade tissue fluids are carried to lymph nodes by lymph. Lymph nodes contain *lymphocytes* and macrophages which are components of the immune system.

Go online to GAMSAT-prep.com for additional chapter review Q&A and forum.

THE IMMUNE SYSTEM

Chapter 8

Memorize	Understand	Not Required*
ɛs in immunity: T-lymphocytes; mphocytes ues in the immune system including e marrow ɛen, thymus, lymph nodes	* Concepts of antigen, antibody, interaction * Structure of antibody molecule * Mechanism of stimulation by antigen	* Advanced level college info * The 5 antibody isotypes * Life cycle of pathogens * Anatomy of lymph nodes * Class switching

GAMSAT-Prep.com

Introduction

The immune system protects against disease. Many processes are used in order to identify and kill various microbes (see Microbiology, Chapter 2, for examples) as well as tumor cells (more detail when you get into medical school!). There are 2 acquired responses of the immune system: cell-mediated and humoral.

Additional Resources

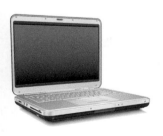

Free Online Q&A + Forum

Video: Online or DVD

Flashcards

Special Guest

* The real GAMSAT may have advanced level information presented (ie. in a passage) but previous knowledge of said information is not required to answer the questions that would follow. Practice ACER and GS practice GAMSATs can help you clarify this point.

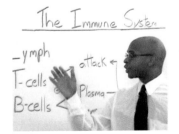

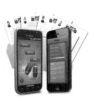

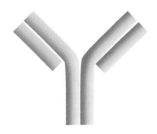

8.1 Overview

The immune system is composed of various cells and organs which defend the body against pathogens, toxins or any other foreign agents. Substances (usu. proteins) on the foreign agent causing an immune response are called **antigens**. There are two acquired responses to an antigen: (1) the **cell mediated response** where T-lymphocytes are the dominant force and act against microorganisms, tumors, and virus infected cells; and (2) the **humoral response** where B-lymphocytes are the dominant force and act against specific proteins present on foreign molecules.

8.2 Cells of the Immune System

B-lymphocytes originate in the bone marrow. Though T-lymphocytes also originate in the bone marrow, they go on to mature in the thymus gland. T-lymphocytes learn with the help of macrophages to recognize and attack only foreign substances (i.e. antigens) in a direct cell to cell manner (= *cell-mediated* or *cellular immunity*). T-lymphocytes have two major subtypes: T-helper cells and T-cytotoxic cells. Some T-cells (T_8, T_C, or T cytotoxic) mediate the apoptosis of foreign cells and virus-infected cells. Some T-cells (T_4, T_H or T *helper*) mediate the cellular response by secreting substances to activate macrophages, other T-cells and even B-cells. {T_H-cells are specifically targeted and killed by the HIV virus in AIDS patients}

B-lymphocytes act indirectly against the foreign agent by producing and secreting antigen-specific proteins called **antibodies**, which are sometimes called immunoglobulins = *humoral immunity*). Antibodies are "designer" proteins which can specifically attack the antigen for which it was designed. The antibodies along with other proteins (i.e. complement proteins) can attack the antigen-bearing particle in many ways:

- **Lysis** by digesting the plasma membrane of the foreign cell

- **Opsonization** which is the altering of cell membranes so the foreign particle is more susceptible to phagocytosis by neutrophils and macrophages

- **Agglutination** which is the clumping of antigen-bearing cells

- **Chemotaxis** which is the attracting of other cells (i.e. phagocytes) to the area

- **Inflammation** which includes migration of cells, release of fluids and dilatation of blood vessels.

The activated antibody secreting B-lymphocyte is called a *plasma cell*. After the first or *primary* response to an antigen, both T- and B-cells produce *memory cells* which are formed during the initial response to an anti-

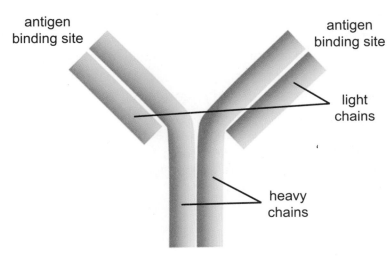

antigen
binding site

antigen
binding site

light
chains

heavy
chains

Figure IV.A.8.1: Schematic representation of an antibody. Antibodies are composed of disulfide bond-linked heavy and light chains. The unique part of the antigen recognized by an antibody is called the epitope. The antigen binding site on the antibody is extremely variable (= hypervariable).

Antibody (= Immunoglobulin = Ig)	Description
IgA	Found in saliva, tears and breast milk. Found in mucosal areas, such as the GI, respiratory and urogenital tracts thus prevents colonization by pathogens.
IgD	Functions mainly as an antigen receptor on B-cells that have not been exposed to antigens. Activates mast cells and basophils (BIO 7.5) to produce antimicrobial factors.
IgE	Binds to particles that induce allergic reactions (= allergens) and triggers histamine release from mast cells and basophils. Also protects against parasitic worms.
IgG	In its four forms, provides the majority of antibody-based immunity against invading germs or pathogens. The only antibody capable of crossing the placenta (BIO 14.6) to give passive immunity to the fetus.
IgM	Expressed on the surface of B-cells (monomer) and in a secreted form (pentamer = complex of 5 monomers). Eliminates pathogens in the early stages of B-cell mediated (humoral) immunity before there is sufficient IgG.

Table IV.A.8.1: Antibody isotypes of mammals. Antibodies are grouped into different "isotypes" based on which heavy chain they possess. The five different antibody isotypes known in mammals are displayed in the table.

genic challenge. These memory cells remain in the circulation and will make the next or secondary response much faster and much greater. {Note: though lymphocytes are vital to the immune system, it is the neutrophil which responds to injury first; BIO 7.5}

T-cells cannot recognise, and therefore react to, 'free' floating antigen. T-cells can only recognize an antigen that has been processed and presented by cells in association will a special cell surface molecule called the major histocompatibility complex (MHC). In fact, "antigen presenting cells", through the use of MHC, can teach both B-cells and T-cells which antigens are safe (*self*) and which are dangerous and should be attacked (*nonself*). MHC Class I molecules present to T_C cells while MHC Class II molecules present to T_H cells.

8.3 Tissues of the Immune System

The important tissues of the immune system are the bone marrow, and the lymphatic organs which include the thymus, the lymph nodes and the spleen. The roles of the bone marrow and the thymus have already been discussed. It is of value to add that the thymus secretes a hormone (= *thymosin*) which appears to help stimulate the activity of T-lymphocytes.

Lymph nodes are often the size of a pea and are found in groups or chains along the paths of the larger lymphatic vessels. Their functions can be broken down into three general categories: i) a non-specific filtration of bacteria and other particles from the lymph using the phagocytic activity of macrophages; ii) the storage and proliferation of T-cells, B-cells and antibody production; (iii) initiate immune response on the recognition of antigen.

The **spleen** is the largest lymphatic organ and is situated in the upper left part of the abdominal cavity. Within its lobules it has tissue called red and white pulp. The white pulp of the spleen contains all of the organ's lymphoid tissue (T-cells, B-cells, macrophages, and other antigen presenting cells) and is the site of active immune responses via the proliferation of T- and B-lymphocytes and the production of antibodies by plasma cells. The red pulp is composed of several types of blood cells including red blood cells, platelets and granulocytes. Its main function is to filter the blood of antigen and phagocytose damaged or aged red blood cells (the latter has a lifespan of approximately 110-120 days). In addition, the red pulp of the spleen is a site for red blood cell storage (i.e. a blood storage organ).

Autoimmunity!

Figure IV.A.8.2: Actually, "autoimmunity" refers to a disease process where the immune system attacks one's own cells and tissues as opposed to one's own car.

8.4 Advanced Topic: ELISA

ELISA, enzyme-linked-immunosorbent serologic assay, is a rapid test used to determine if a particular protein is in a sample and, if so, to quantify it (= assay). ELISA relies on an enzymatic conversion reaction and an antibody-antigen interaction which would lead to a detectable signal – usually a color change. Consequently, ELISA has no need of any radioisotope nor any radiation-counting apparatus.

There are 2 forms of ELISA: (1) direct ELISA uses monoclonal antibodies to detect antigen in a sample; (2) indirect ELISA is used to find a specific antibody in a sample (i.e. HIV antibodies in serum). {Notice the similarity with the concept of "direct" and "indirect" immunofluorescence, BIO 1.5.1}

Go online to GAMSAT-prep.com for additional chapter review Q&A and forum.

THE DIGESTIVE SYSTEM
Chapter 9

Memorize

a as lubrication and enzyme source
ach low pH, gastric juice, mucal
ection against self-destruction

Understand

* Basic function of the upper GI and lower GI tracts
* Bile: storage in gallbladder, function
* Pancreas: production of enzymes; transport of enzymes to small intestine
* Small intestine: production of enzymes, site of digestion, neutralize stomach acid
* Peristalsis; structure and function of villi

Not Required*

* Advanced level college info
* Reading dental x-rays!

GAMSAT-Prep.com

Introduction

The digestive system is involved in the mechanical and chemical break down of food into smaller components with the aim of absorption into, for example, blood or lymph. Thus digestion is a form of catabolism.

Additional Resources

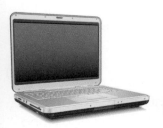

Free Online Q&A + Forum

Video: Online or DVD

Flashcards

Special Guest

* The real GAMSAT may have advanced level information presented (ie. in a passage) but previous knowledge of said information is not required to answer the questions that would follow. Practice ACER and GS practice GAMSATs can help you clarify this point.

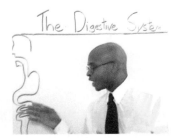

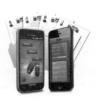

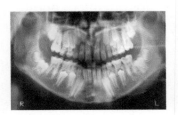

9.1 Overview

The digestive or *gastrointestinal* (= GI) system is principally concerned with the intake and reduction of food into subunits for absorption. These events occur in five main phases which are located in specific parts of the GI system: i) **ingestion** which is the taking of food or liquid into the mouth; ii) **fragmentation** which is when larger pieces of food are *mechanically* broken down; iii) **digestion** where macromolecules are *chemically* broken down into subunits which can be absorbed; iv) **absorption** through cell membranes; and v) **elimination** of the waste products. The GI system secretes enzymes and hormones that facilitate in the process of ingestion, digestion, absorption as well as elimination.

The GI tract (gut or *alimentary canal*) is a muscular tract about 9 meters long covered by a layer of mucosa which has definable characteristics in each area along the tract. The GI tract includes the oral cavity (mouth), pharynx, esophagus, stomach, small intestine, large intestine, and anus. The GI system includes the accessory organs which release secretions into the tract: the salivary glands, gallbladder, liver, and pancreas (*see Figure IV.A.9.1*).

9.2 The Oral Cavity and Esophagus

Ingestion, fragmentation and digestion begin in the oral cavity. Teeth are calcified, hard structures in the oral cavity used to fragment food (= *mastication*). Children have twenty teeth (= *deciduous*) and adults have thirty-two (= *permanent*). From front to back, each quadrant (= *quarter)* of the mouth contains: two incisors for cutting, one cuspid (= *canine*) for tearing, two bicuspids (= *premolars*) for crushing, and three molars for grinding.

Digestion of food begins in the oral cavity when the 3 pairs of salivary glands (*parotid, sublingual*, and *submandibular*) synthesize and secrete saliva. Saliva lubricates the oral cavity, assists in the process of deglutition, controls bacterial flora and initiates the process of digestion. Its production is unique in that it is increased by both sympathetic and parasympathetic innervation. Major components of saliva include salivary amylase, lysozyme, lingual lipase and mucus. Amylase is an enzyme which starts the initial digestion of carbohydrates by splitting starch and glycogen into disaccharide subunits. Lipase is an enzyme which starts the initial digestion of triglyceride (fats). The mucous helps to bind food particles together and lubricate it as it is swallowed.

Swallowing (= *deglutition*) occurs in a coordinated manner in which the tongue and pharyngeal muscles propel the bolus of food into the esophagus while at the same time the upper esophageal sphincter relaxes to permit food to enter. The epiglottis is a small flap of

Basic Dental Anatomy and Pathology

32 Adult Teeth
8 Teeth per Quadrant

3 molars | 2 premolars | 1 canine | 2 incisors

Pathology
- Cavity (C): hole left by infection, tooth decay.
- Filling (F): fills the cavity with metal or composite.
- Bridge (B): false tooth supported by metal.
- Wisdom Tooth (WT; 3rd molar): blocked from erupting (*impaction* likely).

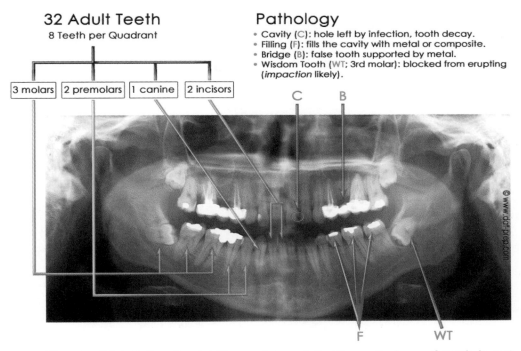

© www.ddfprep.com

C   B

F   WT

Figure IV.A.9.0a: Dental X-ray of an adult. The pathology of teeth is not prerequisite knowledge for the GAMSAT and is only presented for your interest (and as a minor contribution to the future studies of those of you who are studying GAMSAT for dentistry!).

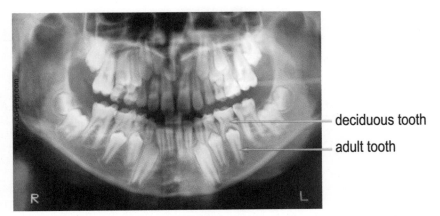

deciduous tooth

adult tooth

R   L

Figure IV.A.9.0b: Dental X-ray of a child showing deciduous (AKA: baby, primary, milk, temporary) teeth and emerging adult (permanent) teeth. Note the "R" on the X-ray indicates the right side of the patient who is facing the observer.

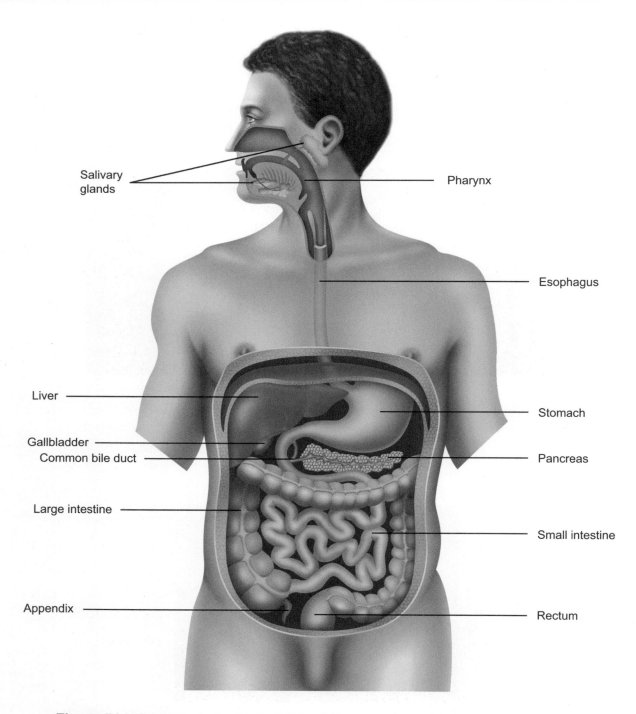

Figure IV.A.9.1: Schematic drawing of the major components of the digestive system.

tissue which covers the opening to the airway (= *glottis*) while swallowing. Gravity and peristalsis help bring the food through the esophagus to the stomach.

The GI system is supplied by both extrinsic innervation and intrinsic innervation. The extrinsic innervation includes the sympathetic and parasympathetic nervous system. The parasympathetic nervous system, mediated by the vagus and pelvic nerves, usually stimulates the functions of the GI tract while the sympathetic nervous system usually inhib-

its the functions of the GI tract. The intrinsic innervation located in the gut wall includes the *myenteric nerve plexus* and *submucosal nerve plexus* which control GI tract motility including peristalsis.

Peristalsis, which is largely the result of two muscle layers in the GI tract (i.e. the inner circular and outer longitudinal layers), is the sequential wave-like muscular contractions which propell food along the tract. The rate, strength and velocity of muscular contractions are modulated by the ANS.

9.3 The Stomach

The stomach continues in fragmenting and digesting the food with its strong muscular activity, its acidic gastric juice and various digestive enzymes present in the gastric juice. The walls of the stomach are lined by thick mucosa which contains goblet cells. These goblet cells of the GI tract protect the lumen from the acidic environment by secreting mucous.

The important components of gastric juice are: i) HCl which keeps the pH low (approximately = 2) to kill microorganisms, to aid in partial hydrolysis of proteins, and to provide the environment for ii) *pepsinogen*, an inactive form of enzyme (= *zymogen*) secreted by gastric chief cells, which is later converted to its active form *pepsin* in the presence of a low pH. Pepsin is involved in the breakdown

of proteins. Both the hormone gastrin, which is produced in the stomach; and parasympathetic impulses can increase the production of gastric juice.

The preceding events turns food into a semi-digested fluid called chyme. Chyme is squirted through a muscular sphincter in the stomach, the *pyloric sphincter*, into the first part of the small intestine, the *duodenum*. Many secretions are produced by exocrine glands in the liver and pancreas and enter the duodenum via the *common bile duct*. Exocrine secretions eventually exit the body through ducts. For example, *goblet cells*, which are found in the stomach and throughout the intestine, are exocrine secretory cells which produce mucus which lines the epithelium of the gastrointestinal tract.

9.4 The Exocrine Roles of the Liver and Pancreas

9.4.1 The Liver

The liver occupies the upper right part of the abdominal cavity. It has many roles including: the conversion of glucose to glycogen; the synthesis of glucose from non-carbohydrates; the production of plasma proteins; the destruction of red blood cells; the deamination of amino acids and the formation of urea; the conversion of toxic ammonia to much less toxic urea (the urea cycle); the storage of iron and certain vitamins; the alteration of toxic substances and most medicinal products (*detoxification*); and its exocrine role - the production of **bile** by liver cells (= *hepatocytes*).

Bile is a yellowish - green fluid mainly composed of water, cholesterol, pigments (from the destruction of red blood cells) and salts. It is the **bile salts** which have a digestive function by the emulsification of fats. Emulsification is the dissolving of fat globules into tiny droplets called *micelles* which have hydrophobic interiors and hydrophilic exteriors (cf. Plasma Membrane, BIO 1.1). Bile salts orient themselves around those lipid droplets with their hydrophilic portions towards the aqueous environment and their hydrophobic portions towards the micelle interior and keep them dispersed. Emulsification also helps in the absorption of the fat soluble vitamins A, D, E, and K.

Thus bile is produced by the liver, stored and concentrated in a small muscular sac, the **gallbladder**, and then secreted into the duodenum via the common bile duct.

9.4.2 The Pancreas

The pancreas is close to the duodenum and extends behind the stomach. The pancreas has both endocrine (*see Endocrine Systems; BIO 6.3.4*) and exocrine functions. It secretes pancreatic juice, which consists of alkaline fluid and digestive enzymes, into the pancreatic duct that joins the common bile duct. Pancreatic juice is secreted both due to parasympathetic and hormonal stimuli. The hormones *secretin* and *CCK* are produced and released by the duodenum in response to the presence of chyme. Secretin acts on the pancreatic ductal cells to stimulate HCO_3^- secretion, whose purpose is to neutralize the acidic chyme. CCK acts on pancreatic acinar cells to stimulate the exocrine pancreatic secretion of digestive enzymes. These enzymes are secreted as enzymes or proenzymes (= *zymogens*; BIO 4.3) that must be activated in the intestinal lumen. The enzymes include pancreatic amylase, which can break down carbohydrates into monosaccharides; pancreatic lipase, which can break down fats into fatty acids and monoglycerides; and nuclease, which can break down nucleic acids. The protein enzymes (proteases) include trypsin, chymotrypsin, carboxypeptidase, which can break down proteins into amino acids, dipeptides or tripeptides.

9.5 The Intestines

The **small intestine** is divided into the duodenum, the jejunum, and the ileum, in that order. It is this part of the GI system that completes the digestion of chyme, absorbs the nutrients (i.e. monosaccharides, amino acids, nucleic acids, etc.), and passes the rest onto the large intestine. Peristalsis is the primary mode of transport. Contraction behind the bolus and simultaneous relaxation in front of the bolus propel chyme forward. Segmentation also aids in small intestine movement - it helps to mix the intestinal contents without any forward movement of chyme. Of course, parasympathetic impulses increase intestinal smooth muscle contraction while sympathetic impulses decrease intestinal smooth muscle contraction.

Absorption is aided by the great surface area involved including the finger-like projections **villi** and **microvilli** (see the Generalized Eukaryotic Cell, BIO 1.1F and 1.2). Intestinal villi, which increase the surface area ten-fold, are evaginations into the lumen of the small intestine and contain blood capillaries and a single lacteal (lymphatic capillary). Microvilli, which increase the surface area twenty-fold, contain a dense bundle of actin microfilaments cross-linked by proteins fimbrin and villin.

Absorption of carbohydrates, proteins and lipids is completed in the small intestine. Carbohydrates must be broken down into glucose, galactose and fructose for absorption to occur. In contrast, proteins can be absorbed as amino acids, dipeptides and tripeptides. Specific transporters are required for amino acids and peptides to facilitate the absorption across the luminal membrane. Lipids are absorbed in the form of fatty acids, monoglycerides and cholesterol. In the intestinal cells, they are re-esterified to triglycerides, cholesterol ester and phospholipids.

The lacteals absorb most fat products into the lymphatic system while the blood capillaries absorb the rest taking these nutrients to the liver for processing via a special vein - the hepatic portal vein [A portal vein carries blood from one capillary bed to another; BIO 7.3]. Goblet cells secrete a copious amount of mucus in order to lubricate the passage of material through the intestine and to protect the epithelium from abrasive chemicals (i.e. acids, enzymes, etc.).

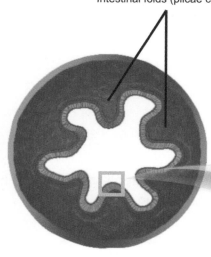

Intestinal folds (plicae circulares)

Cross-section of the small intestine.

Blood vessels

Lacteal

4 intestinal villi.

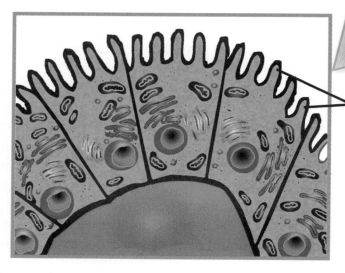

Microvilli

Columnar cells (i.e. intestinal cells arranged in columns)
with microvilli facing the lumen (brush border).

Figure IV.A.9.2: Levels of organization of the small intestine.

9.5.1 The Large Intestines

The large intestine is divided into: the cecum which connects to the ileum and projects a closed-ended tube - the appendix; the colon which is subdivided into ascending, transverse, descending, and sigmoid portions; the rectum which can store feces; and the anal canal which can expel feces (*defecation*) through the anus with the relaxation of the anal sphincter and the increase in abdominal pressure. The large intestine has little or no digestive functions. It absorbs water and electrolytes from the residual chyme and it forms feces. Feces is mostly water, undigested material, mucous, bile pigments (responsible for the characteristic color) and bacteria (= gut flora = 60% of the dry weight of feces).

Essentially, the relationship between the gut and bacteria is mutualistic and symbiotic (BIO 2.2). Though people can survive with no bacterial flora, these microorganisms perform a host of useful functions, such as fermenting unused energy substrates, training the immune system, preventing growth of harmful species, producing vitamins for the host (i.e. vitamin K), and bile pigments.

Go online to GAMSAT-prep.com for additional chapter review Q&A and forum.

THE EXCRETORY SYSTEM
Chapter 10

Memorize

ey structure: cortex, medulla
ron structure: glomerulus,
nan's capsule, proximal tubule, etc.
of Henle, distal tubule,
cting duct
ge and elimination: ureter,
ler, urethra

Understand

* Roles of the excretory system in homeostasis
* Blood pressure, osmoregulation, acid-base balance, N waste removal
* Formation of urine: glomerular filtration, secretion and reabsorption of solutes
* Concentration of urine; counter-current multiplier mechanism

Not Required*

*Advanced level college info

GAMSAT-Prep.com

Introduction

The excretory system excretes waste. The focus of this chapter is to examine the kidney's role in excretion. This includes eliminating nitrogen waste products of metabolism such as urea.

Additional Resources

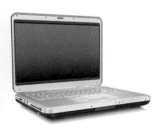

Free Online Q&A + Forum

Video: Online or DVD

Flashcards

Special Guest

* The real GAMSAT may have advanced level information presented (ie. in a passage) but previous knowledge of said information is not required to answer the questions that would follow. Practice ACER and GS practice GAMSATs can help you clarify this point.

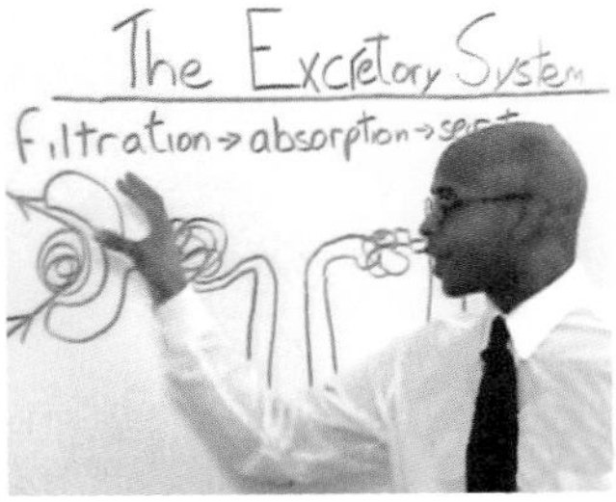

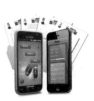

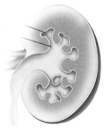

10.1 Overview

Excretion is the elimination of substances (usu. wastes) from the body. It begins at the level of the cell. Broken down red blood cells are excreted as bile pigments into the GI tract; CO_2, an end product of cellular aerobic respiration, is blown away in the lungs; urea and ammonia (NH_3), breakdown products of amino acid metabolism, creatinine, a product of muscle metabolism, and H_2O, a breakdown product of aerobic metabolism, are eliminated by the urinary system. In fact, the urinary system eliminates such a great quantity of waste it is often called the excretory system. It is composed of a pair of kidneys, a pair of ureters and one bladder and urethra.

The composition of body fluids remains within a fairly narrow range. The urinary system is the dominant organ system involved in electrolyte and water homeostasis (*osmoregulation*). It is also responsible for the excretion of toxic nitrogenous compounds (i.e. urea, uric acid, creatinine) and many drugs into the urine. The urine is produced in the kidneys (mostly by the filtration of blood) and is transported, with the help of peristaltic waves, down the tubular ureters to the muscular sack which can store urine, the bladder. Through the process of urination (= *micturition*), urine is expelled from the bladder to the outside via a tubular urethra.

The amount of volume within blood vessels (= *intravascular* or blood volume) and blood pressure are proportional to the rate the kidneys filter blood. Hormones act on the kidney to affect urine formation (see *Endocrine Systems*, BIO 6.3).

10.2 Kidney Structure

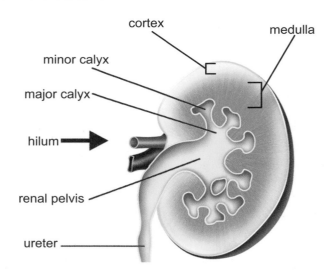

Figure IV.A.10.1: Kidney structure.

The kidney regulates the electrolyte levels in the extracellular fluid and maintains water homeostasis through the production and excretion of urine. The kidney resembles a bean with a concave border (= *the hilum*) where the ureter, nerves, and vessels (blood and lymph) attach. The kidney can be grossly divided into an outer granular-looking **cortex** and an inner dark striated **medulla**. The upper end of the ureter expands into the *renal pelvis* which can be divided into two or three *major calyces*. Each major calyx can be divided into several small branched *minor calyces*. The renal medulla lies deep to the cortex. It is composed of 10-18 medullary pyramids which consist mainly of loop of Henle and collecting tubules. The renal cortex is the superficial layer of the kidney right underneath the capsule. It is composed mainly of renal corpuscles and convoluted tubules.

The kidney is a *filtration-reabsorption-secretion* (excretion) organ. These events are clearly demonstrated at the level of the nephron.

10.3 The Nephron

The nephron is the functional unit of the kidney and consists of the **renal corpuscle** and the **renal tubule**. A renal corpuscle is responsible for the filtration of blood and is composed of a tangled ball of blood capillaries (= *the glomerulus*) and a sac-like structure which surrounds the glomerulus (= *Bowman's capsule*). *Afferent* and *efferent* arterioles lead towards and away from the glomerulus, respectively. The renal tubule is divided into *proximal* and *distal convoluted tubules* with a *loop of Henle* in between. The tube ends in a *collecting duct*.

Blood plasma is **filtered** by the glomerulus through three layers before entering Bowman's capsule. The first layer is formed by the *endothelial cells* of the capillary that possess small holes (= *fenestrae*); the second layer is the *glomerular basement membrane* (BIO 5.3); and the third layer is formed by the negatively charged cells (= *podocytes*) in Bowman's capsule which help repel proteins (most proteins are negatively charged).

The filtration barrier permits passage of water, ions, and small particles from the capillary into Bowman's capsule but prevents pas-

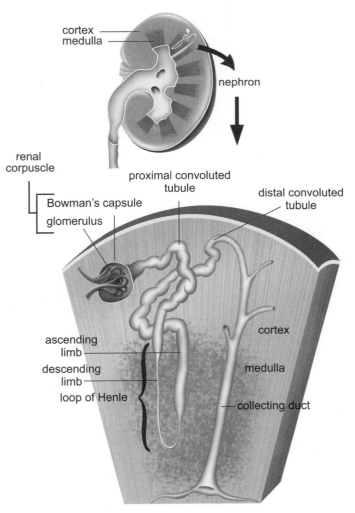

Figure IV.A.10.2: The kidney and its functional unit, the nephron.

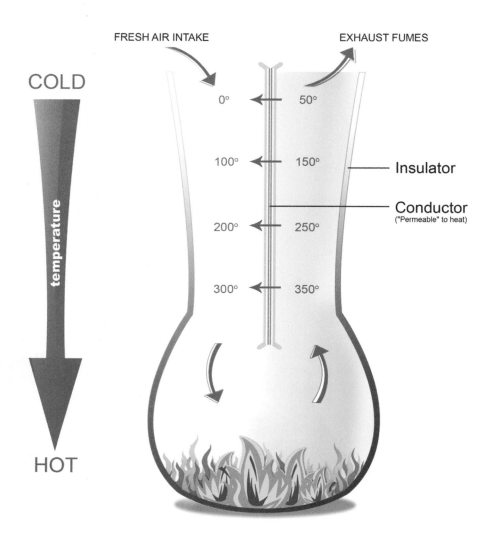

FRESH AIR INTAKE   EXHAUST FUMES

COLD

temperature

0°   50°

100°   150°   Insulator

200°   250°   Conductor
                      ("Permeable" to heat)

300°   350°

HOT

Furnace

The countercurrent principle depends on a parallel flow arrangement moving in 2 different directions (countercurrent) in close proximity to each other. Our example is that of the air intake and exhaust pipe in this simplified schematic of a furnace.

Heat is transferred from the exhaust fumes to the incoming air.

The small horizontal temperature gradient of only 50° is multiplied longitudinally to a gradient of 300°. This conserves heath that would otherwise be lost.

Figure IV.A.10.3: The countercurrent principle (= counter-current mechanism) using a simplified furnace as an example.

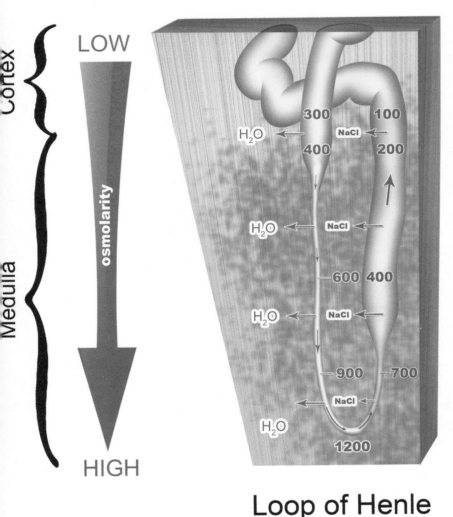

Loop of Henle

The countercurrent system involving the loop of Henle results in an osmotic gradient increasing from cortex to inner medulla (*juxtamedullary* nephrons). Solutes enter and exit at different segments of the nephron. The descending limb of the loop of Henle is highly permeable to water and relatively impermeable to NaCl (thus the filtrate becomes increasingly hypertonic). The ascending limb is impermeable to water but relatively (through active transport) permeable to NaCl.

Due to the increased osmolarity of the interstitial fluid, water moves out of the descending limb into the interstitial fluid by osmosis. Volume of the filtrate decreases as water leaves. Osmotic concentration of the filtrate increases (1200) as it rounds the hairpin turn of the loop of Henle.

Some of the NaCl leaving the ascending limb moves by diffusion into the descending limb from the interstitial fluid thus increasing the solute concentration in the descending limb. Also, new NaCl in the filtrate continuously enters the tubule inflow to be transported out of the ascending limb into the interstitial fluid. Thus this recycling multiplies NaCl concentration.

Figure IV.A.10.4: The countercurrent principle (= counter-current mechanism) in the loop of Henle.

sage of large/negatively charged particles (= *ultrafiltration*) and forms a filtrate in the Bowman's space. The rate of filtration is proportional to the net ultrafiltration pressure across the glomerular capillaries. This net pressure, which is usually positive and favors fluid filtration out of the capillary, can be derived from the difference between glomerular capillary hydrostatic pressure, which favors fluid out of the capillary, and the combined effect of glomerular capillary oncotic pressure and Bowman's space *hydrostatic* pressure, which favor fluid back into the capillary. {The oncotic pressure of Bowman's space is typically zero, so it is ignored here; keep in mind that 'oncotic pressure' is simply the osmotic pressure caused by proteins; see BIO 7.5.2}

The <u>filtrate</u>, which is similar to plasma but with minimal proteins, now passes into the proximal convoluted tubule (PCT). It is here that the body actively **reabsorbs** compounds that it needs (i.e. proteins, amino acids, and especially glucose); and over 75% of all ions and water are reabsorbed by *obligate* (= required) reabsorption from the PCT. To increase the surface area for absorption, the cells of the PCT have a lot of microvilli (= *brush border*; cf. BIO 1.2). Some substances like H^+, urea and penicillin are **secreted** into the PCT.

From the PCT the filtrate goes through the descending and ascending limbs of the loop of Henle which extend into the renal medulla. The purpose of the loop of Henle is to concentrate the filtrate by the transport of ions (Na^+ and Cl^-) into the medulla which produces an osmotic gradient (= *a countercurrent mechanism*). As a consequence of this system, the medulla of the kidney becomes concentrated with ions and tends to "pull" water out of the renal tubule by osmosis.

The filtrate now passes on to the distal convoluted tubule (DCT) which reabsorbs ions actively and water passively and secretes various ions (i.e. H^+). Hormones can modulate the reabsorption of substances from the DCT (= *facultative* reabsorption). Aldosterone acts at the DCT to absorb Na^+ which is coupled to the secretion of K^+ and the passive retention of H_2O.

Finally the filtrate, now called urine, passes into the collecting duct which drains into larger and larger ducts which lead to renal papillae, calyces, the renal pelvis, and then the ureter. ADH concentrates urine by increasing the permeability of the DCT and the collecting ducts allowing the medulla to draw water out by osmosis. Water returns to the circulation via a system of vessels called the *vasa recta*.

Renin is a hormone (BIO 6.3.5) which is secreted by cells that are "near the glomerulus" (= *juxtaglomerular cells*). At the beginning of the DCT is a region of modified tubular cells which can influence the secretion of renin (= *macula densa*). The juxtaglomerular cells and the macula densa are collectively known as the juxtaglomerular apparatus.

10.4 The Bladder

Urine flow through the ureters to the bladder is propelled by muscular contractions of the ureter wall - peristalsis. The urine is stored in the bladder and intermittently ejected during urination, termed micturition.

The bladder is a balloon-like chamber with walls of muscle collectively termed the detrusor muscle. The contraction of this muscle squeezes the urine into the lumen (= *space inside*) of the bladder to produce urination. That part of the detrusor muscle at the base of the bladder, where the urethra begins, functions as a sphincter - the internal urethral sphincter. Beyond the outlet of the urethra is the external urethral sphincter, the contraction of which can prevent urination even when the detrusor muscle contracts strongly.

The basic micturition reflex is a spinal reflex (BIO 6.1.3), which can be influenced by descending pathways from the brain. The bladder wall contains stretch receptors whose afferent fibers enter the spinal cord and stimulate the parasympathetic nerves that supply and stimulate the detrusor muscle. As the bladder fills with urine, the pressure within it increases and the stretch receptors are stimulated, thereby reflexively eliciting stimulation of the parasympathetic neurons and contractions of the detrusor muscle. When the bladder reaches a certain volume, the induced contraction of the detrusor muscle becomes strong enough to open the internal urethral sphincter. Simultaneously, the afferent input from the stretch receptors inhibits, within the spinal cord, the motor neurons that tonically stimulate the external urethral sphincter to contract. Both sphincters are now open and the contraction of the detrusor muscle is able to produce urination.

In summary:

- The internal sphincter is a continuation of the detrusor muscle and is thus composed of smooth muscle under involuntary or autonomic control. This is the primary muscle for preventing the release of urine.

- The external sphincter is made of skeletal muscle is thus under voluntary control of the somatic nervous system (BIO 6.1.4, 6.1.5, 11.2).

Go online to GAMSAT-prep.com for additional chapter review Q&A and forum.

THE MUSCULOSKELETAL SYSTEM
Chapter 11

<table>
<tr><td>Memorize</td><td>Understand</td><td>Not Required*</td></tr>
<tr><td>...ure of three basic muscle types:
...ed, smooth, cardiac
...tary/involuntary muscles;
...athetic/parasympathetic innervation</td><td>* Muscle system, important functions
* Support, mobility, peripheral circulatory assistance, thermoregulation (shivering reflex)
* Control: motor neurons, neuromuscular junctions, motor end plates
* Skeletal system: structural rigidity/support, calcium storage, physical protection
* Skeletal structure: specialization of bone types, basic joint, endo/exoskeleton</td><td>* Advanced level college info</td></tr>
</table>

GAMSAT-Prep.com

Introduction

The musculoskeletal system (= locomotor system) permits the movement of organisms with the use of muscle and bone. Other uses include providing form and stability for the organism; protection of vital organs (i.e. skull, rib cage); storage for calcium and phosphorous as well as containing a critical component to the production of blood cells (skeletal system).

Additional Resources

Free Online Q&A + Forum

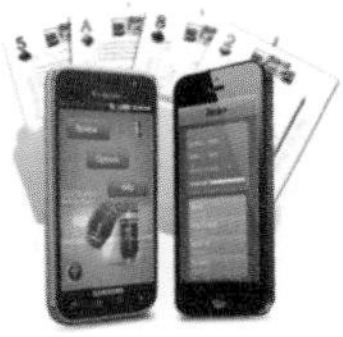

Flashcards

Special Guest

11.1 Overview

The musculoskeletal system supports, protects and enables body parts to move. Muscles convert chemical energy (i.e. ATP, creatine phosphate) into mechanical energy (→ contraction). Thus body heat is produced, body fluids are moved (i.e. lymph), and body parts can move in accordance with lever systems of muscle and bone.

11.2 Muscle

There are many general features of muscle. A latent period is the lag between the stimulation of a muscle and its response. A twitch is a single contraction in response to a brief stimulus which lasts for a fraction of a second. Muscles can either *contract* or *relax* but they cannot actively expand. When muscles are stimulated frequently, they cannot fully relax - this is known as *summation*. Tetany is a sustained contraction (a summation of multiple contractions) that lacks even partial relaxation. If tetany is maintained, the muscle will eventually fatigue or tire. Muscle tone (*tonus*) occurs because even when a muscle appears to be at rest, some degree of sustained contraction is occurring.

The cellular characteristics of muscle have already been described (s*ee Contractile Cells and Tissues,* BIO 5.2). We will now examine the gross features of the three basic muscle types.

Cardiac muscle forms the walls of the heart and is responsible for the pumping action. Its contractions are continuous and are initiated by inherent mechanisms (i.e., they are myogenic) and modulated by the autonomic nervous system. Its activity is decreased by the parasympathetic nervous system and increased by the sympathetic nervous system. The sinoatrial node (SA node) or *pacemaker* contains specialized cardiac muscle cells in the right atrium which initiate the contraction of the heart (BIO 7.2). The electrical signal then progresses to the atrioventricular node (AV node) in the cardiac muscle (myocardium) - between the atria and ventricles - then through the bundle of His which splits and branches out to Purkinje fibers which can then stimulate the contraction of the ventricles (systole; BIO 7.2).

Smooth Muscle has two forms. One type occurs as separate fibers and can contract in response to motor nerve stimuli. These are found in the iris (*pupillary dilation or constriction*) and the walls of blood vessels (*vasodilation or constriction*). The second and more dominant form occurs as sheets of muscle fibers and is sometimes called *visceral muscle*. It forms the walls of many hollow visceral organs like the stomach, intestines, uterus, and the urinary bladder. Like cardiac muscle, its contractions are inherent, involuntary, and rhythmic. Visceral muscle is responsible for peristalsis. Its contractility is usually slow and can be modulated by the autonomic nervous system, hormones, and local metabolites. The activity of visceral muscle is increased by the parasympathetic nervous system and decreased by the sympathetic nervous system.

Skeletal muscle is responsible for voluntary movements. This includes the skeleton and organs such as the tongue and the globe of the eye. Its cells can form a syncytium which is a mass of cells which merge and can function together. Thus skeletal muscle can contract and relax relatively rapidly (*see the Reflex Arc,* BIO 6.1.3).

It should be noted that there are 2 meanings of the word "syncytium" when describing muscle cells. A classic example is the formation of large multinucleated skeletal muscle cells produced from the fusion of thousands of individual muscle cells (= *myocytes*) as alluded to in the previous paragraph ("true syncytium"). However, "syncytium" can also refer to cells that are interconnected by gap junctions (BIO 1.4), as seen in cardiac muscle cells and certain smooth muscle cells, and are thus synchronized electrically during an action potential ("functional syncytium").

Most skeletal muscles act across joints. Each muscle has a movable end (= *the insertion*) and an immovable end (= *the origin*). When a muscle contracts its insertion is moved towards its origin. When the angle of the joint decreases it is called flexion, when it increases it is called extension. Abduction is movement away from the midline of the body and adduction is movement toward the midline. {Adduction is addicted to the middle (= midline)}

Muscles which assist each other are synergistic (for example: while the deltoid muscle abducts the arm, other muscles hold the shoulder steady). Muscles that can move a joint in opposite directions are antagonistic (for example: at the elbow the biceps can flex while the triceps can extend).

Control of skeletal muscle originates in the cerebral cortex. Skeletal muscle is innervated by the somatic nervous system. Motor (*efferent*) neurons carry nerve impulses from the CNS to synapse with muscle fibers at the *neuro-muscular junction*. The terminal end of the motor neuron (motor end plate) can secrete

Skeletal muscle

acetylcholine which can depolarize the muscle fiber (BIO 5.1, 5.2). One motor neuron can depolarize many muscle fibers (= *a motor unit*).

The autonomic nervous system can supply skeletal muscle with more oxygenated blood in emergencies (sympathetic response) or redirect the blood to the viscera during relaxed states (parasympathetic response).

Skeletal muscle can be categorized as Type I or Type II. Type I fibers (= *cells*) appear red because of the oxygen-binding protein myoglobin (BIO 7.5.1). These fibers are suited for endurance and are slow to fatigue since they use oxidative metabolism to generate ATP (BIO 4.7-4.10). Type II fibers are white due to the absence of myoglobin and a reliance on glycolytic enzymes (BIO 4.5, 4.6). These fibers are efficient for short bursts of speed and power and use both oxidative metabolism and anaerobic metabolism depending on the particular sub-type. Type II myocytes are quicker to fatigue.

11.3 The Skeletal System

The microscopic features of bone and cartilage have already been described (*see Connective Cells and Tissues*, BIO 5.4.3/4). We will now examine the relevant gross features of the skeletal system.

The bones of the skeleton have many functions: i) acting like levers that aid in **body movement**; ii) the **storage** of inorganic salts like calcium and phosphorus (and to a lesser extent sodium and magnesium); iii) the production of blood cells (**= hematopoiesis**) in the metabolically active red marrow of the spongy parts of many bones. Bone also has a yellow marrow which contains fat storage cells.

11.3.1 Bone Structure and Development

Bone structure can be classified as follows: i) long bones which have a long shaft, the diaphysis, that is made up mostly of compact bone and expanded ends, like arm and leg bones; ii) short bones which are shaped like long bones but are smaller and have only a thin layer of compact bone surrounding a spongy bone interior; iii) flat bones which have broad surfaces like the skull, ribs, and the scapula and have two layers of compact bones with a layer of spongy bone in the middle; iv) irregular bones like the vertebrae and many facial bones and consist of a thin layer of compact bone covering a spongy bone

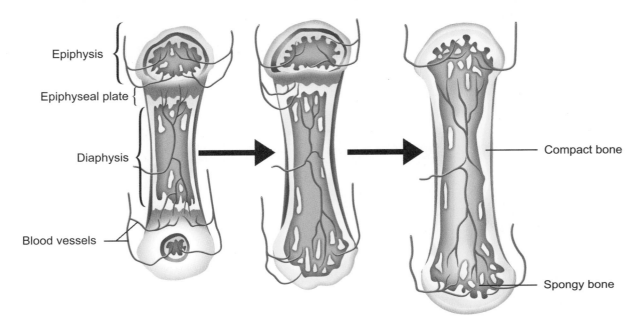

Figure IV.A.11.1: Bone structure and development.

interior. Bone structure can also be classified as: i) <u>primary bone</u>, also known as immature or woven bone, which contains many cells and has a low mineral content; ii) <u>secondary bone</u>, also known as mature or lamellar bone, which has a calcified matrix arranged in regular layers, or lamella.

The rounded expanded end of a long bone is called the *epiphysis* which contains <u>spongy bone</u>. The epiphysis is covered by fibrous tissue (*the periosteum*) and it forms a joint with another bone. Spongy bone contains bony plates called *trabeculae* (= *spicules*). The shaft of the bone which connects the expanded ends is called the *diaphysis.* It is predominately composed of <u>compact bone</u>. This kind of bone is very strong and resistant to bending and has no trabeculae or bone marrow cavities.

Animals that fly have less dense, more light bones (spongy bone) in order to facilitate flying. Animals that swim do not need to have as strong bones as land animals as the buoyant force of the water takes away from the everyday stress on the bones. In the adult, yellow marrow is likely to be found in the diaphysis while red marrow is likely to be found in the epiphysis.

Bone growth occurs in two ways, intramembranous and endochondral bone formation. Both formations produce bones that are histologically identical. Intramembranous bone formation begins as layers of membranous connective tissue, which are later calcified by osteoblasts. Most of the flat bones are formed by this process. Endochondral bone formation is the process by which most of long bones are formed. It begins with hyaline cartilage that functions as a template for the bone to grow on.

Vascularizaton of the cartilage causes the transformation of cartilage cells to bone cells (osteoblasts), which later form a cartilage-calcified bone matrix. The osteoblasts continue to replace cartilage with bone and the osteoclasts create perforations to form bone marrow cavities. In children one can detect an **epiphyseal growth plate** on X-ray. This plate is a disk of cartilage between the epiphysis and diaphysis where bone is being actively deposited (= *ossification*).

11.3.2 Joint Structure

Articulations or joints are junctions between bones. They can be **immovable** like the dense connective tissue sutures which hold the flat bones of the skull together; **partly movable** like the hyaline and fibrocartilage joints on disks of the vertebrae; or **freely movable** like the synovial joints which are the most prominent joints in the skeletal system. Synovial joints contain a joint capsule composed of outer ligaments and an inner layer (= *the synovial membrane*) which secretes a lubricant (= *synovial fluid*).

Freely movable joints can be of many types. For example, ball and socket joints have a wide range of motion, like the shoulder and hip joints. On the other hand, hinge joints allow motion in only one plane like a hinged door (i.e. the knee, elbow, and interphalangeal joints).

11.3.3 Cartilage

The microscopic aspects of cartilage have already been discussed (*see Dense Connective Tissue*, BIO 5.4.2/3). Opposing and mobile surfaces of bone are covered by various forms of cartilage. As already mentioned, joints with hyaline or fibrocartilage allow little movement.

Ligaments attach bone to bone. They are formed by dense bands of fibrous connective tissue which reinforce the joint capsule and help to maintain bones in the proper anatomical arrangement.

Tendons connect muscle to bone. They are formed by the densest kind of fibrous connective tissue. Tendons allow muscular forces to be exerted even when the body (*or belly*) of the muscle is at some distance from the action.

APPENDICULAR SKELETON

AXIAL SKELETON

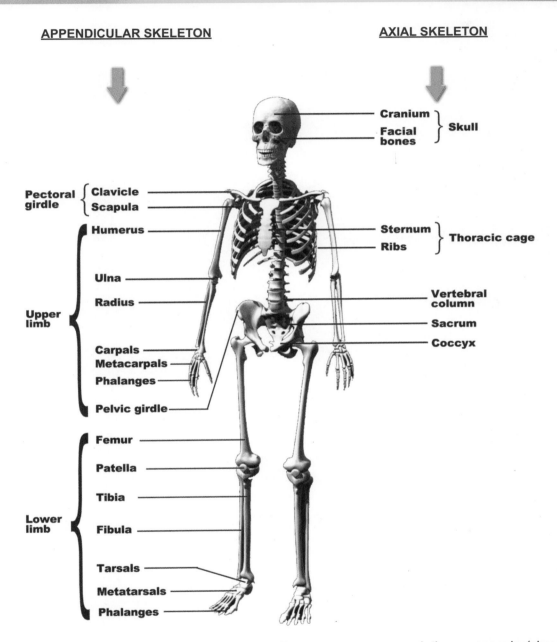

Cranium
Facial bones
} Skull

Pectoral girdle { Clavicle
Scapula

Humerus

Sternum
Ribs
} Thoracic cage

Ulna

Radius

Vertebral column

Upper limb

Sacrum

Coccyx

Carpals
Metacarpals
Phalanges

Pelvic girdle

Femur

Patella

Tibia

Lower limb

Fibula

Tarsals

Metatarsals

Phalanges

Figure IV.A.11.2: Skeletal structure. Note: in brackets some common relations - scapula (shoulder blade), clavicle (collarbone), carpals (wrist), metacarpals (palm), phalanges (fingers), tibia (shin), patella (kneecap), tarsals (ankle), metatarsals (foot), phalanges (toes), vertebral column (backbone). Note that the appendicular skeleton includes the bones of the appendages and the pectoral and pelvic girdles. The axial skeleton consists of the skull, vertebral column, and the rib cage.

Go online to GAMSAT-prep.com for additional chapter review Q&A and forum.

THE RESPIRATORY SYSTEM
Chapter 12

Memorize	Understand	Not Required*
anatomy and order	* Basic functions: gas exchange/thermoreg. * Protection against disease, particulate matter * Breathing mechanisms: diaphragm, rib cage, differential pressure * Resiliency and surface tension effects * The carbonic acid-bicarbonate buffer * Henry's Law	* Advanced level college info

GAMSAT-Prep.com

Introduction ▣▣▣▣

The respiratory system permits the exchange of gases with the organism's environment. This critical process occurs in the microscopic space between alveoli and capillaries. It is here where molecules of oxygen and carbon dioxide passively diffuse between the gaseous external environment and the blood.

Additional Resources

Free Online Q&A + Forum

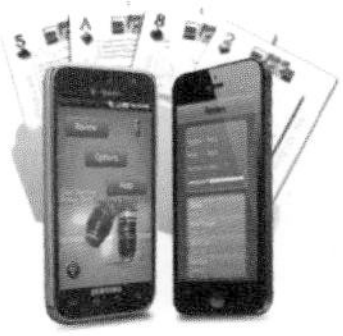

Flashcards

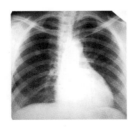

Special Guest

12.1 Overview

There are two forms of respiration: cellular respiration which refers to the oxidation of organic molecules (*see* BIO 4.4 - 4.10) and mechanical respiration where the gases related to cellular respiration are exchanged between the atmosphere and the circulatory system (O_2 in and CO_2 out).

The respiratory system, which is concerned with mechanical respiration, has the following principal functions:

* providing a conducting system for the exchange of gases

* the filtration of incoming particles

* to help control the water content and temperature (= *thermoregulation*) of the incoming air

* to assist in speech production, the sense of smell, and the regulation of pH.

The respiratory system is composed of the lungs and a series of airways that connect the lungs to the external environment, deliver air to the lungs and perform gas exchange.

12.2 The Upper Respiratory Tract

The respiratory system can be divided into an *upper* and *lower respiratory tract* which are separated by the pharynx. The **upper respiratory tract** is composed of the nose, the nasal cavity, the sinuses, and the nasopharynx. This portion of the respiratory system warms, moistens and filters the air before it reaches the lower respiratory system. The nose (*nares*) has receptors for the sense of smell. It is guarded by hair to entrap coarse particles. The nasal cavity, the hollow space behind the nose, contains a ciliated mucous membrane (= a form of *respiratory epithelium*) to entrap smaller particles and prevent infection (this arrangement is common throughout the respiratory tract; for cilia *see the Generalized Eukaryotic Cell*, BIO 1.2). The nasal cavity adjusts the humidity and temperature of incoming air. The nasopharynx helps to equilibrate pressure between the environment and the middle ear via the eustachian tube (BIO 6.2.3).

12.3 The Lower Respiratory Tract

The **lower respiratory tract** is composed of the larynx which contains the vocal cords, the trachea which divides into left and right main bronchi which continue to divide into smaller airways ($\rightarrow$ 2° bronchi $\rightarrow$ 3° bronchi $\rightarrow$ bronchioles $\rightarrow$ terminal bronchioles). The terminal bronchioles are the most distal part of the conducting portion of the respira-

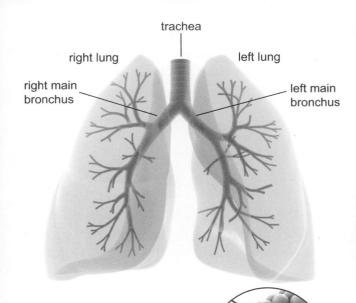

trachea

right lung   left lung

right main
bronchus

left main
bronchus

Figure IV.A.12.1: Illustration representing the lower respiratory tract including the dividing bronchial tree and grape-shaped alveoli with blood supply. Note that "right" refers to the patient's perspective which means the left side from your perspective.

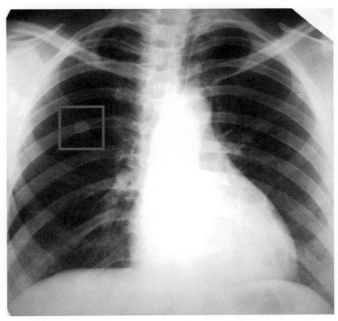

Figure IV.A.12.2: Chest x-ray of an adult male smoker. Notice the coin-shaped shadow in the right lung which presented with coughing blood. Further tests confirmed the presence of a right lung cancer. Cancer-causing chemicals (carcinogens) can irritate any of the cells lining the lower respiratory tract.

tory system. Starting from respiratory bronchioles → alveolar ducts → alveolar sacs until the level of <u>the alveolus</u>, these are considered the respiratory portion of respiratory system, where gas exchange takes place.

It is in these microscopic air sacs called *alveoli* that O_2 diffuses through the alveolar walls and enters the blood in nearby capillaries (where the concentration or *partial pressure* of O_2 is lowest and CO_2 is highest) and CO_2 diffuses from the blood through the walls to enter the alveoli (where the partial pressure of CO_2 is lowest and O_2 is highest). Gas exchange occurs by diffusion across the blood-gas barrier

between the alveolar airspace and the capillary lumen. The blood-gas barrier is composed of three layers: type I pneumocyte cells, fused basal laminae and the endothelium of capillaries. *Alveolar macrophages* are phagocytes which help to engulf particles which reach the alveolus. A *surfactant* is secreted into alveoli by special lung cells (*pneumocytes type II*). The surfactant reduces surface tension and prevents the fragile alveoli from collapsing.

Sneezing and coughing, which are reflexes mediated by the medulla, can expel particles from the upper and lower respiratory tract, respectively.

The **lungs** are separated into left and right and are enclosed by the diaphragm and the thoracic cage. It is covered by a membrane (= *pleura*) which secretes a lubricant to reduce friction while breathing. The lungs contain the air passages, nerves, alveoli, blood and lymphatic vessels of the lower respiratory tract.

12.4 Breathing: Structures and Mechanisms

Inspiration is <u>active</u> and occurs according to the following main events: i) nerve impulses from the <u>phrenic nerve</u> cause the muscular <u>diaphragm</u> to contract; as the dome shaped diaphragm moves downward, the thoracic cavity increases; ii) simultaneously, the intercostal (= *between ribs*) muscles and/or certain neck muscles may contract further increasing the thoracic cavity (the muscles mentioned here are called *accessory respiratory muscles* and under normal circumstances the action of the diaphragm is much more important); iii) as the size of the thoracic cavity increases, its <u>internal pressure</u> decreases leaving it relatively negative; iv) the relatively positive <u>atmospheric pressure</u> forces air into the respiratory tract thus inflating the lungs.

Expiration is <u>passive</u> and occurs according to the following main events: i) the diaphragm and the accessory respiratory muscles relax and the chest wall pushed inward; ii) the elastic tissues of the lung, thoracic cage, and the abdominal organs recoil to their original position; iii) this recoil increases the pressure within the lungs (making the pressure relatively positive) thus forcing air out of the lungs and passageways.

12.4.1 Control of Breathing

Though voluntary breathing is possible (!), normally breathing is involuntary, rhythmic, and controlled by the *respiratory center* in the medulla of the brain stem. The respiratory center is sensitive to pH of the cerebrospinal fluid (CSF). An increase in blood CO_2 or consequently, decrease in pH of the CSF, acts on the respiratory center and stimulates breathing, returning the arterial pCO_2 (partial pressure of carbon dioxide) back to normal. The increase in blood CO_2 and the decrease in pH are two interrelated events since CO_2 can be picked up by hemoglobin forming carbamino-hemoglobin (about 20%, BIO 7.5.1), but it can also be <u>converted into carbonic acid</u> by dissolving in blood plasma (about 5%) or by conversion in red blood cells by the enzyme *carbonic anhydrase* (about 75%). The reaction is summarized as follows:

$$CO_2 + H_2O \leftrightarrow H_2CO_3 \leftrightarrow HCO_3^- + H^+$$

carbonic acid   bicarbonate

According to Henry's Law, the concentration of a gas dissolved in solution is directly proportional to its partial pressure. From the preceding you can see why the respiratory system, through the regulation of the partial pressure of CO_2 in blood, also helps in maintaining pH homeostasis (= a buffer). More generally, the carbonic-acid-bicarbonate buffer is the most important buffer for maintaining acid-base balance in the blood and helps to maintain pH around 7.4.

12.4.2 Henry's Law, Pop and The Bends

Higher gas pressure and lower temperature cause more gas to dissolve in a liquid. When a carbonated drink (soda/pop) is manufactured, water is chilled, optimally to just above freezing, in order to permit the maximum amount of carbon dioxide to dissolve. Then CO_2 is pumped in at high pressure, the pressure is maintained by closing the container (can or bottle), which forces the carbon dioxide to dissolve into the liquid, creating carbonic acid (Le Chatelier's principle; CHM 9.9) and giving 'pop' its tang. Flat soda tastes strange, or at least less pleasant, because of the loss of carbonic acid due to the release of carbon dioxide bubbles/fizz.

So pop is stored in a way to seal pressure, preventing gas escape and maintaining the supersaturation of CO_2 in the solvent.

It is pressure and temperature that drive the outgassing process.

Diving underwater exposes the body to increasing pressure (PHY 6.1). A diving cylinder (scuba tank) is used to store and transport high pressure breathing gas. As the dive becomes deeper, inhaled gas is absorbed into body tissue in higher concentrations than normal (Henry's Law). Surfacing from a deep dive underwater, unused gases (inert) like nitrogen try to do the same thing in your bloodstream that happens when you open a container of pop. The release of these bubbles (outgassing) produces the symptoms of decompression sickness (= 'the bends') that can be painful or even fatal. {Breathing (BIO 12.4), carbon dioxide-carbonic acid, and Henry's Law, are the source of the most likely GAMSAT questions from this chapter.}

Go online to GAMSAT-prep.com for additional chapter review Q&A and forum.

Memorize	Understand	Not Required*
...ture and function of skin, layer ...rentiation ...t glands; nails	* Skin system: homeostasis and osmoregulation * Functions in thermoregulation: hair, erectile musculature, fat layer for insulation * Vasoconstriction and vasodilation in surface capillaries * Physical protection: nails, calluses, hair; protection against abrasion, disease organisms * Relative impermeability to water	* Advanced level college info

GAMSAT-Prep.com

Introduction

Skin is composed of layers of epithelial tissues which protect underlying muscle, bone, ligaments and internal organs. Thus skin has many roles including protecting the body from microbes, insulation, temperature regulation, sensation and synthesis of vitamin D.

Additional Resources

Free Online Q&A + Forum

Flashcards

Special Guest

* The real GAMSAT may have advanced level information presented (ie. in a passage) but previous knowledge of said information is not required to answer the questions that would follow. Practice ACER and GS practice GAMSATs can help you clarify this point.

13.1 Overview

The skin, or *integument*, is the body's largest organ. The following represents its major functions:

* **Physical protection:** The skin protects against the onslaught of the environment including uv light, chemical, thermal or even mechanical agents. It also serves as a barrier to the invasion of microorganisms.

* **Sensation:** The skin, being the body's largest sensory organ, contains a wide range of sensory receptors including those for pain, temperature, light touch, and pressure.

* **Metabolism:** Vitamin D synthesis can occur in the epidermis of skin (*see Endocrine Systems*, BIO 6.3). Also, energy is stored as fat in subcutaneous adipose tissue.

* **Thermoregulation and osmoregulation:** Skin is vital for the homeostatic mechanism of thermoregulation and to a lesser degree osmoregulation. Hair (*piloerection*, which can trap a layer of warm air against the skin's surface) and especially subcutaneous fat (*adipose tissue*) insulate the body against heat loss. Shivering, which allows muscle to generate heat, and decreasing blood flow to the skin (= *vasoconstriction*) are important in emergencies.

On the other hand, heat and water loss can be increased by increasing blood flow to the multitude of blood vessels (= *vasodilation*) in the dermis (cooling by radiation), the production of sweat, and the evaporation of sweat due to the heat at the surface of the skin; thus the skin cools. {Remember: the **hypothalamus** also regulates body temperature (*see The Nervous System*, BIO 6.1); it is like a thermostat which uses other organs as tools to maintain our body temperatures at about 37 °C (98.6 °F)}.

13.2 The Structure of Skin

Skin is divided into three layers: i) the outer **epidermis** which contains a stratified squamous keratinized epithelium; ii) the inner **dermis** which contains vessels, nerves, muscle, and connective tissues; iii) the innermost **subcutaneous layer**, known as hypodermis, which contains adipose and a loose connective tissue; this layer binds to any underlying organs.

The epidermis is divided into several different layers or *strata*. The deepest layer, *stratum basale*, contains actively dividing cells (keratinocytes) which are nourished by the vessels in the dermis. The mitotic activity of keratinocytes can keep regenerating epidermis approximately every 30 days. As these cells continue to divide, older epidermal cells are pushed towards the surface of the skin - *away from the nutrient providing dermal layer*; thus in time they die. Simultaneously, these cells are actively producing strands of a tough, fibrous, waterproof protein called keratin. This process is called *keratinization*. The two preceding events lead to the formation of an outermost layer (= *stratum corneum*) of keratin-filled dead cells which are devoid of organelles and are continuously shed by a process called *desquamation*.

Melanin is a dark pigment produced by cells (= *melanocytes*) whose cell bodies are usually found in the stratum basale. Melanin absorbs light thus protects against uv light induced cell damage (i.e. sunburns, skin cancer). Individuals have about the same number of melanocytes - regardless of race. Melanin production depends on genetic factors (i.e. race) and it can be stimulated by exposure to sunlight (i.e. tanning).

Langerhans cells have long processes and contain characteristic tennis-racket-shaped Birbeck granules. They function as antigen presenting cells in the immune response (BIO 8.2, 8.3).

Merkel cells are present in the richly innervated areas of stratum basale. They are responsible for receiving afferent nerve impulses and function as sensory mechano-receptors (BIO 6.1.1).

The dermis is composed of dense irregular connective tissue including type I collagen fibers and a network of elastic fibers. It contains the blood vessels which nourish the various cells in the skin. It also contains motor fibers and many types of sensory nerve fibers such as fine touch receptors, pressure receptors and cold receptors.

13.3 Skin Appendages

The **appendages** of the skin include hair, sebaceous glands and sweat glands. Hair is a modified keratinized structure produced by a cylindrical downgrowth of epithelium (= *hair follicle*). The follicle extends into the dermis (sometimes the subcutaneous tissue as well). The arrector pili muscle attaches to the connective tissue surrounding a hair follicle. When this bundle of smooth muscle contracts (= *piloerection*), it elevates the hair and "goose bumps" are produced.

The sebaceous glands are lobular acinar glands that empty their ducts into the hair follicles. They are most abundant on the face, forehead and scalp. They release an oily/ waxy secretion called sebum to lubricate and waterproof the skin.

Sweat glands can be classified as either eccrine sweat glands, which are simple tubular glands present in the skin throughout the body or apocrine sweat glands, which are large specialized glands located only in certain areas of the body (i.e. areola of the nipple, perianal area, axilla which is the "armpit") and will not function until puberty.

We have previously explored endocrine glands and saw how they secrete their products - without the use of a duct - directly into the bloodstream (BIO 6.3). Alternatively, endo-

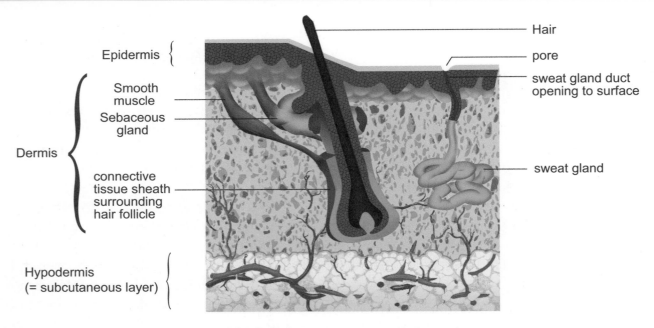

Figure IV.A.13.1: Skin structure with appendages.

crine products may diffuse into surrounding tissue (*paracrine signaling*) where they often affect only target cells near the release site.

An exocrine gland is distinguished by the fact that it excretes its product via a duct to some environment external to itself, either inside the body (BIO 9.3, 9.4) or on a surface of the body. Examples of exocrine glands include the sebaceous glands, sweat glands, salivary glands, mammary glands, pancreas and liver.

Holocrine (= *wholly secretory*) is a type of glandular secretion in which the entire secreting cell, along with its accumulated secretion, forms the secreted matter of the gland; for example, the sebaceous glands. Apocrine concentrates products at the free end of the secreting cell and are thrown off along with a portion of the cytoplasm (i.e. mammary gland, axilla). Eccrine, apocrine and holocrine are subdivisions of exocrine.

13.3.1 Nails, Calluses

Nails are flat, translucent, keratinized coverings near the tip of fingers and toes. In humans, nails grow at an average rate of 3 mm (0.12 in) per month.

A callus is a toughened, thickened area of skin. It is usually created in response to repeated friction or pressure thus they are normally found on the hands or feet.

Go online to GAMSAT-prep.com for additional chapter review Q&A and forum.

REPRODUCTION AND DEVELOPMENT
Chapter 14

Memorize	Understand	Not Required*
and female reproductive structures, tions n, sperm: differences in formation, ive contribution to next generation oductive sequence: fertilization; antation; development r structures arising out of primary layers	* Gametogenesis by meiosis * Formation of primary germ layers: endoderm, mesoderm, ectoderm * Embryogenesis: stages of early development: order and general features of each * Cell specialization, communication in development, gene regulation in development * Programmed cell death; basic: the menstrual cycle	* Advanced level college info

GAMSAT-Prep.com

Introduction

Reproduction refers to the process by which new organisms are produced. The process of development follows as the single celled zygote grows into a fully formed adult. These two processes are fundamental to life as we know it.

Additional Resources

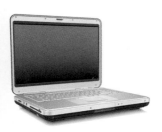

Free Online Q&A + Forum

Video: Online or DVD

Flashcards

Special Guest

* The real GAMSAT may have advanced level information presented (ie. in a passage) but previous knowledge of said information is not required to answer the questions that would follow. Practice ACER and GS practice GAMSATs can help you clarify this point.

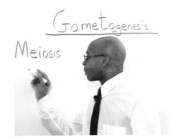

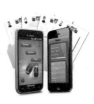

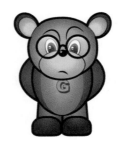

14.1 Organs of the Reproductive System

Gonads are the organs which produce gametes (= germ cells = reproductive cells). The female <u>gonads</u> are the two <u>ovaries</u> which lie in the pelvic cavity. Opening around the ovaries and connecting to the uterus are the <u>Fallopian tubes</u> (= *oviducts*) which conduct the egg (= *ovum*) from the ovary to the <u>uterus</u>. The uterus is a muscular organ. Part of the uterus (= the <u>cervix</u>) protrudes into the <u>vagina</u> or *birth canal*. The vagina leads to the external genitalia. The <u>vulva</u> includes the openings of the vagina, various glands, and folds of skin which are large (= <u>labia majora</u>) and small (= <u>labia minora</u>). The <u>clitoris</u> is found between the labia minora at the anterior end of the vulva. Like the glans penis, it is very sensitive as it is richly innervated. However, the clitoris is unique in being the only organ in the human body devoted solely to sensory pleasure.

The male <u>gonads</u> are the two <u>testicles</u> (= *testes*) which are suspended by spermatic cords in a sac-like <u>scrotum</u> outside the body cavity (this is because the optimal temperature for spermatogenesis is less than body temperature). Sperm (= *spermatozoa*) are produced in the <u>seminiferous tubules</u> in the testes and then continue along a system of ducts including: the <u>epididymis</u> where sperm complete their maturation and are collected and stored; the <u>vas deferens</u> which leads to the <u>ejaculatory duct</u> which in turn leads to the <u>penile urethra</u> which conducts to the exterior. The accessory organs include the <u>seminal vesicles</u>, the <u>bulbourethral</u> and prostate glands. They are exocrine glands whose secretions contribute greatly to the volume of the *ejaculate* (= <u>semen</u> = <u>seminal fluid</u>). The penis is composed of a body or <u>shaft</u>, which contains an erectile tissue which can be engorged by blood; a penile urethra which can conduct either urine or sperm; and a very sensitive head or <u>glans penis</u> which may be covered by foreskin (= *prepuce*, which is removed by circumcision).

Figure IV.A.14.0: An ovulating ovary and a testicle with spermatic cord.

14.2 Gametogenesis

Gametogenesis refers to the production of gametes (eggs and sperm) which occurs by <u>meiosis</u> (*see Mitosis*, BIO 1.3, *for comparison*). Meiosis involves two successive divisions which can produce four cells from one parent cell. <u>The first division</u>, the reduction division, reduces the number of chromosomes from 2N (= *diploid*) to N (= *haploid*) where N = 23 for humans. This reduction division occurs as follows: i) in **prophase I** the chromosomes appear (= *condensed chromatin*), the nuclear membrane and nucleoli disappear and the spindle fibers become organized. Homologous paternal and maternal chromosomes pair[1] (= *synapsis*) forming a tetrad as each pair of homologous chromosomes consists of four chromatids. The exchange of genetic information (DNA) may occur by crossing over between homologous chromosomes at sites called *chiasmata*, therefore redistributing maternal and paternal genetic information ensuring variability; ii) **in metaphase I** the synaptic pairs of chromosomes line up midway between the poles of the developing spindle (= *the equatorial plate*). Thus each pair consists of 2 chromosomes (= 4 chromatids), each attached to a spindle fiber; iii) in **anaphase I** the homologous chromosomes migrate to opposite poles of the spindle, separating its paternal chromosomes from maternal ones. Thus, each daughter cell will have a unique mixture of paternal and maternal origin of chromosomes. In contrast to anaphase in mitosis, the two chromatids remain held together. Consequently, the centromeres do *not* divide; iv) in **telophase I** the parent cell divides into two daughter cells (= *cytokinesis*), the nuclear membranes and nucleoli reappear, and the spindle fibers are no longer visible. Each daughter cell now contains 23 chromosomes (1N).

The first meiotic division is followed by a short interphase I and then the second meiotic division which proceeds essentially the same as mitosis. Thus prophase II, metaphase II, anaphase II, and telophase II proceed like the corresponding mitotic phases.

Gametogenesis in males (= *spermatogenesis*) proceeds as follows: before the age of sexual maturity only a small number of primordial germ cells (= *spermatogonia*) are present in the testes. There are two types of spermatogonia, type A and type B. Type A spermatogonia (2N) are mitotically active and continuously provide a supply of type A or type B spermatogonia. Type B spermatogonia (2N) undergo meiosis and will give rise to primary spermatocytes. After sexual maturation these cells prolifically multiply throughout a male's life.

In the seminiferous tubules, the type B spermatogonia (2N) enter meiosis I and undergo chromosome replication forming primary spermatocytes with 2N chromosomes. Primary spermatocytes complete meiosis I producing two secondary spermatocytes with 1N chromosomes. Secondary spermatocytes quickly enter meiosis II without an intervening S phase to form four spermatids. Spermatids are haploid (1N) cells.

In summary, each primary spermatocyte results in the production of four spermatids. Spermatids undergo a post-meiotic cytodifferentiation whereby spermatids are transformed into **four** motile sperm (1N) through a process called *spermiogenesis*.

Sperm can be divided into: i) a *head* which is oval and contains the nucleus with its 23 chromosomes {since the nucleus carries either an X or Y sex chromosome, sperm determine the sex of the offspring}. The head is partly surrounded by the acrosome which contains enzymes (esp. hyaluronidase) which help the sperm penetrate the egg. The

[1]synapsing homologous chromosomes are often called *tetrads* or *bivalents*.

Spermatogenesis   Oogenesis

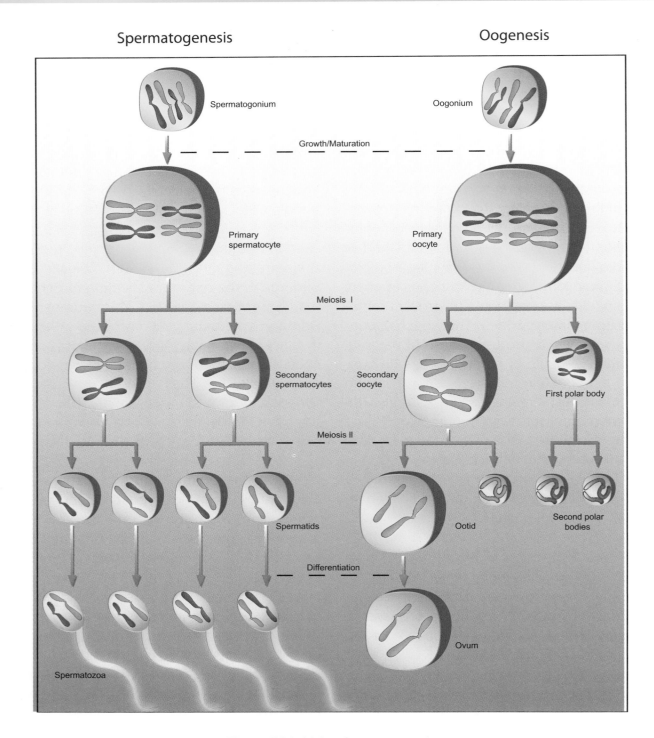

Figure IV.A.14.0a: Gametogenesis.

release of these enzymes is known as the acrosomal reaction; ii) the *body* of the sperm contains a central core surrounded by a large number of mitochondria for power; and iii) the *tail* constitutes a flagellum which is critical for the cell's locomotion. Newly formed sperm are incapable of fertilization until they undergo a process called capacitation, which happens in the female reproductive duct. After removal of its protein coating, the sperm becomes capable of fertilization. Also in the seminiferous tubules are Sertoli cells which support and nourish developing sperm and Leydig cells which produce and secrete testosterone. While LH stimulates the latter, FSH stimulates primary spermatocytes to undergo meiosis. {Remember: LH = Leydig, FSH = spermatogenesis}

Gametogenesis in females (= *oogenesis*) proceeds as follows: in fetal development, groups of cells (= *ovarian or primordial follicles*) develop from the germinal epithelium of the ovary) and differentiate into oogonia (2N). Oogonia (2N) enter meiosis I and undergo DNA replication producing primary oocytes (2N) which are surrounded by epithelia (= *follicular cells*) in the primordial follicle. The oocytes remain arrested in prophase I of meiosis until ovulation which occurs between the ages of about 13 (sexual maturity) and 50 (menopause). Thus, unlike males, all female germ cells are present at birth. Some follicles degenerate and are called *atretic*. During puberty, when the ovarian cycle begins, up to 20 primordial follicles may begin to differentiate to *Graafian follicles*. During this development,

meiosis continues. In response to an LH surge from the pituitary gland, the primary oocyte (2N) completes meiosis I just prior to ovulation to form the secondary oocyte (1N) and the first polar body, which will probably degenerate. The secondary oocyte is surrounded by (from the inside out): a thick, tough membrane (= *the zona pellucida*), follicular cells (= *the corona radiata*), and estrogen-secreting thecal cells. It then enters meiosis II and remains arrested in metaphase of meiosis II until fertilization occurs.

Of the twenty or so maturing follicles, all the remaining secondary follicles will degenerate (= *atresia*) except for one which becomes the Graafian (mature) follicle. In response to the LH surge, the secondary oocyte leaves the ruptured Graafian follicle in the process called ovulation. This ovum, along with its zona pellucida and corona radiata, migrate to and through the Fallopian tube (oviduct) where a sperm may penetrate the secondary oocyte (= *fertilization*). If fertilization occurs then the second meiotic division proceeds, forming a mature oocyte, known as ovum, (1N) and a second polar body; if fertilization does not occur, then the ovum degenerates. Unlike in males, each primary germ cell (oocyte) produces one gamete and not four. This is a consequence of the production of *polar bodies* which are degenerated nuclear material. Up to three polar bodies can be formed: one from the division of the primary oocyte, one from the division of the secondary oocyte, and sometimes the first polar body divides.

14.3 The Menstrual Cycle

The "period" or <u>menstrual cycle</u> occurs in about 28 days and can be divided as follows: i) **Menses:** the first four days (days 1-4) of the cycle are notable for the <u>menstrual blood flow</u>. This occurs as a result of an <u>estrogen</u> and <u>progesterone</u> withdrawal which leads to vasoconstriction in the uterus causing the uterine lining (= *endometrium*) to disintegrate and slough away; ii) **Follicular (ovary)** or **Proliferative Phase** (days 5-14): FSH stimulates follicles to mature, and all but one of these follicles will stop growing, and the one dominant follicle in the ovary will continue to mature into a Graafian follicle, which in turn produces and secretes estrogen. Estrogen causes the uterine lining to thicken (= <u>proliferate</u>); iii) **Ovulation:** a very high concentration of estrogen is followed by an LH surge (estrogen-induced LH surge) at about day 15 (midcycle) which stimulates ovulation; iv) **Luteal** or **Secretory Phase** (days 15-28): the follicular cells degenerate into the <u>corpus luteum</u> which secretes estrogen *and* progesterone. Progesterone is responsible for a transient body temperature rise immediately after ovulation and it stimulates the uterine lining to become more vascular and glandular. Estrogen continues to stimulate uterine wall development and, along with progesterone, inhibits the secretion of LH and FSH (= <u>negative feedback</u>).

If the ovum <u>is fertilized</u>, the implanted embryo would produce the hormone *human chorionic gonadotropin* (= hCG) which would stimulate the corpus luteum to continue the secretion of estrogen and progesterone {hCG is the basis for most pregnancy tests}. If there is <u>no fertilization</u>, the corpus luteum degenerates causing a withdrawal of estrogen and progesterone thus the cycle continues [*see* i) *above*].

Estrous vs. menstrual cycles: Mammals with estrous cycles reabsorb the endometrium if conception does not occur during that cycle. Also, they are generally only sexually active during a specific phase of their cycle ("in heat"). In contrast, females of species with menstrual cycles (i.e. humans) can of course be sexually active at any time in their cycle, and the endometrium is shed monthly.

14.4 The Reproductive Sequence

During sexual stimulation parasympathetic impulses in the male lead to the dilatation of penile arteries combined with restricted flow in the veins resulting in the engorgement of the penis with blood (= *an erection*). In the female, the preceding occurs in a similar manner to the clitoris, along with the expansion and increase in secretions in the vagina. <u>Intercourse</u> or <u>copulation</u> may lead to orgasm which includes many responses from the sympathetic nervous system. In the male, the ejaculation of semen accompanies orgasm. In the female, orgasm is accompanied by many reflexes including an increase in muscular activity of the uterus and the Fallopian tubes. The latter may help in the transport of the already motile sperm to reach the tubes where the egg might be.

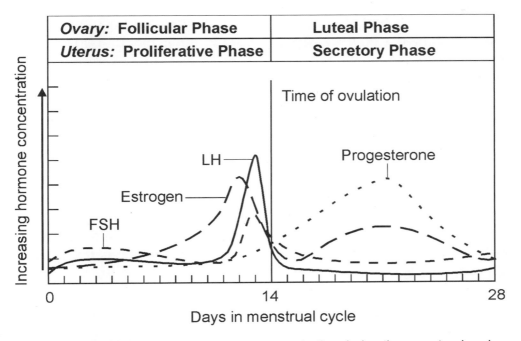

Figure IV.A.14.1: Changing hormone concentration during the menstrual cycle.

14.5 Embryogenesis

The formation of the embryo or *embryogenesis* occurs in a number of steps within two weeks of fertilization. Many parts of the developing embryo take shape during this period (= *morphogenesis*).

Penetration of the zona pellucida leads to the *cortical reaction*, in which the secondary oocyte is no longer permeable to other sperm.

Fertilization is a sequence of events which include: the sperm penetrating the corona radiata and the zona pellucidum due to the release of lytic enzymes from the acrosome known as the <u>acrosome reaction</u>; the fusion of the plasma membranes of the sperm and egg; the egg, which is really a secondary oocyte, becomes a mature ovum by completing the second meiotic division; the nuclei of the ovum and sperm are now called *pronuclei*; the male and female pronuclei fuse forming a <u>zygote</u> (2N). Fertilization, which normally occurs in the Fallopian tubes, is completed within 24 hours of ovulation.

Cleavage consists of rapid, repeated mitotic divisions beginning with the zygote.

Because the resultant daughter cells or blastomeres are still contained within the zona pellucidum, the cytoplasmic mass remains constant. Thus the increasing number of cells requires that each daughter cell be smaller than its parent cell. A morula is a solid ball of about 16 blastomeres which enters the uterus.

Blastulation is the process by which the morula develops a fluid filled cavity (= *blastocoel*) thus converting it to a blastocyst. Since the zona pellucidum degenerates at this point, the blastocyst is free to implant in the uterine lining or endometrium. The blastocyst contains some centrally located cells (= *the inner cell mass*) called the embryoblast which develops into the embryo. The outer cell mass called the trophoblast becomes part of the placenta.

Implantation. The zona pellucida must degenerate before the blastocyst can implant into the endometrium of the uterus. Once implantation is completed, the blastocyst becomes surrounded by layers of cells that further invade the endometrium.

Gastrulation is the process by which the blastula invaginates, and the inner cell mass is converted into a three layered (= *trilaminar*) disk. The trilaminar disk includes the **three primary germ layers**: an outer ectoderm, a middle mesoderm, and an inner endoderm. The ectoderm will develop into the epidermis and the nervous system; the mesoderm will become muscle, connective tissue (incl. blood, bone), and circulatory, reproductive and excretory organs; the endoderm will become the epithelial linings of the respiratory tract, and digestive tract, including the glands of the accessory organs (i.e. the liver and pancreas). During this stage the embryo may be called a gastrula.

Neurulation is the process by which the neural plate and neural folds form and close to produce the neural tube. The neural plate is formed by the thickening of ectoderm which is induced by the developing *notochord*. The notochord is a cellular rod that defines the axis of the embryo and provides some rigidity. Days later, the neural plate invaginates along its central axis producing a central neural groove with neural folds on each side. The neural folds come together and fuse thus converting the neural plate into a neural tube which separates from the surface ectoderm. Special cells on the crest of the neural folds (= *neural crest cells*) migrate to either side of the developing neural tube to a region called the neural crest.

As a consequence, we are left with **three** regions: the surface ectoderm which will become the epidermis; the neural tube which will become the central nervous system (CNS); and the neural crest which will become cranial and spinal ganglia and nerves and the medulla of the adrenal gland. During this stage the embryo may be called a *neurula*.

Though this is a subject which is still poorly understood, it seems clear that morphogenesis relies on the coordinated interaction of genetic and environmental factors. When the zygote passes through its first few divisions, the blastomeres remain indeterminate or uncommitted to a specific fate. As development proceeds the cells become increasingly committed to a specific outcome (i.e. neural tube cells → CNS). This is called **determination**.

In order for a cell to specialize it must differentiate into a committed or determined cell. Since essentially all cells in a person's body have the same amount of genetic information, differentiation relies on the *difference* in the way these genes are *activated*. For example, though brain cells (neurons) have the same genes as osteoblasts, neurons do not activate such genes (otherwise we would have bone forming in our brains!). The general mechanism by which cells differentiate is called **induction**.

Induction can occur by many means. If two cells divide unevenly, the cell with more cytoplasm might have the necessary amount of a substance which could *induce* its chromosomes to activate cell-specific genes. Furthermore, sometimes a cell, through contact (i.e. *contact inhibition*) or the release of a chemical mediator, can influence the development of nearby cells (*recall that the notochord induces the development of the neural plate*). The physical environment (pH, temperature, etc.) may also influence the development of certain cells. Irrespective of what form of induction is used, the signal must be translated into an intracellular message which influences the genetic activity of the responding cells.

Programmed cell-death (PCD = apoptosis) is death of a cell in any form, which is controlled by an intracellular program. PCD is carried out in a regulated process directed by DNA which normally confers advantage during an organism's life-cycle. PCD serves fundamental functions during tissue development. For example, the development of the spaces between your fingers requires cells to undergo PCD.

Thus cells specialize and develop into organ systems (morphogenesis). The embryo develops from the second to the ninth week, followed by the fetus which develops from the ninth week to birth (*parturition*).

14.6 The Placenta

The **placenta** is a complex vascular structure formed by part of the maternal endometrium (= *the decidua basalis*) and cells of embryonic origin (= *the chorion*). The placenta begins to form when the blastocyst implants in the endometrium. A cell layer from the embryo invades the endometrium with fingerlike bumps (= *chorionic villi*) which project into intervillous spaces which contain maternal blood. Maternal spiral arteries enter the intervillous spaces allowing blood to circulate.

The placenta has three main functions: i) the **transfer** of substances necessary for the development of the embryo or fetus from the mother (O_2, H_2O, carbohydrates, amino acids, IgG antibodies - BIO 8.2, vitamins, etc.) and the **transfer** of wastes from the embryo or fetus to the mother (CO_2, urea, uric acid, etc.); ii) the placenta can synthesize substances (i.e. glycogen, fatty acids) to use as an energy source for itself and the embryo or fetus; iii) the placenta produces and secretes a number of hormones including human chorionic gonadotropin (hCG), estrogen and progesterone. The hCG rescues the corpus luteum from regression and stimulates its production of progesterone.

14.7 Fetal Circulation

Consider the following: the fetus has lungs but does not breathe O_2. In fact, the placenta is, metaphorically, the "fetal lung." Oxygenated and nutrient-rich blood returns to the fetus from the placenta via the left umbilical vein. Most of the blood is directed to the inferior vena cava through the ductus venosus. From there, blood joins the deoxygenated and nutrient-poor blood from the superior vena cava and empties into the right atrium. However, most of the blood is diverted from the pulmonary circulation (bypassing the right ventricle) to the left atrium via a hole in the atrial septum: the patent foramen ovale (for adult circulation and anatomy, see chapter 7). Blood then enters the left ventricle and is distributed through the body (systemic circulation) via the aorta.

Some blood in the right atrium enters into the right ventricle and then proceeds into the pulmonary trunk. However, resistance in the collapsed lung is high and the pulmonary artery pressure is higher than it is in the aorta. Consequently, most of the blood bypasses the lung via the ductus arteriosus back to the aorta.

Blood circulates through the body and is sent back to the placenta via right and left umbilical arteries. The placenta re-oxygenates this deoxygenated and nutrient-poor blood and returns it to the fetus through the umbilical vein and the cardiovascular cycle repeats. Notice that in the fetus, oxygenated and nutrient-rich blood can be carried by veins to the right chambers of the heart which cannot occur in normal adult circulation.

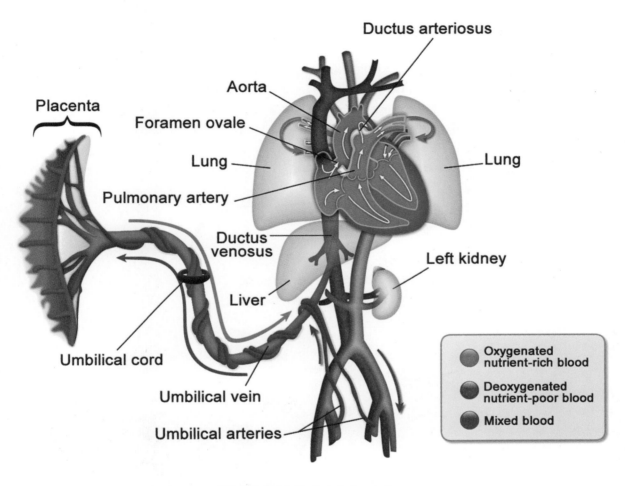

Fig.IV.A.14.2: Fetal circulation.

14.8 Fetal Sexual Development

The normal sexual development of the fetus depends on the genotype (XX female, XY male), the morphology of the internal organs and gonads, and the phenotype or external genitalia. Later, these many factors combine to influence the individual's self-perception along with the development of secondary sexual characteristics (i.e. breast development in females, hair growth and lower pitched voice in males).

Every fetus, regardless of genotype, has the capacity to become a normally formed individual of either sex. Development natu rally proceeds towards "female" unless there is a Y chromosome factor present. Thus the XX genotype leads to the maturation of the Müllerian ducts into the uterus, fallopian tubes, and part of the vagina. The primitive gonad will develop into a testis only if the Y chromosome is present and encodes the appropriate factor and eventually the secretion of testosterone. Thus the XY genotype leads to the involution of the Müllerian ducts and the maturation of the Wolffian ducts into the vas deferens, seminiferous tubules and prostate.

Dear GAMSAT Biology,

If I understand this correctly, reproductive biology is the only science where multiplication and division mean the same thing.

gamsat-prep.com

Go online to GAMSAT-prep.com for additional chapter review Q&A and forum.

Memorize	Understand	Not Required*
: phenotype, genotype, gene, locus, single and multiple /heterozygosity, wild type, recessiveness, ete/co-dominance plete dominance, gene pool nked characteristics, sex determination of mutations: random, translation error, ription error, base subs., etc.	* Importance of meiosis; compare/contrast with mitosis * Segregation of genes, assortment, linkage, recombination * Single/double crossovers; relationship of mutagens to carcinogens * Hardy-Weinberg Principle, inborn errors of metabolism * Test cross: back cross, concepts of parental, F1 and F2 generations	* Advanced level college info

GAMSAT-Prep.com

Introduction

Genetics is the study of heredity and variation in organisms. The observations of Gregor Mendel in the mid-nine-teenth century gave birth to the science which would reveal the physical basis for his conclusions, DNA, about 100 years later.

Hopefully you noticed from the Table of Contents that between Biology chapters 8 and 16, by far, this is the most important chapter. Also, be forewarned: despite the fact that a dihybrid cross (BIO 15.3) is time consuming, it appears in 2 separate ACER GAMSAT practice booklets.

Additional Resources

Free Online Q&A + Forum

Video: Online or DVD

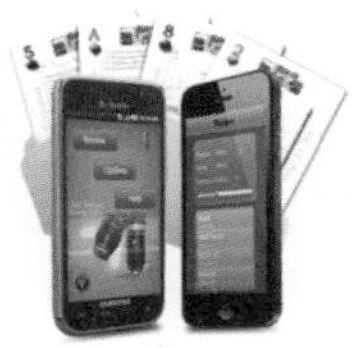

Flashcards

Special Guest

Genetics is a branch of biology which deals with the principles and mechanics of heredity; in other words, the *means* by which *traits* are passed from parents to offspring. To begin, we will first examine some relevant definitions - a few of which we have already discussed.

Chromosomes are a complex of DNA and proteins (incl. histones; BIO 1.2.2). A gene is that sequence of DNA that codes for a protein or polypeptide. A locus is the *position* of the gene on the DNA molecule. Recall that humans inherit 46 chromosomes - 23 from maternal origin and 23 from paternal origin (BIO 14.2). A given chromosome from maternal origin has a counterpart from paternal origin which codes for the same products. This is called a **homologous pair** of chromosomes.

Any homologous pair of chromosomes have a pair of genes which codes for the same product (i.e. hair color). Such pairs of genes are called **alleles**. Thus for one gene product, a nucleus contains one allele from maternal origin and one allele from paternal origin. If both alleles are identical (i.e. they code for the same hair color), then the individual is called **homozygous** for that trait. If the two alleles differ (i.e. one codes for dark hair while the other codes for light hair), then the individual is called **heterozygous** for that trait.

The set of genes possessed by a particular organism is its genotype. The appearance or phenotype of an individual is expressed as a consequence of the genotype and the environment. Consider a heterozygote that expressed one gene (dark hair) but not the other (light hair). The expressed gene would be called dominant while the other unexpressed allele would be called recessive. The individual would have dark hair as their phenotype, yet their genotype would be heterozygous for that trait. The dominant allele is expressed in the phenotype. This is known as Mendel's Law of Dominance.

It is common to symbolize dominant genes with capital letters (A) and recessive genes with small letters (a). From the preceding paragraphs, we can conclude that with two alleles, three genotypes are possible: homozygous dominant (AA), heterozygous (Aa), and homozygous recessive (aa). Note that this only results in two phenotypes since both AA and Aa express the dominant gene, while only aa expresses the recessive gene.

Each individual carries **two** alleles while populations may have many or **multiple alleles**. Sometimes these genes are not strictly dominant or recessive. There may be degrees of blending (= *incomplete dominance*) or sometimes two alleles may be equally dominant (= *codominance*). ABO blood types are an important example of multiple alleles with codominance.

Incomplete dominance occurs when the phenotype of the heterozygote is an intermediate of the phenotypes of the homozygotes. A classic example is flower color in snapdragon: the snapdragon flower color is red for homozygous dominant and white for homozygous recessive. When the red homozygous flower is crossed with the white homozygous flower, the result yields a 100% pink snapdragon flower. The pink snapdragon is the result of the combined effect of both dominant and recessive genes.

15.2 ABO Blood Types

Codominance occurs when multiple alleles exist for a particular gene and more than one is dominant. When a dominant allele is combined with a recessive allele, the phenotype of the recessive allele is completely masked. But when two dominant alleles are present, the contributions of both alleles do not overpower each other and the phenotype is the result of the expression of both alleles. A classic example of codominance is the ABO blood type in humans.

Red blood cells can have various antigens or *agglutinogens* on their plasma membranes which aid in blood typing. The important two are antigens A and B. If the red blood cells have only antigen A, the blood type is A; if they have only antigen B, then the blood type is B; if they have both antigens, the blood type is AB; if neither antigen is present, the blood type is O. There are three allelic genes in the population (I^A, I^B, i^O). Two are codominant (I^A, I^B) and one is recessive (i^O). Thus in a given population, there are six possible genotypes which result in four possible phenotypes:

Genotype	Phenotype
$I^A I^A$, $I^A i^O$	blood type A
$I^B I^B$, $I^B i^O$	blood type B
$I^A I^B$	blood type AB
$i^O i^O$	blood type O

Blood typing is critical before doing a blood transfusion. This is because people with blood type A have anti-B antibodies, those with type B have anti-A, those with type AB have neither antibody, while type O has both anti-A and anti-B antibodies. If a person with type O blood is given types A, B, or AB, the clumping of the red blood cells will occur (= *agglutination*). Though type O can only receive from type O, it can give to the other blood types since its red blood cells have no antigens {type O = universal donor}. Type AB has neither antibody to react against A or B antigens so it can receive blood from all blood types {type AB = universal recipient}.

The only other antigens which have some importance are the Rh factors which are coded by different genes at different loci from the A and B antigens. Rh factors are either there (Rh⁺) or they are not there (Rh⁻). 85% of the population are Rh⁺. The problem occurs when a woman is Rh⁻ and has been exposed to Rh⁺ blood and then forms anti-Rh⁺ antibod-ies (note: unlike the previous case, exposure is necessary to produce these antibodies). If this woman is pregnant with an Rh⁺ fetus her antibodies may cross the placenta and cause the fetus' red blood cells to agglutinate (*erythroblastosis fetalis*). This condition is fatal if left untreated.

15.3 Mendelian Genetics

Recall that in gametogenesis homologous chromosomes separate during the first meiotic division. Thus alleles that code for the same trait are segregated: this is **Mendel's First Law of Segregation. Mendel's Second Law of Independent Assortment** states that different chromosomes (*or factors which carry different traits*) separate independently of each other. For example, consider a primary spermatocyte (2N) undergoing its first meiotic division. It is <u>not</u> the case that all 23 chromosomes of paternal origin will end up in one secondary spermatocyte while the other 23 chromosomes of maternal origin ends up in the other. Rather, each chromosome in a homologous pair separates *independently* of any other chromosome in other homologous pairs.

However, it has been noted experimentally that sometimes traits on the same chromosome assort independently! This non-Mendelian concept is a result of *crossing over* (recall that this is when homologous chromosomes exchange parts, BIO 14.2). In fact, it has been shown that two traits located far apart on a chromosome are more likely to cross over and thus assort independently, as compared to two traits that are close. The propensity for some traits to refrain from assorting independently is called <u>linkage</u>. Double crossovers occur when two crossovers happen in a chromosomal region being studied.

Another exception to Mendel's laws involves **sex linkage**. Mendel's laws would predict that the results of a genetic cross should be the same regardless of which parent introduces the allele. However, it can be shown that some traits follow the inheritance of the sex chromosomes. Humans have one pair of sex chromosomes (XX = female, XY = male), and the remaining 22 pairs of homologous chromosomes are called **autosomes**.

Since females have <u>two</u> X chromosomes and males have only one, a single recessive allele carried on an X chromo-some could be expressed in a male since there is no second allele present to mask it. When males inherit one copy of the recessive allele from an X chromosome, they will express the trait. In contrast, females must inherit two copies to express the trait. Therefore, an X-linked recessive phenotype is much more frequently found in males than females. In fact, a typical pattern of sex linkage is when a mother passes her phenotype to all her sons but **none** of her daughters. Her daughters become *carriers* for the recessive allele. Certain forms of hemophilia, colorblindness, and one kind of muscular dystrophy are well-known recessive sex-linked traits. {In what was once known as Lyon's Hypothesis, it has been shown that every female has a condensed, inactivated X chromosome in her body or somatic cells called a Barr body.}

Let us examine the predictions of Mendel's First Law. Consider two parents, one homozygous dominant (AA) and the other homozygous recessive (aa). Each parent can only form one type of gamete with respect to that trait (*either* A *or* a, *respectively*). The next generation (*called* first filial *or* **F₁**) must then be uniformly heterozygotes or *hybrids* (Aa). Now the F₁ hybrids can produce gametes that can be either A half the time or a half the time. When the F₁ generation is self-crossed, i.e. Aa X Aa, the F₂ generation will be more genotypically and phenotypically diverse and we can predict the outcome in the next generation (F₂) using a Punnett square:

	1/2 A	1/2 a
1/2 A	1/4 AA	1/4 Aa
1/2 a	1/4 Aa	1/4 aa

Here is an example as to how you derive the information within the square: when you cross A with A you get AA (i.e. 1/2 A × 1/2 A = 1/4 AA). Thus by doing a simple *mono*hybrid cross (Aa × Aa) with random mating, the Punnett square indicates that in the F₂ generation, 1/4 of the population would be AA, 1/2 would be Aa (1/4 + 1/4), and 1/4 would be aa. In other words the *genotypic* ratio of homozygous dominant to heterozygous to homozygous recessive is 1:2:1. However, since AA and Aa demonstrate the same *phenotype* (i.e. dominant) the ratio of dominant phenotype to recessive phenotype is 3:1.

Now we will consider the predictions of Mendel's Second Law. To examine independent assortment, we will have to consider a case with two traits (usu. on different chromosomes) or a *di*hybrid cross. Imagine a parent which is homozygous dominant for two traits (AABB) while the other is homozygous recessive (aabb). Each parent can only form one type of gamete with respect to those traits (*either* AB *or* ab, *respectively*). The F₁ generation will be uniform for the dominant trait (i.e. *the genotypes would all be* AaBb). In the gametes of the F₁ generation, the alleles will assort independently.

Consequently, an equal amount of all the possible gametes will form: 1/4 AB, 1/4 Ab, 1/4 aB, and 1/4 ab. When the F$_1$ generation is self-crossed, i.e. AaBb X AaBb, we can predict the outcome in the F$_2$ generation using the Punnett square:

	1/4 AB	1/4 Ab	1/4 aB	1/4 ab
1/4 AB	1/16 AABB	1/16 AABb	1/16 AaBB	1/16 AaBb
1/4 Ab	1/16 AABb	1/16 AAbb	1/16 AaBb	1/16 Aabb
1/4 aB	1/16 AaBB	1/16 AaBb	1/16 aaBB	1/16 aaBb
1/4 ab	1/16 AaBb	1/16 Aabb	1/16 aaBb	1/16 aabb

Thus by doing a dihybrid cross with random mating, the Punnett square indicates that there are nine possible genotypes (*the frequency is given in brackets*): AABB (1), AABb (2), AaBb (4), AaBB (2), Aabb (2), aaBb (2), AAbb (1), aaBB (1), and aabb (1). Since A and B are dominant, there are only four phenotypic classes in the ratio 9:3:3:1 which are: the expression of <u>both</u> traits (AABB + AABb + AaBb + AaBB = 9), the expression of only the <u>first</u> trait (AAbb + Aabb = 3), the expression of only the <u>second</u> trait (aaBB + aaBb = 3), and the expression of <u>neither</u> trait (aabb = 1). Now we know, for example, that 9/16 represents that fraction of the population which will have the phenotype of both dominant traits.

15.3.1 A Word about Probability

If you were to flip a quarter, the probability of getting "heads" is 50% (p = 0.5). If you flipped the quarter ten times and each time it came up heads, the probability of getting heads on the next trial is still 50%. After all, previous trials have no effect on the next trial.

Since chance events, such as fertilization of a particular kind of egg by a particular kind of sperm, occur independently, the genotype of one child has no effect on the genotypes of other children produced by a set of parents. Thus in the previous example of the dihybrid cross, the chance of producing the genotype AaBb is 4/16 (25%) irrespective of the genotypes which have already been produced. For more about probability, see GM 6.1.

15.4 The Hardy-Weinberg Law

The Hardy-Weinberg Law deals with population genetics. A **population** includes all the members of a species which occupy a more or less well defined geographical area and have demonstrated the ability to reproduce from generation to generation. A **gene pool** is the sum of all the unique alleles for a given population. A central component to evolution is the changing of alleles in a gene pool from one generation to the next.

Evolution can be viewed as a changing of gene frequencies within a population over successive generations. The Hardy-Weinberg Law or *equilibrium* predicts the outcome of a randomly mating population of sexually reproducing diploid organisms who are not undergoing evolution.

For the Hardy-Weinberg Law to be applied, the idealized population must meet the following conditions: i) **random mating**: the members of the population must have no mating preferences; ii) **no mutations**: there must be no errors in replication nor similar event resulting in a change in the genome; iii) **isolation**: there must be no exchange of genes between the population being considered and any other population; iv) **large population**: since the law is based on statistical probabilities, to avoid sampling errors, the population cannot be small; v) **no selection pressures**: there must be no reproductive advantage of one allele over the other.

To illustrate a use of the law, consider an idealized population that abides by the preceding conditions and have a gene locus occupied by either A or a. Let p = the frequency of allele A in the population and let q = the frequency of allele a. Since they are the only alleles, p + q = 1. Squaring both sides we get:

$$(p + q)^2 = (1)^2$$

$$OR$$

$$p^2 + 2pq + q^2 = 1$$

The preceding equation (= *the Hardy-Weinberg equation*) can be used to calculate genotype frequencies once the allelic frequencies are given. This can be summarized by the following:

	pA	qa
pA	p^2AA	pqAa
qa	pqAa	q^2aa

The Punnett square illustrates the expected frequencies of the three genotypes in the next generation: AA = p^2, Aa = 2pq, and aa = q^2.

For example, let us calculate the percentage of heterozygous individuals in a population where the recessive allele q has a frequency of 0.2. Since $p + q = 1$, then $p = 0.8$. Using the Hardy-Weinberg equation and squaring p and q we get:

$$0.64 + 2pq + 0.04 = 1$$

$$2pq = 1 - 0.68 = 0.32$$

Thus the percentage of heterozygous (2pq) individuals is 32%.

A practical application of the Hardy-Weinberg equation is the prediction of how many people in a generation are carriers for a particular recessive allele. The values would have to be recalculated for every generation since humans do not abide by all the conditions of the Hardy-Weinberg Law (i.e. *humans continually evolve*).

15.4.1 Back Cross, Test Cross

A back cross is the cross of an individual (F_1) with one of its parents (P) or an organism with the same genotype as a parent. Back crosses can be used to help identify the genotypes of the individual in a specific type of back cross called a test cross. A test cross is a cross between an organism whose genotype for a certain trait is unknown and an organism that is homozygous recessive for that trait so the unknown genotype can be determined from that of the offspring. For example, for P: AA x aa and F_1: Aa, we get:

Backcross #1: Aa x AA
Progeny #1: 1/2 Aa and 1/2 AA

Backcross #2: Aa x aa
Progeny #2: 1/2 Aa and 1/2 aa

15.5 Genetic Variability

Meiosis and mutations are sources of genetic variability. During meiosis I, crossing over occurs between the parental and maternal genes which leads to a recombination of parental genes yielding unique haploid gametes. Thus recombination can result in alleles of linked traits separating into different gametes. However, the closer two traits are on a chromosome, the more likely they will be linked and thus remain together, and vice versa.

Further recombination occurs during the random fusion of gametes during fertilization.

Consequently, taking Mendel's two laws and recombination together, we can predict that parents can give their offspring combinations of alleles which the parents never had. This leads to **genetic variability**.

Mutations are rare, inheritable, random changes in the genetic material (DNA) of a cell. Mutations are much more likely to be either neutral (esp. *silent mutations*) or negative (i.e. cancer) than positive for an organism's survival. Nonetheless, such a change in the genome increases genetic variability. Only mutations of gametes, and not somatic cells, are passed on to offspring.

The following are some forms of mutations:

• **Point mutation** is a change affecting a single base pair in a gene

• **Deletion** is the removal of a sequence of DNA, the regions on either side being joined together

• **Inversion** is the reversal of a segment of DNA

• **Translocation** is when one chromosome breaks and attaches to another

• **Duplication** is when a sequence of DNA is repeated.

• **Frame shift mutations** occur when bases are added or deleted in numbers other than multiples of three. Such deletions or additions cause the rest of the sequence to be shifted such that each triplet reading frame is altered.

A mutagen is any substance or agent that can cause a mutation. A mutagen is not the same as a carcinogen. Carcinogens are agents that cause cancer. While many mutagens are carcinogens as well, many others are not. The Ames test is a widely used test to screen chemicals used in foods or medications for mutagenic potential.

Mutations can produce many types of genetic diseases including inborn errors of metabolism. These disorders in normal metabolism are usually due to defects of a single gene that codes for one enzyme.

15.6 Genetics and Heredity: A Closer Look

The rest of this chapter begins to push into more advanced topics in genetics. However, these topics continue to represent legitimate exam material.

Epistasis occurs when one gene masks the phenotype of a second gene. This is often the case in pigmentation where one gene turns on (or off) the production of pigment, while a second gene controls the amount of pigment produced. Such is the case in mice fur where one gene codes for the presence or absence of pigmentation and the other codes for the color. If C and c represent the alleles for the presence or absence of color and B and b represent black and brown then a phenotype of CCbb and Ccbb would both correspond to a brown phenotype. Whenever cc is inherited the fur will be white.

Pleiotropy occurs when a single gene has more than one phenotypic expression. This is often seen in pea plants where the gene that expresses round or wrinkled texture of seeds also influences the expression of starch metabolism. For example, in wrinkled seeds there is more unconverted glucose which leads to an increase of the osmotic gradient. These seeds will subsequently contain more water than round seeds. When they mature they will dehydrate and produce the wrinkled appearance.

Polygenic inheritance refers to traits that cannot be expressed in just a few types but rather as a range of varieties. The most popular example would be human height which ranges from very short to very tall. This phenomenon (many genes shaping one phenotype) is the opposite of pleiotropy.

Penetrance refers to the proportion of individuals carrying a particular variant of a gene (allele or genotype) that also express the associated phenotype. Alleles which are highly penetrant are more likely to be noticed. Penetrance only considers whether individuals express the trait or not. *Expressivity* refers to the variation in the degree of expression of a given trait.

Nondisjunction occurs when the chromosomes do not separate properly and do not migrate to opposite poles as in normal anaphase of meiosis (BIO 14.2). This could arise from a failure of homologous chromosomes to separate in meiosis I, or the failure of sister chromatids to separate during meiosis II or mitosis. Most of the time, gametes produced after nondisjunction are sterile; however, certain imbalances can be fertile and lead to genetic defects. Down Syndrome (Trisomy 21 = 3 copies of chromosome 21 due to its nondisjunction, thus the person has an extra chromosome making a total of 47 chromosomes); Turner and Klinefelter Syndrome (nondisjunction of sex chromosomes); and Cri du Chat (deletion in chromosome 5) are well known genetic disorders. Hemophilia and red-green color blindness are common sex-linked disorders and are recessive.

Phenylketonuria, sickle-cell anemia and Tay-Sachs disease are common autosomal recessive disorders.

Gene linkage refers to genes that reside on the same chromosome and are unable to display independent assortment because they are physically connected (BIO 15.3). The further away the two genes are on the chromosome the higher probability there is that they will crossover during synapsis. In these cases recombination frequencies are used to provide a linkage map where the arrangement of the genes can be ascertained. For example, say you have a fly with genotype BBTTYY and the crossover frequency between B and T is 26%, between Y and T is 18% and between B and Y is 8%. Greater recombination frequencies mean greater distances so you know that B and T are the furthest apart. This corresponds to a gene order of B-Y-T and since frequencies are a direct measure of distance you know exactly how far apart each allele is and can easily calculate the map distances.

Twin studies (nature vs. nurture) help to gauge the relative importance of environmental and genetic influences on individuals in a sample. Twins can either be monozygotic ("identical"), meaning that they develop from one zygote (BIO 14.5) that splits and forms two embryos, or dizygotic ("fraternal"), meaning that they develop from two separate eggs, each fertilized by separate sperm cells.

Thus fraternal twins are like any 2 siblings from a genetic point of view, but they may share the same environment as they grow up together.

To control for environment, the classical twin study design compares the similarity of monozygotic and dizygotic twins. If identical twins are considerably more similar than fraternal twins (which is found for most traits), this implies that genes play an important role for those specific traits. By comparing hundreds of families of twins, researchers can then understand more about the roles of genetic effects, shared environment, and unique environment in shaping behavior or in the development of disease.

15.6.1   Mitochondrial DNA

Mitochondrial DNA (mtDNA or mDNA) has become increasingly popular as a tool to determine how closely populations are related as well as to clarify the evolutionary relationships among species (= phylogenetics). Mitochondrial DNA is circular (BIO 1.2.2, 16.6.3) and can be regarded as the smallest chro-

mosome. In most species, including humans, mtDNA is inherited solely from the mother. The DNA sequence of mtDNA has been determined from a large number of organisms and individuals (including some organisms that are extinct).

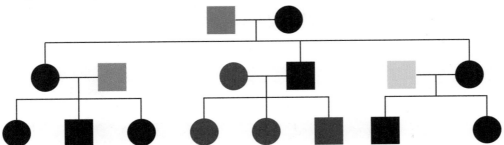

Figure IV.A.15.0: Pedigree ("Family tree"): Maternal inheritance pattern of mtDNA for 3 generations with the grandparents in the top row. As is the standard, circles represent females, squares represent males. Colors show the inheritance of the same mt genome (from mother to offspring, i.e. children). Don't be surprised to see a pedigree of some sort in your practice questions and/or on the real exam.

15.7   DNA Recombination and Genetic Technology

DNA recombination involves DNA that contains segments or genes from different sources. The foreign DNA can come from another DNA molecule, a chromosome or from a complete organism. Most DNA transferred is done artificially using DNA recombination techniques which use restriction enzymes to cut pieces of DNA. These enzymes originate from bacteria and are extremely specific because they only cut DNA at specific recognition sequences along the strand. These recognition sites correspond to different nucleotide sequences and produce sticky and blunt ends when a double stranded DNA segment is cut.

The sticky end is the unpaired part of the DNA that is ready to bind with a complementary codon (sequence of three adjacent nucleotides; BIO 3.0). These cut pieces or **restriction fragments** are often inserted into plasmids (circular piece of DNA that is able to replicate independently of the chromosomal DNA) which are then able to be introduced into the bacteria via transformation (see BIO 2.2).

Treating the plasmid, or replicon, with the same restriction enzymes used on the original fragment produces the same sticky ends in both pieces allowing base pairing to occur when they are mixed together. This attachment is stabilized by DNA ligase. After the ends are joined and the recombinant plasmid is incorporated into bacteria, the bacteria become capable of producing copious amounts of a specific protein that was not native to its species (i.e. bacteria with recombinant DNA producing insulin to treat diabetes).

Bacterium and Vector Plasmid

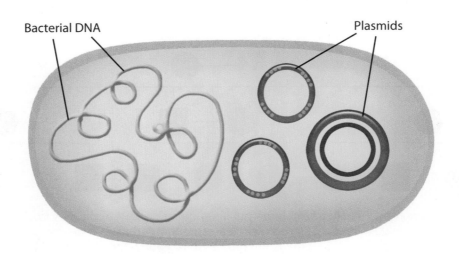

Bacterial DNA

Plasmids

Gel electrophoresis is a method of separating restriction fragments of differing lengths based on their size (as described in the previous section, a restriction fragment is a fragment of DNA cleaved by a restriction enzyme). The DNA fragments are passed through a gel which is under the influence of an electric field. Since DNA is negatively charged it will move towards the cathode (positive electrode). The shorter fragments move faster than the longer ones and can be visualized as a banding pattern using autoradiography techniques.

SDS-PAGE, sodium dodecyl sulfate polyacrylamide gel electrophoresis (ORG 13), also separates proteins according to their electrophoretic mobility. SDS is an anionic detergent (i.e. negatively charged) which has the following effect: (1) linearize proteins and (2) give an additional negative charge to the linearized proteins. In most proteins, the binding of SDS to the polypeptide chain gives an even distribution of charge per unit mass, thus fractionation will approximate size during electrophoresis (i.e. not dependent on charge).

Restriction fragment length polymorphisms or RFLP is a technique that exploits variations in restriction fragments from one individual to another that differ in length due to polymorphisms, or slight differences in DNA sequences. The process involves digest-ing DNA sequences with different restriction enzymes, detecting the resulting restriction fragments by gel electrophoresis, and comparing their lengths. In DNA fingerprinting, commonly used to analyze DNA left at crime scenes, RFLP's are produced and compared to RFLP's of known suspects in order to catch the perpetrator.

Sometimes it is necessary to obtain the DNA fragment bearing the required gene directly from the mRNA that codes for the polypeptide in question. This is due to the presence of introns (non-coding regions on a DNA molecule; BIO 3.0) which prevent transcription of foreign genes in the genome of bacteria, a common problem in recombinant technology. To carry this out one can use reverse transcriptase producing complementary DNA (cDNA) which lack the problematic introns.

Rather than using a bacterium to clone DNA fragments, sometimes DNA is copied directly using the polymerase chain reaction (PCR). This method allows us to rapidly amplify the DNA content using synthetic primers that initiate replication at specific nucleotide sequences. This method relies on thermal cycling (repeated heating and cooling) of the DNA primers and can lead to thousands and even millions of copies in relatively short periods of time.

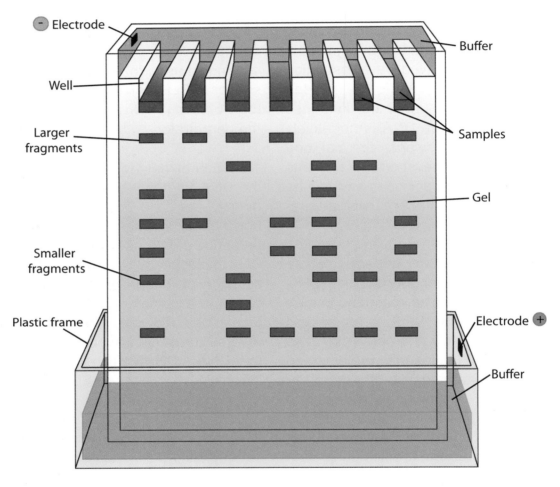

Figure IV.A.15.1: Gel Electrophoresis.

Southern blotting, named after Dr. E. Southern, is the process of transferring DNA fragments from the electrophoresis agarose gel onto filter paper where they are identified with probes. The procedure begins by digesting DNA in a mixture with *restriction endonucleases* to cut out specific pieces of DNA. The DNA fragments are then subjected to gel electrophoresis. The now separated fragments are bathed in an alkaline solution where they immediately begin to denature. These fragments are then placed (or blotted) onto nitrocellulose paper and then incubated with a specific probe whose location can be visualized with autoradiography.

Northern blotting is adapted from the Southern blot to detect specific sequences of RNA by hybridization with cDNA. Similarly, *Western blotting* is used to identify specific amino-acid sequences in proteins. Since this is not required for you to memorize for the GAMSAT, you may want to set aside this mnemonic for when you are attending medical school: SNOW DROP.

SNOW	DROP
Southern	DNA
Northern	RNA
O	**O**
Western	Protein

DNA microarray technology (= DNA chip or biochip or "laboratory-on-a-chip") helps to determine which genes are active and which are inactive in different cell types. This technology evolved from Southern blot-

ting and can also be used to genotype multiple regions of a genome. DNA microarrays are created by robotic machines that arrange incredibly small amounts of hundreds or thousands of gene sequences on a single microscope slide. These sequences can be a short section of a gene or other DNA element that is used to hybridize a cDNA or cRNA (also called anti-sense RNA) sample. The hybridization is usually observed and quantified by the detection of fluorescent tag.

NB: The molecular biology techniques of FRAP (BIO 1.5) and ELISA (BIO 8.4) were described earlier in this book. Electrophoresis and chromatography are discussed in Organic Chemistry Chapter 13.

EVOLUTION

Chapter 16

Memorize	Understand	Not Required*
Define: species, genetic drift Basics: chordates, vertebrates	* Natural selection, speciation * Genetic drift * Basics: origin of life * Basics: comparative anatomy	* Advanced level college info

GAMSAT-Prep.com

Introduction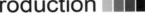

Evolution is, quite simply, the change in the inherited traits of a population of organisms from one generation to another. This change over time can be traced to 3 main processes: variation, reproduction and selection. The major mechanisms that drive evolution are natural selection and genetic drift.

Additional Resources

Free Online Q&A + Forum

Flashcards

Special Guest

* The real GAMSAT may have advanced level information presented (ie. in a passage) but previous knowledge of said information is not required to answer the questions that would follow. Practice ACER and GS practice GAMSATs can help you clarify this point.

16.1 Overview

Evolution is the change in frequency of one or more alleles in a population's gene pool from one generation to the next. The evidence for evolution lies in the fossil record, biogeography, embryology, compara- tive anatomy, and experiments from artificial selection. The most important mechanism of evolution is the **selection** of certain phenotypes provided by the **genetic variability** of a population.

16.2 Natural Selection

Natural selection is the non-random differential survival and reproduction from one generation to the next. Natural selection contains the following premises: i) genetic and phenotypic variability exist in populations: offspring show variations compared to parents; ii) more individuals are produced than live to grow up and reproduce; iii) the population competes to survive; iv) individuals with some genes are more likely to survive (greater fitness) than those with other genes; v) individuals that are more likely to survive transmit these favorable variations (genes) to their offspring so that these genes become more dominant in the gene pool.

It is not necessarily true that natural selection leads to the the Darwin-era expression "survival of the fittest"; rather it is the genes, and not necessarily the individual, which are likely to survive.

Evolution goes against the foundations of the Hardy-Weinberg Law. For example, natural selection leads to non-random mating due to phenotypic differences. Evolution occurs when those phenotypic changes depend on an underlying genotype; thus non- random mating can lead to changes in allelic frequencies. Consider an example: if female peacocks decide to only mate with a male with long feathers, then there will be a selection pressure against any male with a genotype which is expressed as short feathers. Because of this differential reproduction, the alleles which are expressed as short feathers will be eliminated from the population. Thus this population evolves.

The three forms of natural selection are: i) **stabilizing selection** in which genetic diversity decreases as the population stabilizes on an average phenotype (*phenotypes have a "bell curve" distribution*). This is the most common form of natural selection. It is basically the opposite of disruptive selection, instead of favoring individuals with extreme phenotypes, it favors the intermediate phenotype; ii) **directional selection** when an extreme phenotype has a selective advantage over the average phenotype causing the allele frequency continually shifting in one direction (*thus the curve can become skewed to the left or right*). It occurs most often when populations migrate to new areas with environmental pressures; iii) **disruptive selection** where both extremes

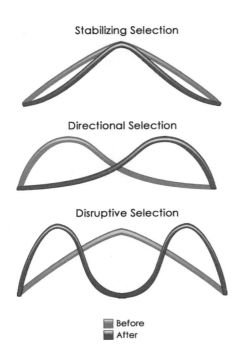

Stabilizing Selection

Directional Selection

Disruptive Selection

■ Before
■ After

are selected over the average phenotype; this would produce a split down the middle of the "bell curve" such that two new and separate "bell curves" would result. For example, if a bird only ate medium sized seeds and left the large and small ones alone, two new populations or groups of seeds would have a reproductive advantage. Thus by selecting against the group of medium sized seeds, two new groups of large and small seeds will result. This is an example of group selection causing *disruptive selection*.

16.3 Species and Speciation

Species can be defined as the members of populations that interbreed or can interbreed under natural conditions. There are great variations within species. A **cline** is a gradient of variation in a species across a geographical area. **Speciation** is the evolution of new species by the isolation of gene pools of related populations. The isolation of gene pools is typically geographic. An ocean, a glacier, a river or any other physical barrier can isolate a population and prevent it from mating with other populations of the same species. The two populations may begin to differ because their mutations may be different, or, there may be different selection pressures from the two different environments, or, *genetic drift* may play a role.

Genetic drift is the random change in frequencies of alleles or genotypes in a population (recall that this is antagonistic to the Hardy-Weinberg Law). Genetic drift normally occurs when a small population is isolated from a large population. Since the allelic frequencies in the small population may be different from the large population (*sampling error*), the two populations may evolve in different directions.

Populations or species can be sympatric, in which speciation occurs after ecological, genetic or behavioral barriers arise within the same geographical boundary of a single population, or allopatric, in which speciation occurs through geographical isolation of groups from the parent population {Sympatric = live together, Allopatric = live apart}. Mechanisms involved in allopatric speciation are represented in the two preceding paragraphs.

The following represents some isolating mechanisms that prevent sympatric populations of different species from breeding together: i) habitat differences; ii) different breeding times or seasons; iii) mechanical differences (i.e. different anatomy of the genitalia); iv) behavioral specificity (i.e. different courtship behavior); v) gametic isolation (= fertilization cannot occur); vi) hybrid inviability (i.e. the hybrid zygote dies before reaching the age of sexual maturity); vii) hybrid sterility; viii) hybrid breakdown: the hybrid offspring is fertile but produces a next generation (F_2) which is infertile or inviable.

16.4 Origin of Life

Evidence suggests that the primitive earth had a reducing atmosphere with gases such as H_2 and the reduced compounds H_2O (vapor), $NH_{3(g)}$ (ammonia) and $CH_{4(g)}$ (methane). Such an atmosphere has been shown (i.e. Miller, Fox) to be conducive to the formation and stabilization of organic compounds. Such compounds can sometimes polymerize (*possibly due to autocatalysis*) and evolve into living systems with metabolism, reproduction, digestion, excretion, etc.

Critical in the early history of the earth was the evolution of: (1) the reducing atmosphere powered with energy (e.g. lightening, UV radiation, outgassing volcanoes) converting reduced compounds (water, ammonia, methane) into simple organic molecules (the 'primordial soup'); (2) self-replicating molecules surrounded by membranes forming protocells (very primitive microspheres, coacervates assembling into the precursor of prokaryotic cells: protobionts); (3) chemosynthetic bacteria which are anaerobes that used chemicals in the environment to produce energy; (4) photosynthesis which releases O_2 and thus converted the atmosphere into an oxidizing one; (5) respiration, which could use the O_2 to efficiently produce ATP; and (6) the development of membrane bound organelles (*a subset of prokaryotes which evolved into eukaryotes,* BIO 16.6.3) which allowed eukaryotes to develop meiosis, sexual reproduction, and fertilization.

It is important to recognize that throughout the evolution of the earth, organisms and the environment have and will continue to shape each other.

16.5 Comparative Anatomy

Anatomical features of organisms can be compared in order to derive information about their evolutionary histories. Structures which originate from the same part of the embryo are called homologous. **Homologous** structures may have similar anatomical features shared by two different species as a result of a common ancestor but with a late divergent evolutionary pattern in response to different evolutionary forces. Such structures may or may not serve different functions. **Analogous** structures have similar functions in two different species but arise from different evolutionary origins and entirely different developmental patterns (see Figure IV.A.16.1).

Vestigial structures represent further evidence for evolution since they are organs which are useless in their present owners, but are homologous with organs which are important in other species. For example, the appendix in humans is a vestige of an organ that had digestive functions in ancestral species. However, it continues to assist in the digestion of cellulose in herbivores.

Taxonomy is the branch of biology which deals with the classification of organisms. Humans are classified as follows:

Kingdom	Animalia
Phylum (= Division)	Chordata
Subdivision	Vertebrata
Class	Mammalia
Order	Primates
Family	Hominidae
Genus	*Homo*
Species	*Homo sapiens*

{Mnemonic for remembering the taxonomic categories: King Philip came over for great soup}

The subphyla Vertebrata and Invertebrata are subdivisions of the phylum Chordata. Acorn worms, tunicates, sea squirts and amphioxus are invertebrates. Humans, birds, frogs, fish, and crocodiles are vertebrates. We will examine features of both the chordates and the vertebrates.

Chordates have the following characteristics at some stage of their development: i) a notochord; ii) pharyngeal gill slits which lead from the pharynx to the exterior; iii) a hollow dorsal nerve cord. Other features which are less defining but are nonetheless present in chordates are: i) a more or less segmented anatomy; ii) an internal skeleton (= *endoskeleton*); iii) a tail at some point in their development.

Vertebrates have all the characteristics of chordates. In addition, vertebrates have: i) a <u>vertebral column</u>; ii) well developed <u>sensory and nervous systems</u>; iii) a <u>ventral heart</u> with a <u>closed vascular system</u>; iv) some sort of a liver, <u>endocrine organs</u>, and <u>kidneys</u>; and v) <u>cephalization</u> which is the concentration of sense organs and nerves to the front end of the body producing an obvious head.

16.6 Patterns of Evolution

The evolution of a species can be divided into four main patterns:

1. Divergent evolution – Two or more species originate from a common ancestor.

2. Convergent evolution – Two unrelated species become more alike as they evolve due to similar ecological conditions. The traits that resemble one another are called analogous traits. Similarity in species of different ancestry as a result of convergent evolution is homoplasty. For example, flying insects, birds and bats have evolved wings independently.

3. Parallel evolution – This describes two related species that have evolved similarly after their divergence from a common ancestor. For example, the appearance of similarly shaped leaves in many genera of plant species.

4. Coevolution – This is the evolution of one species in response to adaptations gained by another species. This most often occurs in predator/prey relationships where an adaptation in the prey species that makes them less vulnerable leads to new adaptations in the predator species to help them catch their prey.

16.6.1 Macroevolution

Macroevolution describes patterns of evolution for groups of species rather than individual species. There are two main theories:

1. **Phyletic gradualism** – This theory argues that evolution occurs through gradual accumulation of small changes. They point to fossil evidence as proof that major changes in speciation occur over long periods of geological time and state that the incompleteness of the fossil record is the reason why some intermediate changes are not evidenced.

2. **Punctuated equilibrium** – This theory states that evolutionary history is marked

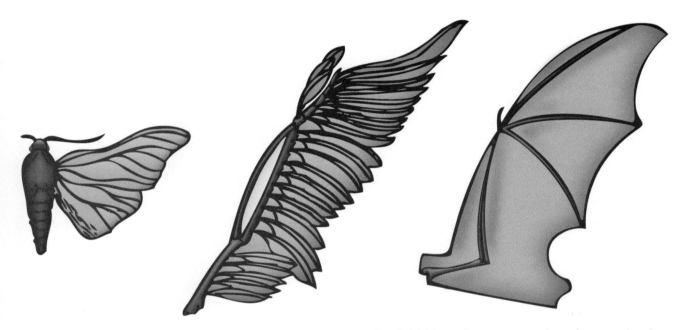

Figure IV.A.16.1: Analogous and homologous structures. The light blue wings represent analogous structures between different species: a flying insect, a bird and a bat, respectively. The bones are homologous structures. For example, green represents the humerus, purple represents the radius and ulna, red represents metacarpals and phalanges. Of course, insects have no bones. See the skeleton in BIO 11.3 to remind yourself of the meaning of some of these bony structures homologous in humans.

by sudden bursts of rapid evolution with long periods of inactivity in between. Punctuated equilibrium theorists point to the absence of fossils showing intermediate change as proof that evolution occurred in short time periods.

16.6.2 Basic Patterns for Changes in Macroevolution

1. Phyletic change (anagenesis): gradual change in an entire population that results in an eventual replacement of ancestral species by novel species and ancestral populations can be considered extinct.

2. Cladogenesis: one lineage gives rise to two or more lineages each forming a "clad". It leads to the development of a variety of sister species and often occurs when it is introduced to a new, distant environment.

3. Adaptive radiation: a formation of a number of lineages from a single ancestral species. A single species can diverge into a number of different species, which are able to exploit new environments.

4. Extinction: more than 99.9% of all species are no longer present.

16.6.3 Eukaryotic Evolution

Eukaryotes evolved from primitive heterotrophic prokaryotes in the following manner:

1. Heterotrophs first formed in the primordial soup (mixture of organic material) present in the early Earth (BIO 16.4). As the cells reproduced, competition increased and natural selection favored those heterotrophs who were best suited to obtain food.

2. Heterotrophs evolved into autotrophs (capable of making own food) via mutation. The first autotrophs were highly successful because they were able to manufacture their own food supply using light energy or energy from inorganic substrates (i.e. cyanobacteria).

3. As a by-product of the photosynthetic activity of autotrophs, oxygen was released into the atmosphere. This lead to formation of the ozone layer which prevented UV light from reaching the earth's surface. The interference of this major autotrophic resource was caused by the increased blockage of light rays.

4. Mitochondria, chloroplasts, and possibly other organelles of eukaryotic cells, originate through the symbiosis between multiple microorganisms. According to this theory, certain organelles originated as free-living bacteria that were taken inside another cell as endosymbionts. Thus mitochondria developed from proteobacteria and chloroplasts from cyanobacteria. This is the belief of the endosymbiotic theory which counts the following as evidence that it bodes true:

A. Mitochondria and chloroplasts possess their own unique DNA which is very similar to the DNA of prokaryotes (circular). Their ribosomes also resemble one another with respect to size and sequence.

B. Mitochondria and chloroplasts reproduce independently of their eukaryotic host cell.

C. The thylakoid membranes of chloroplasts resemble the photosynthetic membranes of cyanobacteria.

16.6.4 The Six-Kingdom, Three-Domain System

Genetic sequencing led to the replacement of the 'old' Five-Kingdom system of taxonomy (BIO 15.5). Under the current system, there are six kingdoms: Archaebacteria (ancient bacteria), Eubacteria (true bacteria; BIO 2.2), Protista (a diverse group of eukaryotic microorganisms), Fungi (BIO 2.3), Plantae ('plants'), and Animalia ('animals'). The Archaea and Bacteria domains contain prokaryotic organisms. The Eukarya domain includes eukaryotes and is subdivided into the kingdoms Protista, Fungi, Plantae, and Animalia.

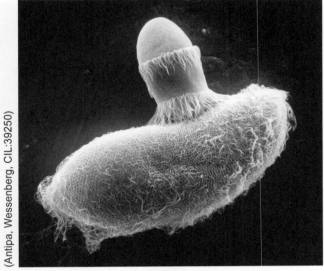

(Antipa, Wessenberg, CIL:39250)

Figure IV.A.16.2: David and Golliath: Two animal-like unicellular, ciliated protists in an epic struggle. The larger of the two carnivores, Paramecium, is attacked from above by the smaller Didinium. In this case, the organisms were preserved for this SEM micrograph (BIO 1.5, 1.5.1) before the outcome could be determined. Like other ciliates (ciliaphora), they can reproduce asexually (binary fission) or sexually (conjugation); osmoregulation is via contractile vacuoles; and, they are also visible using a light microscope.

Six-Kingdom, Three-Domain System

- Archaea Domain
    Kingdom Archaebacteria

- Bacteria Domain
    Kingdom Eubacteria

- Eukarya Domain
    Kingdom Protista
    Kingdom Fungi
    Kingdom Plantae
    Kingdom Animalia

If your Section 3 review is now over, it's time to consolidate your Gold Notes and prepare for full-length (timed) GAMSAT practice exams! Good luck!

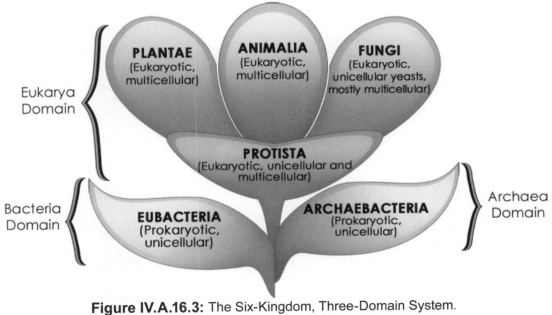

Figure IV.A.16.3: The Six-Kingdom, Three-Domain System.

Go online to GAMSAT-prep.com for additional chapter review Q&A and forum.

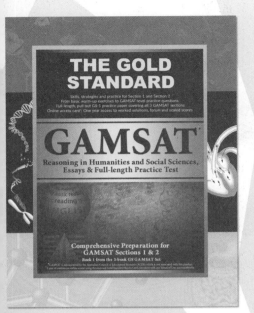